The Vietnamese Economy and the Fourth Industrial Revolution

Vietnam and the Global Economy

Series Editors: **Xuan Vinh Vo**
(University of Economics Ho Chi Minh City, Vietnam)
Dong Phong Nguyen
(University of Economics Ho Chi Minh City, Vietnam)

This book series, Vietnam and the Global Economy, aims to regularly publish theme-oriented special volumes covering various aspects of economic and business development in the institutional context of transitional economy and the global economy. The topics covered include, but are not limited to: transitional economy, global risk, emerging markets, institutional factors, and country and global risks.

Published:

'ol. 2: *The Vietnamese Economy and the Fourth Industrial Revolution*
edited by Dong Phong Nguyen, Dinh Thanh Su, Quang Hung Bui, Bich Nguyet Phan Thi, Viet Tien Ho, Nguyen Phong Nguyen and Xuan Vinh Vo

Recent Developments in Vietnamese Business and Finance
edited by Dong Phong Nguyen, Xuan Vinh Vo, Viet Tien Ho and Mai Dong Tran

Vietnam and the Global Economy – Volume 2

The Vietnamese Economy and the Fourth Industrial Revolution

Editors

Dong Phong Nguyen
Dinh Thanh Su
Quang Hung Bui
Bich Nguyet Phan Thi
Viet Tien Ho
Nguyen Phong Nguyen
Xuan Vinh Vo

University of Economics Ho Chi Minh City, Vietnam

World Scientific

NEW JERSEY • LONDON • SINGAPORE • BEIJING • SHANGHAI • HONG KONG • TAIPEI • CHENNAI • TOKYO

Published by

World Scientific Publishing Co. Pte. Ltd.
5 Toh Tuck Link, Singapore 596224
USA office: 27 Warren Street, Suite 401-402, Hackensack, NJ 07601
UK office: 57 Shelton Street, Covent Garden, London WC2H 9HE

Library of Congress Cataloging-in-Publication Data
Names: Nguyễn, Đông Phong, editor. | Sử, Đình Thành, editor. | Bùi, Quang Hùng, Dr., editor. | Phan Thị, Bích Nguyệt, editor. | Hồ, Viết Tiến, editor. | Nguyễn, Phong Nguyên, editor. | Võ, Xuân Vinh, Dr., editor.
Title: The Vietnamese economy and the fourth industrial revolution / editors, Dong Phong Nguyen, Dinh Thanh Su, Quang Hung Bui, Bich Nguyet Phan Thi, Viet Tien Ho, Nguyen Phong Nguyen, Xuan Vinh Vo, University of Economics Ho Chi Minh City, Vietnam.
Description: New Jersey : World Scientific, [2026] | Series: Vietnam and the global economy ; vol. 2 | Includes bibliographical references.
Identifiers: LCCN 2023026377 | ISBN 9789811262241 (hardcover) | ISBN 9789811262258 (ebook for institutions) | ISBN 9789811262265 (ebook for individuals)
Subjects: LCSH: Vietnam--Economic conditions--1975- | Industry 4.0--Vietnam.
Classification: LCC HC444 .V5746 2026 | DDC 338.9597--dc23/eng/20230705
LC record available at https://lccn.loc.gov/2023026377

British Library Cataloguing-in-Publication Data
A catalogue record for this book is available from the British Library.

For any available supplementary material, please visit
https://www.worldscientific.com/worldscibooks/10.1142/13021#t=suppl

Desk Editors: Aanand Jayaraman/Yulin Jiang

Typeset by Stallion Press
Email: enquiries@stallionpress.com

https://doi.org/10.1142/9789811262258_fmatter

Preface

This book, *The Vietnamese Economy and the Fourth Industrial Revolution*, is a compilation of outstanding papers presented at the International Conference on Business and Finance (ICBF) held in 2020 and 2021, hosted by the University of Economics Ho Chi Minh City, Vietnam. ICBF has become a prestigious event, attracting researchers, experts, and scholars from around the world to exchange ideas and discuss innovative research, emerging trends, and advancements in the fields of business and finance.

We would like to express our sincere gratitude to the anonymous reviewers, as well as to the distinguished guests and scholars, for generously dedicating their time and providing invaluable feedback. Their profound insights and constructive suggestions have significantly enhanced the quality of the papers presented in this volume. The meaningful discussions during the conference also played a crucial role in refining and elevating the value of the research.

We also wish to extend our heartfelt thanks to the team at the Institute of Business Research (IBR), University of Economics Ho Chi Minh City (UEH), and the affiliated departments for their enthusiastic support in organizing the annual International Conference on Business and Finance. We are especially grateful to World Scientific Publishing (Singapore) for their invaluable assistance and significant contributions in helping bring this book to completion.

Lastly, we would like to express our deep appreciation for Mr. Tran Thanh Trung and Ms. Do Thi Thanh Truc, our dedicated editorial assistants. Their tireless support ensured a smooth editing process and played a vital role in the successful completion of this book.

https://doi.org/10.1142/9789811262258_fmatter

About the Editors

Dong Phong Nguyen is a Professor and the Chairman of the Council at the University of Economics Ho Chi Minh City (UEH), Vietnam. With an extensive publication record in prestigious international journals and conference proceedings, his research interests encompass a wide range of fields, including higher education, organizational behavior, e-commerce, and regional socioeconomic development.

Dinh Thanh Su is a Professor and the President of the University of Economics Ho Chi Minh City (UEH), Vietnam. His research focuses on international trade, development economics, and the impact of institutions, with numerous publications in high-ranking journals. His recent work delves into topics such as economic vulnerability, digital infrastructure, entrepreneurship, and the effects of global uncertainty on developing countries.

Quang Hung Bui is an Associate Professor and the Vice President of the University of Economics Ho Chi Minh City (UEH), Vietnam. His research expertise spans accounting, digital transformation, and public sector performance, with numerous publications in high-ranking journals. His recent work examines the adoption of ESG principles, cloud-based accounting, internal control systems, and the impact of leadership in emerging and transition economies.

Bich Nguyet Phan Thi is an Associate Professor and the Chairwoman of the Advisory Council at the University of Economics Ho Chi Minh City (UEH), Vietnam. Her research focuses on digital transformation, innovation, and economic development in Vietnam, with particular emphasis on enterprise performance and regional policy. Her recent projects explore Industry 4.0 and strategic planning at both the institutional and provincial levels.

Viet Tien Ho is an Associate Professor and Co-Director of the French–Vietnamese Center of Management (CFVG). His research interests center on corporate finance, sustainability, and workplace behavior in Vietnam. His recent studies explore topics such as ESG performance, food waste habits, and sexual harassment within organizational settings.

Nguyen Phong Nguyen is an Associate Professor and the Permanent Deputy Head of the Department of Research, Development and Global Engagement. He has made significant contributions to interdisciplinary research in vocational interests, digital transformation, and marketing, with publications in high-ranking journals. His work explores emerging market dynamics, the use of AI in financial services, and user interactions with digital technologies.

Xuan Vinh Vo is a Professor of Finance and the Dean of the Institute of Business Research at the University of Economics Ho Chi Minh City (UEH), as well as a Researcher at CFVG Ho Chi Minh City, Vietnam. He has made significant contributions to energy economics, financial stability, and international business, with numerous studies published in top-tier journals. His research focuses on quantile connectedness in stock and energy markets, the impacts of climate policy, and financial volatility in global markets. Additionally, his expertise spans accounting, finance, and management, further enriching the field with his interdisciplinary approach.

https://doi.org/10.1142/9789811262258_fmatter

About the Contributors

Bao Trung Duong is a Lecturer at the Faculty of Business Administration, Ho Chi Minh City Open University, Vietnam. He has over 5 years of experience in lecturing on the Hospitality and Tourism Management majors at the university level. His research interests include service quality, influencer marketing, tourism behavior, social media, and customer behavior in hospitality. He is a Ph.D. candidate in Business Administration at the International University, Vietnam National University. His research focuses on the impact of social media influencers on the marketing strategy of hospitality firms. He has published a paper in the *African Journal of Hospitality, Tourism and Leisure*, as well as several domestic and international conference proceedings.

Dang Khoa Tran is an Associate Professor and Head of the Strategic Management Department at the Faculty of Business Administration, University of Economics Ho Chi Minh City (UEH). He holds a Ph.D. and has published in reputable international journals indexed in ISI and Scopus, as well as leading domestic academic journals. His main research areas include CSR, HRM, marketing, corporate culture, service quality, and entrepreneurship.

Dinh Tien Minh is an Associate Professor of Marketing and Head of the Department of Marketing in the College of Business, University of Economics Ho Chi Minh City. His field of expertise is marketing, commerce, and international business on which he has written papers for several highly ranked journals.

Gia Luat Diep is an Associate Professor of Finance and Dean of the School of Public Finance at the University of Economics Ho Chi Minh City. His field of expertise is finance and banking.

Hau Trung Nguyen is Deputy Director, Department of General Economics, Vietnam Communist Party's Central Commission for Policy and Strategy. He advises leadership on issues related to finance and monetary policies; policies to promote free trade zones and border economic zones; and a policy framework to develop the private sector. His research interests include financial stability and macroprudential policies, bank governance, public policies and policy analysis, and regulatory frameworks to develop private enterprises and entrepreneurship.

Nguyen Duy Thuc is an Associate Professor, Ph.D., and Senior Lecturer at the Faculty of Fundamental Sciences at Van Lang University, Vietnam. His research interests include economics, econometrics, business, and management.

Nguyen Hai Quang is an Associate Professor who holds a Ph.D. in Economics with a specialization in Business Administration. He currently serves as the Head of the Logistics Department at the Faculty of Commerce, Ho Chi Minh City University of Industry and Trade. His research focuses on publishing issues related to economics and management in the transport sector, tourism, as well as enterprise management and marketing.

Nguyen Xuan Trung is an Associate Professor and Director-General of the Institute for South Asian, West Asian and African Studies (ISAWAAS), Vietnam Academy of Social Sciences (VASS). He is a distinguished scholar with extensive expertise in economic management and international relations. He has authored numerous research publications and played a key role in promoting academic collaboration and policy dialogue on regional and global issues.

Quoc Thy Pham is an Administrative Research Executive at the Institute of Business Research, University of Economics Ho Chi Minh City, and has experience in marketing, digital transformation, e-commerce, management, and finance.

Thanh Truc Do Thi is the Head of the Operations Management Department at the Faculty of Business Administration, Vietnam Aviation Academy. Her primary research areas include human resource management (HRM), quality management, and sustainable development. With extensive experience in academic leadership and research, she has contributed significantly to these fields, particularly in the context of the aviation industry.

Thi Anh Nguyen is the Deputy Head of the Faculty of Law at the College of Economics, Law and Government (CELG), University of Economics Ho Chi Minh City (UEH). She earned her Master's degree in Economic Law from Ho Chi Minh City University of Law and completed her Ph.D. in Law from Yokohama National University in Japan.

Thi Thanh Huong Tran heads the Department of Statistics, Faculty of Accounting – Auditing, at the Banking Academy of Vietnam. Prior to her academic career, she spent ten years at the General Statistics Office of Vietnam, where she was involved in national data analysis and economic reporting. She holds both a Master's degree and a Ph.D. in Economic Statistics from the National Economics University in Hanoi. Her primary research interests include economic statistics, economic restructuring models, economic growth, finance, and investment. Dr. Tran has published and contributed to numerous studies in these fields and remains actively engaged in both academic research and teaching.

Thi Thanh Tra Nguyen is a Lecturer at Ho Chi Minh City University of Foreign Languages – Information Technology, Vietnam. She has research interests in job engagement, leadership, influencer marketing, and logistics services. Her work has been presented and published in International Conference Proceedings such as the International Conference on Finance and Economics, ICFE 2022, International Conference on Business and Finance, ICBF 2023, Annual

World Congress of the Academy for Global Business Advancement, AGBA 2024, and in journals such as *African Journal of Hospitality, Tourism and Leisure*.

Thu Hang Pham is a Lecturer at the Faculty of Economics, Banking Academy of Vietnam. She obtained a Ph.D. in Economics from the National Economic University of Vietnam and an M.Sc. in Development Economics from the Vietnam-Netherlands master's program. Her fields of interest include poverty, income inequality, investment, fiscal decentralization, and market demand analysis.

Thuy Thu Dang is an Associate Professor and Head of the Research Department at the Institute for South Asian, West Asian and African Studies (ISAWAAS), Vietnam Academy of Social Sciences (VASS). She is also a visiting lecturer at the Graduate Academy of Social Sciences. Her field of expertise includes international economics, microfinance, and business management on which she has written papers for numerous academic publications and research projects.

Thuy Trang Thi Pham is a Lecturer at the Faculty of Business Administration at Nguyen Tat Thanh University. She is also a manager in the telecommunications sector. This dual role allows her to integrate academic insights with practical business expertise.

Tran Thanh Trung is a Researcher at the Institute of Business Research, University of Economics Ho Chi Minh City (UEH), Vietnam. He holds a Master of Science degree in Business Administration from UEH and is also pursuing his Ph.D. at Ho Chi Minh City University of Industry and Trade. His research interests span a wide range of topics, including business, marketing, economics, and management.

Tran Thi Thuy Linh, holds Associate Professor Dr. in Finance at University of Economics Ho Chi Minh City. She works at the School of Finance, University of Economics Ho Chi Minh City. With over thirty years of experience in research in corporate finance, the stock market, and banking, her research interests include financial investment, corporate finance, and corporate governance. Her fields of expertise also include the relationship between listed firms and the stock market, and the relationship between listed commercial banks and the stock market. Furthermore, she has also attended many international conferences.

Trung Kien Tran is a Lecturer at the School of Public Finance, CELG, University of Economics Ho Chi Minh City. The primary focus of his teaching and research pursuits includes taxation, customs management, and public finance.

Vo Duy Luong is the Director of PVcomBank (Vietnam Public Joint Stock Commercial Bank), Dong Nai Branch. In addition, he is a Researcher at the Institute of Business Research and a Ph.D. candidate at the University of Economics Ho Chi Minh City (UEH), Vietnam. His research interests include banking, finance, business, and economics.

Vu Tu Anh, Lai Thi Hoai Huong, Pham Hoang Khang, Do Thi Phuong Thao, Le Thi Hoang Thy: They each earned a Bachelor's degree from the University of Economics Ho Chi Minh City (UEH), Vietnam. They participated in this research project during their undergraduate studies at UEH.

https://doi.org/10.1142/9789811262258_fmatter

Contents

https://doi.org/10.1142/9789811262258_fmatter

Introduction

The Vietnamese Economy and the Fourth Industrial Revolution is the second volume in the *Vietnam and the Global Economy* series, published by World Scientific Publishing, Singapore. This volume presents a curated selection of exceptional papers from the International Conference on Business and Finance (ICBF), held in 2020 and 2021 by the Institute of Business Research (IBR) at the University of Economics Ho Chi Minh City (UEH). Over the years, ICBF has become a prominent academic event, attracting scholars, experts, and industry leaders globally, with support from renowned academic journals.

The book covers a broad range of topics, including marketing, behavioral economics, management, leadership, tourism, and law, contributed by a diverse group of authors, university professors, government officials, and successful business leaders. Their collective expertise provides readers with a comprehensive perspective on Vietnam's economic developments, risks, challenges, and emerging opportunities.

The peer-reviewed papers offer in-depth analysis on various aspects of the Vietnamese economy. Notably, topics such as consumer behavior in Ho Chi Minh City supermarkets, university branding based on service quality perceptions, and leadership styles in Vietnamese SMEs are explored. Other areas include the influence of ethical leadership on organizational reputation, the connection between job motivation and organizational commitment, and the impact of capital intensity on labor productivity. This book also examines firm performance, particularly the roles of independent directors and foreign ownership, concluding with a study of inbound tourism's effects on the Mekong Delta region.

Each paper in this volume has undergone a rigorous peer-review process, ensuring the academic integrity of the content. We extend our gratitude to the authors, speakers, and participants whose contributions enriched the discussions at the ICBF conference.

This book is the second volume in the *Vietnam and the Global Economy* series, which also includes the following: Volume 1: *Recent Developments in Vietnamese Business and Finance*; Volume 2: *The Vietnamese Economy and the Fourth Industrial Revolution*; Volume 3: *Business Management in Vietnam*; Volume 4: *Vietnam and the New Era* (currently under development); Volume 5: *Global Perspectives on Legal and Business Reforms in Vietnam* (currently under development).

In conclusion, the ICBF conference and the *Vietnam and the Global Economy* series are organized and led by IBR at the University of Economics Ho Chi Minh City, an institution dedicated to advancing academic research, fostering international collaboration, and promoting global publications in business and finance. This book reflects the successful partnership between IBR and its esteemed collaborator, World Scientific Publishing, furthering the global discourse on Vietnam's economy and its role in the broader global context.

Part I

Banking Studies

https://doi.org/10.1142/9789811262258_0001

Chapter 1

Research on Employees' Perceptions of Banking Activities in the Context of Digital Transformation in Vietnam

Vo Duy Luong and Xuan Vinh Vo

Abstract

The study confirms that digital transformation plays an important role in improving the operational efficiency of banks based on employees' perceptions. The data sample includes 275 employees working at commercial banks in Ho Chi Minh City and neighboring provinces. Using the FsQCA method, the results show that (i) age and educational level strongly influence the outcomes of digital transformation; (ii) digital transformation is comprehensive, involving three different factors: people, internal factors, and external factors of the bank; (iii) certain configurations help banks overcome potential risks of digital transformation, such as budget constraints, lack of communication, or understanding of new processes; and (iv) digital experience is a key factor in overcoming risks arising from banking regulations and compliance.

Keywords: Perception; Commercial bank; Banking activities; Digital transformation.

1. Introduction

With the explosion of 5G technology, big data, artificial intelligence, blockchain, and other digital technologies, a wave of digitization has spread across the globe, ushering the world into the era of the digital economy (Li *et al.*, 2020). Moreover, the emergence of the COVID-19 pandemic accelerated the process of digitalization (Kan *et al.*, 2022). New financial services such as online loan provision and online account management are increasingly prevalent in the banking sector.

As a traditional industry, commercial banking has pioneered computerization (Wang and Wang, 2022). Faced with the rise of the digital economy and the online economy, if the existence and development of commercial banks (CBs) need to adapt to the advancements of the times, they must continue to pursue digital transformation (Khattak and Yousaf, 2021). At the same time, CBs are an essential part of the financial system, undergoing digital transformation (DT) either actively or passively under the influence of the digital economy and financial technology or Fintech (Tian *et al.*, 2022). Therefore, the comprehensive DT of CBs is a significant issue and a continuous task. How does the DT of CBs affect their operational capabilities?

1. The DT of CBs will reduce operational costs and management expenses. After the DT, the number of customers in a bank will decrease, leading the bank to reduce the space used by transaction points, streamline transaction counters, rotate some transaction staff, and invest in new products, thereby improving the bank's operational performance. Simultaneously, the number of product consultants will significantly decrease, as will the number of office staff and new hires, thus reducing personnel costs (Alam *et al.*, 2021).
2. The DT of CBs will increase interest and non-interest income (Bian *et al.*, 2015). Following the bank's DT, optimizing the lending process will enhance credit operation efficiency and increase the number of borrowing customers, while offering a diverse range of loan products will broaden the types of borrowing customers (Zhou and Li, 2023). The launch of online banking will boost loan sales and increase the non-interest income of CBs (Jameaba, 2020).

3. Banks' DT will enhance their operational efficiency. After the DT of banks, the internal audit efficiency of CBs will improve, enhancing the banks' financial efficiency (Chen *et al.*, 2021). After DT, the internal approvals of CBs (office work, personnel), business approvals (loans, service product provision, asset management), and risk control will be more streamlined. This can enhance work efficiency and allow employees to focus more on marketing activities.
4. The DT of banks can be realized through financial sharing (Pramanik *et al.*, 2019). When repaying a loan, customers only need to submit the original invoice, and bank employees will review and upload the documents to the system. The approval and repayment of loans can be directly processed by the higher branch, helping to improve the internal operational efficiency of the bank, saving employee time costs, enhancing marketing activities, improving customer service, and boosting the operational efficiency of CBs. After the bank's DT, the headquarters can know the deposit status of its branches, and the asset and liability management department can conduct centralized lending and investment to maximize asset benefits. The subordinate branches are valued according to the "reallocation capital" of the headquarters, ensuring stable income, avoiding idle cash, enhancing management efficiency, and improving the operational efficiency of CBs (Zhu and Jin, 2022).

Currently, there is limited research on the operations of CBs in the context of DT, with most relying on literature reviews, quantitative research, and case analysis. DT is a mandatory requirement for all businesses, and the banking sector is one of the most affected industries. However, most existing research on DT is based on macro-level industry analysis, there is little research analyzing the perceived impact of DT on employees in commercial banks. This study examines the perceived effect of the DT processes on the dynamic efficiency of CBs from the perspective of bank employees. Research on DT is often applied in enterprises and develops new business models, typically related to changes in governance. However, this research emphasizes the importance of training and education, essential for acquiring new skills and developing new communication capabilities, crucial for adapting people to new working methods (Baskerville *et al.*, 2010). DT often involves adapting products and services to changing customer demands and changing how these products and services are promoted and delivered based on new direct interaction forms with customers (Diener and Spacek, 2021). While most previous studies have been based on macro-level analysis, this research derives from micro-level analysis to investigate the stakeholders in the industry that have the most significant impact on the outcomes of DT in Vietnamese CBs. In this study, the authors employ fuzzy set qualitative comparative analysis (FsQCA) to explore the relationships in the proposed research model.

2. Theoretical

2.1. *The impact of digital transformation on banking operations*

According to Martin and Goggin (2016), DT is understood as the application of information and communication technology and the automation process to develop capabilities for companies, governments, and individuals. Similarly, Fitzgerald *et al.* (2014) state that DT involves using modern technologies such as embedded devices, social networks, and mobile devices to enable businesses to improve their core operations, create new business models, streamline production activities, and enhance customer experience.

Innovative digital financial services, such as robo-advisory and technology-based lending, have gained traction in recent years, accelerating the digitalization of the financial sector (Martin and Goggin, 2016). A survey conducted by the World Bank in 2021 revealed that digital transformation (DT) is now a strategic priority for most commercial banks (Feyen *et al.*, 2023). Despite this, much of the existing research on banks' use of digital technologies for DT, as well as the value it generates, remains largely theoretical. A majority of quantitative studies have centered on computerization or IT applications in banking. For example, (i) research has demonstrated that IT application reduces banking costs; (ii) improves bank profitability; and (iii) mitigates the impact of financial crises or other emergencies (Pierri and Timmer, 2020).

Pierri and Timmer (2020) argue that IT in the early 21st century differs fundamentally from today's digital technology. Consequently, DT in banking goes beyond the mere computerization of processes or the adoption of digital technologies. It ushers in entirely new business models and management practices. In recent years, there has been an emerging body of research that analyzes DT from a Fintech perspective. For instance, (i) Cheng and Qu (2020) investigated the impact of Fintech on credit risk by examining the frequency of Fintech-related keywords in bank annual reports and (ii) Chen *et al.* (2019) explored banks' patent applications in the Fintech domain, finding that Fintech innovations enhance banks' operational efficiency and have a positive influence on the broader banking industry.

2.2. *Developing research hypotheses*

Nadkarni and Prugl (2021) argue that digital transformation (DT) has emerged as one of the most significant management challenges for businesses in recent decades, with this trend likely to continue in the foreseeable future. DT is conceptualized as the strategic implementation of technology to fundamentally enhance organizational performance (Thakor, 2020), necessitating critical support from both employees and leadership. Consequently, DT requires the integration of technological advancements and human resources to optimize organizational performance, particularly in firms that embrace innovation to foster employee motivation toward innovative practices. Fintech companies, in particular, are progressively strengthening their capacity to manage risks and improve the operational efficiency of commercial banks (Zuo *et al.*, 2021). Regarding personal characteristics, the findings should contribute to a better understanding of how the interplay between internal and external factors and the characteristics of bank employees (as intermediaries of DT in banking) may facilitate or impede the success of DT processes. As highlighted in the research by Miles *et al.* (2014), employees' perceptions of their experiences — shaped by factors such as gender, age, and tenure in the bank — play a pivotal role. Moreover, training is instrumental in equipping employees with the knowledge and skills necessary for enhancing operational efficiency, a critical outcome for both individuals and the organization as a whole. The hypothesis is thus formulated as follows:

H_1: The personal characteristics of bank employees affect their perceptions of the impacts of DT

A key internal factor is the level of understanding of the DT process. In a study focused on the board members of German banks, Diener and Spacek (2021) found that employees were often stretched to their limits and experienced significant pressure due to the demands of DT. Initially, employees frequently resisted new developments and were reluctant to embrace change. Another critical internal factor is the communication surrounding the DT process (Porfírio *et al.*, 2024). According to reports from German banks on sustainability, Diener and Spacek (2021) observed that information regarding DT was often incomplete and insufficient, leaving banks considerable discretion in how they presented their reports.

Furthermore, Vermeulen's (2004) research on the financial sector, particularly banks and insurance companies, revealed that many institutions had outsourced essential tasks to information technology, often lacking in-house IT staff. This deficiency became apparent in issues related to product development. The outdated management systems used by many banks were incompatible with newer systems, necessitating the creation of "hybrid products." This highlights the complexity of legacy information systems, where adjustments are often infeasible without the involvement of specialized IT personnel. Consequently, technology-based financial products risk losing their innovative value, potentially diminishing the operational efficiency and business performance of banks (Baskerville *et al.*, 2010; Porfírio *et al.*, 2024).

Nyagadza (2022) underscores the concept of sustainable DT, characterizing it as a progression of IT transformation in terms of its scale, scope, and speed. In a study of multinational banks from developed economies, Forcadell *et al.* (2020) found that the integration of corporate sustainability and DT bolstered banks' credibility and helped blur the boundaries of traditional banking, thereby expanding the scope of their operations. Based on these insights, the second hypothesis for the study is formulated as follows:

H_2*: *Internal DT-related factors, communicated and understood by bank employees, influence perceptions of DT's impacts

Diener and Spacek (2021) identified regulatory requirements as significant external barriers that impede the progression of DT in banks. Additionally, customers represent another key external factor in the DT process. Diener and Spacek (2021) found that customer trust and acceptance of digital technologies varied, reflecting differing expectations, familiarity with DT, and the transition from traditional banking customers to digital users. This diversity in customer perceptions underscores the challenges banks face in navigating these differing levels of trust and technological adoption.

In their research on Italian bank customers, Filotto *et al.* (2021) discovered that during the early stages of technology acceptance, factors such as economic benefits and user-friendliness played a crucial role. Furthermore, maintaining customer loyalty through reliable electronic channels and clearly communicating security policies were essential to fostering customer trust in digital services. Lang and Colgate (2003), in their study of online banking, found that customers who either wanted to use more or less IT felt weaker relationships with the bank compared to those satisfied with their current level of IT use. Interestingly, the study also indicated that both groups — those desiring less and those desiring more IT — felt similarly about their relationship with the bank.

Dimitrova *et al.* (2021), along with Porfírio *et al.* (2024), examined Swedish bank customers and concluded that the greater the perceived barriers related to privacy and access, the lower the customers' intention to use online payment services. These insights point to the critical role of external factors in shaping the success of DT within banks. Based on this understanding, the third hypothesis is proposed as follows:

H_3*: *External factors related to barriers to DT in banking affect perceptions of the impact of DT

3. Research Methodology

3.1. *Research data*

The data used in this study are primary data. Based on previous research, the authors conducted semi-structured interviews with five members, including directors and deputy directors of commercial banks in Ho Chi Minh City and Dong Nai Province (in 7/2024). A pilot survey was then conducted with ten bank employees to assess their understanding of the content meaning of each observed variable in the questionnaire and to make appropriate adjustments. The results of the interviews served as a basis for modifying, supplementing, and finalizing the questionnaire and measurement scale used to survey 275 bank employees (in 7-8/2024) to understand their perceptions of the main factors influencing DT in the banking sector in Vietnam, specifically regarding increasing the operational efficiency and transaction volume of Vietnamese commercial banks. After discussions, the members agreed not to exclude any variables but to add some adjustments to the questions to suit the specific characteristics of the banking sector in Vietnam.

The sampling method primarily used was random sampling for employees at Vietnamese commercial banks, including various subjects, to ensure the objectivity of the research results. The data sample was collected based on the principles of voluntary participation, without coercion, without substituting surveyed employees (unless requested), or intentionally misleading customers regarding the meaning of the survey questionnaire. Hair Jr *et al.* (2014) state that the minimum sample size should be 5 times the survey questions.

However, a larger sample size will gradually reduce the discrepancy between the research and reality, thus enhancing accuracy. Yet, if the sample size is too large, the data collection time will be longer, and costs will increase; therefore, an appropriate sample size also depends on the authors' perspective. This study has 12 observed variables, so the minimum sample size should be $12 \times 5 = 60$ samples. To ensure objectivity and increase accuracy, the authors have used a sample size of 275 survey responses in this research. Table 1 presents the definitions, measurements, and sources of the study variables.

3.2. *Research model and measurement variables*

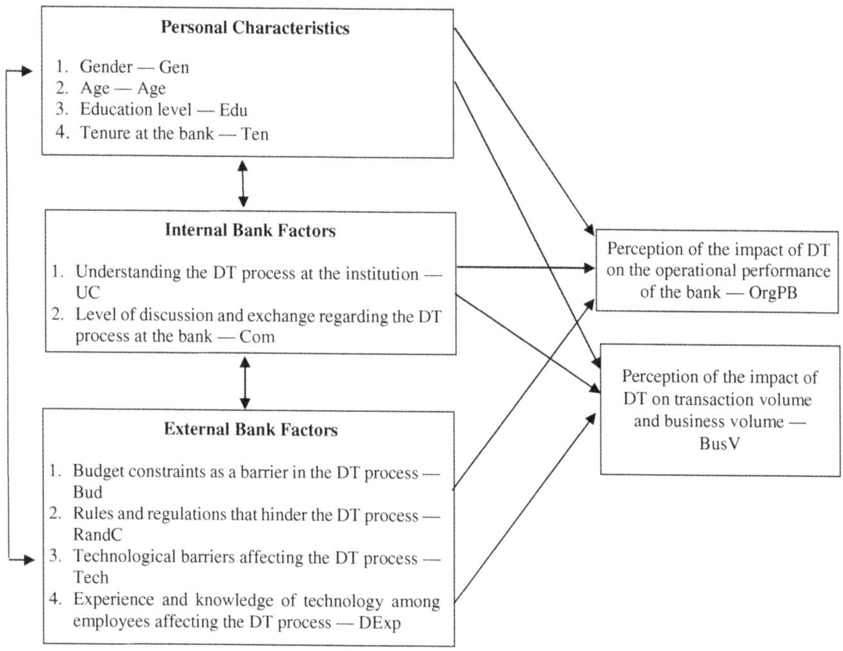

The dependent variables are measured through operational performance, transaction volume, and the bank's business volume (OrgPB and BusV). Operational efficiency relates to business outcomes and is often one of the most challenging theoretical subjects to define (Venkatraman and Ramanujam, 1986; Porfírio *et al.*, 2024). Operational efficiency can be assessed from various perspectives (financial,

Table 1: Description of measurement variables and research hypotheses.

Variable	Definition	Measurement	Previous Research	Expected Sign
Dependent Variables				
OrgPB	Perception of the impact of DT on the operational performance of the bank	1 = Full out; 3 = Maximum ambiguity; 5 = Full in	Venkatraman and Ramanujam (1986), Baskerville *et al.* (2010), Niemand *et al.* (2021), Khaleel *et al.* (2023), and Porfírio *et al.* (2024)	—
BusV	Perception of the impact of DT on the transaction volume and business volume of the bank	—	—	—
Independent Variables				
Personal Characteristics				
Gen	Gender	0 = Male; 1 = Female	Porfírio *et al.* (2024) and Miles *et al.* (2014)	+/−
Age	Age	0 = Under 25 years; 0.3 = From 26 to 35 years; 0.7 = From 36 to 45 years; 1 = From 46 to 55 years	—	+/−
Edu	Education level (Degree)	0 = From grade 9 to 12; 0.499 = College/University Degree; 1 = Postgraduate	—	+/−
Ten	Work experience	0 =< 1 year; 0.25 = From 1 to 5 years; 0.499 = From 5 to 10 years; 0.75 = From 10 to 20 years; 1 = >20 years	—	+/−

Internal Bank Factors				
UC	Level of understanding of the DT process at the bank	2 = Not well understood (Full out); 3.5 = Maximum Ambiguity; 5 = Well Understood (Full in)	Porfírio *et al.* (2024), Diener and Spacek (2021), Vermeulen (2004), Baskerville *et al.* (2010), Nyagadza (2022), and Forcadell *et al.* (2020)	+/−
Com	Level of discussion and exchange about the DT process at the bank	1 = Full out; 3 = Maximum ambiguity; 5 = Full in	—	+/−
External Bank Factors				
Bud	Is budget constraint a barrier in the DT process at the bank?	1 = Yes; 0 = No	Porfírio *et al.* (2024), Diener and Spacek (2021), Filotto *et al.* (2021), Lang and Colgate (2003), and Dimitrova *et al.* (2021)	+/−
RandC	Do rules and regulations hinder the DT process at the bank?	1 = Yes; 0 = No	—	+/−
Tech	Do technological barriers affect the DT process at the bank?	1 = Yes; 0 = No	—	+/−
DExp	Does the experience and knowledge of personnel regarding technology affect the DT process at the bank?	1 = Yes; 0 = No	—	+/−

operational, organizational), leading to numerous indicators that can be examined in different dimensions (financial/profit, operational, effectiveness, efficiency, strategy) (Venkatraman and Ramanujam, 1986).

In a study on banks in Scandinavia and Switzerland, Baskerville *et al.* (2010) found that implementing new knowledge about services often struggles to synchronize technology with business operations, resulting in difficulties in leveraging the business benefits of banks. Integrating business management into this development process becomes more complex due to the increasingly sophisticated information technology for those without in-depth expertise. In research involving banks in Germany, Switzerland, and Liechtenstein, Niemand *et al.* (2021) argue that the levels of operational efficiency relate to banking levels and indicate that the relationship between operational efficiency and a bank's strategic vision for DT is adjusted by business direction. Therefore, enhancing operational efficiency will likely occur if the strategic vision aligns with the bank's development orientation. According to Khaleel *et al.* (2023), in their study of banks in Pakistan, the digital business strategy positively impacts the company's financial performance, with this relationship being mediated by the adoption of blockchain.

4. Research Results

The survey results were compiled using Google Forms. After the survey, observations were encoded with Excel software to process the basic database and calculate the values of the variables according to the proposed research model. From there, a data table of the observations was constructed. Subsequently, the fuzzy-set qualitative comparative analysis (FsQCA) software was used to perform regression estimation and analyze and evaluate perceptions of the impact of DT on the operational performance and transaction volume of Vietnamese commercial banks.

Out of a total of 275 surveyed cases (Table 2), PVcombank accounts for the most significant proportion at 36.4%, indicating a strong presence of this bank in the research sample. Agribank ranks

Table 2: Survey rates for each bank.

Bank	Frequency	Percentage (%)	Valid Frequency (%)	Cumulative Frequency (%)
Agribank	35	12.7	12.7	12.7
PVcombank	100	36.4	36.4	49.1
BIDV	20	7.3	7.3	56.4
Sacombank	17	6.2	6.2	62.5
SCB	16	5.8	5.8	68.4
LPbank	14	5.1	5.1	73.5
NamABank	13	4.7	4.7	78.2
Wooribank	6	2.2	2.2	80.4
Others	54	19.6	19.6	100.0
Total	275	100	100	—

second with 12.7%, reflecting a moderate level of popularity among the banks. BIDV and Sacombank account for 7.3% and 6.2%, respectively, reflecting significant competition but not overly prominent. SCB and LPbank have relatively low proportions, around 5%, while NamABank holds 4.7%, indicating a limited presence in the market. Wooribank has the lowest proportion at just 2.2%, indicating a pretty small position.

The survey results have been integrated using the FsQCA method to study the relationships among the variables in the proposed research model and to identify the most important configurations contributing to the research outcomes. First, it is important to recognize that some variables initially identified in the interviews are duplicates, such as the age of employees compared to their years of service (Age and Ten). Additionally, the gender variable (Gen) and technology barriers (Tech) do not provide significant value for the study. This leads to the creation of four sub-models, each focusing on a specific aspect of the impact of DT. The sub-models considered are as follows:

4.1. *Analysis results of model 1*

The fsQCA model equations used to analyze the conditions affecting organizational performance and business volume are presented in

Table 3: Model equations for fuzzy-set qualitative comparative analysis (fsQCA).

Model	Equation
1	fsOrgP = f(fsAge, fsEdu, fsUC, fsCom, fsBudg)
2	fsBusV = f(fsAge, fsEdu, fsUC, fsCom, fsBudg)
3	fsOrgP = f(fsAge, fsEdu, fsRandC, fsDExp)
4	fsBusV = f(fsAge, fsEdu, fsRandC, fsDExp)

Table 4: Results and configurations of research model 1.

Variable	Configuration 1	Configuration 2	Configuration 3	Configuration 4
fsAge	Z	Z	X	Y
fsEdu	Z	X	X	Y
fsUC	Z	Z	X	Y
fsCom	Y	Z	Z	Z
fsBudg	Y	Y	Z	X
Raw Coverage	0.4150	0.1024	0.1193	0.4196
Unique Coverage	0.4150	0.0152	0.0364	0.4196
Consistency	0.9944	1	1	0.9927
Solution Coverage	0.4150	0.1519	0.1389	0.4196
Solution Consistency	0.9944	1	1	0.9927

Notes: X — Presence of a condition; Y — Absence of a condition; Z — Presence or Absence of a condition.
Source: Results from FsQCA.

Table 3. The fsQCA model analysis results for Model 1 reveal four configurations that lead to similar outcomes, with factors combined in various ways. Table 4 presents the fsQCA results for model 1, including configurations of conditions leading to high organizational performance. Configuration 1, characterized by the absence of discussion and exchange regarding the DT process (fsCom) and budget constraints (fsBudg), has the highest coverage (0.4150) and nearly absolute consistency (0.9944). Similarly, Configuration 4, marked by the absence of age (fsAge), education level (fsEdu), and understanding of the DT process at the agency (fsUC), demonstrates high coverage (0.4196) and high consistency (0.9927), indicating that other factors can compensate for the lack of these elements. Overall, all four configurations play a significant role in explaining the outcomes of the research model. Still, Configurations 1 and 4 yield better results, suggesting multiple combinations can achieve the desired objectives, with education level and budget being the two most critical factors. Model 1 presents the following four configurations:

Configuration 1: When budget issues are not seen as a barrier to DT, the level of discussion and exchange is no longer a problem for achieving the desired banking performance.

Configuration 2: A high level of education tends to reinforce the belief that budget is not an issue in achieving DT outcomes in banking performance.

Configuration 3: Banking employees' suitable age, education level, and understanding of the DT process are simultaneous conditions that enhance positive outcomes in banking performance from DT processes in the banking sector.

Configuration 4: Young banking employees engaged in DT may be key to achieving better outcomes in banking performance from DT processes, even when the overall synthesis suggests that budget may be a barrier to DT, and when employees do not fully understand the DT process and have lower education levels.

4.2. *Analysis results of model 2*

The fsQCA model suggests that there are multiple combinations to achieve similar outcomes, where the presence of factors such as education level, technology use, communication, and budget plays a crucial role (Table 5). Additionally, in some cases, the absence of these factors can be compensated by other elements, depending on the organization's specific context. Configuration 1, characterized by the absence of discussion and exchange regarding the DT process (fsCom) and budget constraints (fsBudg), has the highest coverage (0.4177) and nearly absolute consistency (0.9963). Configuration 3, which also lacks education level (fsEdu), understanding of the DT process at the agency (fsUC), and the level of discussion and

Table 5: Results and configurations of research model 2.

Variable	Configuration 1	Configuration 2	Configuration 3	Configuration 4	Configuration 5
fsAge	Z	X	Z	Z	Z
fsEdu	Z	X	Y	X	X
fsUC	Z	X	Y	Z	X
fsCom	Y	Z	Y	Z	Y
fsBudg	Y	Z	Z	Y	Y
Raw Coverage	0.4177	0.1198	0.4177	0.1714	0.1198
Unique Coverage	0.4177	0.0309	0.4177	0.171	0.0963
Consistency	0.9963	1	0.9963	1	1
Solution Coverage	0.4177	0.1526	0.4177	0.171	0.137
Solution Consistency	0.9963	1	0.9963	1	1

Note: X — Presence of a condition; Y — Absence of a condition; Z — Presence or Absence of a condition.
Source: Results from FsQCA.

exchange about the DT process (fsCom), shows equivalent coverage (0.4177) and high consistency (0.9963), indicating that other factors such as communication and budget can compensate for the absence of these elements. Configurations 2 and 4 have coverage levels of 0.1198 and 0.1714, respectively, with absolute consistency (1.0000). Configuration 5 has the lowest coverage (0.1198) but maintains absolute consistency (1.0000). Model 2 provides the following five configurations:

Configuration 1: When budget issues are not considered barriers to DT, the level of discussion and exchange is no longer a problem for achieving the desired transaction volume and business volume from DT processes in the banking sector.

Configuration 2: The combination of suitable age and high education level of banking employees, along with their understanding of the DT process, simultaneously promotes positive outcomes in transaction volume and business volume from DT processes in banking.

Configuration 3: The combination of banking employees' high education level and understanding of how to communicate and ensure employees grasp the DT process is also a simultaneous condition that fosters positive outcomes in transaction and business volume from DT processes in banking.

Configuration 4: A high education level reinforces the belief that budget is not an issue in achieving DT results in transaction and business volume.

Configuration 5: Understanding and grasping the DT process might indicate that issues related to the level of discussion exchange and budget are less significant for the outcomes of DT on transaction volume and business performance.

4.3. *Analysis results of model 3*

The analysis results of the fsQCA model with Model 3 (Table 6) show three different configurations that lead to similar outcomes: (i) Education level is the only condition present in all three configurations, indicating its essential and consistent role in achieving the desired results. (ii) Different configurations can explain different cases, with Configuration 3 having the highest coverage and explanatory power. (iii) The consistency of all three configurations reaches the maximum

Table 6: Results and configurations of research model 3.

Variable	Configuration 1	Configuration 2	Configuration 3
fsAge	Z	Y	X
fsEdu	X	X	X
fsRandC	X	Z	Y
fsDExp	Z	Y	Y
Raw Coverage	0.1322	0.0756	0.1806
Unique Coverage	0.0520	0.0243	0.0942
Consistency	1	1	1
Solution Coverage	0.1769	0.1108	0.1987
Solution Consistency	1	1	1

Note: X — Presence of a condition; Y — Absence of a condition; Z — Presence or Absence of a condition.
Source: Results from FsQCA.

level (1.0000), demonstrating that the conditions in each configuration are indeed solid and reliable in predicting outcomes. Model 3 provides the following three configurations:

Configuration 1: Bank employees' low education level seems to encourage the idea that rules and regulations are not an issue for achieving better banking performance from DT processes in the banking sector.

Configuration 2: Younger bank employees combined with low knowledge and digital experience reflect better results in banking performance from DT processes in the banking sector.

Configuration 3: A higher level of digital experience is associated with employees who do not view regulatory rules as a barrier, reflected in better banking performance.

4.4. *Analysis results of model 4*

The analysis of the fsQCA model results with research model 4 (see Table 7) indicates that two configurations lead to similar outcomes, even though the conditions are combined in various ways. Configuration 1 shows the presence of DT experience (fsDExp) and the absence of randomness and regulatory rules that hinder DT (fsRandC), explaining 18.15% of the cases with a unique coverage of 0.0947 and

Table 7: Results and configurations of research model 4.

Variable	Configuration 1	Configuration 2
fsAge	Z	Z
fsEdu	Z	Z
fsRandC	Y	X
fsDExp	X	Y
Raw Coverage	0.1815	0.1041
Unique Coverage	0.0947	0.0253
Consistency	1	1
Solution Coverage	0.1997	0.1483
Solution Consistency	1	1

Note: X — Presence of a condition; Y — Absence of a condition; Z — Presence or Absence of a condition.
Source: Results from FsQCA.

achieving absolute consistency of 1.0000. This indicates that this configuration is more prevalent and robust in explaining the outcomes. In contrast, Configuration 2 exhibits the presence of randomness and regulatory rules that hinder DT (fsRandC) and the absence of DT experience (fsDExp), explaining 10.41% of the cases and achieving absolute consistency of 1.0000. Both configurations possess absolute consistency (1.0000), demonstrating that the conditions in each configuration are strong predictors of the outcomes. Configuration 1 has a higher coverage level (0.1815) than Configuration 2 (0.1041), indicating that Configuration 1 is more prevalent among the analyzed cases. Model 4 provides the following two configurations:

Configuration 1: Regulations and competition, combined with low knowledge and digital experience, can challenge banks to achieve higher transaction and business volumes from DT processes.

Configuration 2: Knowledge and digital experience tend to offset the barriers arising from regulations and competition for banks to achieve higher transaction and business volumes from DT processes.

5. Conclusion and Management Implications

The research findings emphasize the importance of bank employees' perceptions and suggest that DT plays a crucial role in increasing transaction volume and improving the operational efficiency of banks. This is evidenced not only through the collected data but also through the analysis of configurations related to people and internal and external factors affecting banking operations. Although the selected sample aimed to ensure a balance in the activities, expertise, and scale of the banks and employee characteristics such as gender, age, and seniority, it cannot be considered representative of all bank employees in Vietnam. With a total number of bank employees in Vietnam estimated at approximately 300,000 to 350,000 by the end of 2023, a sample of 275 employees does not adequately reflect the diversity and characteristics of the entire industry. The results indicate that DT is regarded as essential for increasing transaction volume and enhancing the operational performance of banks, specifically:

The importance of personal characteristics in DT: One of the key ideas explored is that banking operational performance improves from DT processes when employees have higher education levels and are younger. Higher education enables employees to quickly grasp and understand complex DT processes, while younger employees may be associated with dynamism and a faster adaptation to new technologies. This suggests that recruiting and training young employees with high educational qualifications for commercial banks is essential for enhancing banking operational performance through DT. Conversely, the research also shows that good operational performance can be achieved with older employees, provided they also have high education levels and that the DT processes are communicated clearly and understandably. This underscores the importance of effective communication when implementing DT. Older employees may not adapt to new technology as quickly as younger employees, but with adequate support and transparent communication processes, they can still contribute positively to banking operational performance.

The role of internal factors and communication support in DT: The study indicates that internal factors, such as employees' understanding and awareness of the DT process, along with organizational communication support, play a significant role in explaining the overall outcomes of DT. This means that in addition to focusing on employees' education levels and personal characteristics, commercial banks need to pay attention to how they implement and communicate DT processes. Effective communication helps employees better understand the new processes and creates a positive work environment where employees feel supported and motivated to engage in the transformation process. Another important factor identified is employees' understanding of the DT process. When employees clearly understand the goals and benefits of DT, they are more motivated to adopt new technologies and implement related processes. This not only improves individual performance but also enhances the overall operational efficiency of the bank. Therefore, investing in training programs and internal communications about DT is essential.

The impact of external barriers and how to overcome them: The research findings provide evidence of the importance of barriers to DT, primarily external factors such as regulations, rules, technology, budget constraints, or the digital experience of the population, which influence DT outcomes. When these factors are not viewed as barriers, customers' digital experience becomes more critical in leveraging the results of DT processes to enhance banking operational efficiency. This indicates that in the banking context, internal and external factors must be effectively managed to ensure the success of DT. In particular, the research findings highlight that overcoming budget constraints regarding DT processes can be achieved through an appropriate combination of employees' education levels and communication effectiveness. Even with limited budgets, focusing on training and internal communication can compensate for budget limitations. This underscores the importance of developing effective strategies for managing human resources and budgets to successfully implement DT processes.

Acknowledgments

This research was conducted, completed, and financially supported by the University of Economics Ho Chi Minh City (UEH), Vietnam.

Bibliography

Alam, N., Gupta, L., and Zameni, A. (2021). *Fintech and Islamic Finance*. Berlin/Heidelberg, Germany: Springer.

Baskerville, R.L., Cavallari, M., Hjort-Madsen, K., Pries-Heje, J., Sorrentino, M., and Virili, F. (2010). The strategic value of SOA: A comparative case study in the banking sector. *International Journal of Information Technology and Management*, 9(1), 30–53.

Bian, W.L., Wang, X.N., and Sun, Q.X. (2015). Non-interest income, profit, and risk efficiencies: Evidence from commercial banks in China. *Asia-Pacific Journal of Financial Studies*, 44(5), 762–782.

Chen, X., You, X., and Chang, V. (2021). FinTech and commercial banks' performance in China: A leap forward or survival of the fittest? *Technological Forecasting and Social Change*, 166, 120645.

Chen, Y., Wang, Q., Chen, H., Song, X., Tang, H., and Tian, M. (2019, June). An overview of augmented reality technology. *Journal of Physics: Conference Series*, 1237(2), 022082. IOP Publishing.

Cheng, M. and Qu, Y. (2020). Does bank FinTech reduce credit risk? Evidence from China. *Pacific-Basin Finance Journal*, 63, 101398.

Diener, F. and Spacek, M. (2021). Digital transformation in banking: A managerial perspective on barriers to change. *Sustainability*, 13(4), 2032.

Dimitrova, I., Ohman, P., and Yazdanfar, D. (2021). Barriers to bank customers' intention to fully adopt digital payment methods. *International Journal of Quality and Service Sciences*, 14(5), 16–36.

Feyen, E., Natarajan, H., and Saal, M. (2023). *Fintech and the Future of Finance: Market and Policy Implications*. Washington, DC: World Bank Publications.

Filotto, U., Caratelli, M., and Fornezza, F. (2021). Shaping the digital transformation of the retail banking industry. Empirical evidence from Italy. *European Management Journal*, 39(3), 366–375.

Fitzgerald, M., Kruschwitz, N., Bonnet, D., and Welch, M. (2014). Embracing digital technology: A new strategic imperative. *MIT Sloan Management Review*, 55(2), 1.

Forcadell, F.J., Aracil, E., and Ubeda, F. (2020). Using reputation for corporate sustainability to tackle banks digitalization challenges. *Business Strategy and the Environment*, 29(6), 2181–2193.

Hair Jr, J.F., Black, W.C., Babin, B.J., Anderson, R.E., and Tatham, R.L. (1998). Multivariate data analysis. *New Jersey*, 5(3), 207–219.

Jameaba, M.S. (2020). Digitization revolution, FinTech disruption, and financial stability: Using the case of Indonesian banking ecosystem to highlight wide-ranging digitization opportunities and major challenges. FinTech Disruption, and Financial Stability: Using the Case of Indonesian Banking Ecosystem to Highlight Wide-Ranging Digitization Opportunities and Major Challenges (July 16, 2020).

Kan, D., Lyu, L., Huang, W., and Yao, W. (2022). Digital economy and the upgrading of the global value chain of China's service industry. *Journal of Theoretical and Applied Electronic Commerce Research*, 17(4), 1279–1296.

Khaleel, M., Yusupov, Z., Ahmed, A. A., Alsharif, A., Alarga, A., and Imbayah, I. (2023). The effect of digital technologies on energy efficiency policy. *International Journal of Electrical Engineering and Sustainability (IJEES)*, 1(1), 1–8.

Khattak, A. and Yousaf, Z. (2021). Digital social responsibility towards corporate social responsibility and strategic performance of hi-tech SMEs: Customer engagement as a mediator. *Sustainability*, 14(1), 131.

Lang, B. and Colgate, M. (2003). Relationship quality, on-line banking and the information technology gap. *International Journal of Bank Marketing*, 21(1), 29–37.

Li, K., Kim, D.J., Lang, K.R., Kauffman, R.J., and Naldi, M. (2020). How should we understand the digital economy in Asia? Critical assessment and research agenda. *Electronic Commerce Research and Applications*, 44, 101004.

Martin, F. and Goggin, G. (2016). Digital transformations? Gendering the end user in digital government policy. *Journal of Information Policy*, 6, 436–459.

Miles, M. B., Huberman, A. M., and Saldaña, J. (2014). *Qualitative Data Analysis: A Methods Sourcebook* (3rd ed.). Thousand Oaks, CA: SAGE Publications.

Nadkarni, S. and Prugl, R. (2021). Digital transformation: A review, synthesis and opportunities for future research. *Management Review Quarterly*, 71, 233–341.

Niemand, T., Rigtering, J.C., Kallmünzer, A., Kraus, S., and Maalaoui, A. (2021). Digitalization in the financial industry: A contingency approach of entrepreneurial orientation and strategic vision on digitalization. *European Management Journal*, 39(3), 317–326.

Nyagadza, B. (2022). Sustainable digital transformation for ambidextrous digital firms: Systematic literature review, meta-analysis and agenda for future research directions. *Sustainable Technology and Entrepreneurship*, 1(3), 100020.

Pierri, M. N. and Timmer, M. Y. (2020). *Tech in Fin before Fintech: Blessing or Curse for Financial Stability?* Washington, DC: International Monetary Fund.

Porfírio, J.A., Felício, J.A., and Carrilho, T. (2024). Factors affecting digital transformation in banking. *Journal of Business Research*, 171, 114393.

Pramanik, H.S., Kirtania, M., and Pani, A.K. (2019). Essence of digital transformation — Manifestations at large financial institutions from North America. *Future Generation Computer Systems*, 95, 323–343.

Thakor, V. (2020). *Fintech and Banking*. John M. Olin School of Business — European Corporate Governance Institute (ECGI), pp. 1–13.

Tian, X., Zhang, Y., and Qu, G. (2022). The Impact of digital economy on the efficiency of green financial investment in China's provinces. *International Journal of Environmental Research and Public Health*, 19(14), 8884.

Venkatraman, N. and Ramanujam, V. (1986). Measurement of business performance in strategy research: A comparison of approaches. *Academy of Management Review*, 11(4), 801–814.

Vermeulen, P. (2004). Managing product innovation in financial services firms. *European Management Journal*, 22(1), 43–50.

Wang, L. and Wang, Y. (2022). Supply chain financial service management system based on block chain IoT data sharing and edge computing. *Alexandria Engineering Journal*, 61(1), 147–158.

Zhou, Z. and Li, Z. (2023). Corporate digital transformation and trade credit financing. *Journal of Business Research*, 160, 113793.

Zhu, Y. and Jin, S. (2022). The effect of the QR code commission rate on commercial banks in China. *Journal of Digital Convergence*, 20(5), 99–105.

Zuo, L., Strauss, J., and Zuo, L. (2021). The digitalization transformation of commercial banks and its impact on sustainable efficiency improvements through investment in science and technology. *Sustainability*, 13(19), 11028.

Part II

Financial Economics

https://doi.org/10.1142/9789811262258_0002

Chapter 2

Social Performance and Profit: The Case of Vietnam's Microfinance Institutions

Thuy Thu Dang, Hau Trung Nguyen, and Nguyen Xuan Trung

Abstract

The chapter focuses on the relationship between social performance and the profit of microfinance institutions (MFIs) in Vietnam from 2011 to 2016. The authors collect data through statistics of Vietnamese MFIs and the information in the MIX market. Using the ordinary least square (OLS), the results show that social performance positively impacts the profit of MFIs in Vietnam. Thus, the authors concentrate on the solutions, which aim at increasing the assessment of MFIs in the future.

Keywords: Microfinance; Microfinance institutions; Social performance; Profit, Vietnam.

1. Introduction

Sustainable growth is one of the goals globally (Osborn *et al.*, 2015). Governments have initially been paying more attention to inclusive financial development in socio-economic life. One of the biggest concerns is expanding access to multiple sectors. This primary goal is to boost demand for access to essential financial services at a reasonable cost. All segments of the world population, especially low-income, disadvantaged groups in society, are the objectives of this goal. According to the Organization for Economic Co-operation and Development

(OECD, 2013), microfinance is taken into account as one of the key factors for global financial development comprehensively. In addition, microfinance contributes more approaches to financial services to enhance livelihoods and poverty reduction worldwide.

As numerous international organizations penetrated the new microfinance market, microfinance had undergone a remarkable transformation. It is well-known that microfinance flourished in South Asian countries, especially in India and Bangladesh, in the 1970s. South Asia may be regarded as the first cradle of microfinance (Ledgerwood, 1999; Morduch and Haley, 2002; Khandker, 2005). Among South Asian countries, India is considered one of the countries whose microfinance works well because it has neutralized the financial and social goals in its operations.

The proponents of microfinance claim that financial inclusion can help substantially reduce poverty (Dunford, 2006; Littlefield *et al.*, 2003). Financial inclusion through microfinance may contribute to a long-lasting increase in income, an available diversity of income and business activity sources, an accumulation of assets, and smooth consumption; it may reduce the vulnerability due to illness, drought, and crop failures. Moreover, microfinance may contribute to better education, health, and housing for the borrower. It shows that microfinance has a positive spillover in improving livelihoods and tremendous social support for its customers. According to Levine (2005), the correlation and the nature of causality between economic growth and financial development have been analyzed in-depth at the macroeconomic level. Subsequently, several researchers have also pointed out the importance of greater financial leverage because of its ability to affect the poorest group of the world's population (Beck *et al.*, 2007). This is why the development of financial institutions in general and MFIs, in particular, helps to reduce poverty and reduce inequality.

Microfinance has also faced numerous mixed opinions in terms of its benefits. They argued that it does not reach the poorest of the poor (Scully, 2004), or the poorest are consciously eliminated from microfinance programs (Simanowitz and Walter, 2002) for many reasons. *Firstly*, the extremely poor often choose not to take part in microfinance programs due to the lack of confidence or the fear of risky loans (Ciravegna, 2005). Moreover, the poorest, the so-called core poor, are generally too risk-averse to borrow for investment in the future. Thus they will benefit only to a minimal extent from microfinance schemes. *Secondly*, as it is perceived as a group that is likely to be exposed to bad credit risk (Hulme and Mosley, 1996; Marr, 2004), the core poor making group-based micro-loans is less likely to be accepted by other members of in-group lending programs. *Thirdly*, staff members of MFIs may prefer excluding the core poor since lending to them is likely to be extremely risky (Hulme and Mosley, 1996). *Fourthly*, some microfinance programs and projects often require customers to have a minimum amount of savings or collateral, which increases the difficulty for poor customers to access micro-loans (Kirkpatrick and Maimbo, 2002; Mosley, 2001). Microfinance plays a vital role in social and economic development. The UN Capital Development Fund 2004 (UNCDF) points out that microfinance plays three critical roles in development, including (i) helping indigent households meet basic needs and protection against risks, (ii) being associated with improvements in household economic welfare, and (iii) helping to empower women by supporting women's economic participation and so promotes gender equity. The microfinance sector has raised and moved in a new direction for the low-income population supporting traditional banks in accessing the disadvantaged segment in society (World Bank, 2008).

Some MFIs seeking sustainability seek to achieve operational self-sufficiency (OSS), covering all costs without support (Kimando *et al.*, 2012). Globally, 764 microfinance institutions (MFIs) in 87 countries actively provide small and reasonable loans to the target market so that this group of customers can develop small businesses and increase income. Rural residents in these countries face numerous difficulties in farming due to a lack of land, so they tend to move to small businesses (Quayes, 2015). MFIs are very different from traditional banks in the formal sector because they rely on customer deposits, loans, and non-credit services such as capacity building, product marketing, vocational training, and knowledge support in terms of using loans (Hartungi, 2007). These are advantages for MFIs to approach low-income and low-skilled customers in society and gradually increase their operational efficiency. A microfinance institution regarded as successful can effectively allocate credit to the right target customers. Therefore, microfinance activities have both economic implications and profound social implications. MFIs always seek to reach the most target customers possible, whereas they seek to generate capital effectively to help their activities sustain the operation, finance, and institution.

Although it is essential to understand the relationship between social performance and MFIs' profit, especially from a policy perspective, surprisingly few studies have investigated this issue systematically and profoundly. Therefore, this study aims at closing this gap in the literature. In particular, we provide an in-depth analysis of the impact of social performance on MFIs' financial performance (profitability). We use the fixed-effect model with White's heteroskedasticity and robust standard errors (1980) to measure the potential impact. For the analysis, we use data for 28 MFIs in Vietnam in the period 2011–2016.

The study is organized as follows: Section 2 discusses the literature on social performance and financial performance (profitability). Details about data and model specifications are divided in Section 3. Section 4 continues with explaining empirical results, and the summary of the main findings and conclusions derived from the analysis is presented in Section 5.

2. Literature Review

The attention to the poorest populations could cause a decline in profitability. Firstly, small amounts per client are necessary to work within this sector. Therefore, more accounts and customers would be needed to achieve the funds that other entities get. This would increase some fixed costs of operations and hinder the achievement of economies of scale. These poorer customers may also require some extra work due to illiteracy, problems in accessing documentation, and their general lack of experience with this kind of activity, all of which would require greater levels of support. Although it remains debatable, it has also been suggested that late payments could be higher in cases of extreme necessity.

2.1. *Operational performance of MFIs: Social performance and financial performance*

In terms of the effectiveness of MFIs, the most important fact is to assess how microfinance activities have supported poverty reduction and improved social performance for the disadvantaged and poor groups in society (World Bank, 2018). MFIs provide appropriate and proactive products and services to customers by implementing various effective and responsible ways. The study conducted by Collins *et al.* (2009) confirms that an MFI operating improves its financial performance and supports the target customers helping them develop income and guiding them to produce and use capital appropriately. Meanwhile, Armendariz and Labie (2011) say that many MFIs memorized the essential combination of social performance with promoting financial performance during the newly established time. However, in practice, it is challenging to balance. The MFIs may do a trade-off in each stage, such as the institution being newly established. They need to focus more on development than gradually toward social performance. The author emphasizes the task of neutralizing the mission to support the lives of the poor while being more independent of the support funds eventually. However, many MFIs choose their business model through increased competition and commercialization. Studies by Copestake (2007) and Mersland and Storm (2010) confirm that MFIs' growth over the past years has faced financial pressure to survive, so they have excluded the inherent social tasks and their target customers. According to Sinha and Assefa *et al.*, from 2000 to 2005, the average annual growth rate of MFIs in the world was estimated at 50%, whereas from 2006 to 2008, this reached 70–100% annually (Sinha, 2010; Assefa *et al.*, 2013). However, during the global financial crisis, this growth plummeted to a relatively low level (Wagner and Winkler, 2013).

The accessibility of MFI is expressed both economically and socially (Hulme and Mosley, 1996). Social performance understood is how the MFI promotes an approach to its target customer group. Osotimehin *et al.* (2011) review the factors and trends in expanding the approach of MFIs in Southwest Nigeria. The team uses the least square method to analyze the relationship between each factor in the social performance of MFIs. The study shows that social performance positively impacts the average loan size, debt/equity ratio, and loan repayment ratio. The study's new findings suggest that MFIs need to pay more attention to loan size to promote social performance in this area. Shastri (2009) has conducted specific studies on the positive poverty reduction capabilities that MFIs have increased in India. The author points out that microfinance programs in India are a tool to help the poor improve their livelihoods effectively by providing them with each opportunity and guidance on the use of credits most effectively. It is a cyclical activity that creates models of financially sustainable development and increases social performance and the scale of production and business activities for the poor. Rauf and Mahmood (2009) evaluate the effectiveness of the growth strategy in Pakistan when implementing microfinance activities and its impact on the operations of MFIs in some South Asian countries. The study uses the theoretical model and approaches, namely accessibility, to assess the depth and breadth of the target approach. The authors also point out that the microfinance industry in India is gradually shifting from social goals to financial sustainability goals. Following a study in Pakistan, Ghalib (2013) gives a detailed analysis of the operations of MFIs in the Punjab province and concludes that MFIs here reach the target customer group ineffectively. This is due to an expansion of operating costs when reaching the poorest. With high operating costs, MFIs in this area exclude inherent social goals and find ways to overcome financial losses. Similarly, Quayes (2012) asserts that as access levels increase, financial sustainability will decline and *vice versa*. The author points out the inverse correlation between social performance and financial sustainability of MFIs. Similarly, Hermes *et al.* (2011) also carried out in their paper on the social performance of MFIs that are inversely related to financial performance. This relationship itself explains why MFIs need to consider social performance and financial performance when providing financial services to their target customers.

Paxton and Cuevas (2002) shows that MFIs, especially non-governmental organizations (NGOs), face sustainability issues when serving as many customers as possible. However, the poor and the disadvantaged often live in remote areas, so any organization supporting them has to spend a high cost. Therefore, these NGOs often tend to depend on subsidies to cover the high costs incurred. This inverse relationship has created NGOs to trade between their social performance and benefit — financial performance. In another study conducted by Olivares-Polanco (2005) investigating 28 MFIs in Latin America, it was proved that there was a trade-off between social performance and financial performance of MFIs. The more number of served poorest customers, the higher operational costs and the more reduced sustainability level the MFIs bear. Similarly, Piot-Lepetit and Nzongang (2014) analyzed the operations of village banks in Cameroon and showed that 15% of banks faced a trade-off between social performance and operational performance. In addition, 46% of banks do not face any trade-offs. Annim (2012) analyzes 164 MFIs globally and concludes that these organizations need to choose between social performance and profit. In-depth access to each community in remote areas will create challenges in parallel with achieving the financial and social goals. Similarly, the studies of Sun and Im (2015), Cull *et al.* (2007), and Abate *et al.* (2014) also confirm that if organizations want to reach more than target customers in disadvantaged areas aimed at social goals must accept to reduce operational efficiency and sustainable financial goals.

However, there are also numerous studies arguing that there is no correlation between the social performance and financial performance of MFIs (Kereta, 2017; Quayes, 2015; Fajonyomi, 2012) or low correlation, or in the same direction between the accessibility and performance of MFIs (Bassem, 2012; Zerai and Rani, 2012; Amha, 2004; Adhikary and Papachristou, 2014). Zerai and Rani (2012) assessed

85 MFIs in India and figured out a low correlation between loan size (access depth), female borrowers, and sustainability in operations. This low correlation indicates that MFIs in India do not need to trade-off between social performance and profit. Similarly, Adhikary and Papachristou (2014) conclude that social performance (accessibility) positively impacts the profit and performance of MFIs. This study agrees with the studies of Bos and Millone (2015) and Vanroose and D'Espallier (2013). According to Nguyen Kim Anh and Le Thanh Tam (2013), there is a viewpoint that the MFI's performance is evaluated by operational self-sufficiency (OSS), financial self-sufficiency (FSS), institutional self-sufficiency (ISS), and accessibility. They do not affect a lot the performance of MFIs in Vietnam. Similarly, Nghiem Hong Son *et al.* (2006) surveys 46 microfinance projects in Northern and Central Vietnam and use data enveloping analysis (DEA) to evaluate the effectiveness of microfinance programs. In addition, he draws conclusions that the age and location of the program correlate with the performance of microfinance programs.

Ayayi and Sene (2010) identified the factors determining the sustainability of MFIs. They found that a high-quality credit portfolio is the most deciding component of financial sustainability of MFIs, followed by the operation of adequate interest rates and effective management to control personnel expenses. Further, they observed that the social performance of microfinance programs and the age of MFIs, whose coefficients are positive and statistically significant, have a lesser effect on the financial sustainability of MFIs. Kar (2011) found that expansion in leverage raises profit efficiency in MFIs while cost-efficiency deteriorates with a decrease in leverage. Further, he observed a severe impact on social performance.

In the argument between social performance vs. efficiency, Hashemi and Rosenberg (2006) and Weiss and Montgomery (2005) highlight the importance of social performance as the fundamental mission of MFIs, while Christen (2001) and Isern and Porteous (2005) emphasize the status of efficiency and sustainability in securing long term viability of MFIs. Morduch (2005) argues that social performance and sustainability can be compatible under certain conditions. It is hard to reach a coherent conclusion on this issue, as the microfinance sector is still deriving. Besides, more institutions with mixed clientele join the sector, making it harder to conclude. Recent factual studies have started to divide the total sample dataset into subsamples based on specific features that may affect the sustainability–outreach relationship. Cull *et al.* (2007) indicate that MFIs can control social performance and remain profitable, but they observe a trade-off between profitability and social performance to the poorest. Navajas *et al.* (2000) reveal that while MFIs provide loans to many households adjacent to the poverty line, most poor people are also the richest among the poor. Using a modified poverty outreach (social performance) index, Paxton and Cuevas (2002) rebuff the notion of any trade-off between financial sustainability and social performance.

2.2. *Factors affecting the profit of MFIs*

According to Huang (2005) and Vanroose (2008), three factors affect the financial performance (profit) of MFIs: (i) policy, (ii) geography, and (iii) institution. In particular, the mentioned policy factors are income level and instability in the economy (Westley, 2005; Schreiner and Colombet, 2001; Imboden, 2005); the geographic factors affecting the financial performance of MFIs are transaction costs and information costs (Sriram and Kumar, 2005; Schreiner and Colombet, 2001; Hulme and Moore, 2006); and the institutional factor with the education system. Concurrently, Paulson (2002) and Guiso (2004) also pointed out the positives of human capital in the financial sector.

According to the research of Al Mamun (2012), Woller and Woodworth (2001), and Crabb (2008), the factors affecting the profitability of MFIs are leadership, staff training, and motivation, information technology, product and service innovations, lending systems, legal framework. In addition, financial risk management, marketing, corporate governance, and audit systems are also considered to directly affect the financial performance of MFIs (Leonard and Julius, 2016; Chowdhury, 2009; Hulme and Moore, 2006; Chan, 2010; Boateng and Agyei, 2013; Ledgerwood and White, 2006; Hassan, 2002).

The study conducted by Muriu (2011) and Thu Trang Bui (2017) divides the factors affecting the profit of MFIs into two groups: internal and external factors including capital assets and loan portfolio quality, size of the organization, GDP level, rates of inflation and analyzes the relationship of these factors with the profits and performance of MFIs.

In a for-profit MFI, ROE is the strongest profitability indicator; it calculates an MFI's ability to reward its shareholders' investment, build its equity base through retained earnings, and promote additional equity investment. For a non-profit MFI, ROE indicates its capacity to build equity through retained earnings, and increased equity enables the MFI to leverage more financing to grow its portfolio. By excluding donations and non-operating revenues, this ratio demonstrates an institution's ability to achieve income from its core financial service activity. Some mature MFIs have achieved remarkably high ROE exceeding those of banks. Young organizations may take several years to achieve this. Even a mature MFI's ROE can be temporarily depressed due to unplanned events (natural disasters) or planned undertakings (such as expansion). ROE tends to fluctuate more than ROA. Monthly measurements of ROE can be deceiving because many MFI expenditures may not be recorded until the end of the fiscal year. Managers should look for a positive trend over several years and a ratio similar to or better than competitors. Since the market becomes saturated and competition increases, ROE may plateau. MFIs financed solely through equity donations will find this ratio less meaningful because donors rarely base their future investment decisions on ROE. ROE is, however, a good indicator of how well the MFI has used retained earnings and donor money to become sustainable.

3. Methodology and Data

This section provides a discussion of the econometric models, data, and samples used in this study. The model and its main variables are presented in Sub-section 3.1, whereas the data source and sample selection are described in Sub-section 3.2.

3.1. *The impact of social performance on profit*

The following baseline specification is utilized to examine the impact of social performance on profit:

$$\begin{aligned}\text{ROA}_{\text{it}} = \beta_0 &+ \beta_1\text{Age}_{\text{it}} + \beta_2\text{Size}_{\text{it}} + \beta_3\text{Office}_{\text{it}} \\ &+ \beta_4\text{Borrower}_{\text{it}} + \beta_5\text{Aveloanpebor}_{\text{it}} \\ &+ \beta_6\text{Loangrowth}_{\text{it}} + \beta_7\text{Depositratio}_{\text{it}} \\ &+ \beta_8\text{Operexpratio}_{\text{it}} + \beta_9\text{Par}_{\text{it}} + \mu_{\text{it}} \qquad (1)\end{aligned}$$

$$\begin{aligned}\text{ROE}_{\text{it}} = \beta_0 &+ \beta_1\text{Age}_{\text{it}} + \beta_2\text{Size}_{\text{it}} + \beta_3\text{Office}_{\text{it}} + \beta_4\text{Borrower}_{\text{it}} \\ &+ \beta_5\text{Aveloanpebor}_{\text{it}} + \beta_6\text{Loangrowth}_{\text{it}} \\ &+ \beta_7\text{Depositratio}_{\text{it}} + \beta_8\text{Operexpratio}_{\text{it}} \\ &+ \beta_9\text{Par}_{\text{it}} + \mu_{\text{it}} \qquad (2)\end{aligned}$$

Where ROA_{it} and ROE_{it} represent profits of MFI i at year t. Following the literature as Sekabira (2013), Bogan (2012), Kipesha and Xianzhi (2013), and Coleman and Oesi (2008), we use ROA and ROE as the two proxies for MFIs; 9 independent variables include age, size, borrower, office, average loan per borrower, loan growth, deposit ratio, operating expense ratio, PAR > 30. According to the literature overview, nine independent variables can influence ROA and ROE.

MFIs worldwide and in Vietnam are likely to develop through four stages: Start-up, Operational Self-sufficiency, Financial Self-sufficiency, and Development. *During stage 1*, the primary funding sources for MFIs are subsidies, soft loans, and compulsory savings

(Calvin, 2001) because MFIs lack reputation, which erects a barrier to access to other sources of funding. Moreover, due to limited financial capacity, MFIs are unable to afford other higher-cost sources. However, funding from public funds may make MFIs less motivated to monitor debt collection (Ngo, 2012), whereas private finance can help them achieve social goals (Westley, 2006). Therefore, gradually, MFIs tend to replace their capital sources from non-profit institutions to commercial enterprises as MFIs grow to the following stages (Hoque *et al.*, 2011). As these organizations grow to stages 2 and 3, their operations become fully grown, and MFIs will be eligible to meet the requirements of loans from credit institutions. In addition, achieving financial self-sufficiency may support MFIs increase their ability to mobilize capital. *During stage 4*, NGOs and MF officially earn stable growth in after-tax profit, increasing retained earnings and increasing equity. The formal institutions will focus on mobilizing voluntary savings, interbank lending, and issuing bonds and stocks within this stage. These factors will ensure revenue and sustainable development of MFIs.

Notably, in the context of Vietnam, when MFIs are mainly in the start-up and self-sustaining stages of their lifecycle, it is proper to use ROA (the dependent variable) to represent the level of effectiveness in the business portfolio of MFIs. As MFIs are monetary businesses, in which credit activities are the core activities, through the profitability of the loan portfolio, MFIs can develop microfinance activities and expand their customer networks through increasing capital from business activities. The dependent variable ROE shows the management's ability to generate income from the equity available of MFIs.

The MFIs from loan interest are primarily; therefore, the list of loans is the most critical asset. Quality items reflect overdue loans and future income decisions, as well as the organization's ability to increase access and service to existing customers. The most important indicator for assessing portfolio quality is measured by PAR $>$ 30 days.

The MFIs' income is mainly from loan interest; therefore, the loans are the most critical asset. The quality list reflects overdue loans and future income decisions and the institution's ability to increase access and service to existing customers. The most important indicator to measure the portion of the loan portfolio is PAR 30.

Not only affected by the level of access, ROA and ROE of MFIs are also affected by the characteristics of the institutions (size, age, target borrower), effectiveness (average loan per borrower, loan growth, deposit ratio, operating expense ratio), and risk level (PAR > 30).

The GLP is used to measure the size of an institution. It can increase either due to an increase in the number of borrowers without any change in the average loan per borrower or an increase in the average loan size with no increase in the number of borrowers. In the first case, the level of social performance would remain unchanged, while the level of social performance would decline in the latter case. As a result, the size of the institution will hurt social performance. Since the primary goal of an MFI is to provide loans to the very poor, a more significant level of equity would allow it to achieve a greater level of social performance, especially for non-profit MFIs. Following the same thread of logic, the debt-to-equity ratio can also be expected to affect social performance positively. The higher cost of disbursing and administering smaller loans are among the key reasons that prevent formal financial institutions from providing microcredit to the poor. Therefore, a higher total operation ratio would indicate a smaller average loan size and better social performance. Following our logic for the total operation ratio, one would expect the cost per borrower to be positively related to social performance. However, group loans are smaller per borrower in comparison to other loans offered by MFIs. Consequently, the cost per borrower for the smallest loans may be lower than for larger loans. This may result in a positive correlation between loan size and cost per borrower. Otherwise, one would expect social performance to be positively correlated with the average loan per borrower.

3.2. *Data and sample overview*

The research sample is Vietnamese MFIs listed in the MFIs directory by the Vietnam Microfinance Working Group (VMFWG) and financial data on the MIX market. However, due to the continuous fluctuation in the number of organizations joining and withdrawing from Vietnam's microfinance sector from 2011 to 2016, in this study, the authors mainly focused on data of organizations that have yearly operational data for six years. Mainly, 28 organizations (accounting for about 92% of the microfinance market share) include 24 semi-formal MFIs and 04 formal MFIs licensed to operate under the Law on Credit Institutions 2010 by the State Bank.

There are 28 organizations selected as the observed variable and included in the analysis model. Table 1 provides a complete research data description of observed variable data such as age, borrower, average loan per borrower, loan growth, deposit ratio, operating expense ratio, PAR 30 (model 1). It assesses the impact of social performance on ROA of MFIs and ROE with similar variables (model 2) to evaluate the impact of social performance on MFIs' profits.

Two variables used by the authors to evaluate the institution's profit include ROA and ROE. Some studies show that ROA and ROE have a negative impact on the social performance of the poor. MFI increases its focus on sustainability to save self and a few wealthier

Table 1: Summary statistic.

	Obs.	**Mean**	**Std. Dev.**	**Min**	**Max**
Age	150	9.36	6.166896	1	26
Size	150	14.11766	1.768046	5.675513	18.64493
Offices	151	6.807947	11.04096	1	60
Borrower	151	8.746378	1.392162	5.220356	12.64416
Aveloanperbor	151	228.5352	110.8832	43.83	555.93
Loangrowth	147	32.07463	58.80253	−36.34	532.45
Depositratio	151	.2680066	.2145276	0	.878
Operexpratio	146	13.82637	12.16418	1.64	146
PAR	126	.4146032	.9850447	0	7.17

clients since most of the poor cannot pay the market price of the services. Similarly, Kipesha and Zhang (2013) examined the presence of trade-offs between sustainability, profitability, outreach, and social performance using panel data of 47 MFIs for four years from 2008 to 2011 from the Mix market. Data uses an unbalanced panel regression analysis model. After using the Welfarists approach, the study found the presence of negative trade-offs between profitability and social performance to the poor. It did not show the presence of trade-offs between financial sustainability and social performance measures. However, the study found that social performance has a positive relationship with both sustainability and profitability measures.

4. Results and Discussions

The result of this model is checked by applying Hausman Specification Test (Hausman, 1978) to choose whether Fix-effects Model (FEM) or Random-effects Model (REM) for models (1) and (2) is appropriate. In this case, the model is found significant, and then FEM results are taken into consideration.

The results in Tables 2 and 3 show the p-value (Prob > chi2) = 0.0011 and 0.0020 $< \alpha = 0.05$. Therefore, the authors reject the Ho hypothesis and conclude that the model proposed using FEM (used in Model 1 and 2) is more proper and better to explain REM about the impact of social performance on ROA and ROE of MFIs. In order

Table 2: Hausman Specification Test for model (1).

Correlated Fixed Effects — Hausman Test
Equation: Untitled
Test cross-section fixed effects

Test Summary	Chi-Sq. Statistic	Chi-Sq. d.f.	Prob
Cross-section fixed effects	24.02	7	0.0011

Table 3: Hausman Specification Test for model (2).

Correlated Fixed Effects — Hausman Test
Equation: Untitled
Test cross-section fixed effects

Test Summary	Chi-Sq. Statistic	Chi-Sq. d.f.	Prob
Cross-section fixed effects	22.62	7	0.0020

Table 4: The results of FEM and FEM-robust for the models (1) and (2).

	ROA (1)	ROA (2)	ROE (1)	ROE (2)
Offices	−0.2340	−0.2340	−1.0085	−1.0085**
	(0.5595)	(0.4768)	(0.7036)	(0.0253)
Borrower	5.4563**	5.4563***	15.0078***	15.0078***
	(2.5339)	(0.0021)	(3.1869)	(0.0003)
Aveloanperbor	0.0179	0.0179	0.0593***	0.0593***
	(0.0141)	(0.3051)	(0.1777)	(0.0074)
Loangrowth	0.0155	0.0155	−0.0108	−0.0108
	(0.0223)	(0.5662)	(0.0281)	(0.7892)
Depositratio	−18.5149	−18.5149*	7.3204	7.3204
	(13.7349)	(0.0502)	(17.2743)	(0.5710)
Operexpratio	−0.0898	−0.0898	−0.0429	−0.0429
	(0.0749)	(0.3274)	(0.0941)	(0.7108)
PAR	−10.6519***	−10.6519**	−10.1082***	−10.1082**
	(0.1022)	(0.0187)	(1.3861)	(0.0380)
Constant	37.7409*	−37.7409***	−128.3184***	−128.3184***
	(20.6322)	(0.0081)	(25.9488)	(0.0002)
N	117	117	117	117
r2_w	0.5774	0.5774	0.5986	0.5986

Note: Standard error and robust standard error are in parentheses. ***, **, * denote significance at 1%, 5% and 10%, respectively.

to strengthen the persuasion of the model, the authors used White's heteroskedasticity and robust standard errors (1980) for the FEM model (1) and (2). The results obtained with FEM in Table 4 are as follows.

The result of heteroscedasticity and robust standard errors by White (1980) shows an insignificant negative correlation between ROA with several offices and the operating expense ratio. On the other hand, the results show a significant negative correlation between profitability (ROA) and deposit ratio at 10% and PAR 30 at a 5% significant level. The results on ROA showed a positive correlation between ROA and the number of borrowers at 1%. Similarly, ROE has a negative correlation with loan growth and operating expense ratio. Besides, the number of offices and PAR 30 negatively correlated with a significant coefficient with ROE at 5%. The positive correlation results between ROE also support the results on ROE to several borrowers and average loan per borrower at a 1% level of significance.

Financial institutions opening more offices and branches can increase their profits. Financial institutions often seek to expand and benefit more from new markets/areas through reaching more customers, providing more products and services, etc. Different from other financial institutions, the operational expansion of MFIs through offices leads to profit decline (ROA, ROE) due to the characteristics of most customers of MFIs facing poverty and living in remote areas. In order to attract this customer group, instead of opening more transaction offices, MFIs have come up with the solution to let credit officers penetrate these remote areas and directly help customers complete transactions from loans to deposits. This is the most optimal method for MFIs. They do not need to open numerous transaction offices but still reach the most eligible customers possible and increase profits for MFIs.

The increasing number of customers and the average loan per borrower will increase the profit of MFIs (increase in ROA, ROE), which is perfectly reasonable; when the MFIs are popular among individual customers, they can increase profits. Besides, customers of MFIs, after getting access to loans, also receive support for the most effective use of loans such as agricultural production, product consumption, efficient plant species, and handicrafts for export. Besides supporting the use of loans, MFIs in Vietnam also have credit programs, promotional savings, creating incentives for friendly customers such as "Spring giving love," "Saving for the community — Lucky hits" of Capital aid for employment of the poor microfinance institution (CEP) or capacity building and lending programs for members of Tinh Thuong microfinance institution (TYM) or non-financial products and services for community development of Thanh Hoa microfinance institution. In addition, the average loan per borrower also shows the confidence of customers in the institution. The microfinance sector is considered a specific industry since its customers with low levels of education and often build trust in institutions through their relatives and friends. When the loan and the number of customers increase, it is time for MFIs to work towards sustainable development. The emergence of microfinance aims to improve economic conditions for poor customers, provide development opportunities, and improve their lives by providing valuable financial and non-financial services. The reality shows that while accessing formal credit services, poor people and people living in remote areas often have few opportunities to connect or enjoy essential financial services due to several barriers, especially collaterals. MFIs in Vietnam are expecting their customers to access financial and non-financial products and services. Moreover, MFIs also set long-term and sustainable goals in providing specific financial products and services aimed at specific contents: (i) creating more jobs, improving income for the poor, (ii) minimizing the difficulties that the poor face while accessing financial services and products of MFIs and (iii) providing capacity building and support to disadvantaged customers and organizing various community activities.

Loan growth and operating expense ratio are not statistically significant, increasing profits for MFIs. These two factors are significant for the development of MFIs. The deposit rate is statistically significant in the opposite correlation to ROA and positive correlation with ROE. It indicates that each MFI not only increases its profit through deposit mobilization but also undertakes other derivative activities, such as calling for capital investment in each stage of development. Besides, the model results indicate that portfolio at risk (PAR) has an opposite correlation with a significance level of 5%. It is entirely clear that if MFIs want to increase profits, they will continually maintain PAR at a low level. According to international practice, a credit institution will be effective and sustainable if the PAR ratio >30 is less than 5%. According to the regulations of the State Bank of Vietnam, the allowed lousy debt ratio of credit institutions is below 3%. In the context of the period 2011–2016, bad debts of commercial banks increased sharply and are likely to affect banking activities in Vietnam. The very low PAR >30 ratios of formal and semi-formal MFIs (less than 0.5%) show that operational safety is an advantage of MFIs over other types of credit. This result is entirely in line with the expectations of Vanroose *et al.* (2009) and El-Maksoud (2016) and is explained by the economic theory of scale and risk. Accordingly, when risk decreases, profits increase. This also implies that to maximize profits for MFIs, MFIs need to minimize their external risk investments.

5. Conclusion

Results from the two models show that the number of borrowers, operating expense ratio, and PAR have a significant impact on the profit of MFIs. Therefore, the study will focus on providing solutions to help MFIs attract more customers, reduce operating costs, and control PAR, specifically:

(i) MFIs seeking to attract more customers and to develop their products and services should have specific development strategies. Currently, according to the regulations of the Government and the State Bank of Vietnam, MFIs are not allowed to diversify in forms of products and services; thus, they promote credit, savings, and insurance products. Therefore, MFIs need to market more products and services that are suitable for more customer segments. For formal MFIs, it is necessary to increase savings mobilization with different methods and diversifying forms of capital mobilization with different interest rates. For semi-formal MFIs, it is more difficult and risky to raise voluntary deposits, so there is no need to develop this product yet. MFIs that want to attract more borrowers need to find relatively cheap funding sources such as donors, development investors, and trust funds of commercial banks. This is the most crucial basis for MFIs to reduce lending rates, approach customers, reduce operating costs, and increase the ability of sustainable operations. Additionally, MFIs need to strengthen market research and improve and apply new products and services. For instance, it consists of diversifying the method of repaying loan principles and saving to meet a wide range of needs. In addition, piloting some services such as money transfer via mobile or Internet, micro insurance services, third-party agents, etc., can meet the increasing financial needs of poor and low-income households. Along with the number of services, more attention should be paid to the quality, the diversity of services provided, and the availability and accessibility of the services. Promoting investment in non-financial services meets the need to improve the social capacity of customers because this is the most significant difference between MFIs from other credit institutions. These factors are becoming increasingly important in attracting customers that MFIs should strengthen in competition and development.

(ii) The interests of customers and the higher reputation of the institutions are also issues that MFIs in Vietnam face. They should pay attention to attracting customers, cutting operating costs, building customer confidence, and reducing PAR rate through some specific activities: transparency of basic information of MFIs such as interest rates, contract terms, and financial statements. MFIs should publicly list interest rates, especially clearly show the Effective Interest Rates in credit contracts; explain clearly to customers the difference among numerous interest rates; comparably show actual interest rates; make sure all loan terms are known and clearly explained to customers (such as cost, compulsory savings, calculation method, payment frequency ...). The rights and obligations of customers in deposits and loans are clearly stated in the regulations and are publicly listed.

(iii) MFIs should support customers to access credit loans widely and reasonably minimize the asymmetry between borrowers and lenders. Good credit quality allows MFIs to evaluate risks accurately and improve the quality of the customer portfolio. When MFIs analyze their total outstanding loans, they can estimate their repayment capacity. Therefore, MFIs can improve profits, reduce operating costs, increase profit margins, ensure sufficient capital, and meet capital reserve requirements.

Bibliography

Abate, G.T., Borzaga, C., and Getnet, K. (2014). Cost-efficiency and outreach of microfinance institutions: Trade-offs and the role of ownership. *Journal of International Development*, 26(6), 923–932.

Adhikary, S. and Papachristou, G. (2014). Is there a trade-off between financial performance and outreach in South Asian microfinance institutions? *The Journal of Developing Areas*, 48(4), 381–402.

Al Mamun, C.A. (2012). Assessing the factors that led to the management technique reduces MFIs profitability and success of microfinance in Bangladesh: A case study on Grameen Bank. *World Review of Business Research*, 2(2), 75–90.

Amha, W. (2004). Managing growth of microfinance institutions (MFIs): Balancing sustainability and reaching large number of clients in Ethiopia. *Ethiopian Journal of Economics*, 13(2), 61–101.

Annim, S.K. (2012). Microfinance efficiency: Trade-offs and complementarities between the objectives of microfinance institutions and their performance perspectives. *The European Journal of Development Research*, 24(5), 788–807.

Armendariz, B. and Labie, M. (2011). *The Handbook of Microfinance*. World Scientific Publishing.

Assefa, E., Hermes, N., and Meesters, A. (2013). Competition and the performance of microfinance institutions. *Applied Financial Economics*, 23(9): 767–782.

Ayayi, G.A. and Sene, M. (2010). What drives microfinance institution's financial sustainability. *The Journal of Developing Areas*, 44(1), 303–324.

Bassem, B.S. (2012). Social and financial performance of microfinance institutions: Is there a trade off? *Journal of Economics and International Finance*, 4(4), 92–100.

Beck, T., Demirgüç-Kunt, A., and Levine, R. (2007). Finance, inequality and the poor. *Journal of Economic Growth*, 12(1), 27–49.

Boateng, I.A. and Agyei, A. (2013). Microfinance in Ghana: Development, success factors and challenges. *International Journal of Academic Research in Accounting, Finance and Management Sciences*, 3(4), 153–160.

Bogan, V.L. 2012. Capital structure and sustainability: An empirical study of microfinance institutions. *Review of Economics and Statistics*, 94(4), 1045–1058.

Bos, J.W.B. and Millone, M. (2015). Practice what you preach: Microfinance business models and operational efficiency. *World Development*, 70(1), 28–42.

Calvin, B. (2001). Framework for Financing Sources, in an Introduction to Key Issues in Microfinance, on Microfinance Network website.

Chan, S.H. (2010). The influence of leadership and experience on organizational performance: A study of Amanah Ikhtiar Malaysia. *Asia Pacific Business and Review*, 16, 59–77.

Chowdhury, A.M. (2009). *Assessing the Factors that Led to the Success of Microfinance in Bangladesh: A Case Study on Grameen Bank*.

Christen, R.P. (2001). Commercialization and mission drift: The transformation of microfinance in Latin America. *Occasional Paper, No. 5*. CGAP. Washington, DC.

Ciravegna, D. (2005). *The Role of Microcredit in Modern Economy: The Case of Italy*. www.flacso.or.cr/fileadmin/documentos/FLACSO/auCiravegna2.DOC.

Coleman, A. and Osei, K.A. (2008). Outreach and profitability of microfinance institutions: The role of governance. *Journal of Economic Studies*, 35(3), 236–248.

Collins, D., Morduch, J., Rutherford, S., and Ruthven, O. (2009). *Portfolios of the Poor: How the World's Poor Live on $2 a Day*. Princeton University Press.

Copestake, J. (2007). Mainstreaming microfinance: Social performance management or mission drift? *World Development*, 35(10), 1721–1738.

Crabb, P. (2008). Economic freedom and the success of microfinance institutions. *Journal of Developmental Entrepreneurship*, 13(2), 205–219.

Cull, R., Demirguc-Kunt, A., and Morduch, J. (2007). Financial performance and outreach: A global analysis of leading microbanks. *The Economic Journal*, 117(517), F107–F133.

Dunford, C. (2006). *Evidence of Microfinance's Contribution to Achieving the Millennium Development Goals*. Freedom from Hunger.

El-Maksoud S.A. (2016). Performance of microfinance institutions. PhD diss. Cardiff School of Management.

Fajonyomi, O.S., Jegede, C.A., and Akinlabi, B.H. (2012). Relationship between outreach and sustainability of microfinance banks in south-western Nigeria. *OIDA International Journal of Sustainable Development*, 5(11), 51–62.

Ghalib, A.K. (2013). How effective is microfinance in reaching the poorest? Empirical evidence on programme outreach in rural Pakistan. *Journal of Business Economic and Management*, 14(3), 467–480.

Guiso, L., Sapienza, P., and Zingales, L. (2004). The role of social capital in financial development. *American Economic Review*, 94(3), 526–556.

Hartungi, R. (2007). Understanding the success factors of micro-finance institution in a developing country. *International Journal of Social Economics*, 34(1), 388–401.

Hashemi, S. and Rosenberg, R. (2006). Graduating the poor into microfinance: Linking safety nets and financial services. *Focus Note, No. 34*. CGAP. Washington, DC.

Hassan, M.K. (2002). The micro finance revolution and the Grameen Bank experience in Bangladesh. *Financial Markets Institutions & Instruments*, 11(3), 205–265.

Hausman, J.A. (1978). Specification tests in econometrics. *Econometrica*, 46(6), 1251–1271.

Hermes, N., Lensink, R., and Meesters, A. (2011). Outreach and efficiency of microfinance institutions. *World Development*, 39(6), 938–948.

Hoque, M., Chishty, M., and Halloway, R. (2011). Commercialization and changes in capital structure in microfinance institutions: An innovation or wrong turn? *Managerial Finance*, 37(5), 414–425.

Huang Y. (2005). What Determines Financial Development? *Discussion Paper No. 05/580*. University of Bristol.

Hulme, D. and Mosley, P. (1996). *Finance Against Poverty*, Vol. 1. Routledge.

Hulme D. and K. Moore. (2006). Why has microfinance been a development success in Bangladesh (and Beyond). *Global Poverty Research Group (GPRG) Working Paper Series, No. 041*. Institute for Development Policy and Management. University of Manchester.

Imboden K. (2005). Building inclusive financial sectors: The road to growth and poverty. *Journal of International Affairs*, 58(2), 65–86.

Isern, J. and Porteous, D. (2005). Commercial banks and microfinance: Evolving models of success. *Focus Note, No. 28*. CGAP. Washington, DC.

Kar, A.K. (2011). Does capital and financing structure have any relevance to the performance of microfinance institutions? *International Review of Applied Economics*, 26(3), 329–348.

Khandker, S.R. (2005). Micro-finance and poverty: Evidence using panel data from Bangladesh. *The World Bank Economic Review*, 19(2), 263–286.

Kereta, B.B. (2017). Outreach and financial performance analysis of microfinance institutions in Ethiopia. In *African Economic Conference*. Addis Ababa.

Kimando, L.M., Kihoro, J.M., and Njogu, G.W. (2012). Factors influencing the sustainability of microfinance institutions in Murang'a municipality. *International Journal of Business and Commerce*, 1(10), 21–45.

Kipesha E.F. and Zhang X. (2013). Sustainability, profitability and outreach tradeoffs: Evidences from microfinance institutions in East Africa. *European Journal of Business and Management*, 5(8), 136–148 (2013).

Kirkpatrick, C. and Maimbo, M. (2002). The implications of the evolving microfinance agenda for regulatory and supervisory policy. *Development Policy Review*, 20(3), 293–304.

Ledgerwood, J. (1999). *Microfinance Handbook: An Institutional and Financial Perspective*. World Bank.

Ledgerwood, J. and White, V. (2006). *Transforming Microfinance Institutions: Providing Full Financial Services to the Poor*. World Bank.

Levine, R. (2005). Finance and growth: Theory and evidence, in Aghion, P. and Durlauf, S. (Eds.). *Handbook of Economic Growth*, Vol. 1, pp. 865–934. Elsevier.

Littlefield, E., Morduch, J., and Hashemi, S. (2003). Is microfinance an effective strategy to reach the Millennium Development Goals? *Focus Note*, 24, 1–11.

Leonard, M. and Julius, T. (2016). Key success drivers for microfinance institutions in Zimbabwe: Developing core competences for financial inclusion. *International Journal of Business and Social Science*, 7(3), 128–135.

Marr, A.A. (2004). Challenge to the orthodoxy concerning microfinance and poverty reduction. *Journal of Microfinance*, 5(2), 1–35.

Mersland, R. and Storm, R. (2010). Microfinance Mission Drift? *World Development* 38(1), 28–36.

Morduch, J. and Haley, B. (2002). Analysis of the effects of microfinance on poverty reduction. *Working Paper, No. 1014*. NYU Wagner.

Morduch, J. (2005). Smart subsidies for sustainable microfinance: Finance for the poor. *ADB Quarterly Newsletter of the Focal Point for Microfinance*, 6, 1–7.

Mosley, P. (2001). Microfinance and poverty in Bolivia. *Journal of Development Studies*, 37(4), 101–132.

Muriu, P.W. (2011). Microfinance profitability. PhD Diss., University of Birmingham.

Navajas, S., Schreiner, M., and Meyer, R.L. (2000). Microcredit and the poorest of the poor: Theory and evidence from Bolivia. *World Development*, 28, 333–346.

Nghiem Hong Son, Coelli, T. and Rao, P. (2006). The efficiency of microfinance in Vietnam: Evidence from NGO schemes in the North and the Central regions. *International Journal of Environmental, Cultural, Economic and Social Sustainability*, 2(5), 71–78.

Ngo, T.V. (2012). Capital structure and microfinance performance: A cross country analysis and case study of Vietnam. PhD Diss.

Nguyen Kim Anh and Le Thanh Tam (2013). *The Sustainability of Microfinance Institutions in Vietnam: Circumstances and Implications.* Transport Publishing House.

OECD (2013). Promoting Financial Inclusion through Financial Education: OECD/INFE Evidence, Policies and Practice. *Working Papers on Finance, Insurance and Private Pensions, No. 34.* OECD.

Olivares-Polanco, F. (2005). Commercializing microfinance and deepening outreach? Empirical evidence from Latin America. *Journal of Microfinance/ESR Review*, 7(2), 47–69.

Osborn, D., Cutter, A., and Ullah, F. (2015). *Universal Sustainable Development Goals — Understanding the Transformational Challenge for Developed Countries.* Report of a study by stakeholder forum.

Osotimehin, K.O., Jegede, C.A., Akinlabi, B.H., and Hamed, B. (2011). Determinants of microfinance outreach in South-Western Nigeria: An empirical analysis. *International Journal of Management and Business Studies*, 1(1), 1–7.

Paulson, A. (2002). Human capital and the development of financial institutions: Evidence from Thailand. *Working Paper.* Federal Reserve Bank of Chicago.

Paxton, J. and Cuevas, C.E. (2002). Outreach and sustainability of member-based rural financial intermediaries. In *The Triangle of Microfinance: Financial Sustainability, Outreach and Impact.* The Johns Hopkins University Press.

Piot-Lepetit, I. and Nzongang, J. (2014). Financial sustainability and poverty outreach within a network of village banks in Cameroon: A multi-DEA approach. *European Journal of Operational Research*, 234(1), 319–330.

Quayes, S. (2012). Depth of outreach and financial sustainability of microfinance institutions. *Applied Economics*, 44(26), 3421–3433.

Quayes, S. (2015). Outreach and performance of microfinance institutions: A panel analysis. *Applied Economics*, 47(18), 1909–1925.

Rauf, A.S. and Mahmood, T. (2009). Growth and performance of microfinance in Pakistan. *Pakistan Economic and Social Review*, 47(1), 99–122.

Schreiner M. and Colombet, H.H. (2001). From urban to rural: Lessons for microfinance from Argentina. *Development Policy Review*, 19(3), 339–354.

Scully, N. (2004). *Microcredit no Panacea for Poor Women.* Global Development Research Centre.

Sekabira, H. (2013). Capital structure and its role on performance of microfinance institutions: The Ugandan Case. *Sustainable Agriculture Research*, 2(3), 86.

Shastri, K.R. (2009). Microfinance and poverty reduction in India: A comparative study with Asian Countries. *African Journal of Business Management*, 3(4), 136–140.

Simanowitz, A. and Walter, A. (2002). Ensuring impact: Reaching the poorest while building financially self-sufficient institutions and showing improvement in the lives of the poorest women and their families, in Daley-Harris (Eds.), *Pathways Out of Poverty.* Kumarian Press.

Sinha, S. (2010). *How to Calm the Charging Bull — An Agenda for CGAP in the Decade of the "Teenies."* Microfinance Focus.

Sriram M.S. and Kumar, R. (2005). Conditions in which microfinance has emerged in certain regions and consequent policy implications. *Working Paper.* Indian Institute of Management.

Sun, S.L. and Im, J. (2015). Profits and outreach to the poor: The institutional logics of microfinance institutions. *Asia Pacific Journal of Management*, 32(1), 95–117.

Thu Trang Bui. (2017). Factors affecting microfinance development in Vietnam. *Doctoral Sciences Economiques.*

Vanroose, A. (2008). What macro factors make microfinance institutions reach out? *Savings and Development*, 32(3), 153–174.

Vanroose, A. and D'Espallier, B. (2009). Microfinance and financial sector development. *Working Paper, No. 09/040.* CEB.

Vanroose, A. and D'Espallier, B. (2013). Do microfinance institutions accomplish their mission? Evidence from the relationship between traditional financial sector development and microfinance institutions' outreach and performance. *Applied Economics*, 45, 1965–1982.

Wagner, C. and Winkler, A. (2013). The vulnerability of microfinance to financial turmoil — Evidence from the global financial crisis. *World Development*, 51, 71–90.

Weiss, J. and Montgomery, H. (2005). Great expectations: Microfinance and poverty reduction in Asia and Latin America. *Oxford Development Studies*, 33(3–4), 391–416.

Westley G.D. (2005). Microfinance in the Caribbean: How to go further. *Sustainable Development Department Technical Papers Series MSM-129*. Inter-American Development Bank.

Westley, G.D. (2006). *Strategies and Structures for Commercial Banks in Microfinance*. Inter-American Development Bank.

White, H.A. (1980). Heteroskedasticity-consistent covariance matrix estimator and a direct test for heteroscedasticity. *Econometrica*, 48(4), 817–838.

Woller, G. and Woodworth, W. (2001). Microcredit as a grassroots policy for international development. *Policy Studies Journal*, 29(1), 267–283.

World Bank (2008). Finance for all? Policies and pitfalls in expanding access. *A World Bank Policy Research Report*. Washington D.C.

World Bank (2018). *Financial Inclusion*. World Bank.

Zerai, B. and Rani, L. (2012). Is there a tradeoff between outreach and sustainability of micro finance institutions? Evidence from Indian microfinance institutions (MFIs). *European Journal of Business and Management*, 4(2), 90–98.

Part III

Emerging Markets Finance

https://doi.org/10.1142/9789811262258_0003

Chapter 3

The Effects of Remittance and Financial Development on the Economic Growth in Asia-Pacific Countries

Trung Kien Tran and Gia Luat Diep

Abstract

Remittance has become an essential source of foreign income and remarkably influences the current accounts and economies of many nations. However, the relationship between remittance, financial development index, and national economic growth is still controversial. According to the database from 28 countries in the Asia-Pacific region from 1995 to 2018, the effects of remittance and financial development on economic growth are evaluated using empirical methods in this study. The results show that remittance hurts the economy, which can be seen as a constraint on economic growth. Specifically, the credit ratio in the private sector also harms economic development, and the financial development index has a significant effect on the economy.

Keywords: Remittance; Financial development; Economic growth.

1. Introduction

In the last decades, remittance from migrants has been tremendously accounted for and has become one of the significant financial flows of developing countries. Traditional capital sources, such as financial aid or private capital turned secondary (World Bank, 2003; Aggarwal *et al.*, 2010; Bettin *et al.*, 2012; Giuliano and Ruiz-Arranz, 2009; Rao and Hassan, 2011). In 2015, the source of remittance worldwide had been estimated as over 601 billion US dollars, and 411 billion US dollars out of the total belonged to developing countries, which has been tripled than the official development aid. There are two ways of remittance transfers: official and unofficial. Nyamongo and Misati (2011; 2012) stated that the official channel of transferring remittance positively influenced financial development. When the remittance receivers open a bank account in a commercial bank, they can collect the relevant information regarding loans that they could apply for in the future. If the influence on the financial sector is apparent, the financial development is expected to be higher.

According to Adenutsi (2011), Mundaca (2009), Misati and Nyamongo (2010, 2012), financial development relates to private investments and economic growth. Evidence show that financial development is crucial to pushing up the economy. Theories supporting the roles of financial development were indicated in the research of Bagehot (1873), Schumpeter (1911), and Hicks (1969). According to Schumpeter (1911), other augmented services provided by financial intermediation played a vital role in renewability and economic growth. Schumpeter also showed that financial institutes might also increase the changes and economic development by identifying and sponsoring relevant and effective investments.

Based on the research of Aggarwal *et al.* (2010), the high level of financial development leads to a lower level of the marginal impact of remittance. Financial development links to the creation of information on investment opportunities or capital allocation; company regulation and management, commerce, diversification and risk management; mobilizing and synchronizing savings, and easing the exchanges of goods and services. These financial functions lead to saving and investment decisions, technological changes, and finally, economic growth (Misati, 2007; Misati and Nyamongo, 2011).

Besides, research indicated that remittance had negative impacts on development. Firstly, in the information asymmetry situation, the senders could not control the purposes and effectiveness of money transferred to the receivers compared to the primary objective. Secondly, the receivers of remittance used the money for daily consumption, not for investment. They considered remittance as the alternative income, which would lead to negative labor productivity and economic growth in the future. Thirdly, the remittance can increase the foreign exchanges, and the national currency will raise the value. This could be a competitive disadvantage for those nations depending on exporting activities (Amuedo-Dorantes and Pozo, 2004; Chami *et al.*, 2003).

Therefore, the research about "the impacts of remittance and financial development on the economic growths of Asia-Pacific countries" will analyze and criticize the importance of remittance in the structure of capital for economic growth. The evidence could be used to strengthen and solve the controversy of the influence of remittance and financial development on economic growth in previous research. The research includes an introduction, literature reviews, research framework, results, and conclusion.

2. Literature Review

Remittance is defined as the income of migrants that could be sent back to their hometown for any reason (Nyamongo, 2012). In precise meaning, it is an amount that could be sent to but not returned, since it is the marginal amount of money from migrants sent to family members or relatives or friends without any requirements or restrictions, unlike other sources such as loans or shares (Kapur, 2003). WB states that remittance could be sorted into three categories:

Category 1. Workers' remittances: The current cash flow sent by overseas workers or citizens of migrated countries. This source is considered as a part of transactions of the existing account.

Category 2. Overseas employees' compensation: Any workers performing tasks overseas will be compensated a specific amount of money, considered foreign workers' income. The total income from foreign workers will be remittance and become one of the income components in the current account.

Category 3. Migrants' transfers: The corresponding entry of products' categories and changes in financial indicators from migrants, i.e., changing the savings accounts of migrants when they repatriate.

Remittance could be transacted in two ways:

Official transaction: Remittance can be transferred by official institutions or certified individuals/companies working in money transfers such as banks or money transfer companies.

Unofficial transactions: Remittance is transferred in cash by intermediates such as friends, family members, or private companies. The remittance is delivered upon the hometown visitations (Nyamongo, 2012).

2.1. *The effects of remittance on economic growth*

2.1.1. *The positive effects of remittance on economic growth*

Remittance has a significantly positive impact on national economic growth (Solimano, 2003; Aggarwal *et al.*, 2006), increasing the number of bank deposits and bank credits for private sectors (Giuliano and Ruiz-Arranz, 2005). Remittance could replace other financial tools such as credits and insurance, which are not essential in developing countries. It could also stimulate expenditure and investments since it reduces the size of economic depression in some countries and motivates the regional economy. Furthermore, remittance allows households to participate in other business forms, even if the risks could be high the profit could be remarkable. Remittance also helps increase domestic savings and improve the financial intermediations; therefore, it could lead to the potential of the national economy (Ratha, 2013). Besides the positive influences for expenditure and investments, remittance also improves the living standards for receivers by renovating housing areas, educational institutions, and healthcare services.

Remittance also helps to reduce poverty. Since it is a form of income for foreign workers from developing countries working overseas, it is the motivation to escape poverty. In developing countries in the Asia-Pacific, if the ratio of remittance increases by 10%, the poverty ratio reduces by 2.8% (Ravallion and Chen, 1997). The research shows that in 74 developing countries with low and intermediate incomes, 10% of migrants will decrease to 1.9% in the number of people living under 1 US Dollar per day (Adams and Page, 2005). Taylor *et al.* (2005) stated that in the rural areas of Mexico in 2002, there was a significantly contrary impact of remittance on the wealth gap. In the long run, remittance could be the cash flow for asset accumulation, the motivation for agricultural production, and poverty reductions.

Remittance plays a vital role in the financial market development of receiving countries. By increasing the size of cash flow, remittance stretches the sources of money for banks. It helps to increase the financial market and reduce the outsourcing sponsored amount. Economic growth will be evident via (1) economy of scale and (2) political economy influences. The bigger the size of the economy, the higher the pressure for the government to control the financial revolution.

2.1.2. *The adverse effects on economic growth*

In the case of long-term remittance sent to the receivers, households tend to spend rather than invest. Spending demands help to increase the households' benefits, not to grow the economy. Otherwise, when the domestic financial market merges with an international market and the domestic financial system develops, remittance is no longer a domestic private investment. Consumption expenditure only pushes up the economy when the demand is high and aggregate demand increases. As such, the investment capital rises to lead to aggregate supply going up. In this case, aggregate demand tremendously increases because of consumption, but aggregate supply stays unchanged or slightly increases compared to aggregate demand. The result shows no benefits for the national economy from the remittance. And remittance could be a long-term risk if it is considered as permanent income. It leads to a reduction of labor productivity and an increase in private consumption (i.e., imported products) other than investments or domestic savings (Azam and Gubert, 2006; Chami *et al.*, 2012). The rise in consumption could create inflation and turbulent exchange rates (Barajas *et al.*, 2011; El-Sakka and McNabb, 1999). Therefore, macroeconomy principles called "Dutch diseases" could lead to the failure of the domestic economy, current account deficit, and inflation with an uncontrollable monetary system (Kireyev, 2006).

Remittance could be the new illegal channel for money laundering. Even the origin of remittance is clear by official labor that could be proved, and the cash flow from remittance can be used legally. Banks will be the central hub since they can transact a considerable amount of money, and right after remittance is banked into the account, it becomes legal. There will be no doubt of using it regardless of purpose.

Remittance is the primary income of many households. If it is used effectively, the growth of the economy can be noticeable. However, it is mainly considered a secured amount of money that could be a free benefit, even if it may be turned into capital, but there is no hope of using it for investment. The prodigal use of remittance is obviously for high-end products such as houses, automobiles, or relaxation rather than production (Chammi *et al.*, 2005).

2.2. *The effects of remittance and financial development on economic growth*

The relationship between remittance and financial development is based on two substitutes and additional variables to the economic growth. Firstly, the hypothesis stated that remittance and financial development promote each other. With the higher level of financial development, the remittance flow will be sent fast, safely, and economically. Nonetheless, remittance will also be a stimulating factor for financial institutes and authorities. It helps increase the financial intermediation competition and revolutionize the current legislation to promote remittance as investment capital.

Furthermore, the transaction fee will be lower in any country with a developed financial system (Freund and Spatafora, 2008). This case could reduce the number of households prevented from money transactions based on budget limitations and ultimate remittance enhancement from senders. Finally, in the country where the banking system flourishes, remittance can add up credits or mortgaged property. Migrants are recommended to transfer the money to the family with the hope of no-waste use of money from irrelevant activities (Chami *et al.*, 2012).

Otherwise, when the credit market does not grow, the household cannot reach the credit system or loans for investment or projects, or if there is, the interest rate will be very high. In this case, remittance play as an alternative amount of money that can be used to continue business or as a mortgaged property so that the household could ask for official loans from the bank. Furthermore, the remittance will be used as a personal loan from household to household, which could be easier than asking from banks.

The research on the relationship between remittance and financial development focused on accrediting two main hypotheses: replacement or supplement. The replacement hypotheses between remittance and financial development are apparent in some countries' research done with econometric methods. Giuliano and Ruiz-Arranz (2009) showed that official credits and remittances are the forms of replacements, not supplements. Remittance replaces the financial deficit. Ramirez and Sharma (2008) stated that remittance flow had a tremendous effect on economic growth in Latin American and Caribbean countries from 1995 to 2005. The result of remittance was more clearly shown than in other developed countries. Ojapinwa *et al.* (2014) proved that the replacement character of remittance affected the investment and economic growth of receiving countries when the economic downturn happened. Mundaca (2009) also showed a positive relationship between remittance and financial development to economic growth based on databases of 25 Latin American and Caribbean countries from 1970 to 2002.

3. Methodology and Data

3.1. *Empirical model*

The research model is captured by the research of Nyamongo *et al.* (2012). The basic model analyzes the impacts of remittance on the economic growth of Barro (1989, 1991).

$$\mathbf{\Delta yit} = (\beta\mathbf{1} - \mathbf{1})\mathbf{Yt{-}1} + \beta\mathbf{2Xi,t} + \beta\mathbf{t} + \mu\mathbf{i} + \varepsilon\mathbf{i,t} \tag{1}$$

In this model:

Δy: Actual average GDP growth rate
Y: Actual average GDP Rate
X: Vector of variables shown in standard growth model including the ratio of domestic investment upon GDP, inflation ratio, human resource ratio, governmental spending power upon GDP (government based), trade openness
εi,t: Random error in the model
βt: The impacts of mobile variables changed in time but have the same in influences among countries
μi: The effects of different variables in different countries but unchanged by time
β1 − 1: Convergence coefficient

In this research, the impacts of remittance and financial development are obvious on economic growth. The new expanded formula is shown as:

$$\begin{aligned}\mathbf{Ypcg_{i,t}} &= (\beta_1 - \mathbf{1})\mathbf{Ypcr_{i,t-1}} + \beta_2\mathbf{X_{i,t}} + \beta_3\mathbf{Remy_{it}} + \beta_4\mathbf{FD_{it}}\\ &\quad + \beta_5(\mathbf{Remy.FD})_{\mathbf{it}} + \beta_\mathrm{t} + \mu_\mathrm{i} + \varepsilon_{\mathrm{i,t}}\end{aligned}$$

In this model:

$\mathbf{Ypcg_{i,t}}$: The actual average growth rate of GDP in a particular country **(i)** at a specific time **(t)**

$\mathbf{Ypcr_{i,t}}$: Average GDP per capita in a particular country **(i)** at the time (t − **1**) known as a late variable of GPD with the ratio is 1.

Xi,t: Control variables at which remittance has a significant impact on economic growth shown in the standard growth model, including the ratio of domestic investment upon GDP, inflation ratio, human resource ratio, governmental spending power upon GDP (government based), trade openness. In details as below:

Inf: Inflation rate in a country **(i)** at a specific time **(t)**, counted by %. According to Nyamongo *et al.* (2012), inflation creates economic push-ups. However, most of the theories state that the inflation rate has an inverse correlation to economic growth.

Gi: The ratio of total investment upon GDP (% GDP). Most of the theories state that domestic investment has a covariate correlation to economic growth.

Price: Ratio of primary admission (for male and female students) upon GDP (% GDP). Giuliano and Ruiz-Arranz (2005) and Nyamongo *et al.* (2012) showed that this variable representing human resources would be used to predict the relationship between human resource fluctuation and economic growth.

Tr: Trade openness, i.e., the ratio of exportation and importation upon GDP (%GDP). This variable is predicted to have a positive impact on economic growth.

Remyit: The amount of remittance received by a country **(i)** from another country based on GDP in a specific time **(t)**. As shown previously, remittance has played an essential role in economic growth. Giuliano and Ruiz-Arranz (2009) and Rao and Hassan (2001) emphasized that the higher remittance there is, the stronger the economic growth will be. Nevertheless, IMF (2005) stated that remittance may have an inverse or minimum impact on economic growth. Aggarwal *et al.* (2010) also showed that higher financial development would lead to higher implications for remittance.

FDit: The indexes used to measure the financial development of a country **(i)** at the time **(t)**. This corresponding variable is the ratio of (DC = domestic credit/GDP) or monetary supply ($M_2 = M_2$/GDP). According to Calderón and Liu (2003) and King and Levine (1993), the ratio M2/GDP was used popularly to represent the measurement of financial development. The higher M2/GDP, the better elements of finance and legislation will be. This ratio is the actual size of the financial system of a country.

(Remy. FD)it: The corresponding variable representing the impact of remittance on financial development via financial growth elements. This variable plays a crucial role in remittance on economic growth by using the transmission base of the financial region. This is because two variables interact with each other by replacing or supplementing (Calderón *et al.*, 2007; Giuliano and Ruiz-Arranz, 2009; Aggarwal *et al.*, 2010; Martínez *et al.*, 2007).

If the result shows the negative impact and statistical meaning, remittance, and financial development will replace each other in growing the economy. On the other hand, both will be supplements if there is a positive result and the statistical figures are meaningful. The more vital and more significant the nation's financial system, the more advantages of remittance will be shown (Table 1).

Table 1: Descriptions of variables and expected results in the empirical model.

Variables	**Descriptions**	**Expected Results (+/−)**
Ypcg	The actual average growth rate of GPD per capita	
Ypcr	The actual average GPD per capita	+
Remy	The amount of remittance received by a country	+
M_2	Opened monetary supply	+
Dc	The credit of the Private sector	+
Dc.Remy	The corresponding variable of the private sector and the amount of remittance received by a country	+
Inf	Inflation rate	−
Gi	Total investment	+
Gov	Governmental expenditure	+
Pri	The ratio of primary admission	+
Tr	Trade openness	+

Source: Author's summary.

3.2. *Research database*

The primary data was collected based on the databases of 25 countries in the Asia-Pacific region within 24 years (1995–2018) from the World Bank and IMF. The countries chosen were where the remittance had been transferred tremendously, in correspondence with economic size. The reports were fully completed, including Armenia, Azerbaijan, Bangladesh, Bhutan, Cambodia, Fiji, Georgia, India, Indonesia, Iran, Jordan, Kazakhstan, Kyrgyz Republic, Malaysia, Mongolia, Nepal, Oman, Pakistan, Philippines, Sri Lanka, Thailand, Vietnam (excluding Laos, Tonga, Vanuatu (uncompleted reports), Israel, South Korea, and China (developing countries with the vast gap in economic size)). The data were sorted into 10 segments with an average of three years per segment from 1995 to 2018; usually, the previous results were based on five years per segment, but this method could reduce the fluctuation of measured variables in research samples.

3.3. *Research methods*

Based on Nyamongo's (2012) previous research, this research would use a newly formed model and be estimated by pooled, fixed, and random effects from OLS methods with collected data. For the ultimate result and higher reliability, generalized least squares (GLS) and regression analysis named Two-Stage least squares (2SLS) are used to solve the upcoming issues from the model.

4. Results and Discussions

4.1. *Descriptive statistic*

In the case of countries in Asia-Pacific from 1995 to 2018, the variable "economic growth" had the minimum value at −14.35% in Indonesia in 1998 and the maximum value at 32.99% in Armenia in 2006. However, most of the countries' economies increased, so the mean was positive with the value at 4.12751%, and the standard deviation was 3.4315%.

Table 2: Descriptive statistics of the variables in the research.

Variables	Size	Mean	Standard Deviation	Min	Max
Ypcg	132	4.12751	3.4315	−2.814174	22.6529
Ypcr	132	3.475731	3.749365	0.2479496	20.70049
Remy	132	6.574303	7.170327	0.0514124	31.58941
Gi	132	32.53742	18.58252	15.00038	113.0429
Inf	132	6.007082	21.22972	−2.598888	23.39552
Pri	132	103.9896	11.58121	71.46957	147.5328
Gov	132	11.89474	5.079054	0.0209736	26.34746
Tr	132	89.32167	39.53705	26.35466	205.602
M_2	132	60.61006	39.78326	11.98718	209.4513
Dc	132	48.25009	31.8579	4.263765	145.7669
Dc.Remy	132	292.1563	397.7042	0.8796661	2400.343

Source: World Bank and International Monetary Fund.

The Remittance ratio upon GDP was from 0.005% (Kazakhstan, 1997) to 40.7% (Tonga, 2018). As such, the volatility level was around 7.17%, and the mean was 6.57% with the value of variables, the credit ratio of the private sector upon GDP was from 1.16% (Azerbaijan, 1996) to 166.504% (Thailand, 1997). Since the volatility level of remittance ratio upon GDP and other financial development indexes was high, the fluctuation level of other variables increased compared to the standard deviation of M2 (see Table 2). Remy (574.09%) and Dc.Remy (397.70%).

Compared to the mean size at 6%, the inflation rate with a wide range of fluctuation spread from −18.1% (Bhutan, 2004) to 411.76% (Azerbaijan, 1995) with a standard deviation was 21.22%. The fluctuation rates of variables "Total Domestic Investment," "Governmental expenditure," "Ratio of Primary admission," or "trade openness" were not high, and there were no significant differences among these countries. Nonetheless, the variables "Financial development indexes" had a considerable gap. As such, monetary supply M2 ranged from 11.145% in the Kyrgyz Republic in 2011 to 158.27% in Vietnam in 2018.

4.2. *Results and discussions*

To obtain the research objectives, the main models were used to examine: Pool, FEM, REM, by applying Ordinary Least Squares (OLS) and two stages least squares (2SLS). According to the previous results of research (Chami *et al.*, 2003; Catrinescu *et al.*, 2008; Faini, 2007), there was a cause-and-effect impact between remittance and economic growth which would lead to the reliability of variables in the model. As such, the estimation by OLS was replaced by 2SLS since OLS might create internal issues compared to 2SLS. Based on the research of Nyamongo *et al.* (2012), the variable "lagged value of remittance" was chosen to be an instrument in the model. Furthermore, Hausman's Test was also used to select the relevant model, and the result showed that the best model for this research could be REM.

The results of examining the impact of remittance and financial development on economic growth are shown in Tables 3–5. The 1%, 5%, and 10% significance levels are denoted by ***, **, and *,

Table 3: Results of examining the growth model based on average GDP per capita.

	OLS			GLS
	PM (1)	**FEM (2)**	**REM (3)**	**(4)**
Ypcr	−0.3155***	−0.5503***	−0.3824***	−0.2900***
Gi	−0.004	0.1407**	0.0127	0.0094
Infla	0.0406	−0.063	0.0131	0.0101
Pri	0.0309	0.0427	0.0358	0.0428**
Gov	−0.0232	−0.1915	−0.0238	−0.0244
Tr	0.0083	0.0169	0.0097	0.0062**
_cons	1.435	−1.8354	0.6599	−0.0555
R^2	0.1484	0.1891	0.1363	—
Number of Obs	132	132	132	132
Hausman test	—	—	0.0692	—
(Prob > chi2)	—	—	—	—

Note: Symbols **, *** respectively mean 5%, 1%.

Table 4: Results of examining the impact of remittance on growth (average GDP per capita).

	OLS		FEM		REM		GLS
	PM (1)	**PM (2)**	**FEM (3)**	**FEM (4)**	**REM (5)**	**REM (6)**	**(7)**
Ypcr	−0.3564***	−0.4059***	−0.5444***	−0.5441***	−0.3883***	−0.4239***	−0.378***
Gi	−0.0032	−0.0045	0.1381**	0.1612***	0.0122	0.0111	0.0091
Infla	0.039	0.0249	−0.0665	−0.0658	0.0142	0.0131	0.0282
Pri	0.0324	0.0486*	0.0526	0.0532	0.0349	0.0494	0.060***
Gov	−0.0061	0.0234	−0.1911	−0.1708	−0.0213	0.0072	0.0196
Tr	0.0087	0.0079	0.016	0.0215	0.0098	0.0097	0.007***
Remy	—	−0.1034**	—	−0.0895	—	−0.0779	−0.117***
_cons	1.4298	0.1829	−2.9218	−3.6595	0.8114	−0.4102	−1.6481
R^2	0.1564	0.1833	0.1926	0.1958	0.1306	0.1182	—
Hausman test	—	—	—	—	**0.0555**	**0.0563**	
Number of obs	132	132	132	132	132	132	132
				2SLS			
	PM (9)	**PM (10)**	**FM (11)**	**FM (12)**	**RM (13)**	**RM (14)**	
Ypcr	−0.4643***	−0.6505**	−0.6955***	−0.5880*	−0.4643***	−0.6505**	—
Gi	−0.003	−0.0006	0.2033***	0.1669**	−0.003	−0.0006	—
Infla	−0.0076	0.0145	−0.1358	−0.1237	−0.0076	0.0145	—
Pri	0.0561*	0.0368	0.0644	0.0494	0.0561*	0.0368	—
Gov	0.0232	0.0762	−0.2304	−0.212	0.0232	0.0762	—
Tr	0.0092	0.0152	0.0408	0.0328	0.0092	0.0152	—
Remy	−0.1398**	—	−0.3237*	—	−0.1398**	—	—
_cons	0.0368	2.3943	−4.4897	−4.7825	0.0368	2.3943	—
R^2	0.1009	0.0015	0.1955	0.2349	0.1009	0.0015	—
Number of obs	132	132	132	132	132	132	—

Note: Symbols *, **, *** respectively mean 10%, 5%, 1%.
Source: Author's calculation.

Table 5: Results of examining the impact of remittance and financial development on growth (average GDP per capita).

	OLS – Random effects					GLS	GLS
	(1)	(2)	(3)	(4)	(5)	(6)	(7)
Ypcr	−0.305***	−0.3489***	−0.357***	−0.346***	−0.390***	−0.376***	−0.383***
Gi	0.0149	0.0113	0.0134	0.0068	0.0032	0.007	0.0061
Infla	−0.0015	0.0000	−0.0024	−0.0001	0.0004	0.0349	0.0297
Pri	0.0400	0.0519	0.0546*	0.0375	0.0487	0.0675***	0.0649***
Gov	−0.0403	−0.0116	−0.008	−0.0314	−0.0014	0.0308	0.0325
Tr	0.0202*	0.0196*	0.0186*	0.0179*	0.0173*	0.0118**	0.012***
Dc	−0.0279**	−0.0267**	−0.022	—	—	−0.0076	—
Remy	—	−0.0744	−0.0405	—	−0.0747	−0.1103*	−0.115***
Dc.Remy	—	—	−0.0008	—	—	−0.0002	—
M_2	—	—	—	−0.024**	0.0234**	—	−0.0104*
_cons	0.5824	−0.2594	−0.7393	1.4500	0.6839	−2.3922	−1.9142
R^2	0.1409	0.1228	0.1255	0.1166	0.0989	—	—
Number of Obs	132	132	132		132	132	132
				2 SLS			
	PM (8)	**PM (9)**	**PM (10)**	**FM (11)**	**FM (12)**	**FM (13)**	—
Ypcr	−0.401***	−0.439***	−0.4031***	−0.6061**	−0.7256**	−0.5910**	—
Gi	−0.0021	−0.0104	−0.0013	0.2065***	0.204***	0.210***	—
Infla	−0.037	−0.0357	−0.0371	−0.1492	−0.1257	−0.1483	—
Pri	0.0583*	0.0537*	0.0593*	0.0573	0.0641	0.051	—
Gov	−0.0105	−0.0029	−0.0113	−0.194	−0.2429	−0.1925	—
Tr	0.0204**	0.0179**	0.0199*	0.0444	0.0384	0.0424	—
Dc	−0.0301**	—	−0.0276	−0.0181	—	−0.0324	—
Remy	−0.1352**	−0.1281**	−0.116	−0.2851	−0.3390*	−0.404	—
M_2	—	−0.027***	—	—	0.0088	—	—
Dc.Remy	—	—	−0.0004	—	—	0.0021	—
_cons	0.6259	1.7868	0.4245	−4.1963	−4.507	−2.6971	—
R^2	0.1148	0.0926	0.1171	0.2080	0.1927	0.1867	—
Hausman Observations	132	132	132	132	132	132	—

(Continued)

Table 5: (*Continued*)

	2SLS						
	RM (14)	**RM (15)**	**RM (16)**	—	—	—	—
Ypcr	−0.4018***	−0.4398***	−0.4031***	—	—	—	—
Gi	−0.0021	−0.0104	−0.0013	—	—	—	—
Infla	−0.037	−0.0357	−0.0371	—	—	—	—
Pri	0.0583*	0.0537*	0.0593*	—	—	—	—
Gov	−0.0105	−0.0029	−0.0113	—	—	—	—
Tr	0.0204**	0.0179**	0.0199*	—	—	—	—
Dc	−0.0301**	—	−0.0276	—	—	—	—
Remy	−0.1352**	−0.1281**	−0.116	—	—	—	—
M_2	—	−0.027***	—	—	—	—	—
Dc.Remy	—	—	−0.0004	—	—	—	—
_cons	0.6259	1.7868	0.4245	—	—	—	—
R^2	0.1148	0.0926	0.1171	—	—	—	—
Hausman	**0.0938**	**0.0577**	**0.1427**	—	—	—	—
Observations	**132**	**132**	**132**	—	—	—	—

Note: Symbols*, **, *** respectively mean 10%, 5%, 1%.
Source: Author's calculation.

respectively. First, the research estimated the growth model based on variables: Ypcr, Gi, Inf, Pri, Gov, Tr, Equation (1) by OLS and GLS (Table 3). Second, other variables of remittance (Remy) and financial development in the model (Dc, M2) were in Tables 4 and 5.

The regression analysis results by OLS and 2SLS examined the impacts of remittance and financial development on economic growth. The examination was selected and performed by a sequence of independent variables: remittance/GDP, financial development index, and other variables. The results showed that:

The roles of remittance on economic growth are shown with the results in Table 4. After examining the variable "remittance" in the model, regression analysis negatively impacted economic growth with statistical significance. Nonetheless, via FEM and REM, OLS showed insignificant results. Via 2SLS, the coefficient result had a negative impact and significance at 5% and 10%. After inserting the financial development variable into the analysis, it showed the influence of remittance on economic growth, as shown in Table 5. According to the GLS and 2SLS estimation, impact coefficients were negative signs and significances at 1%, 5%, and 10%, but primarily not statistically significant on OLS. The results were aligned with the research of Nyamoingo *et al.* (2012) but opposed to Chami *et al.* (2003, 2008) and in contrast to the expected results. It showed that the remittance could create pressure on the value of the domestic currency, influence the import/export activities, and later affect the work and productivity. In addition, the remittance was considered the income of households which could form the laziness of working and lead to the labor reduction since the households could live without any worries of money. The primary purpose of receivers was to use the remittance as a saving amount, not an investment potential. However, in some countries, remittance is an official cash flow that could help the country develop if there were clear directions for using remittance sources, especially in developing countries.

The impacts of financial development via ratio M2 and domestic credits in the private sector (Dc) showed that: Dc had an inverse effect on economic growth and significance at 5% in case of not examining remittance and its impacts (columns 1,2,8,14 in Table 5). Besides, the monetary supply ratio (M2/GDP), attached to the equation (columns 4,5,7,9,15 in Table 5) with significance at 1%, 5%, and 10% in 2 cases without remittance and its impact variables, showed the negative impact on economic growth. The results declared that the private sectors relied on banks for spending. Working capital or investment amount would negatively influence economic growth since the citizens only save their money in savings accounts for periodical interests, which could restrain the development of the economy.

The corresponding variables in the model resulted in columns 3, 6,10,13,16 in Table 4 having a positive but insignificant impact as such insignificant. This result supported the replacement hypothesis and the same results as Guiliano and Ruiz-Arranz (2005), which showed that remittance had been proved to positively impact countries where credits were burdens and small-scaled financial segments. Remittance replaced the entire underdeveloped financial system and pushed up the economy.

The impacts of actual GDP per capita (Ypcr) on economic growth shown in the research had adverse effects and significances at 1% and 5% in all estimated variables (Ypcr), tremendously influencing economic growth. The result was relevant to other research results of Nyamongo *et al.* (2012), Easterly and Levine (1997), and Sachs and Warner (1997). The researchers stated that low-income countries would develop faster than other high-income countries. And in the future, the low-income nations will catch up with higher-income ones, which was the trend of this research.

The regression coefficient of variable "domestic investment/GDP" had a positive impact and significance at 1% in the models OLS and 2SLS, but other models were insignificant. It showed that domestic investment had a positive influence on economic growth. The higher the investments, the more developing the national economy.

Inflation had a negative correlation to economic growth and no significance in all means and the same expectation. Inflation is the main element restricting the economic growth in the Asia-Pacific from 2001 to 2018. It was relevant that higher economic growth was achieved only when the inflation rate was low and stable.

The human resource variable was measured by the ratio of primary admission upon GDP. It showed the positive relation and significance in some estimated models (columns 7,9,13 in Table 4 and columns 3,6,7,8,9,10,14,15,16 in Table 5) by OLS, GLS, and 2SLS. As a result, the growth of human resources impacted the economic development of the Asia-Pacific countries. The result was aligned with the theories and primary evidence in previous research.

The ratio of Governmental expenditure upon GDP was mostly estimated as negative impact on economic growth, but insignificant. The result was as correct as Nyamongo *et al.*'s (2012) explanation that the higher the governmental expenditure was, the more decreased the economy would be. Since governmental spending was more than private, this could lead to no suitable rooms for the private sector and change other economic fields.

Trade openness represents the total value of imports and exports upon GDP. It showed a positive and significant impact based on GLS and 2SLS (except estimated by OLS and applied permanent estimation by 2SLS). Therefore, countries with high openness levels will push up the economy and simultaneously create more opportunities to attract enormous remittance amounts. The result is accepted to expectations and previous research.

5. Conclusion

The purpose of the research is to examine the relationship between remittance and financial development on economic growth in 22 countries of the Asia-Pacific region from 2001 to 2018, so that suitable choices for human resources and other solutions could be applied for future economic development. The main results showed:

(i) Remittance is the primary source of income of a household, and the use of remittance is mainly for personal purposes, not for investment. Therefore, it created a negative impact on the economy. It was not as crucial as ODA or FDI.
(ii) Financial development had a reverse impact on economic growth and was mainly insignificant in the selected countries when the research was conducted.
(iii) In the relationship between remittance and financial development on economic growth, the link between remittance and ratio of domestic credits and monetary supply M2 showed that the more developed financial systems, the lower the marginal impact of remittance to economic growth.

However, the research also had limitations, such as:

(i) The figures collected from WB and IMF might have errors since the official remittance via financial institutes/ agents was the primary source of information.
(ii) The size of 22 countries was not significant, and the duration was not sufficient to examine on a worldwide scale.
(iii) The lack of information from other countries due to political issues or differences among WB and local banks or IMF figures.
(iv) Dc and M2 only analyzed the financial development indexes, so the impacts of these factors could not be obvious.
(v) Heterogeneous characteristics of research size and economic development situation amongst countries will influence the results.

Bibliography

Adams Jr, R.H., and Page, J. (2005). Do international migration and remittances reduce poverty in developing countries? *World Development*, 33(10), 1645–1669.

Adenutsi, D.E. (2011). Financial development, international migrant remittances, and endogenous growth in Ghana. *Studies in Economics and Finance*, 28(1), 68–89.

Aggarwal, R., Demirguc-Kunt, A., and Martinez Peria, M.S. (2006). *Do Workers' Remittances Promote Financial Development?* The World Bank.

Aggarwal, R., Demigurc-Kunt, A., and Martinez Peria, M.S. (2010). Do remittances promote financial development? *Journal of Development Economics*, 96(2), 255–264.

Amuedo-Dorantes, C., and Pozo, S. (2004). Workers' remittances and the real exchange rate: A paradox of gifts. *World Development*, 32(8), 1407–1417.

Anzoategui, D., Demirgüç-Kunt, A., and Martínez Pería, M.S. (2011). *Remittances and Financial Inclusion: Evidence from El Salvador*. The World Bank.

Azam, J.P. and Gubert, F. (2006). Migrants remittances and the household in Africa: A review of evidence. *Journal of African Economies*, 15(suppl_2), 426–462.

Bagehot, W. (1873). *Lombard Street: A Description of the Money Market*. Henry S. King and Company 65 Cornhill & 12 Paternoster Row.

Barajas, A., Chami, R., Hakura, D., Montiel, P., and Tressel, T. (2011). Workers' remittances and the equilibrium real exchange rate: Theory and evidence [with comment]. *Economia*, 11(2), 45–99.

Barro, R.J. (1989). *A Cross-country Study of Growth, Saving, and Government* (Vol. 2855, p. 55). Cambridge, MA: National Bureau of Economic Research.

Barro, R.J. (1991). Economic growth in a cross section of countries. *The Quarterly Journal of Economics*, 106(2), 407–443.

Bettin, G., Lucchetti, R., and Zazzaro, A. (2012). Financial development and remittances: Micro-econometric evidence. *Economics Letters*, 115(2), 184–186.

Calderón, C. and Liu, L. (2003). The direction of causality between financial development and economic growth. *Journal of Development Economics*, 72(1), 321–334.

Calderón, C., Fajnzylber, P., and López, J.H. (2007). Remittances and growth: The role of complementary policies. *Remittances and Development: Lessons from Latin America*, 335–368.

Catrinescu, N., Leon-Ledesma, M., Piracha, M., and Quillin, B. (2009). Remittances, institutions, and economic growth. *World Development*, 37(1), 81–92.

Chami, R., Fullenkamp, C., and Jahjah, S. (2005). Are immigrant remittance flows a source of capital for development? *IMF Staff Papers*, 52(1), 55–81.

Chami, R., Hakura, D.S., and Montiel, P.J. (2012). Do worker remittances reduce output volatility in developing countries? *Journal of Globalization and Development*, 3(1), 1–25.

Easterly, W. and Levine, R. (1997). Africa's growth tragedy: Policies and ethnic divisions. *The Quarterly Journal of Economics*, 112(4), 1203–1250.

El-Sakka, M.I. and McNabb, R. (1999). The macroeconomic determinants of emigrant remittances. *World Development*, 27(8), 1493–1502.

Faini, R. (2007). Migration and remittances: The impact on countries of origin. *Development Economics*, 21, 185–216.

Freund, C. and Spatafora, N. (2008). Remittances, transaction costs, and informality. *Journal of Development Economics*, 86(2), 356–366.

Giuliano, P. and Ruiz-Arranz, M. (2005). Remittances, financial development and growth. [05/234]. *International Monetary Fund Working Paper.*

Giuliano, P. and Ruiz-Arranz, M. (2009). Remittances, financial development, and growth. *Journal of Development Economics*, 90(1), 144–152.

Hicks, J. (1969). *A Theory of Economic History*, Vol. 9. Oxford University Press.

Kapur, D. (2003). Indian diaspora as a strategic asset. *Economic and Political Weekly*, 445–448.

King, R.G. and Levine, R. (1993). Finance and growth: Schumpeter might be right. *The Quarterly Journal of Economics*, 108(3), 717–737.

Kireyev, M.A. (2006). *The Macroeconomics of Remittances: The Case of Tajikistan.* International Monetary Fund.

Martinez Peria, M.S., Mascaro, Y., and Moizeszowicz, F. (2008). Do remittances affect recipient countries' financial development? *Remittances and Development: Lessons from Latin America*, 171–215.

Misati, R.N. (2007). Liberalization, Stock market development and investment efficiency in Africa. *International Review of Business Research Papers*, 3(4), 183–191.

Misati, R.N. and Nyamongo, E.M. (2011). Financial development and private investment in Sub-Saharan Africa. *Journal of Economics and Business*, 63(2), 139–151.

Mundaca, B.G. (2009). Remittances, financial market development, and economic growth: The case of Latin America and the Caribbean. *Review of Development Economics*, 13(2), 288–303.

Nyamongo, E.M., Misati, R.N., Kipyegon, L., and Ndirangu, L. (2011, November). Remittances and banking sector development in Sub-Saharan African. In *A Paper Presented at the Global Development Forum, Dubai.*

Nyamongo, E.M., Misati, R.N., Kipyegon, L., and Ndirangu, L. (2012). Remittances, financial development and economic growth in Africa. *Journal of Economics and Business*, 64(3), 240–260.

Nyamongo, M.E. and Misati, R. (2010). Modelling the time-varying volatility of equities returns in Kenya. *African Journal of Economic and Management Studies*, 1(2), 183–196.

Ojapinwa, T.V. and Bashorun, O.T. (2014). Do workers' remittances promote financial development in Sub-Sahara Africa countries. *International Journal of Financial Research*, 5(2), 151–159.

Ramirez, M.D. and Sharma, H. (2008). *Remittances and Growth in Latin America: A Panel Unit Root and Panel Cointegration Analysis* (Working Papers 51). Yale University, Department of Economics.

Rao, B.B. and Hassan, G.M. (2011). A panel data analysis of the growth effects of remittances. *Economic Modelling*, 28(1–2), 701–709.

Rao, B.B. and Hassan, G.M. (2012). Are the direct and indirect growth effects of remittances significant? *The World Economy*, 35(3), 351–372.

Ratha, D. (2013). The impact of remittances on economic growth and poverty reduction. *Policy Brief*, 8(1), 1–13.

Ratha, D. (2016). *Migration and Remittances Factbook 2016*. The World Bank.

Ravallion, M. and Chen, S. (1997). What can new survey data tell us about recent changes in distribution and poverty? *The World Bank Economic Review*, 11(2), 357–382.

Richard, A.H.J., and Page, J. (2003). *International Migration, Remittances, and Poverty in Developing Countries*. The World Bank.

Sachs, J.D. and Warner, A.M. (1997). Sources of slow growth in African economies. *Journal of African Economies*, 6(3), 335–376.

Schumpeter, J. (1911). *Theorie der Wirtschaftlichen Entwicklung (transl. 1934). The Theory of Economic Development: An inquiry into Profits, Capital, Credit, Interest and the Business Cycle*. Kyklos.

Solimano, A. (2003). *Remittances by Emigrants: Issues and Evidence*. Santiago de Chile.

Taylor, J.E., Dyer, G.A., and Yúnez-Naude, A. (2005). Disaggregated rural economywide models for policy analysis. *World Development*, 33(10), 1671–1688.

Part IV

Marketing

https://doi.org/10.1142/9789811262258_0004

Chapter 4

Shopping Orientation — Defined Segments Based on Store-Choice Criteria: Case of Supermarkets in Ho Chi Minh City

Dinh Tien Minh, Vu Tu Anh, Lai Thi Hoai Huong, Pham Hoang Khang, Do Thi Phuong Thao, and Le Thi Hoang Thy

Abstract

Although the application of segmentation is a topic of central importance in marketing literature and practice, managers tend to rely on intuition and traditional segmentation techniques based on socio-demographic variables. It is regarded as common sense to separate young and old, rich or poor customers in the retail industry. However, the simplicity of this segmentation logic no longer matches the ever more complex and heterogeneous choices made by customers. Thus, there is a need to re-evaluate the traditional market segmentation criterion. The chapter aims to determine the factors that affect customers' selection decisions in Ho Chi Minh City's supermarkets and then segment shoppers according to these factors. The K-means technique will be used to cluster and ANOVA to test whether there are differences between groups. Ultimately, the segmentation stages will be discussed.

This study revealed five supermarket attractiveness factors from the shoppers' perspective: comfort, location, space, staff, and service. Each segment was profiled in terms of supermarket attractiveness attributes, demographics, and shopping behavior. By analyzing the stated preference data of more than 400 customers, we segmented supermarket customers into four groups: apathetic customers, relaxed customers, convenience-seekers pragmatic customers, and demanding customers.

Keywords: Market segmentation; STP principle; Supermarket; Retail Industry.

1. Introduction

In the Vietnamese economy, the retail industry has always played a significant role. According to the General Statistics Office data, total retail sales of goods would reach 16,563.9 trillion VND in 5 years, representing an increase of around 10.4% per year from 2016 to 2020. Following CSI research, the retail industry provides 42% of the country's GDP, accounting for 142 billion US dollars. Our country's available assets, such as a population of approximately 100 million people, have resulted in a rapidly developing middle class with steadily rising per capita income, high GDP growth, and stable inflation. Retail is a fast-growing business, with annual growth rates ranging from one-and-a-half to double that of the country's GDP. The retail industry increased positively in 2020 though not meeting the predicted growth rate due to the heavy impact of the COVID-19 pandemic. It is expected to grow significantly again soon when the government takes steps to loosen social barriers and prepare for the New Normal.

The supermarkets have also become more competitive as a result of this development. Although there are over a thousand supermarkets, the list of prominent names is limited. Foreign companies gain access to enormous supermarkets and modern shopping malls when they invest in Vietnam. However, one of the reasons these vast supermarket chains fail to remain in the market is that they do not adequately comprehend the difference in Vietnamese consumer habits, which leads to the fact that they have not found suitable groups of target customers. Customer segmentation is an essential task for understanding the market in recent times; yet, it has not been widely applied in the supermarket industry in Ho Chi Minh City.

For a successful marketing strategy, market segmentation is also a significant factor. Understanding the target audience plays a massive role in improving a successful product or service. Companies often use the segmentation market to bring their production and marketing campaigns to a specific target group to grow in a competitive environment. Segmentation allows businesses to make better use of their marketing budgets, gain a competitive edge over rival companies, and, importantly, demonstrate better knowledge of their customers' needs and wants. It can also assist businesses in marketing efficiency, determining new market opportunities, enhancing brand strategy, improving distribution strategies, and customer retention.

Most research publications on supermarket consumer segmentation have relied on demographic factors or the RFM (Recency, Frequency, Monetary) model up to now. These models, however, have some limitations because market needs and customer concerns are constantly changing, necessitating managers to develop new methods to have a good sense of customers' psychology and behavior. This can be done by looking into the factors that influence customers' attraction to supermarkets and classifying customers into different groups based on the importance of the products. Therefore, as for the Vietnamese and global retail industries, this research, titled "Customer segmentation based on the choice of supermarkets: the case of Ho Chi Minh City," will theoretically and practically provide more valuable information, as well as be a resource for further study in the future.

2. Literature Review

2.1. *Segmentation bases and procedure*

Four segmentation bases have emerged as the most popular in segmentation studies (Kotler *et al.*, 2002): Geographic segmentation, Geographic segmentation, Psychographic segmentation, and Behavioral segmentation. Geographic segmentation involves dividing the market by nations, regions, states, countries, cities, and even down to rural and suburban neighborhoods. Geographic segmentation can also involve climate if it pertains to the product and service. Demographic segmentation involves dividing the market by age, gender, family size, life cycle, income, occupation, education, religion, race, generation, and nationality. Demographic segmentation is the most popular basis for segmenting customer markets. Psychographic segmentation is more complicated and requires more market research. Customers within the same demographic group can have very different psychographic characteristics. The variables that form psychographic segmentation are social class, lifestyle, and personality. Behavioral segmentation pertains to knowledge, feelings, and attitudes toward products and services. Behavioral segmentation variables consist of occasions, benefits, user status, user rates, loyalty status, readiness stage, and attitude toward product/service. In reality, much study has been done on segmentation using a hybrid method, which combines different platforms for segmentation, resulting in more outstanding segmentation quality and administrative efficiency (Walsh *et al.*, 2001).

The segmentation process combines six steps according to Lamb *et al.* (2004) as follows:

- The first step is to select a market or product category for study. It may be a market in which the firm has already occupied a new but related market or product category, or a totally new one.
- The second step is to choose a basis for segmenting the market. This step requires managerial insight, creativity, and market knowledge. There are no scientific procedures for selecting segmentation variables.
- The third step is to select the segmentation descriptors. Descriptors identify the specific segmentation variables to use. A successful segmentation plan must produce market segments that meet the four basic criteria: substantiality, identifiably, accessibility, and responsiveness.
- The fourth step is to profile and analyze segments. The analysis should include the segment's size, expected growth, purchase frequency, current brand usage, brand loyalty, and long-term sales and profit potential. This information can then be used to rank potential market segments by profit opportunity, risk, consistency

with organizational tasks and objectives, and other factors that are important to the company.

- The fifth step is to select target markets. This step is not a part of the segmentation process but a natural result of it. It is a major decision that affects and often directly determines the firm's marketing mix.
- The last one is designing, implementing, and maintaining an appropriate marketing mix which is used to bring about mutually satisfying relationships with target markets.

First mentioned by Wind (1978) in *Issues and Advanced in Segmentation Research*, two principal approaches to segmentation are *a priori* segmentation and *post hoc* segmentation. These two approaches, according to Machauer and Morgner, 2001, have paved the way for future segmentation research.

- *A priori* segmentation, in which the researcher chooses some cluster-defining descriptor in advance, customers are then classified into a predefined number of segments and further examined in terms of other characteristics. For example, a segment might be formed based on a favorite brand, and then any differences between the segments in terms of demographics or lifestyle could be studied. But a limitation of priori methods is that they do not directly reflect the customers' needs. For some brands and categories, preexisting characteristics might not yield any useful segments.
- *Post hoc* segmentation, in which the customers are clustered into segments according to the similarity of their multivariate profiles, the segments can then be further examined for differences in other characteristics. The quantity or relative sizes of the segments will not be known before the analysis is completed. Only the set of variables on which customers are to be clustered is pre-specified. For example, the initial clustering might be done based on customer profiles that describe benefits sought from a product and any significant differences between the segments assessed utilizing other segmentation variables.

3. Shopping Orientation

Stone (1954) proposed the concept of "shopping orientation" as a socio-psychological term to describe a consumer's motivations for engaging in shopping activity. The economic shopper, the personalizing consumer, the ethical shopper, and the apathetic shopper were the four sorts of shoppers he identified. This approach is thought to increase the effectiveness in understanding and portraying customers (Moye and Kincade, 2003; Shim and Kotsiopoulos, 1993). Subsequently, Arnold and Reynolds (2003) established six hedonistic purchasing motivations: adventure, sociability, fulfillment shopping, idea shopping, role shopping, and value shopping. Based on Arnold and Reynolds' research, Kim (2006) investigated the hedonistic and pragmatic shopping motivations of urban and suburban shoppers (2003). He divided the pragmatic incentives into two subaspects: "achieving" and "effectiveness," in addition to the six hedonistic motives. The research of Koksal (2019b) revealed three dimensions of shopping motivation: hedonic, achievement, and efficiency. This discovery is in line with Kim's research (2006). Many studies also suggest that different shopping orientations can lead to various store choices and miscellaneous attitudes toward these choices (Gutman and Mills, 1982; Moye and Kincade, 2003). This is applied to customer satisfaction with specific stores as well (McKinney, 2004b).

4. Store-Choice Criteria

"Location" is the first thing to consider. Customers' choice of stores is influenced by the convenience of shopping locations and the ease of access (Wakefield and Baker, 1998; Bhatti *et al.*, 2015). Furthermore, customers prefer shopping sites that are close to their home and have a proper location (Reimers and Clulow, 2009; Jaravaza and Chitando, 2013; Hai Hung and Nguyen, 2020). Service can also be mentioned as a vital factor in choosing a store. An example of store-choice decision-affecting services is a free parking area (Bhatti *et al.*, 2015; Nguyen Hai Hung and Nguyen Thi Hanh Nguyen, 2020).

In order to attract customers, the stores need an appealing physical environment (Ali *et al.*, 2013; Han and Ryu, 2009), a children's indoor playground, as well as a spacious and convenient parking lot (Bhatti *et al.*, 2015). In choosing a shopping mall, while Ward *et al.* (1992) had demonstrated the significance of open space and wide corridors, the impact of the mall size was likewise researched by Wakefield and Baker (1998), as the consequence of comparing a large number of those centers.

Moreover, the store-choice decisions of customers also depend on perceived value and sales promotion (Andreti *et al.*, 2013; Gorji *et al.*, 2020).

Besides, it is impossible not to refer to hygiene factors, called customers' "comfort," which affect customers' choice of stores, shopping malls, or supermarkets. They are all listed as follows: high-quality items (Zulqarnain *et al.*, 2015), knowledgeable staff (Rigopoulou *et al.*, 2008), product variety (Zulqarnain *et al.*, 2015), and sanitation (Singh *et al.*, 2019).

Here are some research articles whose authors have segmented the customers on the basis of store-choice criteria. According to Rigopoulou *et al.* (2008), customers are divided into two segments, which are a group of "fastidious" customers and a group of "easygoing" customers, based on product/price, source of information, and servicescape/personnel. Recently, Oeser *et al.* (2019) have segmented their elderly German customers, based on their selection of nine criteria, including proximity to home; accessibility in terms of good public transportation or car parking; quality-consciousness in terms of freshness, variety, range, provenience, and presentation of products; suitable package sizes; recreational and social dimension of shopping; personal advice from sales staff; price and promotions; waiting times; health-related issues or dietary restrictions. Accordingly, the research subject in this study is grouped into seven segments: indifferent shoppers, leisure shoppers, convenience shoppers, assistance-oriented shoppers, no-frills shoppers, product-oriented shoppers, and service-oriented shoppers. Also, Prashar *et al.* (2019) segmented Indian customers based on the factors that shopping malls have to attract them, and then divided them into three customer segments: hygienic experience seekers, extended experience seekers, and prudent experience seekers.

5. Methodology and Data

There are two main methods for obtaining qualitative research results: in-depth interviews with the specialists of Coop, Big C, AEON, and face-to-face discussions with customers of diverse ages. Besides, the quantitative research will be carried out using a variety of survey methods, including personally administered surveys (in-home interviews), telephone-administered surveys (traditional telephone interviews), and self-administered surveys (online surveys). The sample size is about 400.

Cluster Analysis (K-means) is mainly used to segment the supermarket shoppers. It is one of the clustering algorithms. The input is the data set to be clustered and the number of clusters. At the output, we will get the results of the data distributed to the mentioned clusters. The goal is to segment the data into different groups so that the data in the same cluster can have the same properties. Then, the analysis of variables (ANOVA) is used to determine whether the groups created by the independent variable levels are statistically different by calculating whether the means of the treatment levels are other than the overall mean of the dependent variable. If group means are significantly different from the overall mean, the null hypothesis is rejected. ANOVA uses the F-test for statistical significance. This allows comparing multiple means at once because the error is calculated for the whole set of comparisons rather than for each two-way comparison (which would happen with a t-test).

6. Results and Discussion

A total of 400 shoppers participated in the survey, of which 87 participants were from 15 to 24 years old, 57 participants were from 25 to 29 years old, 174 participants were from 30 to 49 years old, and 82 participants were from 50 to 70 years old.

Cluster analysis (K-means) was used on the five store-choice criteria: comfort, location, service, space, and promotion. Four segments were extracted from the analysis. Based on their mean values in the five store-choice criteria, those four segments were named "apathetic customers" (accounting for 31.25%), "relaxed customers" (accounting for 3.05%), "convenience-seeker and pragmatic customers" (accounting for 27.75%) and "demanding customers" (accounting for 37.95%). Overall, the objective of this research study is divided into two parts. The first step is to determine the attractive features of a supermarket, and the second step is to segment customers into groups based on these factors. Regarding supermarket attractiveness, the results revealed five factors from the shoppers' perspective, namely comfort, location, service, shopping space, and promotion. Of the five factors aforementioned, three factors are consistent with the findings of Wong *et al.* (2001), who had identified five features of mall attractiveness, namely location, quality and variety, popularity, facilities, and sales incentives. This study's "shopping space," "comfort & service," and "location" factors tend to be similar to Wong *et al.*'s (2001) "facilities," "quality and variety," and "location," respectively. The "comfort" and "location" factors in this study are in harmony with the "quality of the center" and "convenience" factors identified by Bellenger *et al.* (1977). The "comfort" and "shopping space & location" factors, to some extent, are in line with "atmosphere leisure" and "accessibility" factors discovered by Frasquet *et al.* (2001). They are also found to be associated with "amenities" and "micro-accessibility" factors concluded by Sit *et al.* (2003). The "shopping space" factor revealed in this study supports the viewpoint of Sit *et al.* (2003) that entertainment deserves to be a distinct factor that comprises multiple items rather than a single one. The "comfort" factor in this study is partially similar to the "retail environment" identified by Ibrahim and Ng (2003). It is also in line with two attractiveness factors of supermarkets, including "environment" and "variety of goods," which were pointed out by Karumba and Ngigi (2018).

As previously mentioned, this study revealed four customer segments based on the attractiveness factors of supermarkets. This study's findings on them, which consist of "apathetic customers," "relaxed customers/shopping enthusiasts," "convenience seeker & pragmatic customers/basic shoppers," and "demanding customers," are pretty consistent with those of authors such as Sit *et al.* (2003), El-Adly (2006), and Ganesh *et al.* (2010). However, in the Vietnamese market, there are still distinctions between each segment, as well as the characteristics of specific customer profiles. For example, the "relaxed customers" do not pay close attention to the location and after-sale services, such as exchange and return. They frequently spend more than two hours at the supermarket. Also, it should be noted that the "apathetic clients" are often a group with a low income of less than 7.5 million.

Validating the four-cluster solution, cluster membership was related to the original five store-choice criteria factors. Between-groups and within-groups, differences were tested using a one-way Analysis of Variances. Due to the sig. of ANOVA < 0.05, it was concluded that clusters differed in relation to the dependent variable (Tables 1 and 2).

6.1. *Segment 1: Apathetic customers*

This is the second most common customer segment, accounting for 31.25% of respondents (Table 1). They consider the "comfort" factor as the priority compared to the remaining three groups. A sanitary supermarket with high-quality products, along with friendly and knowledgeable staff, will attract them. "Location" and "service" are followed by "comfort." They might give priority to supermarkets with convenient transportation and quick delivery and return services. "Space" and "promotion" are assessed to have a normal level. Spacious or delicately decorated areas do not seem to affect their

Table 1: Characteristics of each group (% of each segment).

		Cluster			
Characteristics		**Segment 1 Apathetic Customers**	**Segment 2 the Relaxed Customers**	**Segment 3 the Convenience Seeker and Pragmatic Customers**	**Segment 4 Demanding Customers**
Demographics					
Gender	Male	36.8	25.0	37.8	23.7
	Female	63.2	75.0	62.2	76.3
Age	15–24	25.6	26.1	0.0	17.1
	25–29	12.0	0.0	10.8	19.7
	30–49	32.0	50.0	51.4	46.7
	Over 50	32.0	50.0	11.7	16.4
Family status	Single	45.6	25.0	47.7	47.4
	Married	48.8	41.7	51.4	50.0
	Other (Separated/ divorced/ widowed)	5.6	33.3	0.9	2.6
Job	Student/pupil	24.0	0.0	24.3	20.4
	Trader	8.0	33.3	18.0	17.8
	Officers	44.0	58.3	46.8	44.7
	Housewife/ pensioner	22.4	8.3	9.0	16.4
	Other	1.6	0.0	1.8	0.7
Income	Under 5 million	24.0	8.3	27.9	24.0
	5–7.5 million	24.0	16.7	9.0	19.1
	7.5–15 million	36.0	75.0	33.3	34.9
	15–30 million	11.2	0.0	18.0	17.8
	30–45 million	4.0	0.0	6.3	4.6
	Over 45 million	0.8	0.0	5.4	3.3
Behavior					
Shopping frequency	< 1 time/week	38.4	41.7	36.0	32.2
	1–2 times/week	42.4	50.0	45.9	45.4
	3–4 times/week	14.4	8.3	13.5	19.7
	> 5 time/week	4.8	0.0	4.5	2.6
Time for a shopping trip	< 1 hour	43.2	8.3	35.1	29.6
	1–2 hours	42.4	41.7	43.2	52.6
	> 2 hours	14.4	50.0	21.6	17.8
Spend for a shopping trip	< 200.000 VND	16.8	0.0	13.5	11.2
	200.000–500.000 VND	53.6	33.3	40.5	45.4
	> 500.000 VND	29.6	66.7	45.9	43.4

(*Continued*)

Table 1: (*Continued*)

Characteristics	Cluster			
	Segment 1 Apathetic Customers	Segment 2 the Relaxed Customers	Segment 3 the Convenience Seeker and Pragmatic Customers	Segment 4 Demanding Customers
Shopping Style				
– Often buy unnecessary things	4.0	16.7	5.4	13.8
– Think carefully before buying something	56	66.6	52.3	55.2
– Only buy things that have been planned at home and often don't buy more	36.0	16.7	38.7	28.9
– Other	4.0	0.0	3.6	2.0
– Often listen to staff advice when buying goods	4.0	16.7	3.6	2.0
– Consider the reviews of other customers instead of staff when choosing products	34.4	50.0	34.2	36.8
– Only buy things based on needs and don't consider the suggestions of others	59.2	33.3	60.4	51.3
– Other	2.4	0.0	1.8	0.7

Source: Research result of 400 respondents.

decisions in choosing supermarkets, nor do advertisements on social media. The most significant difference between this group and the others is that the impact of those factors on the customers' choice is not too strong. They appear to be unconcerned with the factors relating to the supermarket.

Demographically, more than half of the customers in this segment (62.4%) are more than 30 years old, and nearly half of them are in marital status. Females make up about 63.2% of this segment. Most participants (36%) have an income of between 7.5 million and 15 million VND, followed by those with incomes ranging from 5 million to 7.5 million VND (24%), and the remaining have a revenue

Table 2: Characteristics of each group (% of total segment).

Characteristics		Cluster: Segment 1 Apathetic Customers	Segment 2 the Relaxed Customers	Segment 3 the Convenience Seeker and Pragmatic Customers	Segment 4 Demanding Customers
Demographics					
Gender	Male	11.50	0.75	10.5	9.0
	Female	19.75	2.25	17.25	29.0
Age	15–24	8.0	0.0	7.25	6.5
	25–29	3.75	0.0	3.0	7.5
	30–49	10.0	1.5	14.25	17.75
	Over 50	9.5	1.5	3.25	6.25
Family status	Single	14.25	1.25	13.25	18.0
	Married	15.25	0.75	14.25	19.0
	Other (Separated divorced/ widowed)	1.75	1.0	0.25	1.0
Job	Student/pupil	7.5	0.0	6.75	7.75
	Trader	2.5	1.0	5.0	6.25
	Officers	13.75	1.75	13.0	17.0
	Housewife/ pensioner	7.0	1.0	2.5	6.75
	Other	0.5	0.0	0.5	0.25
Income	Under 5 million	7.5	0.25	7.75	7.75
	5–7.5 million	7.5	0.5	2.5	7.25
	7.5–15 million	11.25	2.25	9.25	13.25
	15–30 million	3.5	0.0	5.0	6.75
	30–45 million	1.25	0.0	1.75	1.75
	Over 45 million	0.25	0.0	1.5	1.25
Behavior					
Shopping frequency	< 1 time/week	12.0	1.25	10.0	12.25
	1–2 times/week	13.25	1.5	12.75	17.25
	3–4 times/week	4.5	0.25	3.75	7.5
	> 5 time/week	1.5	0.0	1.25	1.0
Time for a shopping trip	< 1 hour	13.5	0.25	9.75	11.25
	1–2 hours	13.25	1.25	12.0	20.0
	> 2 hours	4.5	1.5	6.0	6.75
Spend for a shopping trip	< 200.000 VND	5.25	0.0	3.75	4.25
	200.000–500.000 VND	16.75	1.0	11.25	17.25
	> 500.000 VND	9.25	2.0	12.75	16.5

(*Continued*)

Table 2: (*Continued*)

Characteristics	Segment 1 Apathetic Customers	Segment 2 the Relaxed Customers	Segment 3 the Convenience Seeker and Pragmatic Customers	Segment 4 Demanding Customers
	Cluster			
Shopping Style				
– Often buy unnecessary things	1.25	0.5	1.5	5.25
– Think carefully before buying something	17.5	2.0	14.5	21.0
– Only buy things that have been planned at home and often don't buy more	11.25	0.5	10.75	11.0
– Other	1.25	0.0	1.0	0.75
– Often listen to staff advice when buying goods	1.25	0.5	1.0	4.25
– Consider the reviews of other customers instead of staff when choosing products	10.75	1.5	9.5	14.0
– Only buy things based on needs and don't consider the suggestions of others	18.5	1.0	16.75	19.5
– Other	0.75	0.0	0.5	0.25

Source: Research result of 400 respondents.

of less than 5 million VND (24%). Therefore, more than half of the respondents said they only spent 200,000 VND to 500,000 VND per trip to the supermarket (Table 2).

Most customers in this group are officials or employees, accounting for 44%, and students only comprise 24%. That they are all inherently quite busy is why 80.8% of the total respondents go to the market less than twice per week, and 85.6% use less than two hours per purchase. The customers of this segment tend to be reasonably confident about their knowledge since nearly all of them think carefully before buying something without consulting the salesperson.

6.2. *Segment 2: Relaxed customers*

This segment has the lowest quantity of customers (only 3.05% of the total respondents). Likewise three other groups, its customers prioritize the "comfort" factor. Specifically, they highly prefer supermarkets that have a wide range of new and high-quality products from diverse brands, meet the standard of sanitation, as well as have knowledgeable and always ready-to-help staff toward their products and customers' needs. For this segment, the "space" factor cannot be ignored. Shopping areas must be spacious and beautifully decorated, the parking lot must be convenient, and the children's indoor playground is needed as well. The remaining factors, including "location," "service," and "promotion," do not affect their choice of supermarket.

Demographically, all of the shoppers of this segment are more than 30 years old, of which 41.7% are in marital status, and 33.3% are separated/divorced/widowed. About 75% of this segment is females. This group's income is primarily ranging from 7.5 million to 15 million VND, so it can be said that their income has an influence on the amount of money they spend on each purchase. According to the survey/interview results, 66.7% of the group's total customers often spend over 500,000 VND, while the remaining spend about 200,000 to 500,000 VND (33.3%).

Simultaneously, those customers frequently spend more than two hours at the supermarket. Inferred, they tend to wander around the supermarket while shopping. This group of customers often think carefully before making a buying decision, though sometimes, they buy unnecessary things that are not intended.

6.3. *Segment 3: Convenience seeker and pragmatic customers*

The customers in this segment choose the supermarkets that are located close to where they live. This helps them go to the supermarket more quickly and conveniently from home or working/studying places without worrying about traffic jams. They also highly appreciate supermarkets with many new and high-quality products from various brands; free parking lot; fast delivery, along with quick return and exchange services.

Demographically, more than half of the customers in this segment (51.4%) are more than 30 years old and in marital status. About 62.2% of this segment are females. Their frequency of going to supermarkets is quite a lot, usually once or twice a week (45.9%). Every time they go to the supermarket, they typically spend one to two hours (43.2%) or even more (21.60%). The amount of money those customers spend on each purchase usually ranges from 200.000 to 500.000 VND (40.5%) and may even be over 500,000 VND (45.9%).

This group of people often thinks very carefully and makes a shopping list before going to the supermarket. Therefore, they hardly have the habit of buying additional junk items during shopping. They are usually very confident in their own knowledge and only buy things they consider suitable for them. Even though they sometimes think of their relatives or customers' advice, consulting the salespeople in the supermarkets will never be in their minds.

6.4. *Segment 4: Demanding customers*

This segment has the highest number of customers, which accounts for 37.95%. They require all five factors, including "comfort," "space," "location," "service," and "promotion." They are the perfectionists, demanding the supermarkets' staff to be professional, products to be high-quality, the sanitation standards to be met, and the shopping areas to be beautifully decorated and fully equipped. Those customers also focus on the quality of services and highly evaluate the advertisements and their friends' suggestions in choosing a supermarket. They prefer supermarkets that are near their house and meet all the requirements above. Most of them have a shopping style that emphasizes subjectivity and is based on their desires, needs, and interests. Another part of this segment is primarily influenced by outside factors, mainly from people they know and trust, such as their family and friends. Demographically, more than half of the shoppers in this segment (63.1%) are more than 30 years old, and exactly half of them are in marital status. About 76.3% of this segment are females. This segment is also the group of customers with the highest number of people having an income of over 15 million VND per month (25.7%). Their shopping frequency is relatively sparse, from one to two times per week (45.4%, and with each shopping trip, they usually spend from one to two hours (5.6%. The amount of money they pay for each purchase usually ranges from 20,000 to 500,000 VND (45.4%) and might be over 50,000 VND (43.4%).

They often think carefully or plan what to buy before every shopping at the supermarket. This group of people often relies on their own knowledge and experience to make choices and considerations in shopping, so disorganized salespeople or shoppers rarely dominate them.

7. Conclusion

7.1. *Segment 1: Apathetic customers*

This group includes customers who do not have a clear motivation. They often go to the supermarket only for reference. Apathetic customers might be more accessible because they do not have any negative experiences. It is recommended that the level of their emotional engagement needs a boost. Their expectations and reference points need to be understood to know how to satisfy them, and more importantly, make them surprised and delighted if their expectations are exceeded. All the factors were barely rated differently, though the "comfort" factor was more prioritized than the others. Therefore, an apathetic and ambivalent customer can be engaged and enthusiastic if the quality of products, space, and sanitation of the supermarket are all improved, for instance, by preparing decorations for festive occasions. Concerning the staff, they also play an essential role. They should actively communicate and introduce to customers the unique things of the supermarket or the happening promotions.

Then, following the customers' reaction, they need to be flexible in what to do next, give them more information, or lead them to other things.

7.2. *Segment 2: Relaxed customers*

This is a group of customers who often go shopping randomly in the supermarket. They are easily attracted by supermarkets' "space" factor, apart from the "comfort." Nowadays, various display advertising strategies directly affect the customers' buying decisions, along with the supermarket's profit. In terms of the marketing field, product placement is a fantastic subject. "Product to shelf placement" is a vital retailing strategy that has a significant impact on the financial performance of supermarkets. Managing this problem successfully will result in the blooming in overall supermarket's profit. Therefore, beautifully decorating areas, displaying high-quality products in the most visible places, and organizing many vibrant activities will attract more customers in this segment. Satisfying these customers will be an advantage to turn them into loyal customers since they usually go shopping and are willing to pay high prices.

7.3. *Segment 3: Convenience seeker and pragmatic customers*

Customers of this segment are mainly concerned about the "convenience" factor. Therefore, the board of directors should consider expanding their business to where near the residential area. Besides, in choosing a supermarket, they only care for things relating to a supermarket's attributes, which are the quality of products, the popularity, and the variety of stores. Accordingly, it is suggested that supermarkets should display the price tags transparently for customers to compare prices and quality. Moreover, to satisfy this customer segment, supermarkets can offer mall-wide sales off, gifts with purchase, a quantity discount, or vouchers once the minimum purchase amount is reached. Other features, such as parking lot, sanitation, and ease of access, are also considered necessary. On the contrary, the "entertainment" factor can be ignored. The existence of large food courts and cinemas, as well as the supermarket's popularity on social media, are unimportant in their point of view.

7.4. *Segment 4: Demanding customers*

This is a group of customers who have high demands on choices and shopping. More high-quality and diverse products, better services, along with secure and convenient shopping facilities are the necessary conditions to attract those customers. Therefore, in building strategies and implementation, it is essential to comprehend those customers' psychology and buying habits, especially knowing the product origin and the production process. The stage of product display should be ensured to be eye-catching, neat, and easy to find. Moreover, customer service needs to be taken care of, especially in product search, shopping advice, and so on. Yet, it is necessary to avoid causing the feeling of unnaturalness and discomfort to those customers with too many offers or advice.

Bibliography

Ali, F., Omar, R., and Amin, M. (2013). An examination of the relationships between physical environment, perceived value, image and behavioural intentions: A SEM approach towards Malaysian resort hotels. *Journal of Hotel and Tourism Management*, 27(2), 9–26.

Andreti, J., Zhafira, N.H., Akmal, S.S., and Kumar, S. (2013). The analysis of product, price, place, promotion and service quality on customers' buying decision of convenience store: A survey of young adult in Bekasi, West Java, Indonesia. *International Journal of Advances in Management and Economics*, 2(6), 72–78.

Arnold, M.J. and Reynolds, K.E. (2003). Hedonic shopping motivations. *Journal of Retailing*, 79(2), 77–95.

Baltas, G. and Papastathopoulos, P. (2003). Shopper characteristics, product and store choice criteria: A survey in the Greek grocery sector. *International Journal of Retail & Distribution Management*, 31(10), 498–507.

Bellenger, D., Robertson, D., and Greenberg, B. (1977). Shopping centre patronage motives. *Journal of Retailing*, 53(2), 29–38.

Bhatti, K.L., Latif, S., and Latif, R. (2015). Factors affecting consumer's store choice behavior. *International Journal of Application or Innovation in Engineering & Management (IJAIEM)*, 4(9), 71–77.

El-Adly, M.I. (2007). Shopping malls attractiveness: A segmentation approach. *International Journal of Retail & Distribution Management*, 35(11), 936–950.

Frasquet, M., Gil, I., and Moll'a, A. (2001). Shopping-centre selection modelling: A segmentation approach. *International Review of Retail, Distribution & Consumer Research*, 11(1), 23–38.

Ganesh, J., Reynolds, K.E., Luckett, M., and Pomirleanu, N. (2010). Online shopper motivations, and e-store attributes: An Examination of Online Patronage Behavior and Shopper Typologies. *Journal of Retailing*, 86(1), 106–115.

Gorji, M. and Siami, S. (2020). How sales promotion display affects customer shopping intentions in retails. *International Journal of Retail & Distribution Management*, 48(12), 1337–1355.

Gutman, J. and Mills, M.K. (1982). Fashion lifestyle, self-concept, shopping orientation and store patronage: An integrative analysis. *Journal of Retailing*, 58(2), 64–86.

Hung, D.H., Nguyen, N.T.H. (2020). Factors affecting the choice of supermarket for shopping by consumers in Hanoi Capital in Vietnam. *European Journal of Business and Management*, 12(3), 42–47.

Ibrahim, M. and Ng, C. (2003). Determinants of entertaining shopping experiences and their link to consumer behaviour: Case studies of shopping centres in Singapore. *Journal of Leisure Property*, 2(4), 338–357.

Jaravaza, D.C. and Chitando, P. (2013). The role of store location in influencing customers' store choice. *Journal of Emerging Trends in Economics and Management Sciences*, 4(3), 302–307.

Karumba, T. and Ngigi, P. (2018). Factors that influence customer choice of supermarkets in Karatina Town Nyeri County, Kenya. *Scholars Journal of Economics: Business and Management*, 5(4), 286–294.

Koksal, M.H. (2019a). Food choice motives for consumers in Lebanon: A descriptive study. *British Food Journal*, 121(11), 2607–2619.

Koksal, M.H. (2019b). Shopping motives, mall attractiveness, and visiting patterns in shopping malls in the Middle East: A segmentation approach. *Contemporary Management Research*, 15(1), 1–23.

Kotler, P., Armstrong, G., Saunders, J., and Wong, V. (2002). *Principles of Marketing*. 3rd European Edition, Prentice-Hall.

Lamb, C.W., Hair, J.F., and McDaniel, C.D. (2004). *Marketing*. Thomson/South-Western, USA.

Lamb, C.W., Hair, J.F., and McDaniel, C. (2011). *Essentials of Marketing*. Cengage Learning.

Machauer, A. and Morgner, S. (2001). Segmentation of bank customers by expected benefits and attitudes. *International Journal of Bank Marketing*, 19(1), 6–18.

Minh, T. (2015). Xây dựng mô hình nghiên cứu các yếu tố quyết sự thu hút khách hàng mua sắm các trung tâm thương mại tại Thành Phố Hồ Chí Minh: Tham mô hình Châu Âu. *Tạp chí Nghiên cứu Châu Âu*, 8(179), 58–71.

Moye, L.N. and Kincade, D.H. (2003). Shopping orientation segments: Exploring differences in store patronage and attitudes toward retail store environments among female apparel consumers. *International Journal of Consumer Studies*, 27(1), 58–71.

Oeser, G., Aygün, T., Balan, C.L., Paffrath, R., and Schuckel, M.T. (2019). Segmenting elder German grocery shoppers based on shopping motivations. *International Journal of Retail & Distribution Management*, 47(2), 129–156.

Prashar, S., Singh, H., Parsad, C., and Vijay, T.S. (2019). Segmenting Indian shoppers on mall attractiveness factors. *International Journal of Services Technology and Management*, 25(1), 18–35.

Reimers, V. and Clulow, V. (2009). Retail centres: It's time to make them convenient. *International Journal of Retail & Distribution Management*, 37(7), 541–562.

Rigopoulou, I.D., Tsiotsou, R.H. and Kehagias, J.D. (2008). Shopping orientation-defined segments based on store-choice criteria and satisfaction: An empirical investigation. *Journal of Marketing Management*, 24 (9–10), 979–995.

Sit, J., Merrilees, B., and Birch, D. (2003). Entertainment-seeking shopping centre patrons: The missing segments. *International Journal of Retail & Distribution Management*, 31(2), 80–94.

Shim, S. and Kotsiopoulos, A. (1993). A typology apparel shopping orientation segments among female consumers. *Clothing and Textiles Research Journal*, 12(1), 73–85.

Stone, G.P. (1954). City shoppers and urban identification: Observations on the social psychology of city life. *American Journal of Sociology*, 60(1), 36–45.

Tsiotsou, R.H., Rigopoulou, I.D., and Kehagias, J.D. (2010). Tracing customer orientation and marketing capabilities through retailers' websites: A strategic approach to internet marketing. *Journal of Targeting, Measurement and Analysis for Marketing*, 18(2), 79–94.

Walsh, G., Hennig-Thurau, T., Wayne-Mitchell, V., and Wiedmann, K.P. (2001). Consumers' decision-making style as a basis for market segmentation. *Journal of Targeting, Measurement and Analysis for Marketing*, 10(2), 117–131.

Wind, Y. (1978). Issues and advances in segmentation research. *Journal of Marketing Research*, 15(3), 317–337.

Wakefield, K.L. and Baker, J. (1998). Excitement at the mall: Determinants and effects on shopping response. *Journal of Retailing*, 74(4), 515–539.

Wong, G., Yu, L., and Yuan, L. (2001). SCATTR: An instrument for measuring shopping centre attractiveness. *International Journal of Retail & Distribution Management*, 29(2), 76–86.

Zulqarnain, H., Zafar, A.U., and Shahzad, M. (2015). Factors that affect the choice of Consumers in selecting retail store, for grocery shopping. *International Journal of Multidisciplinary and Current Research*, 3(1), 1167–1172.

Part V

Behavioral Economics Business

https://doi.org/10.1142/9789811262258_0005

Chapter 5

The Impact of Independent Directors on Firm Performance on the Vietnamese Stock Market

Tran Thi Thuy Linh

Abstract

This chapter aims to study the impact of independent directors (IDs) on firm performance on the Vietnamese stock market using both market-based performance measures (Tobin's Q ratio and EVA) and accounting-based ratios (ROA and ROE). The chapter analyzed the balance data of 80 firms on the Ho Chi Minh Stock Exchange from 2015 to 2018 with the Generalized Method of Moments (GMM). We find that the independent directors (PERIND) have an impact on firm performance with ROA and ROE. Besides, the effect of independent directors (NIND) adds value to the firm performance with ROA, ROE, and Tobin's Q or performance as long as they are the minority on a board of listed companies in Vietnam. The stewardship theory, the agency theory, and Enterprise Law 2014 (guidelines on independent directors) were used to analyze the impact of IDs on the performance of Vietnamese firms. This study provides additional evidence to the literature regarding the relationship between independent directors (IDs) and firm performance.

Keywords: Independent director; Outside director; Independent board; Board structure; Performance.

Contribution/Originality: This study uses a new estimation methodology, GMM method analysis, to measure the impact of independent directors (IDs) on firm performance in the Vietnamese stock market. These exhaustive empirical methods combined with theories like the stewardship theory, the agency theory, and Enterprise Law 2014 (guidelines on independent directors) were used to analyze the impact of IDs on the performance of Vietnamese firms.

1. Introduction

In corporate governance, the board of directors (BOD) plays a central role in the operating system of a joint-stock company. As a representative for shareholders, the board of directors ensures the company's strategic direction and performs the function of consulting and monitoring the effectiveness of the company's management. For businesses to maintain operational efficiency, the company's management and operation are essential factors to increase the value of the business. Therefore, BOD members need to implement the principles of Corporate Governance well to improve operational efficiency.

According to the Organization for Economic Cooperation and Development (OECD, 1999), principles of Corporate Governance should lay out a vision of the board's responsibilities: "The corporate governance framework should ensure the strategic guidance of the company, the effective monitoring of the board, and the board's accountability to the company and the shareholders." The characteristics of the BOD have an impact on the advisory and oversight of the Board's responsibilities. Therefore, corporate governance significantly affects firm performance (Larcker and Tayan, 2011).

Board members are expected to exhibit independence to be effective in an advisory and oversight capacity. From a regulatory standpoint, independence is evaluated by the degree to which a director is free from conflicts of interest that might compromise their ability to act solely in the firm's interest. Independence is critical in ensuring that directors can take positions in opposition to those of management when necessary.

The characteristics of the BOD have a significant influence on corporate performance, such as size, professional information, and demographics of members of the BOD, independent members, etc. Many studies around the world have analyzed the impact of independent members on corporate performance. Bozcuk (2011) shows a positive correlation between the presence of independent members in BOD, and the firm performance calculated in book value and market value. Eisenberg *et al.* (1998) note that the critical role of external independent directors in the BOD can improve the efficiency of businesses. Studying from the US companies, Duchin *et al.* (2010) show that there is a statistically significant relationship between independent members and firm performance. Other studies in European countries (Krivogorsky, 2006), New Zealand (Hossain *et al.*, 2001), and South Korea (Black *et al.*, 2006) have similar results. Nwokwu *et al.* (2019) use the accounting measure (ROE) to study the influence of independent members on firm performance in Nigeria. The results find a positive correlation between the ratio of independent members and the return on equity. However, Pham *et al.* (2011) employ economic value-added (EVA) measures as an alternative performance measure. Their results show that there is not a significant relationship between firm performance and corporate governance.

In Vietnam, the Ho Chi Minh Stock Exchange (HOSE) has had 382 companies with capitalization reaching 3.28 VND billion in 2019, which increased to 14.05% compared to 2018 and accounted for nearly 60% of GDP in 2018. Market liquidity was recorded with a daily average trading value of VND 4,128 billion and an average trading volume of about 182.5 million shares, decreased by 25% and 10% compared to 2018. This could be an opportunity for investors to choose good stocks in their portfolio to achieve the target return rate. Since the Enterprise Law 2014 issued and edited with Decree No 71/2017/ND-CP (it is replaced Decree No. 155/2020/ND-CP) about Guidelines on the Governance of Public companies, the BOD of a listed company must ensure at least 1/3 of the total members of the BOD that are an independent member. Decree No. 71/2017/ND-CP has had many new regulations aimed at improving corporate governance. In fact, the activities of independent Board members in many firms are not practical, as they act as gatekeepers and critics of the enterprise. Therefore, businesses need to promote the role and the voice of the independent members of the BOD to encourage criticisms in the company, protecting the enterprises themselves and their owners.

In this situation, the main objective of the chapter is to study two issues: *(i) the impact of independent members on the performance of Vietnamese listed companies; (ii) whether the independent directors add value for firms when they are the minority in a board of listed companies in Ho Chi Minh Stock Exchange.*

The remainder of this chapter consists of Section 2 which analyzes the empirical studies. The research methodology is presented in Section 3. Section 4 shows experimental results, and the final Section 5 concludes the chapter.

2. Theory Framework and Empirical Studies

2.1. *Theory framework (background)*

2.1.1. *Stewardship theory*

Corporate finance is the collection of control mechanisms that an organization adopts to prevent or dissuade potentially self-interested managers from engaging in activities detrimental to the welfare of shareholders and stakeholders (Larcker and Tayan, 2011).

Stewardship theory was introduced by Donaldson and Davis (1989, 1991) as a normative alternative to the agency theory. This agency theory led to the birth of corporate governance issues. The incomplete nature of the contract between shareholders and the company makes it relatively easier to violate ethical norms. Hence, shareholders need to find other ways to protect their interests. Shareholders can use this by assuring the corporate entities fulfill their responsibilities toward shareholders' interests (Shleifer and Vishny, 1997).

The executive manager, under stewardship theory, far from being an opportunistic shirker, essentially wants to do a good job, to be a good steward of the corporate assets. Grounded in psychology, sociology, and leadership theories, stewardship theory argues for the possible alignment between the principals and agents, which is reflective of a psychological contract or a close relationship with the agent behaving in a community-focused manner, directing trustworthy moral behavior toward the firms and its shareholders (Davis *et al.*, 2007). Thus, stewardship theory holds that there would be no inherent, general problem of executive motivation (Donaldson and Davis, 1991).

Managerial theory shows that executives are not opportunity evaders. They basically want to do a good job, to become a good manager (Subramanian, 2018). Based on this theory, shareholders can feel secure when putting their assets in the hands of the leaders and executives of the company.

2.1.2. *The agency theory*

Jensen and Meckling (1976) initiated agency theory by redefining the agency relation among the shareholders (principal) and manager (agent) and argued that there is always a conflict between shareholders and managers. This conflict issue raises shareholders' expenses due to the representative's actions — called agency cost. However, according to Jensen and Meckling (1976), an increase in the proportion of internal ownership will also lead to a decrease in firm value because the act of pursuing the interests of internal ownership groups will lead to decisions to occupy the claims of external shareholders and extract firm's resources.

According to the agency theory, the importance of corporate governance (CG) is to reduce the conflicts between controlling shareholders and minority shareholders in a company. CG is considered a mechanism to help align management objectives with stakeholders' goals to increase a business's operational efficiency. Therefore, it can be said that agency theory is considered as opposed to the stewardship theory. It encourages shareholders to find ways to curb the representative's abuses and is the premise of the idea of independent members in BOD. Accordingly, the independent members in the BOD play a pivotal role in improving the effectiveness of the BOD as well as reducing costs through increased management oversight (Hermalin *et al.*, 1991).

2.2. *Empirical researches*

Independent Directors (IDs) or Outside Directors (ODS) is not just a topic in the field of management and economics that has become a legal regulation. From the perspective of the corporate governance doctrine, IDs are supposed to critique the decisions of representatives — executives who run independently and rely solely on the company's interests. In one of the earliest studies, Fama (1980) suggests that the development of behavioral theories leads to the rejection of a classical management model. The theory shows that the manager, the owner, and the executive are not the owners who unilaterally run the company to maximize profits, supporting the arguments of a manager.

Internationally, there have been many controversial studies related to the correlation between independent directors and firm performance. Demsetz *et al.* (1985) and Linck *et al.* (2008) suggest that independent directors assist executives in making investment decisions and ensure that the performance of the executives is scrutinized. However, Hermalin *et al.* (1991) analyzed the companies listed on the New York Stock Exchange but could not find the link between IDs and the firm's performance. Similarly, Bhagat and Black (2002) did not succeed in finding the relationship between IDs in the BOD and the performance of the US companies in 1991.

Eisenberg *et al.* (1998) note that independent outsiders' critical role in improving board effectiveness. These independent directors oversee management activities. Their activities can reduce the asymmetric issues of costs and information of members of the BOD. The IDs give their multidimensional perspective on the same issue based on the knowledge gained in other areas. Besides, Beasley and Mark (1996) ran their study throughout the United States, and suggest that a more significant percentage of outside members on the BOD significantly reduces the likelihood of fraudulent financial statements. Also, when outside directors' ownership in the business and the outsider's term in the BOD increase, the possibility of financial reporting fraud decreases.

Dahya and McConnell (2007) studied in the United Kingdom the impact of proposals from the Cadbury Committee on corporate governance and the BOD. They also demonstrate that there is a very significant correlation between outsiders and firm performance. Duchin *et al.*'s (2010) research on companies in the US shows a statistically significant relationship between IDs and firm performance. Other studies in European countries (Krivogorsky, 2006), New Zealand (Hossain *et al.*, 2001), and Korea (Black *et al.*, 2006) all show similar results. Eslihan (2011) demonstrates that there is a significant positive relationship between the presence of IDs, the number of IDs in the BOD, to the firm's performance both in terms of accounting (ROE) and market value (IAPP). Research by Bhabra and Li (2011) is about the impact of the IDs on the performance of Chinese companies using Tobin's Q to reflect the market value also gave similar results. The results of Li *et al.* (2015) are robust to a battery of endogeneity checks and are more substantial with market-based (Tobin's Q) performance measures compared to accounting-based estimates (ROA). Their results support the notion of high ownership concentration, which has a moderating influence on board effectiveness, but the effect also depends on ownership types and the country's institutional environment. In contrast, Maharani (2018) shows that independent directors do not affect the performance of listed businesses in Indonesia. Bhagat and Black (2002) found evidence that low-profitability firms increase the independence of their BOD. However, there is no evidence that this strategy works. Firms with more independent boards do not perform better than other firms. With the sample of Australian companies, Pham *et al.* (2011) said that there is no correlation between IDs and the performance of listed companies. Crespí-Cladera and Pascual-Fuster (2014) find no correlation between independent members and the implementation of businesses in Spain. Haldar *et al.* (2019) find that independent board directors in Indian companies had no significant effect on financial performance.

In recent years, according to Tulung *et al.* (2018), the results show a positive relationship between IDs in the BOD and firm performance in Indonesia. The research by Nwokwu *et al.* (2019) shows a positive correlation between the proportion of independent directors and ROE on the performance of enterprises in Nigeria. According to Rashid (2018), this study also finds that board size has a significant favorable influence on both board independence and firm performance.

In summary, empirical studies have shown that independent directors have a significant influence on the performance of enterprises. A lot of empirical evidence shows that independent directors have a statistically positive correlation with an enterprise value based on accounting criteria and market value. However, many studies have found no correlation between independent directors and firm performance.

In Vietnam, Enterprise Law 2014 has already had regulations and guidelines on independent directors, encouraging the appointment of independent members to the BOD of the enterprise. On December 31, 2020, for public companies and listed companies, the appointment of independent directors was no longer an incentive, but this is mandatory, as provided in Decree No. 155/2020/ND-CP. For public companies, it is required to have 1/5 of the number of independent directors in the BOD. This figure for listed companies is 1/3 and always ensures at least 01 independent directors in the BOD. However, from the 2018 corporate scoring report organized by the SSC, only 47 listed companies currently fully meet the provisions of Decree No. 155/2020/ND-CP.

3. Methodology and Data

3.1. *Researching data*

The sample consists of companies listed on the HOSE, composed of 80 non-financial companies with data from 2015 to 2018, gathered from websites such as Vietstock, CafeF, and cophieu68. Because of the research data in 2015–2018, the authors only analyze Decree No. 71/2017/ND-CP guidelines on corporate governance of public companies.

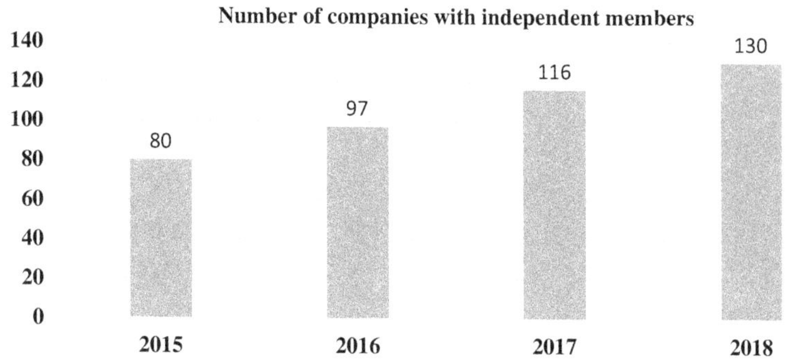

Figure 1: Chart of the number of companies having independent directors on HOSE.

Source: Authors' data and calculation.

We collect data from eligible listed companies for conditions of samples:

- The company ends the fiscal year on 31/12 and unchanged fiscal year during the observations period and has an uninterrupted business.
- Companies must have IDs in the BOD before Decree No. 71/2017/ND-CP about Guidelines on Governance of Public Companies is issued.
- The selected companies do not have a negative Beta coefficient.

We collected the change in the number of companies with independent directors in 4 years (2015–2018). In 4 years, only 130 companies on HOSE had the presence of independent directors in the BOD (about 34% of 382 companies listed on HOSE). Since 2015, there were only 80 companies satisfied the conditions of the samples (Figure 1).

3.2. *Expected hypothesis*

In Vietnam, the concept of non-executive independent members is specified in Decision No. 12/2007/QD-BTC dated March 15, 2007, of the Ministry of Finance and Circular 121/2012/TT-BTC. As stipulated in these documents, the total number of non-executive independent members in the BOD must account for 1/3 of the members. However, the number of listed companies with independent members who are not operating in the BOD is minimal, and there are no sanctions for not implementing. Until the Enterprises Law 2014 was enacted and Decree No. 71/2017/ND-CP, there was only a whole institution and specific sanctions on this issue in Vietnam. According to studies by Duchin *et al.* (2010), Eslihan (2011), Koerniadi and Tourani-Rad (2012), Tulung *et al.* (2018), and Nwokwu *et al.* (2019), the results showed a positive relationship between IDs in the BOD and the effectiveness of the company. Also, Beasley (1996), studying the United States, said that a more significant percentage of independent directors to the BOD could significantly reduce the possibility of fraudulent financial statements, improving firm performance, which is consistent with Eslihan (2011). Koerniadi and Tourani-Rad (2012) showed that this finding is important given the increasing trend of independence in New Zealand firm boards and suggests that board independence is considered a better monitoring function. Therefore, we expected the research results as follows:

H_1*: *Independent members have a positive impact on the performance of Vietnamese listed companies

H_2*: *Independent directors add value or performance as long as they are the minority aboard

3.3. *The description of variables in the model*

3.3.1. *Dependent variables: Measuring firm performance*

We measure the performance of enterprises using a combination of accounting and market measures.

3.3.1.1. Accounting-based ratios performance measures (ROA, ROE)

- The two of these ratios are quite a comprehensive picture of the company's efficiency from an accounting perspective. Nwokwu *et al.* (2019) used ROE to assess the impact of the BOD on corporate profits. Jiao *et al.* (2013) used ROA as an indicator to evaluate the performance.

- ROA is calculated by net income divided by the total asset. ROA represents asset efficiency.
- ROE is calculated by net income divided by total equity, while ROE reflects the effective use of equity.

3.3.1.2. Market-based performance measures (Tobin's Q, EVA)

- Tobin's Q is calculated by the total market value of equity and the book value of debt is divided by total assets. In the study of Eslihan (2011) in Turkey on the influence of independent directors on business activities, the author used Tobin's Q to evaluate the market value aspect of companies listed on the Istanbul Stock Exchange, similar to Li *et al.* (2015).
- EVA is used next to Tobin's Q. The EVA measures a company's financial performance based on the residual assets calculated by deducting the cost of capital from operating profit, which is tax-adjusted based on cash. Sharma *et al.* (2012), studied EVA and compared it with traditional methods (EPS, ROA, ROE, OCF, NOPAT, NI, RI).

EVA will accurately reflect the additional impact of independent directors on the enterprise value. Elali (2006) showed that EVA surpassed Tobin's Q in explaining shareholder wealth, in line with the study of Koerniadi and Tourani-Rad (2012) and Haldar *et al.* (2018).

3.3.2. *Explaining variables*

The author describes the following independent variables in Table 1.

When we analyze IDs in the case of a majority in the BOD which can increase performance and a trend of independence in Vietnamese firm boards and suggests that board independence, which is considered to be a better monitoring function (Haldar, 2018), the PERIND variable will replace by NIND variable.

Table 1: Variables of the research model.

Variables	Explaining Variables	How to Calculate Variable	Authors
ROE	The return rate on equity	$\text{ROE} = \frac{Net\, revenue}{Equity}$	Nwokwu *et al.* (2019); Koerniadi and Tourani-Rad (2012)
ROA	The return rate on asset	$\text{ROA} = \frac{Net\, revenue}{Total\, assets}$	
TOBINQ	Tobin's Q-factor: The ratio between the market price and the replacement value of a tangible asset	$\text{Tobin's Q} = \frac{EMV + LMV}{EBV + LBV}$ Of which: – EMV: Market value of Equity – LMV: Market value of Liabilities – EBV: Book value of Equity – LBV: Book value of Liabilities	Eslihan (2011); Bhabra and Li (2011); Li *et al.* (2015)
EVA	Economic value added	EVA = NOPAT – (TC × WACC) – NOPAT: Taking profit before interest and tax NOPAT = Profit after tax + Interset × (1 – tax rate corporate) – TC: Investment capital is determined by the total average assets on the balance sheet – WACC: Weighted average weighted interest rate (including loans and equity)	Elali (2006); Sharma (2012); Pham *et al.* (2011); Koerniadi and Tourani-Rad (2012); Haldar *et al.* (2018)
WACC		– $\text{debt cost} = \frac{interest}{total\, debt}$ – ri: equity cost – $\text{ri} = \text{r}_\text{f} + \beta \times (\text{r}_\text{m} - \text{r}_\text{f})$	Sharma and Kumar (2012)

PERIND	The ratio of independent members to the total number of members of the BOD	PERIND = $\frac{the\, number\, of\, independent\, directors}{Total\, members\, in\, the\, BOD}$	Rashid (2018)
NIND	The minority independent directors	Dummy variable: the value of 1 if independent directors are the minority and take 0 otherwise	Haldar *et al.* (2018); Koerniadi and Tourani-Rad (2012)
BDSIZE	Number of Board members	BDSIZE = total number of the BOD	Eslihan (2011); Nwokwu *et al.* (2019)
BUSY	The busy independent members	Dummy variable: receive value 1 if the independent member is a member of the BOD or a BOD of 2 other companies or more. Get 0 in other cases	Nwokwu *et al.* (2019); Koerniadi and Tourani-Rad (2012)
ACSIZE	The number of members of the Control Board	ACSIZE = The number of members of the Control Board	Koerniadi and Tourani-Rad (2012); Bhagat and Black (2002)
BLOCK	The cumulative ratio of large shareholders owning more than 5% of the shares	BLOCK = $\sum_1^n ti$ Where it is the number of shares held by a major shareholder	Rashid (2018)
LEV	Long-term debt ratio	LEV = $\frac{Total\, long - term\, debt}{Total\, assets}$	Haldar *et al.* (2018)
B/M	The ratio of market values to book values	B/M = $\frac{Market\, value}{Book\, value}$	Koerniadi and Tourani-Rad (2012)
SIZE	Natural logarithm of stock market prices	SIZE = Ln(market prices)	Haldar *et al.* (2018)

Source: Author's calculation.

3.3.3. *Reaching model*

We analyze the main objective of the paper with two reaching models, such as:

- **Model 1:** Do independent members of the BOD affect the business performance of Vietnamese listed companies?

Performance (ROA, ROE, TOBINQ, EVA) $= \alpha + \beta 1$ PERIND $+$ $\beta 2$ BDSIZZE $+ \beta 3$ BUSY $+ \beta 4$ ACSIZE $+ \beta 5$ BLOCK $+ \beta 6$ LEV $+$ $\beta 7$ B/M $+ \beta 8$ SIZE $+ e_{i,t}$

- **Model 2:** How do Independent directors add value or performance as long as they are the minority on a listed company board in Vietnam?

Performance (ROA, ROE, TOBINQ, EVA) $= \alpha + \delta 1$ NIND $+$ $\delta 2$ BDSIZE $+ \delta 3$ BUSY $+ \delta 4$ ACSIZE $+ \delta 5$ BLOCK $+ \delta 6$ LEV $+$ $\delta 7$ B/M $+ \delta 8$ SIZE $+ e_{i,t}$

We use the Fixed Effects Model (FEM) and Random Effects Model (REM) with the balanced panel data. The Hausman Tests (Hausman, 1978) are used in the chapter to select the appropriate model.

Simultaneously, the Variance Inflation Factor (VIF) test is used to test for multicollinearity among variables, and the Wald test is used to test for heteroscedasticity. The Wooldridge test (Wooldridge, 2010) is tested for correlation test. The authors use the GMM Estimation of Arellano and Bond (1991) to overcome autocorrelation, heteroscedasticity, and endogenous variable violations, resulting in unbiased, stable, and the most efficient estimation results.

4. Empirical Results

4.1. *Descriptive statistics and variables of Pearson correlation*

4.1.1. *Descriptive statistics*

According to Table 2, the average return on asset (ROA) of companies listed on the HOSE is 7.22%, and ROE is 14.54%, indicating that companies operate effectively. The data are an outlier to ROA, ROE because of the data of ROA, ROE of the Savina firm. Table 2's results show the maximum and minimum values of ROA and ROE in the whole research sample after the author has processed Outlier by Winsorrize technique. The results of other countries in the region are relatively good such as Indonesia with ROE of 8.4%, ROA of 4.1% (Maharani, 2018), or China with ROA of 3.2%. Similarly, Tobin's Q has an average value of nearly 1.5, suggesting that its market value is greater than its asset value. The B/M shows that the company's market value is more significant than its book value. The positive EVA also indicates that the profits generated by the company exceed the cost of capital. The leverage rate of the companies surveyed is relatively low. The average value of LEV is 12.27% which is lower than China's 44.6% (Bhabra and Li, 2011) and New Zealand's 42.2% (Koerniadi and Tourani-Rad, 2012). Even a country in the region (Indonesia) has a very high leverage ratio of 59.29% (Maharani, 2018). The average value of PERIND is 26.76% independent members of the Board. The value is not enough to meet the provisions of the Enterprise Law in 2014, and is also very low compared to countries such as India's 40.73% (Haldar *et al.*, 2018),

Table 2: Descriptive statistics of board involvement and corporate performance.

	Observation	Mean	STD. Dev.	Min	Max
ROA	320	0.0722	0.0576	0.0034	0.2227
ROE	320	0.1454	0.1041	0.0077	0.4078
TobinsQ	320	1.5628	1.7001	−1.7255	12.8543
EVA	320	0.0000	0.0000	0.0000	0.0000
BDSIZE	320	6.365	1.3553	3.0000	11.0000
PERIND	320	0.2676	0.1250	0.1111	8.0000
NIND	320	0.0344	0.1825	0.0000	1.0000
BUSY	320	0.1156	0.3203	0.0000	1.0000
ACSIZE	320	3.0781	0.5458	0.0000	6.0000
BLOCK	320	0.4590	0.2276	0.0000	0.9780
LEV	320	0.1227	0.1404	0.0000	0.6108
B/M	320	1.1055	0.9707	−1.3843	7.0667
SIZE	320	9.8884	0.9434	7.2862	12.3545

Source: Author's statistical output.

New Zealand's 51.9% (Koerniadi and Tourani-Rad, 2012), USA' 60% (Bhagat and Black, 2002), or China's 36% (Jiao *et al.*, 2013). However, Vietnam is not a country having the lowest percentage of independent directors in the world. Some countries are even lower such as Turkey at 10% (Eslihan, 2011) or Indonesia at 13.7% (Maharani, 2018). This shows that companies in Vietnam currently did not pay much attention to adding IDs to the BOD during 2015–2018.

In addition, only about three companies out of 80 surveyed companies have more than half of the independent directors in the BOD. The average of NIND equals 3.4%, reflecting that the companies have not complied with the regulation of independent directors in the BOD of Vietnamese companies.

4.1.2. *Variables of Pearson correlation*

According to Table 3, the correlation between the two variables PERIND and NIND is 0.619 because they are calculated based on the number of independent members. ROE and ROA are 0.8777 reflecting the firm performance. For the remaining variables in the model, the correlation matrix shows that the variables are not strongly correlated with each other. The correlation coefficients are less than 0.8, and the VIFs of the two models are smaller than 10. Therefore, the multi-collinear phenomenon is not severe.

The author performed the Variance Inflation Factor (VIF) test in Table 4, which shows that the Variance Inflation Factor (VIF) of the independent variables in the models is all less than 10, indicating that there is no multicollinearity.

4.2. *Results of regression analysis and model selection*

4.2.1. *Checking appropriate model selection*

The chapter uses Hausman (1978) test to select an appropriate regression model between FEM and REM (Table 5).

Table 3: Correlation matrix variables (Pearson correlation).

	ROA	ROE	TOBINQ	EVA	BDSIZE	PERIND	NIND	BUSY	ACSIZE	BLOCK	LEV	B/M	SIZE
ROA	1	—	—	—	—	—	—	—	—	—	—	—	—
ROE	0.8777	1	—	—	—	—	—	—	—	—	—	—	—
TOBINQ	0.3794	0.3926	1	—	—	—	—	—	—	—	—	—	—
EVA	0.3631	0.3385	0.6444	1	—	—	—	—	—	—	—	—	—
BDSIZE	0.1741	0.2136	0.2146	0.2226	1	—	—	—	—	—	—	—	—
PERIND	(0.0696)	(0.0645)	(0.1123)	(0.0236)	(0.0159)	1	—	—	—	—	—	—	—
NIND	(0.1102)	(0.1198)	(0.0603)	(0.0572)	(0.0252)	0.6185	1	—	—	—	—	—	—
BUSY	(0.1200)	(0.0541)	(0.1086)	(0.0578)	0.0042	0.0180	(0.0682)	1	—	—	—	—	—
ACSIZE	(0.1570)	(0.0956)	(0.0493)	(0.1198)	0.1311	(0.0931)	0.0044	0.0737	1	—	—	—	—
BLOCK	0.0045	(0.0330)	0.0535	(0.0294)	(0.0013)	0.0747	0.1083	0.0293	0.2173	1	—	—	—
LEV	(0.2462)	(0.1878)	(0.1170)	(0.0308)	0.1140	0.1192	0.0805	0.0512	(0.0044)	0.1038	1	—	—
B/M	(0.3279)	(03908)	(0.4423)	(0.2569)	(0.1852)	0.1582	0.0538	0.1423	(0.0464)	(0.1316)	(0.0775)	1	—
SIZE	0.3961	0.4663	0.5912	0.4422	0.2348	(0.1288)	(0.0870)	(0.1396)	0.0011	0.1055	(0.0505)	(0.7366)	1

Source: Author's statistical output.

Table 4: VIF of Independence variables.

MODEL 1			MODEL 2		
Independence Variables	**VIF**	**1/VIF**	**Independence Variables**	**VIF**	**1/VIF**
PERIND	1.07	0.9344	NIND	1.04	0.9652
BDSIZE	1.15	0.8702	BDSIZE	1.15	0.8701
BUSY	1.08	0.9231	BUSY	1.09	0.9154
ACSIZE	1.14	0.8743	ACSIZE	1.13	0.8869
BLOCK	1.14	0.8777	BLOCK	1.14	0.8780
LEV	1.24	0.8097	LEV	1.23	0.8133
B/M	2.41	0.4143	B/M	2.39	0.4184
SIZE	2.74	0.3645	SIZE	2.75	0.3631

Source: Author's statistical output.

4.2.2. *Testing the effectiveness of research models*

In order to test the effectiveness of the two research models, the author performed the Wald test to detect the Heteroscedasticity and Wooldridge test (Wooldridge, 2010) to test autocorrelation for the appropriate model. Specific results are shown in Table 6a and 6b.

In summary, Model 1 has heteroscedasticity and autocorrelation with dependent variables (TOBINQ, EVA).

So, Model 2 has heteroscedasticity and autocorrelation with dependent variables (TOBINQ, EVA).

4.2.3. *Regression results of the effect of independent members on the performance of Vietnamese listed companies*

Because Models 1 and 2 have heteroscedasticity and autocorrelation. So, the author used GMM regression model to fix it. GMM regression results of model 1 with four dependent variables

- **Model 1:** *Do independent members of the BOD affect the business performance of Vietnamese listed companies?*

$$Performance\ (ROA, ROE, TOBINQ, EVA) = \alpha + \beta 1\ PERIND + \beta 2\ BDSIZZE + \beta 3\ BUSY + \beta 4\ ACSIZE + \beta 5\ BLOCK + \beta 6\ LEV + \beta 7\ B/M + \beta 8\ SIZE + e_{i,t}$$

Table 5: Hausman test for regression model between FEM and REM.

	Model 1				**Model 2**			
	(1a)	**(1b)**	**(1c)**	**(1d)**	**(2a)**	**(2b)**	**(2c)**	**(2d)**
p-value	0.0020	0.0330	0.8829	0.1195	0.0022	0.0326	0.9932	0.1085
Conclusion	Rejected H_0	Rejected H_0	Accepted H_0	Accepted H_0	Rejected H_0	Rejected H_0	Accepted H_0	Accepted H_0
An appropriate regression model	FEM	FEM	REM	REM	FEM	FEM	REM	REM

Source: Author's statistical output.

Table 6a: Testing result of Model 1.

Test	Model 1			
	(1a) **ROA**	(1b) **ROE**	(1c) **TOBINQ**	(1d) **EVA**
Heteroscedasticity test (Wald test)	Chi2(80) = 8.1e + 05 Prob > Chi2 = 0.000	Chi2(80) = 1.2e + 06 Prob > Chi2 = 0.000	Chi2(80) = 3.1e + 06 Prob > Chi2 = 0.000	Chi2(80) = 7.0e + 06 Prob > Chi2 = 0.000
Serial correlation test (Wooldridge test)	F(1.79) = 0.183 Prob > F = 0.6697	F(1.79) = 0.188 Prob > F = 0.6658	F(1.79) = 17.712 Prob > F = 0.0001	F(1.79) = 16.150 Prob > F = 0.0001
Conclusion	Model 1, which has ROA as the dependent variable, has heteroscedasticity but no autocorrelation	Model 1, which has ROE as the dependent variable, has heteroscedasticity but no autocorrelation	Model 1, which has TOBINQ as the dependent variable, has heteroscedasticity and autocorrelation	Model 1, which has EVA as the dependent variable, has heteroscedasticity and autocorrelation

Source: Author's statistical output.

Table 6b: Testing result of Model 2.

Test	Model 2 (2a) ROA	(2b) ROE	(2c) TOBINQ	(2d) EVA
Heteroscedasticity test (Wald test)	Chi2(80) = 9.3e + 06 Prob > Chi2 = 0.000	Chi2(80) = 1.4e + 06 Prob > Chi2 = 0.000	Chi2(80) = 2.7e + 07 Prob > Chi2 = 0.000	Chi2(80) = 1.1e + 07 Prob > Chi2 = 0.000
Serial correlation test (Wooldridge test)	F(1.79) = 0.094 Prob > F = 0.7594	F(1.79) = 0.086 Prob > F = 0.7702	F(1.79) = 17.657 Prob > F = 0.0001	F(1.79) = 16,476 Prob > F = 0.0001
Conclusion	Model 2, which has ROA as the dependent variable, has heteroscedasticity but no autocorrelation	Model 2, which has ROE as the dependent variable, has heteroscedasticity but no autocorrelation	Model 2, which has TOBINQ as the dependent variable, has heteroscedasticity and autocorrelation	Model 2, which has EVA as the dependent variable, has heteroscedasticity and autocorrelation

Source: Author's statistical output.

Table 7: Regression results of the effect of independent members on the performance of Vietnamese listed companies with Model 1.

	ROA	ROE	TOBINQ	EVA
PERIND	0.0808^{***}	0.1560^{***}	-0.1620	0
BDSIZE	0.0173^{***}	0.0229^{***}	0.0878^{***}	0
BUSY	-0.2388^{***}	0.0548^{***}	0.2385^{**}	0
ACSIZE	-0.0065^{***}	-0.0059	0.1647^{**}	0
BLOCK	0.0469^{***}	0.0934^{***}	1.0438^{***}	0
LEV	-0.2494^{***}	-0.2892^{***}	-0.4398^{*}	0
B/M	-0.0231^{***}	-0.0058	-0.0823^{*}	0
SIZE	-0.0049	0.0650^{***}	0.5663^{***}	$-7.79e+09^{***}$
_cons	0.0433	-0.6708^{***}	-6.3896^{***}	0
Observation	320	320	320	320
AR(1) (p-value)	0.251	0.208	0.094	0.213
AR(2) (p-value)	—	—	—	—
Hansen test (p-value)	0.607	0.269	0.225	0.000

Notes: *significant at 10% level; **significant at 5% level; ***significant at 1% level.
Source: Author's statistical output.

According to Table 7, most IDs have a positive impact on firm performance. They are only statistically significant at the 1% level for ROA, ROE, and consistent with H1, as per the study by Haldar *et al.* (2018). Tobin's Q and EVA do not have a statistically significant relationship with IDs, which is consistent with the research of Pham *et al.* (2011). The positive impact of independent directors on the performance is that there is no strict regulation on IDs in the BOD of Vietnamese enterprises before Decree No. 71/2017/ND-CP. IDs may be indifferent to seeking out company information, often having little interest in their role for the company and judging the information supplied by the managers.

The BDSize positively impacts firm performance and is only statistically significant at the 1% level for ROA, ROE, Tobin's Q, consistent with Haldar *et al.* (2018) study. EVA does not have a statistically significant relationship with BDSize.

The result showed that block holders (BLOCK) are positively correlated and significantly at 1% with performance (except EVA).

This result is similar to those reported (Hossain *et al.*, 2001) that show high firm ownership concentration has a somewhat positive impact on firm performance.

The ACSIZE has a negative impact on firm performance and is only statistically significant at the 1% level for ROA but positively with Tobin's Q (except ROE and EVA).

LEV and B/M negatively correlate with a statistical significance to the firm performance based on both accounting or market methods, consistent with Koerniadi's research. Koerniadi and Tourani-Rad (2012) suggest that high debt levels can lead to a decrease in firm performance.

4.2.4. *Regression results of an impact of independent directors add value or performance as long as they are the minority on a board of listed companies in Vietnam*

Koerniadi and Tourani-Rad (2012) show the effects of the presence of independent directors on firm value (Tobin's Q ratio and EVA) and performance (ROA and ROE). These findings are given the increasing trend of independence in New Zealand firm boards and suggest board independence, which is considered a better monitoring function. We test model 2, replacing the PERIND variable with a dummy variable NIND.

- **Model 2:** *How do independent directors add value or performance as long as they are the minority on a listed company board in Vietnam?*

$Performance\ (ROA,\ ROE,\ TOBINQ,\ EVA) = \alpha + \delta 1\ NIND + \delta 2\ BDSIZE + \delta 3\ BUSY + \delta 4\ ACSIZE + \delta 5\ BLOCK + \delta 6\ LEV + \delta 7\ B/M + \delta 8\ SIZE + e_{i,t}$

According to Table 8, the study finds a negative and statistically significant relationship between the NIND variable and the ROA, ROE, Tobin Q (except EVA), opposite to H2, which is consistent with the research of Black *et al.* (2010) and Koerniadi and Tourani-Rad (2012).

Table 8: Regression results of the impact of independent directors add value or performance as long as they are the minority on a listed company board in Vietnam.

	ROA	ROE	TOBINQ	EVA
NIND	−0.0315***	−0.0455***	−0.3385***	0
BDSIZE	0.0191***	0.0286***	0.1029***	0
BUSY	0.0002	0.0375**	0.2140**	0
ACSIZE	−0.0091***	−0.0042	0.1964***	0
BLOCK	0.0306***	0.0060	0.9389***	0
LEV	−0.2406***	−0.1006	0.0850	0
BM	−0.2354***	0.0010	−0.1282***	0
SIZE	−0.0077	0.0648***	0.5060***	−1.11e + 10***
_cons	0.0963*	−0.6504***	−6.0594***	0
Số quan sát	320	320	320	320
AR(1) (*p*-value)	0.246	0.221	0.091	0.200
AR(2) (*p*-value)	—	—	—	—
Hansen test (*p*-value)	0.491	0.686	0.212	0.000

Notes: *significant at 10% level; **significant at 5% level; ***significant at 1% level.
Source: Author's statistical output.

The study finds a positive and statistically significant relationship between the BDSIZE variable and the ROA, ROE, and Tobin's Q (except EVA). The ACSIZE has a negative impact on firm performance and is statistically significant at the 1% level for ROA but positively with Tobin's Q (except ROE and EVA). The BUSY has a positive impact on firm performance and is statistically significant at the 5% level for ROE, Tobin's Q.

The BLOCK positively impacts firm performance and is statistically significant at the 1% level for ROA, Tobin's Q. This result is similar to those reported (Hossain *et al.*, 2001) that show high firm ownership concentration has a somewhat positive impact on firm performance.

In summary, through the regression, GMM suggests that independent directors (PERIND) impact the company's performance with accounting-based ratios (ROA and ROE). Besides, the impact of independent directors (NIND) adds value to firm performance using both market-based performance measures (Tobin's Q) and accounting-based ratios (ROA and ROE) or version as long as they are the minority on a board of listed companies in Vietnam.

5. Conclusion

This chapter has two objectives. First, study the impact of independent members on the performance of Vietnamese listed companies, and second, study the independent directors add value or performance as long as they are the minority on a board of listed companies in Vietnam with the sample of 80 listed companies in HOSE in the period of 2015–2018.

We have found the impact of the presence of IDs on the Board on the firm performance of Vietnamese listed companies in both market-based performance measures (Tobin's Q ratio and EVA) and accounting-based ratios (ROA and ROE). However, the IDs represent the minority shareholders. These results are consistent with Hermalin *et al.*'s (1991) research, analyzing companies listed on the New York Stock Exchange. Similarly, Bhagat and Black (2002) were unsuccessful in finding the relationship between IDs in the BOD to the performance of companies in the US in 1991, which is also consistent with the study of Pham *et al.* (2011) for Australian companies. Maharani (2018) on the Indonesian market, the market very similar to Vietnam in terms of geography and level of development, also has identical results.

This study also found that the use of leverage in Vietnam is not effective, as well as the Supervisory Board has a negative effect on the firm performance. We also found that company size has a significant impact on performance. The theory of economies of scale explains this.

The reason is that Decree No. 71/2017/ND-CP about Guidelines on the Governance of Public companies has not been well implemented by Vietnamese listed companies. Therefore, we expect that further studies will confirm a positive and statistically significant effect of independent members on the performance of Vietnamese listed companies.

Bibliography

Arellano, M. and Bond, S. (1991). Some tests of specification for panel data: Monte Carlo evidence and an application to employment equations. *Review of Economic Studies*, 58, 277–297.

Beasley, M.S. (1996). An empirical analysis of the relation between Board of Director composition and financial statement fraud. *The Accounting Review*, 71(4), 443–465.

Bhabra, H.S. and Li, T. (2011). Independent directors and corporate performance: Evidence from listed firms in China. *Corporate Ownership & Control*, 8(3), 145–169.

Bhagat, S. and Black, B.S. (2002). The non-correlation between board independence and long-term firm performance. *Journal of Corporation Law*, 27, 232–273.

Black, B.S., Jang, H., and Kim, W. (2006). Does corporate governance predict firms' market values? Evidence from Korea. *Journal of Law, Economics, & Organization*, 22, 366–413.

Bozcuk, A.E. (2011). Performance effects of outside directors on corporate boards. *International Journal of Business and Social Science*, 2, 20.

Crespí-Cladera, R. and Pascual-Fuster, B. (2014). Does the independence of independent directors matter? *Journal of Corporate Finance*, 28, 116–134.

Dahya, J. and McConnell, J. (2007). Board composition, corporate performance, and the Cadbury Committee Recommendation. *The Journal of Financial and Quantitative Analysis*, 42(3), 535–564.

Davis, J., Frankforter, S., Vollrath, D., and Hill, V. (2007). An empirical test of stewardship theory. *Journal of Business & Leadership: Research, Practice, and Teaching (2005–2012)*, 3(1), Article 6.

Davis, J.H., Schoorman, F.D., and Donaldson, L. (1997). Towards a stewardship theory of management. *Academy of Management Review*, 22(1), 20–47.

Demsetz, H. and Lehn, K. (1985). The structure of corporate ownership: Causes and consequences. *Journal of Political Economy*, 33, 3–53.

Donaldson, L. and Davis, J.H. (1989). CEO governance and shareholder returns: Agency theory or stewardship theory. *Paper Presented at the Annual Meeting of the Academy of Management.*

Donaldson, L. and Davis, J.H. (1991). Stewardship theory or agency theory: CEO governance and shareholder return. *Australian Journal of Management*, 16(1), 49–64.

Duchin, R., Matsusaka, J.G., and Ozbas, O. (2010). When are outside director effective? *Journal of Financial Economics*, 96, 195–214.

Eisenberg, T., Sundgren, S., and Wells, M.T. (1998). Larger board size and decreasing firm value in small firms. *Journal of Financial Economics*, 48(1), 35–54.

Elali. W. (2006). Contemporaneous relationship between EVA and shareholder value. *International Journal of Business Governance and Ethics*, 2, 237–253.

Eslihan, E.B. (2011). Performance effects of outside directors on corporate boards. *International Journal of Business and Social Science*, 2(20).

Fama, E.F. (1980). Agency problem and the theory of the firm. *Journal of Political Economy*, 88(2), 288–308.

Fama, E.F. and Jensen, M.C. (1983). Separation of ownership and control. *The Journal of Law and Economics*, 26, 301–325.

Guidelines No. 102. (2001). Guidelines for establishing independent director system in listed firms. *Chinese Securities Regulatory Commission CSRC*; Marketplace Rules 4000A. (n.d.). NASDAQ.

Haldar, A., Shah, R., Rao, N., Stokes, P., Demirbas, D., and Dardour, A. (2018). Corporate performance: Does board independence matter? Indian evidence. *International Journal of Organizational Analysis*, 26(1), 185–200.

Hausman, J. (1978). Specification tests in econometrics. *Econometrica*, 46, 1251–1271.

Hermalin, B.E. and Weisbach, M.S. (1991). The effects of board composition and direct incentives on firm performance. *Financial Management*, 20, 101–112.

Hossain, M.A., Prevost, M.A., and Roa, R. (2001). Corporate governance in New Zealand: The effect of the 1993 companies act on the relation between board composition and firm performance. *Pacific Basin Finance Journal*, 9(2), 119–145.

Jensen, M. (1986). Agency cost of free cash flow, corporate finance, and takeovers. *American Economic Review Papers and Proceedings*, 76, 323–329.

Jensen, M.C. and Meckling, W.H. (1976). Theory of the firm: Managerial behavior, Agency cost and ownership structure. *Journal of Financial Economics*, 3, 305–360.

Jensen. M.C. and Meckling, W.H. (1976). Can the corporation survive? *Center for Research in Government Policy and Business Working Paper no.* PPS 76-4, University of Rochester, Rochester, NY.

Jiao, H., Dong, Y., Hou, W., and Lee, E. (2013). Independent directors and corporate performance in China. In D. Cumming, A. Guariglia, W. HOU, and E. Lee (Eds.), *Developing China's Capital Market: Experiences and Challenges* (pp. 176–190).

Koerniadi, H. and Tourani-Rad, A. (2012). Does board independence mater? Evidence from New Zealand. *Australasian Accounting, Business and Finance Journal*, 6(2), 3–18.

Krivogorsky, V. (2006). Ownership, board structure, and performance in continental Europe. *International Journal of Accounting*, 41, 176–196.

Larcker, D. and Tayan, B. (2011). *Corporate Governance Matters: A Closer Look at Organizational Choices and their Consequences*, 2nd Ed. FT Press.

Li, K., Lu, L., Mittoo, U.R., and Zhang, Z (2015). Board independence, ownership concentration and corporate performance-Chinese evidence. *International Review of Financial Analysis*, 41(C), 162–175.

Linck, J.S., Netter, J.M., and Yang, T. (2008). The determinants of board structure. *Journal of Financial Economics*, 87(2), 308–328.

Maharani P.S.N. (2018). An impact of independent director on board of the directors on the performance of the firm, evidence from Indonesia. *Faculty of Economy and Business*, 69–82.

Nwokwu, T.C., Rathnasingha, D.L.P.M., and Randiwela, P. (2019). Corporate governance, board participation and firm performance of the listed companies in Nigeria. *Journal of Finance and Bank Management*, 7(1), 7–16.

OECD. (1999). *OECD Principles of Corporate Governance.* Paris: OECD Publishing.

Pham, P.K., Suchard, J.-A., and Zein, J. (2011). Corporate governance and alternative performance measures: Evidence from Australian firms. *Australian Journal of Management, Australian School of Business*, 36(3), 371–386.

Rashid, A. (2018). Board independence and firm performance: Evidence from Bangladesh. *Future Business Journal*, 4(1), 34–49.

Sharma, A.K. and Kumar, S. (2012). EVA versus conventional performance measures — Empirical evidence from India. *Paper Presented at the ASBBS Annual Conference, Las Vegas.*

Shleifer, A. and Vishny, R.W. (1997). A survey of corporate governance. *Journal of Finance, American Finance Association*, 52(2), 737–783.

Subramanian, S. (2018). Stewardship theory of corporate governance and value system: The case of a family-owned business group in India. *Indian Journal of Corporate*, 11(1), 88–102.

Tulung, J.E. and Ramdani, D. (2018). Independence, size and performance of the board: An emerging market research. *Corporate Ownership & Control*, 15(2–1), 201–208.

Wooldridge, J.M. (2010). *Econometric Analysis of Cross Section and Panel Data*, 2nd Ed. The MIT Press.

https://doi.org/10.1142/9789811262258_0006

Chapter 6

Impact of the Strategic Incremental Perspective on the Business Performance of Small and Medium-Sized Hospitality Enterprises

Thi Thanh Tra Nguyen, Bao Trung Duong, and Xuan Vinh Vo

Abstract

The business performance of small and medium-sized hospitality firms has been receiving particular attention in the Vietnamese market. This study aims to evaluate the impacts of the strategic incremental perspective on business performance. Around 342 samples are analyzed through the PLS-SEM method. Findings reveal that organizational knowledge acquisition, firm competitive advantage, and employee commitment significantly impact business performance. Furthermore, a strategic incremental perspective contributes significantly to the positive performance of businesses. In addition, this study will offer practical suggestions for hoteliers and hospitality managers to enhance performance from the strategic as well as theoretical point of view for this field. It could be helpful for policymakers to create innovative ideas and achieve good performance. This study also has certain limitations.

Keywords: Business performance; Hospitality; Small and medium-sized businesses; Strategic incremental perspective.

1. Introduction

The sector's small and medium-sized businesses (SMEs) are essential to the health of many developing nations' economies, including Vietnam. These SMEs make a substantial contribution to the creation of jobs, the growth of the local economy, and the development of tourism (Hsu, 2020; Pham and Doan, 2021). They must constantly adjust to changing consumer tastes and economic conditions, as well as fierce market competition and resource constraints (O'Gorman, 2001; Kwortnik and Thompson, 2009). For SMEs to effectively handle these issues and improve their company performance, they need to embrace strategic approaches that allow them to expand and compete successfully.

A viable strategy for improving corporate performance in the fast-paced hospitality industry is the strategic incremental perspective, which calls for making little, ongoing improvements as opposed to big, abrupt changes (Pettigrew, 1990). This viewpoint is especially important for SMEs that have to gradually adjust to changing market conditions and resource limitations (Helfat and Peteraf, 2003). Despite its potential advantages, empirical research on the effects of strategic incrementalism on business performance is not resourceful, particularly when it comes to Vietnamese SMEs in the hotel industry. Furthermore, there has not been enough research done on the roles that employee engagement, organizational knowledge acquisition, and firm competitive advantage play as mediators in this relationship (Zahra and George, 2002; Barney, 1991). This study aims to address these gaps by exploring the influence of a strategic incremental perspective on business performance and identifying the mediating roles of these key variables in Vietnamese hospitality SMEs.

In this research, the dependent variable is business performance, which encompasses various dimensions such as financial performance (customer acquisition, profitability) and non-financial performance (customer satisfaction, employee satisfaction) (Menter *et al.*, 2023; Nunes and Val Pereira, 2021). The independent variable is the strategic incremental perspective, characterized by a step-by-step approach to strategy implementation and adaptation, allowing firms to make ongoing improvements in response to internal and external changes (Quinn, 1980).

The study also examines three mediating variables: organizational knowledge acquisition, firm competitive advantage, and employee commitment. Organizational knowledge acquisition refers to the processes through which firms acquire, assimilate, and utilize knowledge to enhance their operations and decision-making (Cohen and Levinthal, 1990). Firm competitive advantage involves the unique capabilities and resources that enable a firm to outperform its competitors (Barney, 1991). Employee commitment denotes the degree of employees' attachment and loyalty to the organization, which can influence various organizational outcomes, including performance (Meyer and Allen, 1991).

The study will focus on a sample of hospitality SMEs in Vietnam, known as small hotels. This selection provides a pertinent context for exploring the relationships between strategic incrementalism, organizational knowledge acquisition, firm competitive advantage, employee commitment, and business performance in a rapidly growing and competitive market environment. It is essential to look into these factors in the context of Vietnamese hospitality SMEs in order to comprehend how small strategic moves might boost company performance. Because SMEs are dynamic and resource-constrained, the strategic incremental viewpoint offers a framework for ongoing adaptation and improvement (Helfat and Peteraf, 2003). Through an examination of the mediating functions of employee commitment, firm competitive advantage, and organizational knowledge acquisition, this research will provide insights into how incremental strategies can successfully improve business performance and support the overall prosperity of small and medium-sized enterprises (SMEs) in the hospitality industry (Zahra and George, 2002; Barney, 1991).

The theoretical framework for this study is grounded in the Resource-Based View (RBV) and Dynamic Capabilities Theory. The RBV posits that firms achieve competitive advantage through the effective utilization of valuable, rare, inimitable, and non-substitutable resources (Barney, 1991). Dynamic Capabilities Theory extends this by focusing on a firm's ability to adapt, integrate, and reconfigure its resources to respond to changing market conditions (Teece *et al.*, 1997). These theories are relevant for understanding how incremental strategic changes can impact business performance, especially in the context of SMEs operating in a dynamic and competitive environment (Helfat and Peteraf, 2003). By offering empirical data on the effect of strategic incrementalism on company performance within Vietnamese hospitality SMEs, this study adds to the body of literature. It provides a thorough understanding of how incremental methods affect performance results by clarifying the mediating roles of employee commitment, firm competitive advantage, and organizational knowledge development. This study adds to our knowledge of SMEs' strategic management and offers useful recommendations for enhancing corporate performance in developing economies.

The remainder of this paper is organized as follows: The next section reviews the relevant literature on strategic incrementalism, business performance, and the mediating variables under investigation. The subsequent section describes the research methodology, including the sample, data collection methods, and analytical techniques. This is followed by the presentation of findings and a discussion of the results in relation to the theoretical framework and existing literature. The paper concludes with practical implications, study limitations, and recommendations for future research.

2. Theoretical Background

2.1. *Resource-based view theory*

The Resource-Based View (RBV) of the firm is a foundational theory in strategic management that emphasizes the role of a firm's internal resources and capabilities in achieving and sustaining competitive advantage (Barney, 1991; Peteraf, 1993; Wernerfelt, 1984). RBV posits that firms can achieve superior performance by leveraging resources that are valuable, rare, inimitable, and non-substitutable

(VRIN criteria) (Barney, 1991; Grant, 1996a; Teece *et al.*, 1997). Rare resources are scarce in comparison to demand, inimitable resources are challenging for rivals to imitate because of special qualities or past circumstances, and valuable resources allow businesses to take advantage of opportunities and reduce risks (Barney, 1991; Helfat and Peteraf, 2003; Peteraf, 1993). Non-substitutable resources are those for which there are no equivalent replacements that can provide the same benefits (Barney, 1991; Teece *et al.*, 1997).

The RBV has been further developed through the concept of dynamic capabilities, which emphasizes a firm's ability to adapt, integrate, and reconfigure its resources to meet changing market conditions (Teece *et al.*, 1997; Eisenhardt and Martin, 2000). Dynamic capabilities are crucial for firms to sustain competitive advantage over time by responding to shifts in the external environment and leveraging internal capabilities effectively (Teece, 2009; Helfat and Peteraf, 2003). This perspective highlights the importance of continuous renewal and innovation in maintaining a competitive edge (Eisenhardt and Martin, 2000; Kraaijenbrink *et al.*, 2010; Wright *et al.*, 2005).

Recent expansions of RBV theory have examined organizational culture, knowledge management, and human capital as key organizational resources and capabilities. Research has indicated that organizational culture can have a substantial effect on how well a company uses its resources (Wright *et al.*, 2005). Knowledge management practices enhance a firm's absorptive capacity and innovation potential, contributing to competitive advantage (Zahra and George, 2002; Grant, 1996a). Human capital, including skills, expertise and the competencies of employees, plays a critical role in effectively utilizing resources and sustaining performance (Barney, 1991; Coff, 1997; Wright *et al.*, 2005).

The theory has evolved to incorporate dynamic capabilities and various resource dimensions, offering a comprehensive framework for understanding competitive advantage in a dynamic business environment (Barney, 1991; Teece *et al.*, 1997; Helfat and Peteraf, 2003).

2.2. *Dynamic capabilities theory*

Dynamic Capabilities Theory, a significant extension of the Resource-Based View (RBV), focuses on a firm's ability to integrate, build, and reconfigure internal and external competencies to address rapidly changing environments (Teece *et al.*, 1997). This theory highlights that having resources that are valuable, rare, inimitable, and non-substitutable (VRIN) is not enough in dynamic marketplaces. Additionally, businesses need to create dynamic capabilities — organizational procedures that permit adaptability and flexibility (Eisenhardt and Martin, 2000; Teece, 2007). These capabilities enable firms to innovate, respond to market changes, and sustain competitive advantage in environments characterized by rapid technological advancements and shifting consumer preferences (Teece, 2007; Zollo and Winter, 2002; Winter, 2003).

According to Teece (2007), there are three primary categories of dynamic capabilities: sensing, seizing, and transforming. Sensing is the process of recognizing and evaluating environmental opportunities and dangers; seizing is the mobilization of resources to seize opportunities; and transforming is the ongoing renewal of a firm's capabilities and resources (Teece, 2007; Helfat *et al.*, 2007). These procedures are specific to each business since they are ingrained in routines and influenced by the firm's prior experiences (Winter, 2003; Zollo and Winter, 2002). Research has demonstrated that firms with strong dynamic capabilities are better positioned to innovate and maintain a competitive edge in volatile markets (Eisenhardt and Martin, 2000; Ambrosini and Bowman, 2009; Helfat and Peteraf, 2009).

Furthermore, dynamic skills depend on the external context in which they are used; therefore, their benefits are not constant in all situations (Eisenhardt and Martin, 2000; Winter, 2003). Businesses may depend more on their current capabilities in stable settings, but in extremely turbulent markets, the capacity to quickly reallocate resources becomes essential (Teece, 2007; Helfat and Peteraf, 2009). The relationship between market dynamics and dynamic capabilities emphasizes how crucial organizational learning, path dependencies, and strategic decision-making are to maintaining competitive advantage (Zollo and Winter, 2002; Teece, 2007; Ambrosini and Bowman, 2009).

2.3. *Small and medium-sized hospitality enterprises*

Small and medium-sized enterprises (SMEs) in the hospitality sector are critical to the global economy, contributing significantly to employment, regional development, and innovation within the tourism industry (Morrison and Teixeira, 2004; Thomas *et al.*, 2011). SMEs in hospitality typically include hotels, restaurants, and travel agencies, which are characterized by their flexibility, personalized services, and deep local market knowledge (Jones *et al.*, 2016; Gilmore *et al.*, 2001). Despite their importance, these businesses face unique challenges such as limited access to finance, high competition, and the need for continuous innovation to remain competitive in a fast-paced market (Getz and Carlsen, 2005; Pikkemaat and Peters, 2005).

The hospitality SMEs' ability to adapt and respond to changing consumer demands and market conditions is often constrained by their smaller size and resource limitations (Morrison and Teixeira, 2004; Thomas *et al.*, 2011). However, their agility and ability to offer unique, authentic experiences often provide them with a competitive edge, particularly in niche markets (Gilmore *et al.*, 2001; Getz and Carlsen, 2005). Strategic management and marketing practices tailored to the specific needs and characteristics of SMEs in hospitality are crucial for their success and sustainability in the competitive tourism industry (Jones *et al.*, 2016; Pikkemaat and Peters, 2005).

2.4. *Strategic incremental perspective*

The strategic incremental perspective emphasizes the gradual and continuous development of a firm's strategy through small, adaptive changes rather than radical transformations (Quinn, 1978; Lindblom, 1959). This approach is particularly relevant in dynamic and uncertain environments where flexibility and responsiveness are crucial for sustaining competitive advantage (Mintzberg, 1990; Floyd and

Wooldridge, 2000). Firms adopting a strategic incremental approach focus on experimentation, learning, and adaptation, allowing them to refine their strategies incrementally in response to evolving market conditions (Burgelman, 1991; Brown and Eisenhardt, 1997). This process fosters organizational resilience and the capacity to navigate complex, rapidly changing environments by leveraging small wins and learning from failures (Eisenhardt and Brown, 1998; Hart, 1992).

Strategic incrementalism contrasts with more traditional, comprehensive strategic planning methods that rely on long-term forecasts and rigid plans (Quinn, 1980; Mintzberg, 1994). Instead, it supports a more emergent strategy development process, where strategic decisions are made progressively, enabling firms to adjust and optimize their strategies over time (Mintzberg and Waters, 1985; Burgelman, 1991). This approach is particularly beneficial for small and medium-sized enterprises (SMEs), which may lack the resources to implement large-scale strategic changes but can benefit from continuous, small-scale improvements (Floyd and Wooldridge, 2000; Brown and Eisenhardt, 1997).

2.5. *Business performance*

Business performance refers to the assessment of how well an organization achieves its goals and objectives, often measured through financial and non-financial indicators (Kaplan and Norton, 1992; Richard *et al.*, 2009). Financial metrics like profitability, revenue growth, and return on investment (ROI) are traditional measures of performance, providing insight into a firm's economic health (Venkatraman and Ramanujam, 1986; Kaplan and Norton, 1996). However, non-financial indicators, such as customer satisfaction, employee engagement, and innovation capability, are increasingly recognized as critical components of comprehensive performance evaluation, reflecting the broader dimensions of business success (Neely *et al.*, 1995; Kaplan and Norton, 2001).

The multidimensional nature of business performance necessitates a balanced approach to measurement, combining financial outcomes with operational efficiency, strategic alignment, and market competitiveness (Venkatraman and Ramanujam, 1986; Kaplan and Norton, 1996). Performance measurement systems, like the Balanced Scorecard, integrate these diverse indicators, enabling organizations to monitor and improve their strategic performance holistically (Kaplan and Norton, 1992; Neely *et al.*, 1995). This comprehensive approach ensures that companies not only focus on short-term financial gains but also on long-term sustainability and competitive advantage, which are essential for enduring success in dynamic markets (Richard *et al.*, 2009; Kaplan and Norton, 2001).

2.6. *Organizational knowledge acquisition*

Organizational knowledge acquisition refers to the processes through which firms obtain, assimilate, and utilize knowledge to enhance their capabilities and competitiveness (Zahra and George, 2002; Grant, 1996a). This process is crucial for innovation, as it allows organizations to leverage both internal and external sources of knowledge, facilitating learning and adaptation in dynamic environments (Cohen and Levinthal, 1990; Nonaka, 1994). Effective knowledge acquisition involves not only the absorption of information but also its integration into organizational routines and practices, thereby improving decision-making and strategic performance (Tsai, 2001; Argote and Ingram, 2000).

Firms employ various mechanisms for knowledge acquisition, including collaboration with external partners, investing in research and development, and creating knowledge-sharing cultures within the organization (Lane *et al.*, 2001; Huber, 1991). The effectiveness of these mechanisms depends on the firm's absorptive capacity — the ability to recognize, assimilate, and apply new knowledge — which is shaped by prior knowledge, learning orientation, and organizational structure (Cohen and Levinthal, 1990; Zahra and George, 2002). Moreover, the dynamic nature of knowledge acquisition requires continuous effort to update and refine the knowledge base, ensuring that organizations remain competitive in rapidly changing markets (Nonaka and Takeuchi, 1995; Grant, 1996a).

2.7. *Firm competitive advantage*

Firm competitive advantage refers to the unique position a company achieves by implementing strategies that create more value than its competitors, allowing it to outperform rivals (Porter, 1985; Barney, 1991; Stutz and Warf, 2009). Central to the concept is the ability of a firm to sustain its competitive edge over time through resources and capabilities that are valuable, rare, inimitable, and non-substitutable (VRIN) (Barney, 1991; Peteraf, 1993). These resources can be tangible, such as technology and capital, or intangible, such as brand reputation, intellectual property, and organizational culture (Amit and Schoemaker, 1993; Dierickx and Cool, 1989). These qualities or features can include access to natural resources such as high-quality materials, low-cost labor, or access to highly trained human resources. Powell (2001) asserts that a business strategy is a tool for managing resources and generating competitive advantage.

The resource-based view (RBV) argues that firms gain competitive advantage by effectively managing and leveraging their unique internal resources and capabilities (Barney, 1991; Wernerfelt, 1984). However, achieving and sustaining competitive advantage also require firms to be dynamic and adaptable, continuously innovating and responding to changes in the external environment (Teece *et al.*, 1997; Eisenhardt and Martin, 2000). Moreover, strategic positioning within the industry, as well as the firm's ability to create and capture value through differentiation or cost leadership, also plays a critical role in maintaining a competitive edge (Porter, 1985; Grant, 1991).

2.8. *Employee commitment*

Employee commitment refers to the psychological attachment and loyalty that employees feel toward their organization, significantly influencing job satisfaction, performance, and retention (Meyer and Allen, 1991; Mowday *et al.*, 1979). It is often conceptualized through three dimensions: affective commitment, which is based on emotional attachment; continuance commitment, which involves the costs associated with leaving the organization; and normative commitment, which reflects a sense of obligation to stay (Meyer and

Allen, 1991). High levels of employee commitment are associated with positive organizational outcomes, including higher productivity, reduced turnover, and improved organizational citizenship behaviors (Meyer*et al.*, 2002; Mathieu and Zajac, 1990).

Factors influencing employee commitment include organizational support, leadership styles, job satisfaction, and opportunities for personal and professional growth (Allen and Meyer, 1996; Mowday *et al.*, 1979). Effective leadership and supportive work environments are critical in fostering affective commitment, where employees feel valued and aligned with the organization's goals (Bass and Riggio, 2006). Additionally, training and development opportunities can enhance normative commitment, as employees perceive a reciprocal obligation to contribute to the organization's success (Meyer *et al.*, 2002). Understanding and enhancing employee commitment is crucial for organizations aiming to maintain a motivated and dedicated workforce, thereby achieving long-term success (Mowday *et al.*, 1979; Allen and Meyer, 1996).

3. Hypotheses and Conceptual Framework

Strategic incremental perspective and organizational knowledge acquisition

The strategic incremental perspective emphasizes gradual, small-scale changes that align with long-term goals, promoting adaptability within organizations (Johnson *et al.*, 2003). This approach allows for continuous learning, which is crucial for organizational knowledge acquisition (Grant, 1996b). Research suggests that organizations adopting an incremental strategy tend to cultivate a culture of ongoing learning, fostering knowledge accumulation and dissemination (Mintzberg and Waters, 1985; Nonaka, 1994). By integrating new knowledge gradually, these organizations can adapt to environmental changes more effectively (Burgelman, 1991). Furthermore, incrementalism supports the dynamic capability of organizations, enhancing their ability to acquire, integrate, and reconfigure knowledge in response to external shifts (Teece *et al.*, 1997). The synergy between incremental strategy and knowledge acquisition thus contributes to sustained competitive advantage (Zollo and Winter, 2002).

***H_1*: The strategic incremental perspective has a positive impact on organizational knowledge acquisition**

Strategic incremental perspective and firm competitive advantage

The strategic incremental perspective, which involves making gradual, small-scale changes, has been linked to enhancing firm competitive advantage by fostering adaptability and innovation (Mintzberg and Waters, 1985). This approach allows firms to respond to environmental changes more flexibly, enabling them to maintain or enhance their competitive position (Grant, 1996a). By continuously adjusting and fine-tuning strategies, firms can capitalize on emerging opportunities and mitigate risks (Quinn, 1980; Burgelman, 1991). Research indicates that firms employing an incremental strategy are better equipped to exploit their existing resources while simultaneously developing new capabilities, contributing to sustained competitive advantage (Teece *et al.*, 1997). Furthermore, incrementalism supports a learning culture within firms, facilitating continuous improvement and innovation, which are critical for maintaining competitiveness in dynamic markets (Zollo and Winter, 2002; D'Aveni, 1994).

***H_2*: The strategic incremental perspective has a positive impact on firm competitive advantage**

Strategic incremental perspective and employee commitment

The strategic incremental perspective, characterized by gradual and continuous changes, positively influences employee commitment by fostering a stable yet evolving work environment (Quinn, 1980). Employees tend to feel more secure and engaged when changes are implemented incrementally, as this approach reduces uncertainty and allows for gradual adaptation (Mintzberg and Waters, 1985). Research suggests that when employees are involved in incremental strategy processes, their sense of ownership and commitment to organizational goals increases (Burgelman, 1991). Furthermore, incrementalism facilitates continuous learning and development opportunities for employees, which enhances their commitment to the organization (Grant, 1996b). By aligning individual growth with organizational changes, firms can maintain high levels of employee commitment, which is crucial for long-term success (Teece *et al.*, 1997; Meyer and Allen, 1991).

H_3*: *The strategic incremental perspective has a positive impact on employee commitment

Organizational knowledge acquisition and firm competitive advantage

Organizational knowledge acquisition is crucial for achieving and sustaining a firm's competitive advantage. By continuously acquiring and integrating knowledge, firms can enhance their capabilities, innovate, and respond effectively to market changes (Grant, 1996b). Knowledge acquisition allows firms to develop unique competencies that are difficult for competitors to imitate, thus contributing to a sustainable competitive advantage (Nonaka, 1994). Moreover, the dynamic capability framework suggests that the ability to acquire, integrate, and reconfigure knowledge is central to maintaining a competitive edge in rapidly changing environments (Teece *et al.*, 1997). Studies indicate that firms with robust knowledge acquisition processes are better positioned to exploit new opportunities and improve operational efficiency, which directly impacts their competitive standing (Davenport and Prusak, 1998; Zollo and Winter, 2002). Thus, the strategic acquisition and management of knowledge are pivotal for long-term success and competitiveness.

H_4*: *Organizational knowledge acquisition has a positive impact on firm competitive advantage

Employee commitment and firm competitive advantage

Employee commitment plays a vital role in enhancing firm competitive advantage by driving higher productivity, reducing turnover, and fostering innovation (Meyer and Allen, 1991). Committed employees are more likely to invest in the firm's success, contributing to superior performance and a stronger competitive position (Porter, 1985). Studies show that firms with high levels of employee commitment experience greater organizational stability, which supports consistent strategic execution and competitive resilience (Becker *et al.*, 1996). Additionally, committed employees are more willing to go beyond their formal roles, leading to enhanced customer service and operational efficiency, key factors in sustaining competitive advantage (Barney, 1991). The alignment of employee goals with organizational objectives through commitment fosters a unified effort toward innovation and market responsiveness, further strengthening competitive positioning (Huselid, 1995).

H_5*: *Organizational knowledge acquisition and Business Performance

Organizational knowledge acquisition is critically linked to improved business performance by enhancing a firm's ability to innovate, adapt, and optimize processes (Grant, 1996a). Firms that effectively acquire and integrate knowledge are better positioned to respond to market demands and technological changes, leading to improved operational efficiency and innovation (Nonaka, 1994). This knowledge-driven adaptability contributes to superior business performance by enabling firms to maintain competitive advantages in dynamic environments (Teece *et al.*, 1997). Moreover, the effective transfer and application of acquired knowledge across the organization can lead to enhanced decision-making and strategic execution, directly impacting financial and market performance (Zahra and George, 2002). Research suggests that businesses that prioritize knowledge acquisition and learning cultures tend to exhibit higher profitability and market share growth (Davenport and Prusak, 1998; Cohen and Levinthal, 1990).

H_6*: *Organizational knowledge acquisition has a positive impact on business performance

Firm competitive advantage and business performance

The correlation between firm competitive advantage and business performance is well documented in strategic management literature.

A firm's competitive advantage, derived from unique resources, capabilities, or strategic positioning, directly influences its business performance, including profitability, market share, and growth (Barney, 1991). Firms with a sustainable competitive advantage are better able to achieve superior financial outcomes by leveraging their distinct strengths in the marketplace (Porter, 1985). Research indicates that competitive advantage, particularly when rooted in firm-specific capabilities like innovation or operational efficiency, leads to improved business performance metrics (Grant, 1991). Additionally, firms that continuously renew and adapt their competitive advantages through dynamic capabilities are more likely to maintain high performance levels over time (Teece *et al.*, 1997). The alignment of competitive strategies with market conditions further enhances a firm's ability to outperform competitors (Prahalad and Hamel, 1990).

H_7*: *Firm competitive advantage has a positive impact on business performance

Employee commitment and business performance

Employee commitment is strongly correlated with enhanced business performance, as it drives higher productivity, innovation, and organizational stability (Meyer and Allen, 1991). Committed employees are more likely to exert discretionary effort, leading to improved operational efficiency and customer satisfaction, which are critical for superior business outcomes (Huselid, 1995). Studies suggest that organizations with high levels of employee commitment experience lower turnover rates and reduced absenteeism, resulting in cost savings and consistent performance (Mathieu and Zajac, 1990). Moreover, committed employees are more engaged in continuous improvement initiatives, contributing to sustained competitive advantage and better financial performance (Porter, 1985). The alignment of employee goals with organizational objectives, fostered by strong commitment, enhances overall business performance, including profitability and market share (Becker *et al.*, 1996).

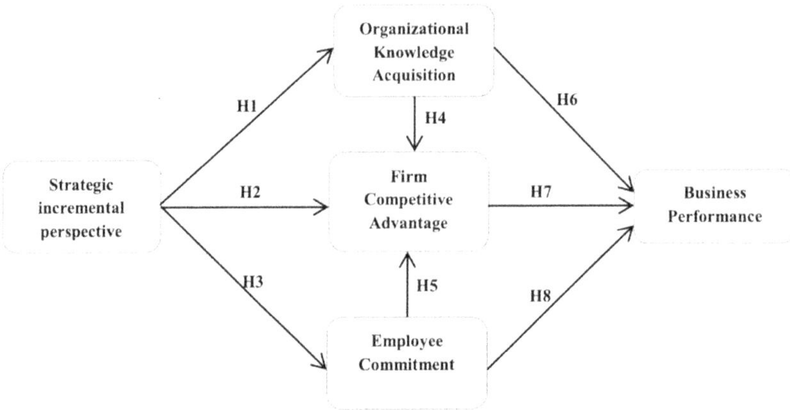

Figure 1: Proposed model.

H_8: Employee commitment has a positive impact on business performance

The model (Figure 1) illustrates a conceptual framework linking a strategic incremental perspective to business performance through various mediating variables. The arrows denote hypothesized relationships, each labeled (H1 to H8). Starting from the Strategic Incremental Perspective, the framework suggests that incremental, step-by-step strategic approaches lead to improvements in Organizational Knowledge Acquisition (H1), Firm Competitive Advantage (H2), and Employee Commitment (H3).

Subsequently, Organizational Knowledge Acquisition (H4) and Employee Commitment (H5) are hypothesized to bolster the Firm Competitive Advantage. Ultimately, Firm Competitive Advantage (H6), Organizational Knowledge Acquisition (H7), and Employee Commitment (H8) directly contribute to Business Performance.

4. Methodology

4.1. *Sampling*

To investigate the impact of the strategic incremental perspective on the business performance in the hotel industry, hoteliers and heads of department are chosen to deliver a questionnaire via online channels. Social media platforms are preferred to send an online survey with the snowballing method. There are two parts in the questionnaire design: The first section aims to collect the demographic information, while the rest of the survey focuses on questions regarding theoretical constructs of business performance (see Table A1: Measurement scales and sources). Respondents are requested to answer 18 items for five factors following a five-point Likert scale (1 — totally disagree, 5 — totally agree). 342 adequately answered forms were selected out of 382 collected forms for the analysis. Descriptive information of all respondents is shown in Table 1. The most striking feature is that the highest education of the respondents was university level with 67.5%. In terms of position within the company, the respondents were mainly owners and department heads with 29.8% and 30.4% respectively. The highest surveyed company type was private companies with 69.0%.

Table 1: Descriptive statistics.

Construct	Items	Frequency	Percent (%)
Gender	Male	218	63.7
	Female	124	36.3
Highest education level	High School & Vocational School	20	5.8
	College level	43	12.6
	University level	231	67.5
	Master's level	38	11.1
	Doctoral level	10	2.9
Position in the company	Company owner	102	29.8
	Chief Executive Officer	52	15.2
	Vice Director	46	13.5
	Management Board Assistant	38	11.1
	Head of Department	104	30.4
Company type	State-Owned Company	95	27.8
	FDI Company	10	2.9
	Private Company	236	69.0
	5.00	1	0.3
Company industry	Trade and Service	206	60.2
	Production	97	28.4
	Real Estate	30	8.8
	Others	9	2.6

4.2. *Measurement*

This study applied partial least squares structural equation modeling (PLS-SEM) to evaluate the unpremeditated influence of the strategic incremental perspective on business performance in the hotel industry. SEM analysis method supports research by simultaneously modeling and evaluating complex correlations among multiple dependent and independent variables (Hair *et al.*, 2022). Moreover, SEM is affordable and can measure the direct and indirect relationships among variables as well as examine interactions among latent variables. In evaluating the correlations, SEM is allowed to estimate errors in observed variables; hence, this method is considered a more comprehensive examination of the theoretical concepts of interest. PLS-SEM is a rapid statistical modeling tool, which has been proven by numerous preliminary articles. In this study, PLS-SEM is used to estimate the reliability and validity of the five latent variables, before testing the proposed model to indicate the relationships among variables. Moreover, a blindfolding technique shows the predictive and exploratory power of the proposed structural model. Finally, the mediating effect is tested in this study.

5. Data Analysis and Findings

5.1. *Measurement model evaluation*

This study conducts reliability and validity testing to evaluate the measurement model (Barclay *et al.*, 1995). Table 2 reveals the results of reliability and convergent validity testing with the indicators of factor loading, Cronbach's alpha, Composite Reliability (CR), and Average variance extracted (AVE). In detail, all the factor loading values exceed the threshold of 0.60 (Hair *et al.*, 1998). Cronbach's alpha values for each construct are also higher than the recommended values of 0.70 (Hair *et al.*, 2009), except for the variable items of COMAD (0.699) and INCREPER (0.608). However, as exploratory research, a Cronbach's alpha higher than 0.60 is acceptable for this study (Nunnally, 1967; Hair *et al.*, 2022). Hair *et al.* (2021) suggested

Table 2: Construct reliability and validity testing.

Construct	Code	Loading	Alpha	CR	AVE
Business Performance (BUPER)	BUPER1	0.830	0.791	0.865	0.616
	BUPER2	0.833	—	—	—
	BUPER3	0.769	—	—	—
	BUPER4	0.701	—	—	—
Employee commitment (EMCO)	EMCO1	0.749	0.783	0.861	0.608
	EMCO2	0.799	—	—	—
	EMCO3	0.850	—	—	—
	EMCO4	0.714	—	—	—
Firm Competitive Advantage (COMAD)	COMAD1	0.744	0.699	0.816	0.527
	COMAD2	0.757	—	—	—
	COMAD3	0.741	—	—	—
	COMAD4	0.657	—	—	—
Organizational Knowledge Acquisition (OLKA)	OLKA1	0.768	0.718	0.841	0.638
	OLKA2	0.835	—	—	—
	OLKA3	0.792	—	—	—
Strategic Incremental Perspective (INCREPER)	INCREPER1	0.774	0.608	0.789	0.557
	INCREPER2	0.651	—	—	—
	INCREPER3	0.806	—	—	—

that CR values should be greater than 0.7 and AVE indicators for each construct should exceed 0.5. The findings in Table 2 indicates that the reliability and convergent validity of the model constructs meet the measurement threshold evaluation.

To test discriminant validity, this study employs the results of the Heterotrait–Monotrait Ratio (HTMT) and the Fornell–Larcker criterion (Table 3). Henseler *et al.* (2015) proposed that HTMT values of each pair of constructs should be lower than the threshold value of 0.90 for conceptually similar constructs, with 0.85 for conceptually different constructs. Moreover, Fornell and Larker (1981) also suggested that the square root of the AVE of a latent variable should be greater than the correlation between the remainder of the latent variables. The findings in Table 3 show satisfactory discriminant testing for the measurement model valuation. Therefore, overall measurement items demonstrate acceptable item dependability.

Table 3: Discriminant validity testing.

Heterotrait–Monotrait Ratio (HTMT)					
	BUPER	EMCO	COMAD	OLKA	INCREPER
Business Performance	—	—	—	—	—
Employee Commitment	0.598	—	—	—	—
Firm Competitive Advantage	0.720	0.834	—	—	—
Organizational Knowledge Acquisition	0.585	0.573	0.658	—	—
Strategic Incremental Perspective	0.414	0.300	0.489	0.451	—
Fornell–Larcker Criterion					
	BUPER	EMCO	COMAD	OLKA	INCREPER
Business Performance	*0.785*	—	—	—	—
Employee Commitment	0.469	*0.780*	—	—	—
Firm Competitive Advantage	0.541	0.621	*0.726*	—	—
Organizational Knowledge Acquisition	0.446	0.434	0.468	*0.799*	—
Strategic Incremental Perspective	0.296	0.215	0.323	0.309	*0.747*

5.2. *Structural model evaluation*

Initially, potential collinearity issues should be examined for structural model regressions (Sarstedt and Mooi, 2019). This study employs variance inflation factor (VIF) values to recognize the collinearity problem in the model. Table 4 indicates that all the inner VIF values are lower than the benchmark of 3.0; hence, collinearity

Table 4: Inner VIF values.

	BUPER	**EMCO**	**COMAD**	**OLKA**	**INCREPER**
Business Performance	—	—	—	—	—
Employee Commitment	1.701	—	1.243	—	—
Firm Competitive Advantage	1.767	—	—	—	—
Organizational Knowledge Acquisition	1.337	—	1.311	—	—
Strategic Incremental Perspective	—	1.000	1.116	1.000	—

Table 5: Predictive and explanatory power testing.

	SSO	**SSE**	Q^2**(=1-SSE/SSO)**	R**-square**	R**-square Adjusted**
Business Performance	1,368.000	1,080.905	0.210	0.356	0.351
Employee Commitment	1,368.000	1,330.617	0.027	0.046	0.043
Firm Competitive Advantage	1,368.000	1,054.079	0.229	0.455	0.450
Organizational Knowledge Acquisition	1,026.000	969.841	0.055	0.096	0.093
Strategic Incremental Perspective	1,026.000	1,026.000	—	—	—

is not a problematic issue for this structural model (Becker *et al.*, 2015; Mason and Perreault, 1991).

In the next step, to measure the model's explanatory power, this study will calculate the coefficient of determination (R^2), which indicates the variance explained in each of the endogenous constructs (Shmueli and Koppius, 2011). Based on the findings in Table 5, the model explained 35.6% of the variance in business performance. The R^2 values of COMAD (45.5%) can be considered moderate, whereas the R^2 value of EMCO (4.6%) and OLKA (9.6%) are weak. So that Employee Commitment and Organizational Knowledge Acquisition should be always measured as a multi-item construct. As a general guideline, these R^2 values are considered to have weak explanatory power (<0.5) for this model (Hair *et al.*, 2011).

To estimate the predictive relevance, this study applies the Stone–Geisser Q^2 (cross-validated redundancy) value from a blindfolding process performed using PLS. The predictive relevance demonstrates that the worth of $Q2$ is above zero (Chin, 2010). According to Table 5, the $Q2$ values of all constructs range from 0.027 to 0.210, which means that all $Q2$ values are higher than zero. Therefore, the results show a good fit and a high predictive relevance to the model.

This study applies the bootstrapping method to measure the significance of the path coefficients (Wetzels *et al.*, 2009). Table 6 illustrates the results of structural model assessments with remarks on hypothesis testing. In detail, all *p*-values of each path are lower than the significance level of 0.05 (Hair *et al*, 2022). Thus, INCREPER

Table 6: Hypotheses testing.

	Original Sample (O)	**Standard Deviation**	***T*-Statistics**	***p*-values**	**2.5%**	**97.5%**	**Remark**
EMCO -> BUPER	0.164	0.068	2.420	**0.016**	0.035	0.307	Significant
EMCO -> COMAD	0.500	0.052	9.692	**0.000**	0.388	0.593	Significant
COMAD -> BUPER	0.339	0.076	4.484	**0.000**	0.182	0.480	Significant
OLKA -> BUPER	0.217	0.052	4.190	**0.000**	0.113	0.311	Significant
OLKA -> COMAD	0.203	0.051	3.957	**0.000**	0.103	0.303	Significant
INCREPER -> EMCO	0.215	0.062	3.465	**0.001**	0.081	0.324	Significant
INCREPER -> COMAD	0.153	0.049	3.094	**0.002**	0.050	0.246	Significant
INCREPER -> OLKA	0.309	0.049	6.279	**0.000**	0.201	0.401	Significant

has a relationship with COMAD, OLKA, and EMCO. Similarly, COMAD, OLKA, and EMCO have a relationship with BUPER. OLKA and COMAD also have a relationship with COMAD. Moreover, there is no zero value in the bias confidence interval for each path. The original sample (O) values represent the effect size of each path coefficient, with all values higher than zero. From eight direct hypotheses — H1, H2, H3, H4, H5, H6, H7, and H8 — are supported.

5.3. *Mediating effect evaluation*

To test the mediating effect, this study will use the results shown in Table 7. First, the total indirect effect is 0.212 with a *p*-value lower than 0.05, and the confidence interval bias excludes zero. This result indicates that there are mediating effects on this structural model. Next, this study investigates the relationship of INCREPER and BUPER through the mediating roles of COMAD, EMCO, and OLKA. Specifically, EMCO did not have a mediating significance in the impact relationship between INCREPER and BUPER as the *p*-value of specific indirect effect was greater than 0.05 (0.093). By contrast, these values satisfy the specific indirect effect of OLKA and COMAD, with the *p*-values being 0.002 and 0.027, respectively. Moreover, these confidential interval biases do not include zero with the ranges being [0.029; 0.112] and [0013; 0.102]. Thus, COMAD and OLKA have a mediating effect on the relationship between INCREPER and BUPER.

Table 7: Mediating effect.

	Effect	**Sd**	*t*	*p*	**2.5%**	**97.5%**
Total indirect effects						
INCREPER → BUPER	0.212	0.038	5.542	0.000	0.135	0.284
Specific Indirect Effects						
INCREPER → COMAD → BUPER	0.052	0.023	2.214	0.027	0.013	0.102
INCREPER → EMCO → BUPER	0.035	0.021	1.681	**0.093**	0.006	0.091
INCREPER → OLKA → BUPER	0.067	0.022	3.113	0.002	0.029	0.112

6. Discussion

To test the impact of the strategic incremental perspective on business performance in hospitality SMEs, this study proposed eight hypotheses. Using empirical research, this study reveals that all hypotheses are supported and can be used as a comprehensive structural model in the field of business performance evaluation. According to the studies of Menter *et al.* (2023) and Nunes and Val Pereira (2021), several financial and non-financial attributes have a significant impact on business performance. In this study, the findings show that there are three dimensions related to non-financial aspects that have a positive effect on business performance in hospitality SMEs (H6, H7, H8): employee commitment, firm competitive advantage, and organizational knowledge acquisition. Among the three dimensions, the advantage of firm competitiveness has the highest impact on performance with the effect size of 0.339, followed by the ability to acquire knowledge and the commitment of employees. Moreover, employee commitment and knowledge acquisition also impact a firm's competitive advantage (H4, H5). Competitiveness can be impacted by robust knowledge acquisition processes, which create more opportunities and enhance operational effectiveness (Zollo and Winter, 2002). Similarly, this study also confirms that high commitment from employees leads to high competitiveness for the firms.

The incremental perspective has a positive impact on employee motivation and firm competitiveness. In detail, the findings of testing for hypotheses H1 and H3 reveal that the strategic instrumental perspective has a good relationship with organizational knowledge acquisition and employee commitment, with effect sizes of 0.309 and 0.215, respectively. Hypothesis H2 indicates a significant relationship of strategic instrumental perspective of corporate competitiveness, but the lowest level with the correlation coefficient of 0.153. From the above results, it can be concluded that incremental perspective has a higher impact on employee knowledge acquisition and commitment than on corporate competitive performance.

This study tests the mediation roles of employee commitment, knowledge acquisition, and competitive advantage on the path of strategic incremental perspective and business performance. Although business performance is the final outcome that all hospitality SMEs desire to achieve, it does not depend directly on strategic perception (Helfat and Peteraf, 2003). This study indicates that the strategic incremental perspective must impact several dimensions, hence positively developing business performance. Through empirical research, firm competitive advantage and organizational knowledge acquisition are shown to be mediating factors influencing strategic perspective on business performance. Nevertheless, it is recognized that employee commitment does not have a mediating effect. Business performance can be nurtured by the strategic incremental awareness of the organization through the knowledge gained by employees and the perceived increased competitiveness.

7. Conclusion

7.1. *Theoretical implications*

The findings of this study hold significant theoretical implications for the strategic management of small and medium-sized enterprises (SMEs), particularly in the hospitality sector. The study emphasizes the value of the strategic incremental approach and how it may be used to improve organizational performance over time instead of making drastic, large-scale changes (Pettigrew, 1990). This theory supports the Resource-Based View (RBV) and Dynamic Capabilities Theory, which emphasize how businesses must integrate, adapt, and reorganize their resources in order to stay competitive in changing markets (Barney, 1991; Teece *et al.*, 1997).

The study further validates the critical roles of mediating variables, such as employee commitment, organizational knowledge acquisition, and competitive advantage. This reflects how an incremental strategic approach fosters knowledge acquisition, enabling firms to adapt to environmental changes through a continuous learning culture (Zahra and George, 2002). The research also contributes to the understanding of the link between incrementalism and organizational performance, as it empirically demonstrates that small, strategic changes lead to improved competitive positioning and employee commitment (Helfat and Peteraf, 2003).

Additionally, by fusing firm competitiveness with incremental strategic planning, the study adds to the body of knowledge on competitive advantage. It suggests that strategic incrementalism gives SMEs the flexibility they need to constantly improve their capabilities and resources (Teece *et al.*, 1997). Specifically, it validates the idea that this kind of strategy fosters innovation and results in long-term competitive advantages, particularly in resource-constrained industries like hospitality (Mintzberg, 1990; Grant, 1996b). Based on how tiny, ongoing adjustments contribute to business success in the context of a market that is changing quickly, these insights deepen the corpus of knowledge already in existence.

7.2. *Practical implications*

Hotel managers gain many suggestions from this study, which investigates the effect of a strategic incremental perspective on hospitality business performance. Data collection from SME leaders contribute to comprehensive operational knowledge, which assists managers in making decisions effectively. In the tech age, hospitality enterprises have to be motivated to accept digital transformation to adapt to complex markets. Information systems can help firms arrange and analyze data efficiently. However, hotel managers will still have many issues in terms of decision-making without strategic management. Hotel managers could benefit from this study by applying strategic incremental perspectives in practical environments.

First, managers must focus on training and knowledge acquisition for employees to improve the performance of the business. Human resources play an important role in many aspects of an organization (Cohen and Levinthal, 1990; Nonaka, 1994), particularly in the service industry where the human touch is appreciated in the working environment. Research and development activities should be considered as a core value task in hospitality human management. By providing both internal and external sources of knowledge and facilitating learning, employees are inspired to engage closely with firms, thereby implementing excellent performance. Furthermore, knowledge acquisition can help create a knowledge-sharing culture within the organization (Lane *et al.*, 2001). Hotel managers should invest time and resources to organize effective training courses and motivate employees to better themselves by learning. Second, hotel managers should invest in developing the incremental perspective toward competitive advantage. Competitiveness is built from technology transformation, capital, brand reputation, intellectual property, and organizational culture (Amit and Schoemaker, 1993; Dierickx and Cool, 1989). A strategic perspective contributes to enriching the organizational culture, which is necessary for an intangible product such as the hospitality industry. Third, hotel managers should increase employee commitment. By providing good compensation, a clear promotion path, and an attractive working environment, hotels could enhance employee commitment. Once hotel staff commit to their work, the performance is positively improved. This can be experienced in terms of customer service, services delivery, and working collaboratively.

7.3. *Limitations*

This study has shown that adopting a strategic incremental perspective significantly enhances the business performance of hospitality SMEs by fostering organizational learning, increasing employee commitment, and enhancing competitive advantage. Through a methodical approach to incremental strategy, firms are able to navigate complex and dynamic environments, making small yet impactful improvements that lead to sustained business success. The research underscores the importance of continuous strategic adaptation and offers a valuable framework for understanding the mechanisms through which incremental changes contribute to improved organizational outcomes. Future research should explore the long-term effects of this approach in other sectors, as well as investigate potential cultural and contextual factors that might influence the effectiveness of strategic incrementalism in diverse business environments.

Acknowledgments

This research was supported by the University of Economics Ho Chi Minh City (UEH), Vietnam.

Bibliography

Allen, N.J. and Meyer, J.P. (1996). Affective, continuance, and normative commitment to the organization: An examination of construct validity. *Journal of Vocational Behavior*, 49(3), 252–276. https://doi.org/10.1006/jvbe.1996.0043.

Ambrosini, V. and Bowman, C. (2009). What are dynamic capabilities and are they a useful construct in strategic management? *International Journal of Management Reviews*, 11(1), 29–49. https://doi.org/10.1111/j.1468-2370.2008.00251.x.

Amit, R. and Schoemaker, P. J. (1993). Strategic assets and organizational rent. *Strategic Management Journal*, 14(1), 33–46. https://doi.org/10.1002/smj.4250140105.

Argote, L. and Ingram, P. (2000). Knowledge transfer: A basis for competitive advantage in firms. *Organizational Behavior and Human Decision Processes*, 82(1), 150–169. https://doi.org/10.1006/obhd.2000.2893.

Barclay, D., Higgins, C., and Thompson, R. (1995). The partial least squares (PLS) approach to causal modeling: Personal computer adoption and use as an illustration. *Technology Studies*, 2, 285–309.

Barney, J. (1991). Firm resources and sustained competitive advantage. *Journal of Management*, 17(1), 99–120. https://doi.org/10.1177/014920639101700108.

Bass, B.M. and Riggio, R.E. (2006). *Transformational Leadership* (2nd ed.). New York, NY: Psychology Press.

Becker, T.E., Billings, R.S., Eveleth, D.M., and Gilbert, N. L. (1996). Foci and bases of employee commitment: Implications for job performance. *Academy of Management Journal*, 39(2), 464–482. https://doi.org/10.2307/256788.

Becker, J.M., Ringle, C.M., and Sarstedt, M. (2015). How to apply multi-group analysis in PLS-SEM: Lessons from the automotive industry. *Long Range Planning*, 48(1), 1–12.

Brown, S.L. and Eisenhardt, K.M. (1997). The art of continuous change: Linking complexity theory and time-paced evolution in relentlessly shifting organizations. *Administrative Science Quarterly*, 42(1), 1–34. https://doi.org/10.2307/2393807.

Burgelman, R.A. (1991). Intraorganizational ecology of strategy making and organizational adaptation: Theory and field research. *Organization Science,* 2(3), 239–262. https://doi.org/10.1287/orsc.2.3.239.

Chin, W.W. (2010). How to write up and report PLS analyses. In V.E. Vinzi, W.W. Chin, J. Henseler, and H. Wang (Eds.), *Handbook of Partial Least Squares* (pp. 655–690). Berlin, Germany: Springer-Verlag.

Cohen, W.M. and Levinthal, D.A. (1990). Absorptive capacity: A new perspective on learning and innovation. *Administrative Science Quarterly,* 35(1), 128–152. https://doi.org/10.2307/2393553.

Coff, R.W. (1997). Human assets and management dilemmas: Coping with hazardous circumstances. *Organization Science,* 8(3), 424–442. https://doi.org/10.2307/259327.

Davenport, T.H. and Prusak, L. (1998). *Working Knowledge: How Organizations Manage What They Know.* Boston, Massachusetts: Harvard Business School Press.

Dierickx, I. and Cool, K. (1989). Asset stock accumulation and sustainability of competitive advantage. *Management Science,* 35(12), 1504–1511. https://doi.org/10.1287/mnsc.35.12.1504.

Eisenhardt, K.M. and Brown, S.L. (1998). Competing on the edge: Strategy as structured chaos. *Long Range Planning,* 31(5), 786–789. https://doi.org/10.1016/S0024-6301(98)00092-2.

Eisenhardt, K.M. and Martin, J.A. (2000). Dynamic capabilities: What are they? *Strategic Management Journal,* 21(10–11), 1105–1121. https://doi.org/10.1002/1097-0266(200010/11)21:10/11<1105::AID-SMJ133>3.0.CO;2-E.

Floyd, S. W., and Wooldridge, B. (2000). *Building Strategy from the Middle: Reconceptualizing Strategy Process.* Thousand Oaks, CA: SAGE Publications.

Getz, D. and Carlsen, J. (2005). Family business in tourism: State of the art. *Annals of Tourism Research,* 32(1), 237–258. https://doi.org/10.1016/j.annals.2004.07.006.

Gilmore, A., Carson, D., and Grant, K. (2001). SME marketing in practice. *Marketing Intelligence & Planning,* 19(1), 6–11. https://doi.org/10.1108/02634500110363583.

Grant, R.M. (1991). The resource-based theory of competitive advantage: Implications for strategy formulation. *California Management Review,* 33(3), 114–135. https://doi.org/10.2307/41166664.

Grant, R.M. (1996a). Prospering in dynamically-competitive environments: Organizational capability as knowledge integration. *Organization Science,* 7(4), 375–387. https://doi.org/10.1287/orsc.7.4.375.

Grant, R.M. (1996b). Toward a knowledge-based theory of the firm. *Strategic Management Journal,* 17(S2), 109–122. https://doi.org/10.1002/smj.4250171110.

Hair, J.F., Hult, G.T.M., Ringle, C.M., and Sarstedt, M. (2022). *A primer on partial least squares structural equation modeling (PLS-SEM)* (3rd ed.). Thousand Oaks, CA: Sage.

Hart, S.L. (1992). An integrative framework for strategy-making processes. *Academy of Management Review*, 17(2), 327–351. https://doi.org/10.5465/amr.1992.4279547.

Helfat, C.E. and Peteraf, M.A. (2003). The dynamic resource-based view: Capability lifecycles. *Strategic Management Journal*, 24(10), 997–1010. https://doi.org/10.1002/smj.332.

Helfat, C.E. and Peteraf, M.A. (2009). Understanding dynamic capabilities: Progress along a developmental path. *Strategic Organization*, 7(1), 91–102. https://doi.org/10.1177/1476127008100133.

Helfat, C.E., Finkelstein, S., Mitchell, W., Peteraf, M.A., Singh, H., Teece, D.J., and Winter, S.G. (2007). *Dynamic Capabilities: Understanding Strategic Change in Organizations*. Malden, MA; Oxford, UK: Blackwell Publishing.

Henseler, J., Ringle, C.M., and Sarstedt, M. (2015). A new criterion for assessing discriminant validity in variance based structural equation modeling. *Journal of the Academy of Marketing Science*, 43(1), 115–135. https://doi.org/10.1007/s11747-014-0403-8.

Hsu, D.K. (2020). Exploring the relationship between entrepreneurial orientation and firm performance in the hospitality industry: The role of innovation and knowledge acquisition. *Journal of Hospitality & Tourism Research*, 44(2), 230–250. https://doi.org/10.1177/1096348020911426.

Huber, G.P. (1991). Organizational learning: The contributing processes and the literatures. *Organization Science*, 2(1), 88–115. https://doi.org/10.1287/orsc.2.1.88.

Huselid, M.A. (1995). The impact of human resource management practices on turnover, productivity, and corporate financial performance. *Academy of Management Journal*, 38(3), 635–672. https://psycnet.apa.org/doi/10.2307/256741.

Johnson, G., Scholes, K., and Whittington, R. (2005). *Exploring Corporate Strategy: Text and Cases* (7th ed.). Harlow, England: Prentice Hall.

Jones, P., Hillier, D., and Comfort, D. (2016). Sustainability in the global hotel industry. *International Journal of Contemporary Hospitality Management*, 28(1), 36–67. https://doi.org/10.1108/IJCHM-10-2012-0180.

Kaplan, R.S. and Norton, D.P. (1992). The balanced scorecard—measures that drive performance. *Harvard Business Review*, 70(1), 71–79.

Kaplan, R.S. and Norton, D.P. (1996). Using the balanced scorecard as a strategic management system. *Harvard Business Review*, 74(1), 75–85.

Kaplan, R.S. and Norton, D.P. (2001). Transforming the balanced scorecard from performance measurement to strategic management: Part I.

Accounting Horizons, 15(1), 87–104. https://doi.org/10.2308/acch.2001.15.1.87.

Kraaijenbrink, J., Spender, J.C., and Groen, A.J. (2010). The resource-based view: A review and assessment of its critiques. *Journal of Management,* 36(1), 349–372. https://doi.org/10.1177/0149206309350775.

Kwortnik, R.J. and Thompson, G.M. (2009). Unifying service marketing and operations management with service experience management. *Journal of Service Research,* 11(4), 389–406. https://doi.org/10.1177/1094670508324263.

Lane, P.J., Salk, J.E., and Lyles, M.A. (2001). Absorptive capacity, learning, and performance in international joint ventures. *Strategic Management Journal,* 22(12), 1139–1161. https://doi.org/10.1002/smj.206.

Lindblom, C.E. (1959). The science of "muddling through." *Public Administration Review,* 19(2), 79–88. https://doi.org/10.2307/973677.

Mason, C.H., and Perreault, W.D., Jr. (1991). Collinearity, power, and interpretation of multiple regression analysis. *Journal of Marketing Research,* 28(3), 268–280.

Mathieu, J.E. and Zajac, D.M. (1990). A review and meta-analysis of the antecedents, correlates, and consequences of organizational commitment. *Psychological Bulletin,* 108(2), 171–194. https://doi.org/10.1037/0033-2909.108.2.171.

Menter, M., Göcke, L., Zeeb, C., and Clauss, T. (2023). Disentangling the complex longitudinal relationships between business model innovation and firm performance. *Journal of Business Research,* 168, 114229.

Meyer, J.P. and Allen, N.J. (1991). A three-component conceptualization of organizational commitment. *Human Resource Management Review,* 1(1), 61–89. https://doi.org/10.1016/1053-4822(91)90011-Z.

Meyer, J.P., Stanley, D.J., Herscovitch, L., and Topolnytsky, L. (2002). Affective, continuance, and normative commitment to the organization: A meta-analysis of antecedents, correlates, and consequences. *Journal of Vocational Behavior,* 61(1), 20–52. https://doi.org/10.1006/jvbe.2001.1842.

Mintzberg, H. (1990). The design school: Reconsidering the basic premises of strategic management. *Strategic Management Journal,* 11(3), 171–195. https://doi.org/10.1002/smj.4250110302.

Mintzberg, H. (1994). *The Rise and Fall of Strategic Planning.* Free Press.

Mintzberg, H. and Waters, J.A. (1985). Of strategies, deliberate and emergent. *Strategic Management Journal,* 6(3), 257–272. https://doi.org/10.1002/smj.4250060306.

Morrison, A. and Teixeira, R. (2004). Small business performance: A tourism sector focus. *Journal of Small Business and Enterprise Development,* 11(2), 166–173. https://doi.org/10.1108/14626000410537100.

Mowday, R.T., Steers, R.M., and Porter, L.W. (1979). The measurement of organizational commitment. *Journal of Vocational Behavior,* 14(2), 224–247. https://doi.org/10.1016/0001-8791(79)90072-1.

Neely, A., Gregory, M., and Platts, K. (1995). Performance measurement system design: A literature review and research agenda. *International Journal of Operations & Production Management,* 15(4), 80–116. https://doi.org/10.1108/01443579510083622.

Nonaka, I. (1994). A dynamic theory of organizational knowledge creation. *Organization Science,* 5(1), 14–37. https://doi.org/10.1287/orsc.5.1.14.

Nonaka, I. and Takeuchi, H. (1995). *The Knowledge Creating Company: How Japanese Companies Create the Dynamics of Innovation.* New York, NY: Oxford University Press.

Nunes, M.P. and Val Pereira, R. (2021). Business model innovation and business performance in an innovative environment. *International Journal of Innovation Management,* 25(6), 2140021. https://doi.org/10.1142/S1363919621500365.

Nunnally, J.C. (1967). *Psychometric theory.* New York, NY: McGraw Hill.

Peteraf, M.A. (1993). The cornerstones of competitive advantage: A resource-based view. *Strategic Management Journal,* 14(3), 179–191. https://doi.org/10.1002/smj.4250140303.

Pettigrew, A.M. (1990). Longitudinal field research on change: Theory and practice. *Organization Science,* 1(3), 267–292. https://doi.org/10.1287/orsc.1.3.267.

Pikkemaat, B. and Peters, M. (2005). Towards the measurement of innovation — A pilot study in the small and medium-sized hotel industry. *Journal of Quality Assurance in Hospitality & Tourism,* 6(3–4), 89–112. https://doi.org/10.1300/J162v06n03_06.

Porter, M.E. (1985). *Competitive Advantage: Creating and Sustaining Superior Performance.* New York, NY: Free Press.

Powell, T.C. (2001). Competitive advantage: Logical and philosophical considerations. *Strategic Management Journal,* 22(9), 875–888. http://dx.doi.org/10.1002/smj.173.

Prahalad, C.K. and Hamel, G. (1990). The core competence of the corporation. *Harvard Business Review,* 68(3), 79–91.

Quinn, J.B. (1978). Strategic change: "Logical incrementalism." *Sloan Management Review,* 20(1), 7–21.

Quinn, J.B. (1980). *Strategies for Change: Logical Incrementalism.* Homewood, IL: Richard D. Irwin.

Richard, P.J., Devinney, T.M., Yip, G.S., and Johnson, G. (2009). Measuring organizational performance: Towards methodological best practice. *Journal of Management,* 35(3), 718–804. https://doi.org/10.1177/0149206308330560.

Sarstedt, M. and Mooi, E. (2019). *A concise guide to market research: The process, data, and methods using IBM SPSS statistics* (2nd ed.). Cham, Switzerland: Springer.

Shmueli, G. and Koppius, O.R. (2011). *Predictive analytics in information systems research.* MIS Quarterly, 35(3), 553–572.

Stutz, F.P. and Warf, B. (2009). *The World Economy.* Upper Saddle River, NJ: Prentice Hall.

Teece, D.J. (2007). Explicating dynamic capabilities: The nature and microfoundations of (sustainable) enterprise performance. *Strategic Management Journal,* 28(13), 1319–1350. https://doi.org/10.1002/smj.640.

Teece, D.J. (2009). *Dynamic Capabilities and Strategic Management: Organizing for Innovation and Growth.* Oxford, UK: Oxford University Press.

Teece, D.J., Pisano, G., and Shuen, A. (1997). Dynamic capabilities and strategic management. *Strategic Management Journal,* 18(7), 509–533. https://doi.org/10.1002/(SICI)1097-0266(199708)18:7509::AID-SMJ882⟩3.0.CO;2-Z.

Thomas, R., Shaw, G., and Page, S.J. (2011). Understanding small firms in tourism: A perspective on research trends and challenges. *Tourism Management,* 32(5), 963–976. https://doi.org/10.1016/j.tourman.2011.02.003.

Tsai, W. (2001). Knowledge transfer in intraorganizational networks: Effects of network position and absorptive capacity on business unit innovation and performance. *Academy of Management Journal,* 44(5), 996–1004. https://doi.org/10.5465/3069443.

Venkatraman, N. and Ramanujam, V. (1986). Measurement of business performance in strategy research: A comparison of approaches. *Academy of Management Review,* 11(4), 801–814. https://doi.org/10.2307/258398.

Wernerfelt, B. (1984). A resource-based view of the firm. *Strategic Management Journal,* 5(2), 171–180. https://doi.org/10.1002/smj.4250050207.

Wetzels, M., Odekerken Schröder, G., and van Oppen, C. (2009). Using PLS path modeling for assessing hierarchical construct models: Guidelines and empirical illustration. *MIS Quarterly,* 33(1), 177–195.

Winter, S.G. (2003). Understanding dynamic capabilities. *Strategic Management Journal,* 24(10), 991–995. https://doi.org/10.1002/smj.318.

Wright, P.M., Dunford, B.B., and Snape, E.S. (2005). Human resources and the resource-based view of the firm. *Journal of Management,* 31(6), 981–1000. https://doi.org/10.1177/014920630102700607.

Zahra, S.A. and George, G. (2002). Absorptive capacity: A review, reconceptualization, and extension. *Academy of Management Review,* 27(2), 185–203. https://doi.org/10.5465/amr.2002.6587995.

Zollo, M. and Winter, S.G. (2002). Deliberate learning and the evolution of dynamic capabilities. *Organization Science,* 13(3), 339–351. https://doi.org/10.1287/orsc.13.3.339.2780.

Appendix: Questionnaire

Table A1: Measurement scales and sources.

Construct	Definitions	Items	Code	Source
Strategic incremental perspective	The incremental process of strategy formation results in coordinated and conscious action toward a certain goal	Making detailed strategic plans is a waste of time	INCREPER1	Quinn (1980)
		Successful managers set a general strategic direction and then fill in the details along the way	INCREPER2	
		A good strategy is not a detailed long-term plan, but a guideline for the further exploration of opportunities	INCREPER3	
Employee commitment	Employees believe in the goals and values of the organization and hold a strong desire to retain membership in the organization, which can be observable and evaluated by managers	The employee appears to be "emotionally attached" to the organization	EMCO1	
		The employee views organizational problems as his or her problems	EMCO2	
		The employees really care about the fate of this organization	EMCO3	
		The employees share the difficulties of the organization	EMCO4	

Organizational knowledge acquisition	Firms employ various mechanisms for knowledge acquisition, including collaboration with external partners, investing in research and development, and creating knowledge-sharing cultures within the organization	The employees attend fairs and exhibitions regularly There is a consolidated and resourceful R&D policy New ideas and approaches to work performance are experimented with continuously	OLKA1 OLKA2 OLKA3	Pérez López *et al.* (2005)
Firm competitive advantage	Firms can achieve competitive advantage in different areas such as gaining market share, knowledge and know-how, employee commitment, brand reputation, and image	Customer experience overall the company is excellent Customers are optimistic about the long-term future of this corporate entity Employees appear to be highly committed to the organization In comparison with competitors, the net profit margin has increased COMAD1	COMAD2 COMAD3 COMAD4	
Business performance	Business Performance is an outcome of Business Model Innovation, which is identified as the correlation between innovation and performance enhancement	Customers are satisfied with the value delivering to them The business acquires new customers Current profitability helps the company reach its financial goals Employees are satisfied with their work	BUPER1 BUPER2 BUPER3 BUPER4	Menter *et al.* (2023) Nunes and Val Pereira (2021)

Part VI

Economics, Business, and Law

https://doi.org/10.1142/9789811262258_0007

Chapter 7

Evaluating the Impact of Capital Intensity, Capital Productivity, and Other Factors on Labor Productivity in Different Sectors in Vietnam

Thi Thanh Huong Tran, Thu Hang Pham, and Xuan Vinh Vo

Abstract

This study examines the impact of capital intensity, capital productivity, average equipped fixed assets per employee, and other factors on labor productivity in Vietnam's economic sectors during 2013–2017 using Two-Stage Least Square (2SLS) and Minimum Bayes Factor. Unlike other previous studies, this study uses 2SLS to solve the endogenous problem among the impact factors. Moreover, the Minimum Bayes Factor is used to verify the validity of the quantitative results. The results show that capital intensity and capital productivity positively impact labor productivity in non-state economic and FDI sectors. Meanwhile, the scale of implemented investment and the average equipped fixed assets per employee are the key factors influencing labor productivity for the state-owned sector. Additionally, improving corruption control has a crucial impact on the labor productivity of the foreign-invested sector.

Keywords: Labor productivity; Economic sectors; Impact factors; 2SLS; Minimum Bayes Factor.

1. Introduction

Increasing labor productivity is one of the significant factors contributing to improving the competitiveness of a business as well as an economy. In particular, in the context that Vietnam is a country with low per capita income with traditional competitive advantages such as low raw material costs and cheap labor, productivity is always a severe problem. Low labor productivity is a major impediment to attracting foreign direct investment, international integration, and economic growth. Moreover, in the gradual transition of the economic growth model from width to depth, the inevitable consequence is that the factors affecting labor productivity have significant fluctuations. Therefore, promoting productivity growth and identifying motivating factors for productivity growth is one of the core issues for Vietnam.

Increasing labor productivity is one of the significant factors contributing to improving the competitiveness of a business as well as an economy. In particular, given Vietnam's low per capita income and traditional competitive advantages such as low raw material costs and cheap labor, productivity is always a significant issue. Low labor productivity severely impedes attracting foreign direct investment, international integration, and economic growth. Moreover, in the gradual transition of the economic growth model from width to depth, the inevitable consequence is that the factors affecting labor productivity have significant fluctuations. Therefore, promoting productivity growth and identifying motivating factors for productivity growth is one of the core issues for Vietnam.

The labor productivity of Vietnam has been enhanced significantly and tends to increase from 2013 to 2017. In 2013, Vietnam's labor productivity was only 48.72 million VND per person but rose to 60.75 million VND/person (at 2010 prices) in 2017 (GSO, 2018). Labor productivity in all economic sectors increased as well during this period. However, also in this phase, the pace of overall labor productivity and each economic sector, in particular, was always lower than Vietnam's GDP growth rate. Moreover, according to Nguyen (2018), Vietnam's labor productivity was very low compared to those of Southeast Asia's countries. According to PPP 2011, in 2016, the labor productivity of Vietnam was up to 9,894 US dollars. This figure equaled 7.0% of the productivity level of Singapore and 17.6% of Malaysia's. The gap was even wider than Indonesia's and the

Philippines' (42.3% and 56.7%, respectively). For Vietnam to not be left behind by other countries in the region, improving labor productivity has been a challenge.

To the extent of labor productivity by type of ownership, there is a big gap in labor productivity among economic sectors. There has been a shift in the components contributing to the overall economy in recent years, coinciding with the development of Vietnam's economy. From a labor productivity perspective, the non-state economic sector has the lowest labor productivity. The labor productivity of foreign-invested economic sectors has decreased sharply in recent years. According to statistics from the 2018 Statistical Yearbook (GSO, 2018), the growth rate of labor productivity in all economic sectors is lower than each of their value-added growth rates. Therefore, to promote economic growth in Vietnam, it is necessary to encourage labor productivity growth in all economic sectors. It is also essential to research the factors influencing the productivity growth of each economic sector of Vietnam.

This study approaches the impact of factors on labor productivity in Vietnam's economic sectors. On the aspect of ownership, Vietnam's economy is divided into three areas: state-owned, non-state, and foreign-invested sectors, in which the state-owned sector includes: state-owned enterprises, administrative and non-business agencies; the non-state sector has non-state enterprises (collective), collective economic units (collective), private (private) and individuals (households); and the foreign-invested sector includes: enterprises with 100% foreign investment (100% foreign-invested enterprises), joint ventures between Vietnam and foreign countries (joint ventures between foreign parties and domestic partners).

The chapter's objective is to define the differences in the factors affecting labor productivity across the economic sector and the reasons for those dissimilarities.

The main findings show the factors that affect the productivity of each ownership sector differ. Capital intensity (CI) and capital productivity (CP) have an impact on labor productivity in the non-state sector and foreign-invested sector, in which capital productivity

(CP) has a substantial influence on labor productivity in the foreign-invested sector. The most significant factors affecting the productivity of the state-owned sector are the size of implemented capital (IIF) and the average fixed asset per employee (FAPE). Corruption control (PAPI4) only has a positive impact on the labor productivity of the foreign-invested sector.

This chapter's remainder is structured as follows: literature review, data and methodology, results and discussion, and conclusion.

2. Literature Review

Labor productivity has been studied so far because of its indispensable role in socio-economic issues. Labor productivity studies are researched in various aspects. Most of these studies focus on the enterprise perspective, and others concentrate on the nation's labor productivity or labor productivity according to economic structure.

From an enterprise perspective, some of the main factors affecting the firm's labor productivity are *skilled labor, capital, fixed assets, R&D, information, and location.*

The quality of the workforce has a positive impact on labor productivity, confirmed by almost all studies surrounding this issue. The quality of labor expressed in the proportion of trained workers is considered a vital factor affecting labor productivity (Lucas, 1988; Baptista and Swann, 1998; Firouzi *et al.*, 2010; Shinada, 2011). This conclusion is quite similar to the research in the context of Vietnam. Nguyen *et al.* (2016) investigated 2,000 enterprises in seven economic sectors into three groups: *low technology*, *medium technology*, and *high technology.* The survey results show that highly skilled workers are highly productive. However, another unexpected result from Papadogonas and Voulgaris (2005) is that the factors affecting negative labor productivity are *the proportion spent on human resource training* and *industrial fees*, implying that the more capital available for labor training, the less productive labor is. This result contrasts with the studies of human resources and can be understood by evaluating the effectiveness of training programs. This phenomenon shows the enterprise's weakness in the process of investing in human resources when the training quality is not matched with that investment.

Apart from the quality of labor, labor income also has a positive impact on labor productivity (Firouzi *et al.*, 2010). Tran (2019) also points out that the average monthly payment of labor had a beneficial effect on Vietnam's labor productivity growth during 2012–2015. From an enterprise perspective, its fixed assets are also an essential factor affecting labor productivity (Papadogonas and Voulgaris, 2005; Nguyen, 2018).

The most crucial factor that contributes to labor productivity growth is capital. Most studies point to the positive role of money (Shinada, 2011; Firouzi *et al.*, 2010; Papadogonas and Voulgaris, 2005). This factor is also considered in many aspects. Shinada (2011) uses data on Japanese enterprises in the period of 1977–2008 to demonstrate the impact of capital on labor productivity, while Firouzi *et al.* (2010) and Papadogonas and Voulgaris (2005) focus on capital intensity. The positive effect implies that firms with high capital intensity will yield high labor productivity.

The impact of geographical position on enterprise efficiency is also studied in many research papers. Audretsch and Feldman (1996) find that geographical location also enhances innovation activities. Baptista and Swann (1998) use data from 248 enterprises in the UK to conclude that "an enterprise can be renewed if its employees are qualified." This is explained by the fact that some business clusters attract new businesses more and grow more rapidly than other groups. Besides, CIEM and UNDP research (2011) shows that labor productivity is higher when companies are in urban areas or larger cities than in rural areas or smaller towns. The percentage of businesses with improvement is certainly higher. However, most of these improvements are applied to satisfy customers' needs rather than meet market demand.

Growth analysis plays a principal role in increasing labor productivity in the "technological process." To illustrate this concept, many studies focus on the part of R&D (Guellec and Potterie, 2001; Scarpetta and Tressel, 2002), the level of education (Lucas, 1988), and the role of public infrastructure (Aschauer, 1989). Many economic debates have been broadening to more new factors than traditional ones, such as information and communication technology factors (ICT). Many outstanding articles — such as the ones by Jorgenson and Stiro (2000) or by Oliner and Sichel (2000) — show the role of ICT in TFP growth as well as ICT investment in increasing labor productivity.

Labor productivity research from the perspective of the economic structure is often considered through the economic structure or economic ownership structure. From this aspect, in addition to the factors mentioned above, public administration is a critical factor in promoting labor productivity growth (Aschauer, 1989; Nguyen, 2018). According to another research on labor productivity in Vietnam, according to Nguyen (2018), the leading cause of inefficient labor productivity in Vietnam is the efficiency of public administration. Tran (2019) proposes that labor restructuring be applied to better administration for higher productivity as one solution for improving labor productivity.

Thus, theoretical and empirical studies show many factors affecting labor productivity. These factors can be divided into groups: *labor size and quality, workers' income, fixed assets, capital intensity, management efficiency, R&D activities*, and *technology in the production process*.

However, in accordance with various researches, among the groups of factors affecting labor productivity mentioned above, there is always a reciprocal relationship. Numerous studies show that capital and administrative management efficiency in enterprises and localities are closely related. Luan *et al.* (2016) conclude that if the management is more transparent, investors are more likely to engage in investing and increasing capital. Research by Drabek and Payne (2002) suggests that transparency in a country's administrative management creates a great attraction for increasing foreign investment and capital. Batra *et al.* (2001) and Emery (2003) draw the same conclusions: ineffective administrative management is an important element of private investment and has an impact on labor productivity. Lambsdorff (2003) also asserts that corruption adversely affects capital flows. The research paper by Kelly (2014) also shows that corruption is one factor that significantly reduces the nation's economic productivity.

In addition, many studies show a short-term and long-term correlation between labor and capital. Juselius (2005) uses various quantitative methods to estimate the relationship between workforce and capital in the long run to find the law of change in substitution and the ratio of these two factors. This correlation has also been studied in terms of economics and politics in many theoretical and empirical studies (Moseley, 2014; Patnaik, 2014; Syll, 2014).

In summary, there are many studies on the factors impacting labor productivity growth. However, there are no substantial studies on how these factors affect the labor productivity growth in each economic sector against the backdrop of Vietnam. Moreover, there are endogenous conditions among the influencing factors that the studies have not mentioned. This study is expected to make a small contribution to the result of research on the mentioned factors.

3. Data and Methodology

3.1. *Data and model*

Studies on economic growth and labor productivity, in particular, are often affected by endogenous variables. This study is concerned with the endogenous variables between labor productivity and capital productivity. As shown by the results of many studies, capital productivity is supposed to be one of the influential factors for enhancing labor productivity. On the other hand, capital productivity is also affected by many economic elements, such as the quality of labor or regional governance. To overcome the endogenous problem, two-stage least square methods are used with capital as an endogenous variable.

According to previous studies, the impact of factors on labor productivity is assessed based on the following equations:

$$\mathrm{LP}_{ij} = \alpha_0 + \alpha_1\ \mathrm{RTE}_{ij} + \alpha_2\ \mathrm{AIE}_{ij} + \alpha_3\ \mathrm{FAPE}_{ij} + \alpha_4\ \mathrm{IIF}_{ij} + \alpha_5\ \mathrm{CI}_{ij} + \alpha_6\ \mathrm{PAPI}_{4ij} + \alpha_7\ \mathrm{CP}_{ij} + u_{ij} \quad (1)$$

with constraints:

$$\mathrm{CP}_{ij} = \beta_0 + \beta_1\ \mathrm{RTE}_{ij} + \beta_2\ \mathrm{PAPI}_{2ij} + \beta_3\ \mathrm{PCI}_{ij} + \beta_4\ \mathrm{PAPI}_{6ij} + \beta_5\ \mathrm{LB}_{ij} + v_{ij} \quad (2)$$

where i is province i; j is year j; LP is a measure of productivity (Millions VND/person); RTE is the rate of trained employees (%); AIE is the average income per employee (Thousand VND/person); FAPE is the average equipped fixed assets per employee (Millions VND/person); IIF is the implemented investment at constant price 2010 (Billions VND); CI is the capital intensity (Millions VND/person); CP is the capital productivity (Times); LB is the labor force (Person); PCI is the provincial competitiveness index (%); PAPI2 is the transparency index (Points); PAPI4 is the Control of corruption index (Points); PAPI6 is the public service Delivery index (Points); u_{ij}, v_{ij} is the error term. All variables are summarized in the Table 1 and Tables A1 in the Appendix.

Data for labor productivity (LP), rate of trained employee (RTE), average income per employee (AIE), average equipped fixed assets per employee (FAPE), capital intensity (CI), capital productivity (CP), and implemented investment (IIF) of state-owned and non-state economic, as well as FDI sectors, are collected from the Statistical Yearbook of 39 provinces in Vietnam. Data for these variables in the foreign direct investment sector is collected from the Statistical Yearbook of 34 provinces in Vietnam. The Vietnam Chamber of Commerce and Industry (VCCI) provides data for the provincial competitiveness index (PCI). Data for public administration performance indicators (corruption control indexes — PAPI4) are collected from the website: http://papi.org.vn/.

Table 1: Measurement of variables in the research model.

Variables		Unit	Measurement
Labor productivity — LP		Millions VND/person	Value-added of the economy/Total labor of the economy
Labor force — LB		People	Number of working labors
Rate of trained employee — RTE		%	Trained labor of the economy/Total labor of the economy
Average income of employee per month — AIE		Thousands VND/person	Total income of employees/Total labor of the economy
Average equipped fixed assets per employee — FAPE		Millions VND/person	Total fixed assets/total labor of the economy
Capital intensity — CI		Millions VND/person	Capital implemented per month in the economy/total labor in the economy
Implemented investment — IIF		Billions VND	Implemented investment at constant price 2010
Capital productivity — CP		Times	Value-added of the economy/capital of the economy
Provincial Competitiveness Index — PCI		%	Use a scale from 10 (highest) to 1 (lowest) for the following ten criteria: Market entry; Land access; Transparency; Time cost; Unofficial costs; Incentives with foreign enterprises; Dynamism; Private economic development policy; Labor training; Legal institutions
The Provincial Governance and Public Administration Performance Index — PAPI	Transparency — PAPI2	Points	Including sub-dimensions: Access to information, poverty lists, communal budget and expenditure, land-use plans/Price frames
	Control of corruption — PAPI4	Points	Including sub-dimensions: Limits on public sector corruption, equity in employment, limits on corruption in service delivery, and willingness to fight corruption
	Public service Delivery — PAPI6	Points	Including sub-dimensions: Health, Education, Infrastructure, Law and order

Data sources for the provincial registering index (PCI) are collected from the Vietnam Chamber of Commerce and Industry (VCCI). Data sources on the efficiency index of public administration (transparency index (PAPI2), corruption control component index (PAPI4), and public service delivery index (PAPI6) are collected from the webpage: http://papi.org.vn/.

3.2. *Methodology*

In the scope of the research and data, a regression model for panel data is used. The panel data regression method not only increases the likelihood of the model because of the number of observations but also helps the processing of heterogeneity in datasets between units. The unevenness between provinces relates to economic development, infrastructure, socio-economic policies, geographical location, and resources.

However, a disadvantage of panel data with large numbers of observations in a short time series is that it often causes heteroskedasticity, and it is difficult to overcome this problem. Moreover, in research models of economic growth, endogenous variables usually exist. Endogenous issues lead to omitting variables or simultaneity. In these cases, the REM and FEM estimates are no longer consistent with the reliable estimates. The general method to solve this problem is to predict the instrumental variables estimator, especially evaluating by two-step least squares (2SLS).

After the estimating process, the following tests need to be carried out to examine the validity of the results, including Durbin, Wu–Hausman test for endogeneity, and Sargan and Basmann test for overidentifying restrictions.

However, there is much research focusing on the disadvantages of p-value in estimating processes. The most concerning issue is that the p-value is not an accurate measurement of the probability of the hypothesis occurring without regard to the likelihood of the selected sample (Nguyen, 2019). Hence, to retest the evaluated results above, Minimum Bayes Factor (MBF) is used. Goodman (1999) addresses the objectivity and calculations of MBF through four steps. The process for translating the p-value to MBF is performed as below:

Step 1: p-value values are calculated from the observed values of the sample. Thus, this value results from two probabilities: $P(Evidence|H_0)$ and $P(Evidence|H_\alpha)$.

Step 2: For smaller p-values, hypothesis H_0 is less supported. Therefore, in the same manner, MBF can be formulated as:

$$MBF = P(Evidence|H_0)/P(Evidence|H_\alpha) \quad (3)$$

Step 3: For calculation purposes, MBF should be converted into an approximation form of Gauss' law (Standard Normal Distribution form)

$$MBF = P(Evidence|H_0)/P(Evidence|H_\alpha) = e^{-z^2/2} \quad (4)$$

Then, z represents the corresponding z-value from the given null effect instead of the p-value.

4. Results and Discussion

4.1. *Results*

The estimation results are described in Table 2 as follows.

The estimation and testing results in Table 2 and Tables A2–A4 in the Appendix show that:

For the state-owned sector, the model has an endogenous existence, and the use of the 2SLS method is appropriate. The results obtained through the estimation of 2SLS are as follows: The average equipped fixed assets per employee (FAPE) is of great significance for labor productivity growth in the state-owned sector, followed by implemented investment (IIF). The results show that if the average equipped fixed assets per employee increased by a unit, labor productivity would increase by 0.012 units in the state-owned sector. Similarly, if the size of the implemented investment increases by a unit, labor productivity will increase by about 0.004.

For the non-state sector, average income per employee (AIE), average equipped fixed assets per employee (FAPE), capital intensity

Table 2: Results of estimating the impact of factors on labor productivity in different sectors in Vietnam.

Explanatory Variables	State-Owned Sector	Non-State Sector	Foreign-Invested Sector
RTE	−0.3795249	−0.0390268	−4.340867
	(0.6399665)	(0.0770969)	(3.802374)
AIE	0.000425	0.0015255**	0.0092945
	(0.0024868)	(0.0007342)	(0.0221031)
FAPE	0.0108942***	−0.0081769**	−0.0018028
	(0.0024796)	(0.0041922)	(0.0045788)
IIF	0.0042545**	0.0002844	0.0025912
	(0.0017018)	(0.0001274)	(0.0025245)
CI	−0.1314817	1.127186***	0.0648003***
	(0.1020819)	(0.1087719)	(0.0154213)
PAPI4	−6.898684	0.6065456	146.3789*
	(8.714575)	(1.128656)	(85.88524)
CP	13.48584	3.603952***	16.43746***
	(13.48584)	(0.8830873)	(0.7063339)
Cons	155.7039**	−6.149924	−683.446*
	(74.58473)	(8.096625)	(411.8703)

Notes: *Standard error in parentheses: **Significant at the 5% level; ***Significant at the 1% level.

(CI), and capital productivity (CP) all impact labor productivity. Through 2SLS estimates, only the average equipped fixed assets per employee (FAPE) negatively impacts labor productivity; other factors have a positive effect.

For the foreign-invested sector, the Durbin and Wu–Hausman test shows that the model has no endogenous status. Therefore, to estimate the impact of factors on labor productivity growth in the foreign-invested sector, the Breusch–Pagan test is performed to choose between the POLS model and the FEM and REM models. Breusch–Pagan test results show that the OLS model is appropriate for estimating the impact of factors on labor productivity growth in the foreign-invested sector. To increase the reliability of OLS estimates and the results obtained are stable, OLS with robustness is the fairest method. Table 2 shows the results of assessing the impact of factors on labor productivity in this sector. It can be seen that the factors of capital intensity (CI), capital productivity (CP), and the control of corruption index (PAPI4) have implications for labor productivity increase in this sector.

To increase the coherence, the Minimum Bayes Factor test is conducted to select suitable variables for endogenous models for different sectors. Bayes test results are quoted in Table 3 as follows.

The test result with the Minimum Bayes Factor shows the average equipped fixed assets per employee (FAPE) and the size of implemented investment (IIF) have a Minimum Bayes Factor of less than 10% (Table 3). This means two core factors are significant and increase labor productivity in the state-owned sector.

Bayesian results show that factors that affect labor productivity in the non-state sector include capital productivity (CP) and capital intensity (CI) because there is a Minimum Bayes Factor of less than 10%. The Bayesian test shows that the average income per employee (AIE) and the average equipped fixed assets per employee (FAPE) have a Minimum Bayes Factor greater than 10%, so these factors are removed. Consequently, it can be seen that for the non-state sector, capital productivity (CP) has the most significant impact on labor productivity. Specifically, each increase in capital productivity results in a considerable increase in labor productivity of about 3.6 units. Similarly, the increase of a unit in capital intensity raises labor productivity by about 1.12 (about 1/3 of capital productivity).

The test result with Minimum Bayes Factor shows that, in reality, capital productivity (CP), capital intensity (CI), and the control of corruption index (PAPI4) have an impact on labor productivity in the foreign-invested sector. Specifically, if capital productivity (CP) increases by a unit, labor productivity in the foreign-invested sector increases by approximately 16.5 units. The impact of capital intensity (CI) is relatively small, corresponding to an increase in capital intensity, leading to a rise of only 0.65 units of labor productivity in the foreign-invested sector. The control of corruption index (PAPI4) has the most substantial impact on labor productivity in the foreign-invested sector. Each increase in the (PAPI4) score increases labor productivity in the foreign-invested sector by about 146.38.

Table 3: Relation between p-value and minimum Bayes factors.

Explanatory Variables	State-Owned Sector		Non-State Sector		Foreign-Invested Sector	
	p-value (Z Score)	Minimum Bayes Factor	p-value (Z Score)	Minimum Bayes Factor	p-value (Z Score)	Minimum Bayes Factor
CP	0.627	(0.95)	0.000	0.0045	0.000	0.0045
	(−0.324)	1/1.05	(3.29)	(1/224)	(3.29)	(1/224)
RTE	0.553	(0.99)	0.613	(0.96)	0.256	(0.81)
	(−0.133)	1/1.01	(−0.287)	1/1.04	(0.656)	1/1.24
AIE	0.864	0.56	0.038	0.21	0.675	0.9
	(−1.098)	(1/1.8)	(1.774)	(1/4.8)	(−0.454)	(1/1.11)
FAPE	0.000	0.0045	0.051	(0.26)	0.694	0.88
	(3.29)	(1/224)	(1.635)	1/3.8	(−0.507)	(1/1.14)
IIF	0.012	(0.08)	0.026	(0.15)	0.307	0.88
	(2.257)	1/12.77	(1.943)	1/6.6	(0.504)	(1/1.14)
CI	0.198	0.70	0.000	0.0045	0.000	0.0045
	(0.849)	(1/1.43)	(3.29)	(1/224)	(3.29)	(1/224)
PAPI4	0.429	0.98	0.591	0.97	0.0091	0.041
	(0.179)	(1/1.02)	(−0.23)	(1/1.02)	(1.335)	(1/2.4)

Source: The authors' calculation.

Thus, it can be seen that factors that strongly affect labor productivity in different ownership sectors are also quite distinct. For state ownership, the factor affecting productivity is the scale of implemented investment (IIF) and the average equipped fixed assets per employee (FAPE). Meanwhile, the non-state and foreign-invested sectors have significant similarities: the only factors affecting labor productivity are capital productivity (CP) and capital intensity (CI). In particular, in the non-state sector and foreign-invested sector, the role of capital productivity (CP) is much larger than the role of capital intensity (CI). In addition, improving control of the corruption index (PAPI4) has tremendous implications for improving labor productivity in the foreign-invested sector.

4.2. *Discussion*

Through the results of the study on the overview and quantitative research, it can be seen that the factors affecting labor productivity growth in three economic sectors (state-owned, non-state, and foreign-invested) have the following characteristics:

Capital intensity (CI) has a crucial impact on the pace of labor productivity growth in all three economic sectors, indicating that the labor productivity growth of these sectors depends on the increase of investment capital per worker. The results show that the capital intensity (CI) of the non-state sector has the most considerable impact on labor productivity (1.13 million VND per person), followed by the foreign-invested sector (about 0.06 million VND per person). It proves that the implemented investment per employee of the foreign-invested sector is the highest, but its efficiency is lower. Implemented investment per worker in non-state sectors is used more effectively. Thus, continuing to increase the implemented investment is necessary to promote labor productivity growth, especially growing the implemented investment of non-state sectors. The rate of trained workers (RTE) does not affect the labor productivity of economic sectors. Thus, the growth of Vietnam's economic sectors in labor productivity is still primarily based on the change in width through increasing investment per labor. It is necessary to have a strategy for training and retraining workers to develop their skills in all economic sectors so that labor productivity can be soon improved in parallel with growing investment capital.

Capital productivity (CP) impacts the labor productivity of both groups of non-state and foreign-invested sectors. All economic sectors in Vietnam need to use investment effectively. The estimation results affirm that the foreign-invested sector's capital productivity (CP) is the highest, and the gap is quite large compared to the rest (five times). The foreign-invested sector uses capital most effectively and has the greatest impact on labor productivity (the coefficient is about 16.437).

Particularly for the state-owned sector, the average equipped fixed assets per employee (FAPE) and the size of implemented investment (IIF) are of great significance for increasing labor productivity in this sector. The average equipped fixed assets per employee (FAPE) is significant in improving labor productivity growth in the state-owned sector but has no significance in non-state and foreign-invested sectors. This estimation partly shows the dependence of state enterprises on economic growth in the width model and has not shifted to the economic growth in-depth model. Labor productivity in the non-state and foreign-invested sectors does not obviously link the increase in average equipped fixed assets per employee and labor productivity.

This is especially evident when the second factor affecting labor productivity in the state-owned sector is measured by the size of implemented investment at constant prices. Non-state and foreign-invested sectors do not show a clear link between increasing the average equipped fixed assets per employee and labor productivity. It can be said that, basically, the state-owned sector still grows in width with the tendency of expanding capital and labor factors contributing to economic growth.

The rate of trained employees (RTE) has no significance in all three economic sectors in the labor productivity growth. It shows inefficiencies in labor training in all three economic sectors. The underlying causes can be the poor quality of training and lack of association with economic enterprise activities. On the other hand, the forecast of employment growth is highly volatile in industrialization, which leads to highly trained workers being forced to fall into structured unemployment and do the jobs for which they were not initially trained. This has terrible consequences, not only slowing down productivity growth but also wasting social resources.

Similarly, the average income per employee (AIE) has no impact on the pace of labor productivity in all three sectors. This suggests that the increase in wages and the improvement of bonus regimes are not yet a strong motivation for workers to increase productivity. Although the basic salary tends to increase, the average income has consistently grown relatively high in recent years in Vietnam. However, if income growth is insufficient to offset the increase in costs due to the impact of inflation, then it is only nominal and has no practical meaning. Of the three sectors, the foreign-invested sector has the highest average income. Still, the change in the average income level does not affect employee productivity.

Finally, the surprising thing is that controlling the corruption index (PAPI4) is only significant for the foreign-invested sector. With many efforts in administrative reform, Vietnam hopes that it will improve socio-economic indicators, labor productivity, and overall economic growth. However, the estimation results show that, for the state-owned and non-state sectors, the improvement in corruption control has no impact on labor productivity. The foreign-invested sector is unique in its response to the local government's effective corruption control. It can be seen that controlling corruption in public service provision for foreign-invested enterprises is one factor that significantly affects their decisions when choosing where to invest. When attracting FDI, provinces should focus on improving infrastructure and public services to meet these businesses' requirements. The results show that the foreign-invested sector appears to be the most affected area of corruption in current management. Improving control of corruption will contribute to increasing productivity for the foreign-invested sector.

5. Conclusion

Through the research results, it can be seen that each sector is affected by different factors. However, the non-state and foreign-invested sectors still have similar similarities. These two sectors are heavily influenced by capital productivity (CP) and capital intensity (CI), in which capital productivity in the foreign-invested sector greatly impacts labor productivity. Moreover, the control of corruption index (PAPI4) also significantly enhances labor productivity in the foreign-invested sector. At the same time, it seems that better control of corruption means nothing for the state-owned sector. Remarkably, the state-owned sector differs from the other two groups. The most significant factor affecting the productivity of the state-owned sector is the size of implemented investment (IIF) and the average equipped fixed assets per employee (FAPE). In addition, other factors have minimal effect on labor productivity in this sector.

To enhance the labor productivity of economic sectors in Vietnam in the coming period, businesses and socio-economic organizations need to:

Firstly, improve the quality of human resources; promote training and retraining for workers in all economic sectors to meet international integration needs.

Secondly, improve the quality of training institutions to provide the economy with high-quality labor resources. There should be policies that focus on scaling up and improving the quality of vocational training systems, in combination with theory and practice, to overcome the situation of untrained labor quickly. Higher education needs to enhance investment in developing research activities and applying science and technology to production activities.

Thirdly, reform the market-based wage policy to ensure the appropriateness of raising wages while increasing labor productivity.

Fourthly, improve the efficiency of using fixed assets in enterprises across all economic sectors. The technology level of Vietnamese enterprises is still inferior; meanwhile, the ones participating in creative projects are still limited and not yet deeply involved in global supply chains. Accordingly, they cannot take advantage of the spread of knowledge, labor productivity, and technology from transnational corporations into domestic enterprises. Therefore, enterprises must invest in modern science and technology applications in production. There should be preferential credit policies for businesses using production lines with high and modern technology.

Fifthly, improve the efficiency of businesses in economic sectors by using investment capital.

Sixthly, implement effective policies to attract FDI to create a new impetus for economic growth. Vietnam needs to continue improving the investment environment, create favorable conditions for businesses, especially FDI enterprises, create a fair and competitive environment, and regard all economic sectors equally.

Seventhly, to increase social labor productivity, it is necessary to create a driving force for developing strong private enterprises. The private economy should provide the momentum to increase productivity. A well-developed private economy creates positive values, such as creating a labor market that requires workers to have high qualifications and applying modern science and technology to production to improve competitiveness. It is necessary to drastically reform the state-owned business sector, which holds a notable portion of the economy's capital but uses it inadequately.

Eighthly, improve provincial competitiveness in economic management quality and build a favorable business environment for the development of private enterprises.

Ninthly, continue to supervise and limit corruption in the economy.

Lastly, Vietnam needs the support and consultation of development partners and the business community to find appropriate and effective policies as well as solutions.

Acknowledgments

This research was supported by the University of Economics Ho Chi Minh City (UEH), Vietnam.

Appendix

Table A1: Summary of variables.

Variable	Obs	Mean	Std. Dev.	Min	Max
State-Owned Sector					
LP	156	118.4375	52.85331	7.552098	399.1184
RTE	156	18.0572	7.752371	8	47.2
AIE	156	6380.689	1729.427	2730	10940
FAPE	156	1211.581	1792.532	131.4	16201.11
IIF	156	5079.192	3853.298	1300.763	20865.34
CI	156	113.7483	89.54019	33.15406	795.4359
PAPI4	156	5.975513	.5097846	4.74	7.27
CP	156	1.793714	1.072627	0.0518558	5.638874
PAPI2	156	5.700577	.5000429	4.7	7.24
LB	156	60236.22	22908.62	18517	122200
PCI	156	58.29026	3.073863	48.96	70
PAPI6	156	6.945705	.3286436	6.01	8.03
Non-State Sector					
LP	156	33.76494	12.37745	0.5425171	83.40983
RTE	156	18.0572	7.752371	8	47.2
AIE	156	4557.131	800.9467	2792.692	7082
FAPE	156	295.6901	129.7142	112.2784	749.267
IIF	156	8350.823	5264.404	772.766	32684.12
CI	156	17.39328	9.143975	4.626349	55.80667
PAPI4	156	5.975513	0.5097846	4.74	7.27
CP	156	2.908135	1.390023	.0433766	8.30074
PAPI6	156	6.945705	0.3286436	6.01	8.03
PAPI2	156	5.700577	0.5000429	4.7	7.24
LB	156	638000.8	324287	184674	2005172
PCI	156	58.29026	3.073863	48.96	70
Foreign-Invested Sector					
LP	136	339.559	938.4974	15.11312	9517.717
RTE	136	17.73609	6.922886	8	41.62079
AIE	136	5489.403	2169.958	3.709	12756.6
FAPE	136	649.1869	2849.154	41.05263	33428

Table A1: (*Continued*)

Variable	Obs	Mean	Std. Dev.	Min	Max
IIF	136	5634.083	11310.87	8.034	52277.03
CI	136	455.6963	1460.335	5.718139	11188.82
PAPI4	136	6.011176	.495975	4.76	7.27
CP	136	7.671864	49.82818	.0262522	580.7808
PAPI2	136	5.7446	.57994	5.0	7.0
PAPI6	136	6.986765	.3231371	6.01	8.03
PCI	136	58.71831	2.987312	48.96	70
LB	136	38854.354448	88049.31491	109.0000	520510.000

Table A2: Results of estimating the impact of the influencing factors labor productivity in the state-owned sector.

Explanatory Variables	2SLS	SE
RTE	−0.3795249	0.6399665
AIE	0.000425	0.0024868
FAPE	0.0108942***	0.0024796
IIF	0.0042545**	0.0017018
CI	−0.1314817	0.1020819
PAPI4	−6.898684	8.714575
CP	13.48584	13.48584
Cons	155.7039**	74.58473

Tests of endogeneity
Ho: variables are exogenous
Durbin (score) chi2(1) = 19.6439(p = 0.0000)
Wu–Hausman F(1, 147) = 21.1773(p = 0.0000).

Tests of overidentifying restrictions:
Sargan (score) chi2(3) = 7.73792(p = 0.0518)
Basmann chi2(3) = 7.56767(p = 0.0558).

Testing of instrumental variables CP:
R-sq. = 0.3958 Adjusted R-sq. = 0.3542 Partial R-sq. = 0.1148
F (4,145) = 4.70317 Prob. = 0.0013.

Notes: Standard error in parentheses: **Significant at the 5% level; ***Significant at the 1% level.

Table A3: Results of estimating the impact of the influencing factors labor productivity in the non-state sector.

Explanatory Variables	**2SLS**	**SE**
RTE	−0.0390268	0.0770969
AIE	0.0015255**	0.0007342
FAPE	−0.0081769**	0.0041922
IIF	0.0002844	0.0001274
CI	1.127186***	0.1087719
PAPI4	0.6065456	1.128656
CP	3.603952***	0.8830873
Cons	−6.149924	8.096625

Tests of endogeneity
Ho: variables are exogenous
Durbin (score) chi2(1) = 12.9936(p = 0.0003)
Wu–Hausman F(1,147) = 13.3565(p = 0.0004).

Tests of overidentifying restrictions:
Sargan (score) chi2(3) = 5.58637(p = 0.1336)
Basmann chi2(3) = 5.3853(p = 0.1457).

Testing of instrumental variables CP:
R-sq. = 0.5348 Adjusted R-sq. = 0.5028 Partial R-sq. = 0.2523
F(4,145) = 12.231 Prob. = 0.0000.

Notes: Standard error in parentheses: **Significant at the 5% level; ***Significant at the 1% level.

Table A4: Results of estimating the impact of the influencing factors labor productivity in the foreign-invested sector.

Explanatory Variables	**2SLS**	**SE**
RTE	−2.738599	7.471191
AIE	0.0141892	0.00267416
FAPE	0.0006777	0.0183172
ICF	0.0035859	0.0055862
CI	0.0738166*	0.0417667
PAPI4	23.13402	199.5897
CP	23.13402***	10.07705
Cons	−64.31985	1090.853

Tests of endogeneity
Ho: variables are exogenous
Durbin (score) chi2(1) = 0.870032(p = 0.3509)
Wu–Hausman F(1,127) = 0.817688(p = 0.3676).

Tests of overidentifying restrictions:
Sargan (score) chi2(3) = 0.79862(p = 0.8498)
Basmann chi2(3) = 0.738362(p = 0.8641).

Testing of instrumental variables CP:
R-sq. = 0.0468 Adjusted R-sq. = −0.0294 Partial R-sq. = 0.0091
F(4,145) = 0.287031 Prob. = 0.8859.

Notes: Standard error in parentheses: **Significant at the 5% level; ***Significant at the 1% level.

Bibliography

Aschauer, D. (1989). Is public expenditure productive? *Journal of Monetary Economics*, 23(2), 177–200.

Audretsch, D. and Feldman, M. (1996). R&D spillovers and the geography of innovation and production. *American Economic Review*, 86(3), 630–640.

Baltagi, B.H. (2005). *Econometric Analysis of Panel Data.* John Wiley & Sons Ltd.

Baptista, R. and Swann, G. (1998). Do firms in clusters innovate more? *Research Policy*, 27(5), 525–540.

Batra, G., Kaufmann, D., and Stone, A. (2001). *Voices of the Firms 2000: Investment Climate and Governance Findings of the World Business Environment Survey.* World Bank.

CIEM and UNDP (2011). *Researching a New Height: Review of Policy on Private Enterprises.* CIEM and UNDP.

Drabek, Z. and Payne, W. (2002). The impact of transparency on foreign direct investment. *Journal of Economic Integration*, 17(4), 777–810.

Emery, J. (2003). Governance, transparency and private investment in Africa. *Global Forum on International Investment, OECD-Africa Investment Roundtable*, November 19, 2003.

Firouzi, F., Sakireh, S., Nasim, M., and Aslaninia (2010). *Determinants of Labour Productivity in Iran's Manufacturing Firms: Emphasizing on Labour Education and Training.* University of Tabriz.

General Statistics Office (2015). *Statistical Yearbook.* Statistical Publishing House.

Goodman, S.N. (1999). Toward evidence-based medical statistics. *Annals of Internal Medicine*, 130(12), 1005–1113.

GSO (2018). *Statistical Yearbook of Vietnam 2018.* Statistical Publishing House.

Guellec, D. and Potterie, B. (2001). R&D and productivity growth: Panel data analysis of 16 OECD Countries. *OECD Science, Technology and Industry Working Papers 2001/03.*

Jorgenson, D. and Stiroh, K. (2000). Raising the speed limit: US economic growth in the information age. *OECD Economics Department Working Papers 261*, OECD Publishing.

Juselius, M. (2005). Long-run relationships between labor and capital: Indirect Evidence on the elasticity of substitution. *Yrjö Jahnsson Foundation and the Research Unit on Economic Structures and Growth (University of Helsinki)*, HECER Discussion Paper No. 57.

Kelly, C. (2014). *Corruption and Productivity.* A Thesis Presented to the Graduate School of Clemson University.

Lambsdorff, J.G. (2003). How corruption affects persistent capital flows. *Journal of Economics of Governance*, 229–243.

Luan, C., and Jiang, H., and Tien, C. (2016). Does governance transparency lead to more supportive foreign investment? *Journal of Asian Business Strategy*, 6(6), 113–124.

Lucas, R. (1988). On the mechanics of economic development. *Journal of Monetary Economics*, 22(1), 3–42.

Moseley, F. (2014). A critique of the marginal productivity theory of the price of capital. *Real World Economics Review*, 59, 131–137.

Nguyen, B.L. (2018). Report on Vietnam's labor productivity. Forum "Improving labor productivity, leveraging economic growth," Hanoi.

Nguyen, H.T. (2019). How to test without *p*-value. *Thailand Statistician*, 17(2), i–x.

Nguyen, T.H. and Nguyen, T.L.H. (2016). Situation and factors affecting Vietnam's labor productivity through surveys of industrial production enterprises.

Nguyen, T.N.L. (2018). Vietnam's labor productivity growth rate and the effects of FDI attraction. *Review of Finance.*

Nguyen, V.Đ. (2016). Factors affecting labor productivity and problems raised. *Review of Finance*, 12(5), 13.

Oliner, S. and Sichel, D. (2000). The resurgence of growth in the late 1990s: Is information technology the story? *Journal of Economic Perspectives*, 14(4), 3–22.

Page, R. and S. Eiki (2017). Beyond *p*-value and hypothesis testing: Using the Minimum Bayes Factor to teach statistical inference in undergraduate introductory statistic Courses. *Journal of Education and Learning*, 6(4), 254–266.

Papadogonas, T. and Voulgaris, F. (2005). Labor productivity growth in Greek manufacturing firms. *Operational Research*, 5(3), 459–472.

Patnaik, P. (2014). Capitalism, inequality and globalization: Thomas Piketty's capital in the twenty-first century. *The Marxist*, 30(2), 55–69.

Scarpetta, S. and Tressel, C. (2002). The role of policy and institutions for productivity and firm dynamics: Evidence from micro and industry data. OECD Economic Department Working Papers 329, OECD Publishing.

Shinada, N. (2011). Quality of labor, capital, and productivity growth in Japan: Effects of employee age, seniority, and capital vintage. RIETI Discussion Paper Series, 11–E–036.

Syll, L.P. (2014). Piketty and the limits of marginal productivity theory. *Real-World Economics Review*, 69, 36–43.

Tran Thi Thanh Huong (2019). *Impact of Factors on Vietnam's Labor Productivity Growth, International Workshop: Economics and Statistical Methods — Application in Economics and Finance*. Information and Communications Publishing House, pp. 215–236.

https://doi.org/10.1142/9789811262258_0008

Chapter 8

Environmental Impact Assessment: A Gap between Theory and Practice in Vietnam

Thi Anh Nguyen

Abstract

Environmental Impact Assessment (EIA) is considered a common tool for addressing environmental concerns in proposed projects. In Vietnam, EIA has been legally implemented since 1993. The first law on environmental protection was adopted to reduce the pressure on environmental components and pollution caused by the Industrial Revolution and economic modernization. Nowadays, EIA is governed by the Law on Environmental Protection 2014 and regulations specifying the EIA process. Apart from some benefits to the environment and society, EIA still has some challenges in reality and exists the gap between theory and practice. To address this problem, the chapter analyzes the process of EIA in Vietnam. This analysis is based on the review of the relevant literature, legal provisions, and EIA reports. The conclusion finally shows that Vietnam's EIA process should be improved in the future.

Keywords: EIA; Environment; Environmental protection; Vietnam.

1. Introduction

The Vietnamese government's aim has been to encourage economic growth with harmonious consideration of environmental issues.[1]

[1]Resolution No.11/NQ-TW dated June 6, 2017 of the 5th Plenum of the Party Central Committee, 12th Tenure on perfecting a socialist-oriented market economy.

From the 1980s, some studies of EIA were conducted in many development projects in Vietnam. With the efforts of Vietnamese experts as well as the assistance of international organizations, such as UNEP, UNDP, IUCN, and ADB (Can, 1997; Doberstein, 2003), the Law on Environment Protection was officially adopted by the National Assembly on December 27, 1993.[2] In efforts to have an effective EIA in practice, the Government[3] and the Ministries issued some legal documents for the implementation of EIA. While significant results of environmental protection have been achieved in EIA policy and law, there has been a gap between EIA theory and practice in Vietnam. Based on an analysis of the current laws on EIA in Vietnam and its application, in reality, some recommendations would introduce to solve the existing gap. Hence, firstly, this chapter demonstrates the definition of EIA to identify the purposes of this tool. In this research, EIA is intended to supply information for the "players" (Munn, 1975) or the "actors" (Glasson *et al.*, 2013, 24) in the decision-making from which the current environmental issues, as well as potential environmental concerns, are well understood. Secondly, the history of Vietnam's EIA, some legal regulations on EIA, and its application in real-life situations will be analyzed to show some drawbacks in the current EIA provisions of Vietnam and give some suggestions for improvement in the future.

2. What Is Environmental Impact Assessment?

It is said that human survival depends on the environment, resources, and raw materials. However, economic growth, rapid industrialization, urbanization, and human needs at high levels of human

[2]See Law on environmental protection of 1993 of Vietnam's National Assembly Law. Retrieved on August 26, 2016 from http://www.moj.gov.vn/vbpq/Lists/Vn%20bn%20php%20lut/View_Detail.aspx?ItemID=10443 (Vietnamese version only).

[3]See Decree No.175-CP dated October 18, 1994, of Vietnamese Government on guiding implementation of the law on environmental protection. Retrieved on August 27, 2016 from http://www.kenfoxlaw.com/resources/legal-documents/governmental-decrees/2199-vbpl-sp-29100.html.

development have been affecting the environmental components leading to rapid loss of natural resources, and environmental pollution. People have been increasingly suffering from natural disasters. Natural disasters (floods, drought, and desertification), poverty, and hunger have been adverse impacts of climate change. As a result, EIA is formally approved as an effective tool for protecting the environment and harmonizing economic growth with environmental protection following the basic principle of "it is better to prevent a problem than to cure it." This tool would help stakeholders find the measures to restrict potentially adverse impacts at an early stage of the specific project. Barrow (1997) explained that EIA is "an approach which seeks to improve development by *a priori* assessment."

From the early 1960s, several proposals for a national environmental policy were discussed in the US (Glasson *et al.*, 2013) because pollution, environmental degradation, and other environmental problems were both complex and interrelated (Wood, 2003). In 1969, NEPA was adopted by the US as the first country to develop a system of EIA. This act was passed to ensure that environmental concerns received adequate attention at all levels of government planning, decision-making, and action in the US (Burton *et al.*, 1983). Many countries have provided that EIA has been a mandatory process (Burton *et al.*, 1983). Concurrently, in the international sphere, the EIA can be easily recognized in a large number of international conventions, protocols, and agreements (Morgan, 2012).

Forty-five years after its first official appearance, the EIA is now universally recognized as a key instrument for environmental management, firmly embedded in domestic and international environmental law (Morgan, 2012). However, definitions of EIA abound in literature and legislation (Glasson *et al.*, 2013), and up to now, there has been no universally accepted definition of EIA. Although NEPA represented the first formal law on EIA, there was no definition of EIA in this law.

The UN Conference on the Human Environment, having met in Stockholm from June 5–16, 1972, proclaims at the 21st principle that according to the national environmental policies, countries have the right to exploit their natural resources and the responsibility to ensure that development activities do not cause damage to the environment.[4] Concurrently, the Convention on EIA in a transboundary context defines EIA as a national procedure for evaluating the likely impact of a proposed activity on the environment.[5] Consequently, at the UN Conference on Environment and Development in Rio de Janeiro, the 1992 Rio Declaration proclaimed that "environmental impact assessment, as a national instrument, shall be undertaken for proposed activities that are likely to have a significant adverse impact on the environment and are subject to a decision of a competent national authority."[6]

In addition, WB also defines EIA, which was applied to projects proposed for WB financing, as "EIA is an instrument to identify and assess the potential environmental impacts of a proposed project, evaluate alternatives, and design appropriate mitigation, management, and monitoring measures" (WB 1999, revised 2011, Annex A-Definitions (2)). Environmental impacts shall be predicted and assessed on the project's likely positive and negative impacts in quantitative terms to the extent possible (WB 1999, revised 2011, Annex 2, 2(e)).

According to OECD (1992), EIA is a procedure used to examine the environmental consequences, both beneficial and adverse, of a proposed development project and to ensure that these consequences are taken into account in the project design. The EIA evaluates the expected effects on human health, the natural environment, and the property. The EIA should consider alternative project designs (including the "no-action" alternative), as well as mitigation

[4]See Principle 21 of United Nations Conference on the Human Environment. Retrieved on December 26, 2016 from http://www.encyclopedia.com/environment/energy-government-and-defense-magazines/united-nations-conference-human-environment-1972.

[5]See Article 1 (vi) of Convention on Environmental Impact Assessment in a Transboundary Context. Retrieved on December 26, 2016 from https://treaties.un.org/pages/ViewDetails.aspx?src=IND&mtdsg_no=XXVII-4&chapter=27&clang=_en.

[6]See supra note 6.

measures or environmental safeguards that should be incorporated into the project design to offset adverse impacts.

JICA guidelines for environmental and social considerations emphasize the impacts not only on the environment but also on the society of the proposed project. EIA includes evaluating the environmental and social impacts that projects are to have, analyzing alternative plans, and preparing adequate mitigation measures and monitoring plans following the laws or guidelines of host countries (JICA, 2010).

The above illustration of the notion of EIA displays that EIA is an important assessment process for projects. With the emphasis on the environmental consequences of a proposed project, some scientists conclude that EIA is a decision tool employed to identify and evaluate the probable environmental consequence of certain proposed development actions to facilitate informed decision-making and sound environmental management (Cashmore, 2004; Cashmore *et al.*, 2004). Other scholars consider EIA as a document for decision-makers and highlight that EIA is a systematic and integrative process for considering possible impacts before a decision is made on whether or not a proposal should be approved to proceed (Wood, 2003). Munn (1975) also defines EIA as "an activity designed to identify and predict the impact of an action on the bio-geophysical environment and human health and well-being, and to interpret and communicate information about the impacts."

In line with Lawrence (2003), in this research, EIA is defined as a systematic process of:

- Determining and managing (identifying, describing, measuring, predicting, interpreting, integrating, communicating, involving, and controlling) the
- potential (or real) impacts (direct and indirect, individual and cumulative, the likelihood of occurrence) of
- proposed (or existing) human actions (projects, plans, programs, legislation, activities) and their alternatives on the
- environment (physical, chemical, biological, ecological, human health, cultural, social, economic, built, and interrelations).

This definition demonstrates that EIA is a process that embeds numerous activities. However, EIA in developing countries tends to be very different from EIA in developed nations (Wood 2003). It is a fact that in some developing countries, EIA has been carried out because of the pressure from donor agencies rather than demand for environmental protection. Although EIA was introduced later and is different from the EIA's origin, the concept of EIA is the same. Particularly, in Japan, EIA shall mean the process of (a) surveying, predicting, and assessing the likely impact that a project will have on various aspects of the environment; (b) studying possible environmental protection measures relating to the project; (c) assessing the likely overall environmental impact of such measures.[7] In Vietnam, according to Law on Environmental Protection No.55/2014/QH13, EIA refers to the analysis and prediction of environmental impacts of specific investment projects to take preventive measures to protect the environment during the implementation of such projects.[8]

All views of EIA's concept mentioned above display that EIA is a process to produce the documentation used to predict environmental protection activities (Glasson *et al.*, 2013). In this research, EIA is understood as a fence, helping to screen and eliminate the activities, which shall harmfully affect the environment, society, and human beings. EIA is a systematic process through which the public shall participate to give opinions on the potential impacts of proposed projects on the environment, society, and humans. Through the EIA process, the environmental rights shall be fully enhanced.

In conclusion, while there is no common definition of EIA, it is generally agreed that EIA is a systematic process used to predict, not prevent, the adverse environmental consequences of a proposed activity, through which the public has the right to participate.

---

[7]See supra note 6. Environmental Impact Assessment Act 1997 (Japan). Retrieved on February 17, 2016 from http://www.env.go.jp/en/laws/policy/assess.

[8]See supra note 2.

3. History of Environmental Impact Assessment in Vietnam

Efforts of the Vietnamese Government to escape from poverty and to boost economic growth had begun since ending the devastating war in 1975. However, along with the achievement in economic development, Vietnam experienced environmental degradation and pollution (Quyen *et al.*, 1995; Quy, 1997; Can, 2002; Obbard *et al.*, 2002; Doberstein, 2004; Toan, 2015). Particularly, according to Can (2002), there have been some serious environmental problems in Vietnam as follows:

- Deterioration of forest resources;
- Decrease in agricultural land and deterioration of soil quality;
- Inefficiency in the conservation and use of water resources;
- Irrational use of mineral resources;
- Degradation of biological resources;
- Environmental pollution.

Hence, the conflicts between economic growth and environmental protection activities for a good living environment in environmental management in Vietnam have emerged. Consequently, EIA was officially introduced as a valuable tool for promoting sustainable development in legal documents and ensuring environmental rights. Concurrently, to harmonize the benefits among proponents, the public, and decision-makers in the EIA process, public participation shall be formally provided as a vital component.

Depending on the viewpoint of each author, the development of EIA in Vietnam can be divided into different phases. Obbard *et al.* (2002), for example, divided the development of EIA in Vietnam into three phases: (i) from 1983 to 1993: preparation for EIA procedures; (ii) from 1993 to mid-1996: implementation of EIA procedures; (iii) from mid-1996 to current: improvement of EIA. Similar to Obbard *et al.* (2002), Doberstein (2003) also divides the history of EIA into three relatively distinct periods: the learning phase (pre-1990); the formalization phase (1990–1994); and the implementation and capacity-building phase (1995–present). However, from the perspective of Vietnamese experts in EIA, the history and development of the EIA system in Vietnam can be divided into four phases (Toan, 2015). They are (i) pre-December 27, 1993 (the learning phase); (ii) from December 27, 1993 to July 1, 2006 (the first legislation on EIA); (iii) from July 1, 2006 to December 31, 2014 (the improvement of EIA); (iv) from January 1, 2015 to current (the revision of EIA).

In addition, based on the EIA implementation in practice, Can (1997) divided the development of Vietnam's EIA into three phases: (1) preparation for implementation, (2) implementation, and (3) improvement of implementation. Following this line of thinking, I divided the development of EIA in Vietnam into two phases since the late 1970s. They are (i) pre-1993 (the research and learning phase in which EIA was not officially provided with any laws); (ii) from 27/12/1993 to the current time (the legal formalization in which EIA was formally provided in law).

In short, from 1993 to 2016, significant changes in Vietnam's EIA legislation have taken place. The legal documents have been gradually improved and amended to meet the requirements of economic growth and environmental protection policy. Particularly, the EIA process was legally described clearly to ensure the EIA report's quality for sustainable development. However, one of the shortcomings of the current EIA legislation is the procedure of public consultation in the EIA process (Toan, 2016). Thus, to promote sustainable development and environmental rights, it is necessary to improve the current EIA system, particularly public participation in the EIA process.

4. Vietnam's Environmental Impact Assessment: Analysis of the Legal Regulations and Their Application in Reality

4.1. *Projects required to conduct EIA: Too many but not enough*

According to Clause 2 Article 19, Law on Environmental Protection 2014, the environmental impact assessment must be performed in the preparatory stage of the project.[9] The environmental impact assessment objects consist of:[10] (a) Projects subject to the decision on investment intentions made by the National Assembly, Government, and the Prime Minister; (b) Projects that use land parcels situated in wildlife sanctuaries, national parks, historical-cultural monuments, world heritage sites, biosphere reserves, scenic beauty areas that have been ranked; (c) Projects that can cause bad effects on the environment. To specify the above provisions, Decree No.40/2019/ND-CP[11] listed 107 projects that the proponent shall conduct EIA.

Based on the current legal provisions, EIA has been performed in the specific proposed project. Hence, there are no requirements provided on the combination of the EIA of projects, current actions, and proposed actions. All projects have not forecasted the integrated impacts yet. This is one of the reasons causing environmental pollution.

4.2. *Proponent intervention in the contents of EIA report*

"Who should prepare the EIA report?" is a difficult question for legislators and the scholars who study the EIA system. Hollick (1984) argues that the proponent shall be responsible for EIA preparation by using the consultants listed by the Environmental Protection Agency. Following this line of thinking, in Vietnam, LEP 2014 also provided that the proponents or consultancies hired by the proponents shall carry out the EIA process. However, the proponents shall take statutory responsibility for the conclusive result after conducting an environmental assessment. The proponent shall cover expenses incurred from the formulation and inspection of the report on EIA.

In the first case, the proponent shall prepare the EIA report and hold a public meeting to receive objective opinions and reasonable requests from the relevant public. The proponent has extremely

---

[9]Clause 2 Article 19, Law on Environmental Protection 2014.

[10]Clause 1 Article 18, Law on Environmental Protection 2014.

[11]See Appendix II, Decree No.40/2019/ND-CP dated May 13, 2019 on amendments to decrees on guidelines for the law on environment protection.

expressed his ideas in the EIA report. Thus, this shall favor the proponent when interpreting the contents of the EIA report. As aforementioned, the proponent will try to persuade the public of environmental information and the given alternatives in the EIA report. It is very hard for the public to interfere in the EIA process. Consequently, the owner of the project shall control the EIA process.

In the second case, the proponent has to pay the money for hiring the consultants to elaborate on the EIA report. The proponent does not want to waste money and time without getting a smooth EIA report. Therefore, when consultancies elaborate on the EIA report, the proponent still intervenes in the contents of the EIA report and sometimes distorts the information. It means that because the consultancies are employed, they will speak the voice of the proponents who pay money for hiring them. It is difficult for consultants to give their opinions, which puts proponents at a disadvantage. It is said that dependent finance should influence the quality of the opinions strongly. It is reasonable for proponents to have a smooth EIA process because they pay money for hiring consultants. Hence, proponents have the right to know the EIA process, leading to intervention in EIA contents. As a result, the EIA report shall reflect opinions that are subjective rather than what is objective. Limitation of intervention in the EIA process is a challenge for EIA legislation in Vietnam.

4.3. *EIA process: In need of changing for improvement of the quality*

The way to conduct the EIA process would solely determine the quality of the EIA report. Based on the Law on Environmental Protection 2014 and relevant legal documents, the proponent/consultant prepares the EIA report for their proposed projects. As a result, they can easily intervene in the contents of EIA and just disclose the mandatory information, which brings benefits for them. The public meeting is compulsorily held only once during the EIA process, at the stage of EIA preparation. If citizens do not attend this only public meeting, they will not have any opportunity to give opinions on the EIA report. Especially, implementation of notice for the public meeting is still limited.

Nowadays, it takes about six months to complete the EIA process, so the time for consulting public opinions is also too short. Especially, communication among the proponent/consultant, the responsible authority, and the public is mainly one-way; as a result, the quality of public opinions is often low. However, the proponent wants to end the procedure of public consultation as soon as possible because of the time-consuming. For them, this procedure aims to provide information to the public and fulfill their obligation for the submission of the EIA report.

The cost has been a burden to the proponent. According to Sinclair and Doelle (2003), EIA legislation shall set the quality standard for public participation, such as requirements for authorities, proponents, and the public regarding the notice, access to information, and participation. Thus, to solve the above drawbacks in the current EIA process in Vietnam, I suggested that the EIA legislation should be improved. *Firstly*, the EIA process should start from the first stage of the decision-making process when the Strategic Environmental Assessment is already completed. The public could access the planning document and express their opinions on the environmental issues from the earliest stage of the EIA process (such as Primary Environmental Impact Consideration), even with no options. *Secondly*, it is necessary to establish independent consultancies so that the EIA report is a scientific work of specific experts. Hollick (1984) suggests that environmental agencies should maintain a register of acceptable environmental consultants so that the proponent can select one of them from a register of those known to be honest, unbiased, technically competent, and capable of working with a design team. Hollick (1984) proposes that it might be better to form two committees to identify important environmental issues. The first committee includes expert representatives from the proponent, relevant agencies, and outside organizations. The second one comprises the decision-maker's representatives and public interest groups. These committees can receive support from the government, and they will be empowered by responsible authorities to make decisions independently. It is logical and reasonable for the proponents to pay the direct costs of the EIA. In Vietnam, LEP 2014 provided that the project owner shall cover all expenses incurred from the elaboration and appraisal EIA report. However, the cost for the procedure of public meetings should be subsidized by the state to support the proponent, saving costs and time in the EIA process. *Thirdly*, the public meeting should be held several times during the EIA process instead of one time under the current EIA process. This will be more reasonable if the government supports the cost of public meetings. Before submitting the EIA report to the responsible authorities, the relevant parties should convene one or more public meetings to explain the proposed project and receive opinions from people of diverse socioeconomic backgrounds if they miss the first public meeting. As a result, the conflicts among the proponent, the governments, and the public will be reduced, and the implementation of the project will achieve success and effectiveness. *Fourthly*, to develop sustainability and guarantee a sound environment for the people, it is necessary to provide a specific period for consultation. Particularly, for the aim of inviting comments, proponent and/or local governments should make the documents of each stage (such as the planning document, the draft EIA report, and the final EIA report) available for public comments in the local areas for one month from the date on which these documents are made known to the public. Additionally, anyone can submit comments and opinions to the proponent and/or the responsible authorities within 45 days from the date on which the above documents are made known to the public. On the other hand, this period starts when these documents are announced publicly and ends 15 days after the termination of the period during which these documents are made known to the public. *Finally*, the notice is the most important for implementing the procedure of public participation. Doelle and Sinclair (2006) propose that the ultimate responsibility for initial notice requirements should belong to the proponent. In contrast to this suggestion, in

Vietnam, notice for public meetings has not been provided in any legal documents. In reality, notwithstanding the lack of these provisions, notice has still been conducted by the responsible parties in Vietnam. Normally, the proponent sends the notice to the People's Committee of the commune. Then this local government will issue a notice inviting the public to come to the public meeting for public opinions. Thus, a direct party making the notice for public meetings and/or for public comments is the People's Committee of the commune, not a proponent; but the proponent still bears the full responsibility for the failure of the public meeting. The People's Committee of the commune, a local government, provides the actual notice through websites created for this announcement, public announcement at the bulletin boards, public areas, and social media easily to the local people under the direct governance of the People's Committee of the commune. If the EIA process was changed under my proposal, the requirement for a notice period would be 30 days from the date on which these documents for public comments are made known to the public. I contend that responsibility for the notice should be provided by both proponent and local governments early in the planning stage with initial purposes and alternatives of the proposed project. Based on this, lawmakers can establish the new EIA process to achieve the effectiveness of this procedure.

4.4. *One-way flow of environmental information in the EIA process*

In Vietnam, to give an impulse to economic development, the industrialization and economic modernization programs have been carried out since the late 1980s. As a result, the Vietnamese government and public authorities occasionally fail to consider essential environmental concerns, increasing the conflicts between the economic benefits and the demand for a good living environment. To harmonize this conflict, the government should greatly facilitate citizens to give opinions in the decision-making process. However, the right to access information is not implemented fully, accurately, and punctually in the EIA process. People receive information passively (one-way flow of information), which leads to the quality of public opinions. The proponent should recognize that both the quality of the EIA report and the success of the project will increase through public participation. Besides, the proponent shall get a higher level of consensus on the project which can avoid environmental disputes in the future (Del Furia and Wallace-Jones, 2000).

It is vital that environmental information is the key element in whether it helps stakeholders participate in the EIA process. Some authors have already discussed the definition of "environmental information" (Changhua, 2005; Yousefi-Sahzabi *et al.*, 2014) and other issues relating to environmental information (Stephan, 2002; Hakla, 2003; Yousefi-Sahzabi *et al.*, 2014). In addition, in both the international and national sphere, the notion of environmental information is officially provided in the legal documents. Information can be stored and transmitted in a variety of forms (Israel and Perry, 1991). Therefore, according to the Aarhus Convention, environmental information means any information in written, visual, aural, electronic, or any other material form (UNECE, 2014). In Vietnam, representatives of local communities have the right to ask the owners of companies to provide information on environmental protection through direct dialogues or in writing and have the right to ask the responsible authorities to supply results of the investigation, inspection, and handling of the entities.[12] The supply of environmental information to the community is on the environmental state management authorities. If environmental information refers to legal documents, environmental reports, information about proposed and existing activities, they may significantly affect the environment, harmful waste sources, result of inspection, examination and handling of violation and specialized environmental publications. On the

[12]See more details in Article 146 LEP 2014, supra note 2.

other hand, if environmental information refers to their environmental protection activities and license related to the extraction, use, and protection of natural resources and the environment, it will be on the companies.

The flow of information in the EIA process is one way from the proponent to the public. According to theory, public participation can help the proponent collect local information to produce a good EIA report and make the EIA process more transparent. Therefore, supplying environmental information plays a key role in improving the transparency of the EIA process. The responsible authorities and the proponent have to facilitate the public's access to environmental information. Moreover, the public actively searches and updates environmental information through the given forms provided by responsible authorities and companies. However, most environmental information is stored in computerized information systems (Haklay, 2003). In Vietnam, the computer system has not been adequately equipped yet. Especially, some large proposed projects have often been located in remote areas with poor infrastructure. The distance from the People's Committee to the community is very far and inconvenient for transportation. Additionally, the low public awareness level is challenging the environmental information transfer. As a result, the public capability of assessing environmental information fully from the storage unit would have been limited. The public often knows the proposed project's information when the consultants come to each household to disseminate environmental information. But it has never happened in reality. It is, therefore, not surprising that the public is willing to agree with the proposed projects because proponents have already drawn the good prospect.

In short, to change the one-way flow of environmental information into a two-way flow of environmental information for transparency and effectiveness of the EIA process, it is necessary to increase public environmental awareness and improve the infrastructure system and environmental information system. After that, the proponent and the public can exchange the environmental information for the valuable EIA report with a strong consensus.

5. Conclusion

In this chapter, I have conducted the analysis of EIA in theory and practice in Vietnam. The results show that Vietnam's EIA process needs improvement. Combining the EIA's current actions and proposed actions is necessary to reduce the potential environmental impacts in real-life situations. Also, changing a one-way flow of environmental information into a two-way flow of environmental information for transparency and effectiveness of the EIA process is very important. Besides, it is necessary to amend the current legal provisions to prevent the proponent control in the EIA process and the EIA report.

Bibliography

Barrow, C.J. (1997). *Environmental and Social Impact Assessment: An Introduction*. Arnold, Hodder Headline, PLC.

Burton, I. *et al.* (1983). Environmental impact assessment: National approaches and international needs. *Environmental Monitoring and Assessment*, 3(2), 133–150.

Can, L.T. (1997). The development of Environmental impact assessment in Vietnam. Environmental policy and management, in H. Mercker, and Hoang, V.P. (Eds.), *Vietnam*. German Foundation for International Development, Public Administration Promotion Centre.

Can, L.T. (2002). Environmental capacity building in Vietnam. Capacity building in national environmental policy: A comparative study of 17 countries. *Environmental Policy*, 393–407.

Cashmore, M. (2004). The role of science in environmental impact assessment: Process and procedure versus purpose in the development of theory. *Environmental Impact Assessment Review*, 24(4), 403–426.

Cashmore, M. *et al.* (2004). The interminable issue of effectiveness: Substantive purposes, outcomes and research challenges in the advancement of environmental impact assessment theory. *Impact Assessment and Project Appraisal*, 22(4), 295–310.

Changhua, W. (2005). Improving the legal and policy foundation for public access to environmental information in China. *Temple Journal of Science, Technology & Environmental Law*, 24, 291.

Del Furia, L. and Wallace-Jones, J. (2000). The effectiveness of provisions and quality of practices concerning public participation in EIA in Italy. *Environmental Impact Assessment Review*, 20(4), 457–479.

Doberstein, B. (2003). Environmental capacity-building in a transitional economy: The emergence of EIA capacity in Vietnam. *Impact Assessment and Project Appraisal*, 21(1), 25–42.

Doberstein, B. (2004). EIA models and capacity building in Vietnam: An analysis of development aid programs. *Environmental Impact Assessment Review*, 24(3), 283–318.

Doelle, M. and Sinclair, A.J. (2006). Time for a new approach to public participation in EA: Promoting cooperation and consensus for sustainability. *Environmental Impact Assessment Review*, 26(2), 185–205.

Glasson, J. *et al.* (2013). *Introduction to Environmental Impact Assessment*. Routledge.

Haklay, M.E. (2003). Public access to environmental information: Past, present and future. *Computers, Environment and Urban Systems*, 27(2), 163–180.

Hollick, M. (1984). Who should prepare environmental impact assessments? *Environmental Management*, 8(3), 191–196.

Israel, D.J. and Perry, J. (1991). What is information? in P. Hanson (Ed.), *Information, Language and Cognition*. University of British Columbia Press, 1–19.

JICA (2010). *Guidelines for Environmental and Social Considerations*. JICA.

Lawrence, D.P. (2003). *Environmental impact Assessment: Practical Solutions to Recurrent Problems*. John Wiley & Sons, Inc.

Morgan, R.K. (2012). Environmental impact assessment: The state of the art. *Impact Assessment and Project Appraisal*, 30(1), 5–14.

Munn, R.E. (1975). Environmental impact assessment; principles and procedures. SCOPE report, 5.

Obbard, J.P. *et al.* (2002). Environmental assessment in Vietnam: Theory and practice. *Journal of Environmental Assessment Policy and Management*, 4(3), 267–295.

OECD (1992). OECD Development Assistance Committee — Guidelines on Aid and Environment, No. 1. Good Practices for Environmental Impact Assessment of Development Projects.

Quy, V. (1997). Environmental issues in Vietnam: An overview, in V.P.H. Hinrich Mercker. German Foundation for International Development, Public Administration Promotion Centre, pp. 5–30.

Quyen, P.B. *et al.* (1995). Environmental pollution in Vietnam: Analytical estimation and environmental priorities. *TrAC Trends in Analytical Chemistry*, 14(8), 383–388.

Sinclair, A.J. and Doelle, M. (2003). Using law as a tool to ensure meaningful public participation in environmental assessment. *Journal of Environmental Law and Practice*, 12, 27.

Stephan, M. (2002). Environmental Information disclosure programs: They work, but why? *Social Science Quarterly*, 83(1), 190–205.

Toan, M.T. (2015). Strategic Environmental Assessment and Environmental Impact Assessment in Vietnam. *The 4th National Environment Conference*, Ha Noi.

Toan, M.T. (2016). A proposal of perfectibility of EIA system during appraisal the investment project.

UNECE (2014). *The Aarhus Convention — An Implementation Guide.* UNECE.

WB (1999, revised 2011). *Environmental Assessment. Operational Policy, Bank Procedure and Good Practice 4.01.* World Bank.

Wood, C. (2003). Environmental impact assessment in developing countries: An overview. *Conference on New Directions in Impact Assessment for Development: Methods and Practice.*

Wood, C. (2003). *Environmental Impact Assessment: A Comparative Review.* Pearson Education.

Yousefi-Sahzabi, A. *et al.* (2014). Some thoughts on the notion of environmental information science. *Electronic Green Journal*, 1(37), 1–16.

Part VII

Tourism

https://doi.org/10.1142/9789811262258_0009

Chapter 9

The Different Elasticity of Inbound Tourism Demand in the Mekong Downstream Nations: Evidence from the Chinese Market

Nguyen Hai Quang

Abstract

Although numerous studies have investigated tourism demand's income and price elasticities, prior studies usually estimated the demand from different international markets to one specific country. This chapter determines the price and income elasticity of tourism demand from the primary inbound market (China) to five Mekong downstream nations — Cambodia, Laos, Myanmar, Thailand, and Vietnam to spot the varying influences of these factors. These differences are evidence that in addition to price and income, the destination choice of Chinese tourists to these countries depends on other factors attracting tourists. The results reveal that income level in China positively affects tourism demand in all these five countries, while the impact of relative price on the demand is only found in the case of Cambodia and Myanmar; the effect of substitute prices is only found in Myanmar and Thailand.

Keywords: Inbound tourism demand; Income; Prices; Different influences; Mekong downstream nations.

1. Introduction

Nowadays, many studies have been conducted to determine which factors impact tourism demand and its findings noticed by researchers and policymakers. Researchers applied various techniques, using both qualitative and quantitative research methods to propose tourism demand models. For quantitative research, the most commonly used factors affecting tourism demand include income (e.g., Tea *et al.*, 2013; Li *et al.*, 2006; Seetaram *et al.*, 2016; Dogru and Sirakaya-Turk, 2017) and price (e.g., Song and Li, 2008; Teresa, 2009; Baldigara *et al.*, 2013; Li *et al.*, 2006; Neelu *et al.*, 2016).

While current studies tend to concentrate on measuring the price and income elasticity of inbound tourism demand from different international markets to a specific country, there is a limited number of empirical works comparing the elasticity of demand to individual countries in an area in order to find out the different effects of the factors between countries.

Tourism plays a vital role in leading to the economic growth of many countries, contributing to the development of related services and infrastructure. International tourists bring foreign currencies to destination countries, increase residents' incomes, create jobs, improve their living standards, and contribute to expanding and strengthening international economic relations. Therefore, analyzing inbound tourism demand is crucial, providing practical evidence to assist countries in formulating policies and proposing effective action plans to attract tourists. With the significant contribution of the tourism industry to annual GDP, the lower Mekong countries, including Cambodia, Laos, Myanmar, Thailand, and Vietnam, have also focused on finding sustainable tourism development strategies. These countries have launched tourism policies and have been organizing annual conferences such as the "Development of Mekong sub-region tourism resources workshop" since 2009 with the participation of the World Tourism Organization (UNWTO), Asia-Pacific Regional Tourism Exchange (APTEC), Tokyo Development Training Center, and World Bank. Thanks to their diverse cultural identities, precious history, and beautiful landscapes, these countries have numerous tourist attractions, with dozens of natural and cultural heritages recognized by UNESCO as world heritage sites.

China is the most important international tourism market to Mekong countries. The proportion of Chinese tourists in total international visitor arrivals is high, far exceeding other markets, and increasing continuously, especially from 2015 to 2019 (Figure 1).

The number of Chinese tourists coming to the Mekong countries in 2019 is shown in Table 1. Accordingly, the number of tourists from China is the highest for most of these countries (except Laos, with the number ranked third). Specifically, the total Chinese visitor arrivals is nearly 21 million, accounting for 17.18% (in Myanmar) and up to 35.73% (in Cambodia) of total international tourists. Chinese tourists are from 1.12 times (in Myanmar) to 2.20 times (in Thailand) higher than South Korean tourists, ranking second in 2019. Moreover, China's spending on outbound tourism is the highest globally, reaching 1,850 US dollars/trip (World Tourism Organization, 2019). Therefore, Chinese tourists play a crucial role in the tourism industry of these countries (Table 1).

Given the influence of the Chinese market, it is clear that the Lower Mekong countries should pay attention and add attractive

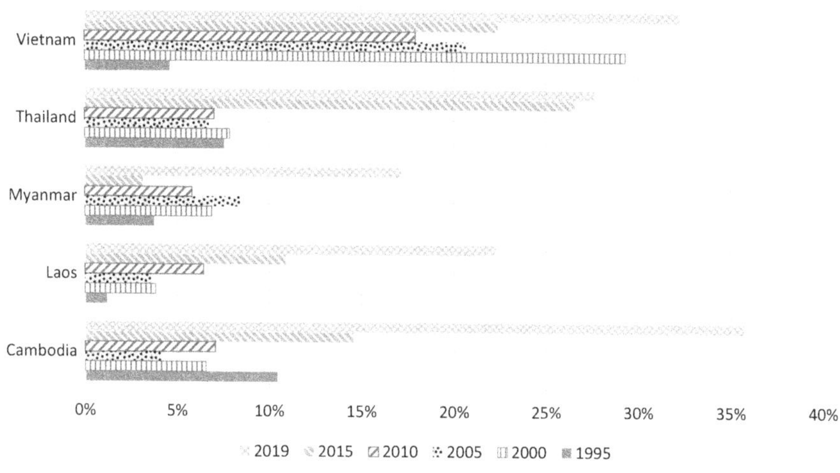

Figure 1: The proportion of Chinese tourists in total international visitor arrivals to the Mekong downstream nations.
Source: Analysis from data of UNWTO and the tourism authorities of the countries.

Table 1: Chinese tourism statistics to the Mekong downstream nations in 2019.

Countries	Inbound Tourist (Million)	From China (Million)	Proportion (%)	Rank	Compared to the Leading Tourism Market (Time)
Cambodia	6.61	2.36	35.73	1	2.60
Laos	4.58	1.02	22.27	3	0.50
Myanmar	4.36	0.75	17.18	1	1.12
Thailand	39.80	10.99	27.63	1	2.20
Vietnam	18.01	5.81	32.24	1	1.35
Total	**73.36**	**20.93**			

Source: Analysis from data of UNWTO and the tourism authorities of the countries.

forces to seduce them. Competition between countries to captivate this enormous market is increasingly fierce among destinations, especially in Southeast Asia, including the Mekong countries (Mai, 2018).

By understanding the factors affecting Chinese tourism demand, policymakers have the foundation for proposing effective ways to attract tourists. Surprisingly, there has been almost no previous research on the price and income elasticity of Chinese Tourism Demand to lower Mekong countries. Based on Song *et al.* (2010) summary of tourism demand articles from 2000 to 2009 and the authors' review from 2010 to the present, the studies were mainly conducted in destinations such as the US, Europe, Australia (Australia and New Zealand), North Asian countries (Hong Kong, China, Korea, Taiwan, Japan) and some other countries such as Thailand, Carbine island, etc. This is the motivation for the authors to exploit this research. This study aims to estimate the different effects of income and price elasticities on Chinese tourism demand in the lower Mekong countries, including Cambodia, Laos, Myanmar, Thailand, and Vietnam. The findings yield both academic and practical contributions, adding to the number of studies on tourism demand.

The following section introduces theoretical foundations and outlines our proposed research model, data collection, and descriptive variables. The chapter then presented data analysis methods, estimated coefficients in the model, and discussed the research results. The article ends with the conclusion.

2. Literature Review and Research Model

2.1. *Literature review*

Tourism has currently become one of the main economic sectors of many countries. Therefore, the identification of factors affecting tourism demand is of interest to both government and researchers. However, the demand model has differences in terms of dependent and independent variables. There are also differences in data collection, research methods, country of origin, and destination pairs.

Specific indicators can measure tourism demand. Song *et al.* (2010) summarized and presented four main groups used as tourism demand proxies: (1) tourist arrivals/number of tourists per population; (2) monetary-related groups such as tourist spending; (3) groups related to the time of travel such as travel days, tourist nights at the destinations; (4) final group relates to travel distance between the country of origin and destination. However, Song *et al.* (2010) showed that tourist arrivals are an appropriate proxy for demand. Similarly, Crouch (1992), through a meta-analysis of 51/80 studies published from 1961 to 1992, showed that visitor arrivals are commonly used in tourism demand studies as the dependent variable. This conclusion was also agreed by Lim (1997) and Song and Li (2008). Song and Li (2008) summed up 53/84 studies published from 1994 to 2004 and concluded that tourist arrivals are appropriate for tourism demand. Precisely, this variable is measured by the total number of tourists coming from one country to another.

Tourism demand is fundamentally a function of certain factors such as income, prices, exchange rates, transportation costs, and marketing expenses (Dogru and Sirakaya-Turk, 2017). On the other hand, Seetaram (2012) also argued that non-economic factors relating to geographical conditions such as climate and culture also affect tourism demand. However, transportation costs are referred to as the additional travel price index because the cost accounts for a large proportion of total travel costs, and high transportation costs may be due to long distances to destinations. Marketing expenditure is rarely used in tourism demand studies due to a lack of available or reliable data (Crouch, 1994a), and the impact of this factor on tourism demand is also shallow (Song and Li, 2008). According to Song and Li (2008), previous studies also used dummy variables to capture the impact of seasonality on demand. With seasonal dummy variables, the researchers could determine breakpoints endogenously and consider the effect of each period on the change of regression coefficients.

On the other hand, Song and Li (2008) also suggested that seasonal dummy variables in the tourism demand model remain controversial regarding its predictive ability. Even though quarterly or monthly data contain richer information than annual data, quarterly and monthly data are limited due to the inaccessibility of detailed data. As a result, most studies tend to use annual data (Song and Li, 2008), which cannot capture the seasonality effect. Word of mouth, in addition, is also used as a factor that influences tourism demand. Tourists, after the end of their trips, return home and spread their express about the destination. In the regression model, this variable is a lagged dependent variable, such as tourist arrivals or travel receipts (Song and Witt, 2003). However, this measurement is quite simple to capture the impact of spreading the destination's information on other visitors' choice behavior (Kumar *et al.*, 2020).

The results of Li *et al.* (2006) concluded that econometric studies on tourism demand indicated tourists' income, travel price from a country i to country j year t (Relative price), and prices of alternative destinations from a country i to country j year t (Substitute price). They are the most important determinants of demand. The impact of these factors is also confirmed through the subsequent synthesis of tourism researches by Song and Li (2008) and is consistent with Lim's conclusions (1997).

According to Crouch (1994a), income is the most critical factor in the tourism demand model. Tourists' income is usually measured through GDP or GNP. Besides, another proxy for income that is rarely used is the Industrial Production Index (IIP) (Dogru and Sirakaya-Turk, 2017). According to Lim (1997), discretionary income is the best measure of income. This data, however, is often unavailable. Researchers often use natural or nominal GDP/GNP data as a suitable proxy for income (Peng *et al.*, 2014). Travel abroad is still considered a luxury good (Crouch, 1994a). Tourists' demands are often sensitive when income changes. In other words, as incomes rise, people tend to increase their overseas travel. Thus, tourism demand for a destination country has a positive correlation with tourist income.

Tourism demand relates to the consumption of goods and services at a destination, tourists are transported across locations, and the consumption of tourism services coincides with production (Kumar *et al.*, 2020). Many studies also showed that price is the main factor affecting tourism demand, including the cost of living at a destination (Relative price) and the cost of living at a competitive destination (Substitute Price). Ideally, private and alternative destination prices should be measured using the tourist price index, a combination of goods and services tourists consume (Martin and Witt, 1989). However, this index is not always available. Moreover, according to Martin and Witt (1989), the difference between the travel price index and the consumer price index is negligible.

Consequently, the consumer price index (CPI) is mainly used to measure relative and substitute prices. Relative and substitute prices are also standardized by the exchange rate, which relates to the currency difference between the country of origin and destination pairs. Moreover, tourists use the exchange rate to compare the price of a destination to the price in their country (Dogru and Sirakaya-Turk, 2017). Dogru and Sirakaya-Turk (2017) also suggested a contradiction in researchers' views when using the exchange rate as an independent variable. Some studies only used standardized prices by an applicable exchange rate, affecting tourism demand (e.g., Song and Witt, 2006; Song and Wong, 2003). At the same time, others used both exchange rates and prices standardized by an applicable exchange rate as independent variables in the research model (for example, Uysal and Crompton, 1985; Martin and Witt, 1989; Qiu and Zhang, 1995; Dogru and Sirakaya-Turk, 2017). However, applying the exchange rate as a separate independent variable raises serious analytical and empirical problems. The exchange rate is used separately as an independent variable that does not convey enough information to compare prices between the country of origin and destination due to the difference in inflation rates can be offset by exchange rates and vice versa (Dogru and Sirakaya-Turk, 2017). Martin and Witt (1989) argued that the exchange rate, independently, is not an appropriate indicator when analyzing the impact on tourism demand.

As such, the factors affecting tourism demand may vary depending on research contexts. However, most studies have shown that inbound tourism demand is strongly linked to economic variables such as income, relative price (prices related to travel services), and substitute price. These variables influence consumer travel decisions. Therefore, the tourism demand function for a specific destination country is given according to Eq. (1).

$$D_t = f(IT_t, PT_t, PS_t) + U_t \tag{1}$$

where

D_t: The quantity of the tourism product demanded at time t
IT_t: Tourists' level of income at time t
PT_t: The price of the tourism product/service at time t
PS_t: The price for substitute destinations at time t
U_t: The disturbance term captures all of the other factors that may influence the quantity of the tourism product demanded at time t

2.2. *The long-run tourism demand model*

The long-run tourism demand model applied in this chapter is based on the theory of direct demand, which assumes that tourism arrivals depend on the income of potential tourists and the tourism relative price level at origin, destination, and substitute destinations (Eq. (2)).

$$LnDT_{j,t} = \beta_{0j} + \beta_{1j} lnIT_t + \beta_{2j} lnPT_{j,t} + \beta_3 lnPS_{j,t} + \varepsilon \qquad (2)$$

where:

$LnDT_{j,t}$: Natural logarithm of tourist arrivals from China to j country in year t

$LnIT_t$: Natural logarithm of income of Chinese tourists in year t

$LnPT_{j,t}$: Natural logarithm of prices of tourism from China to country j in year t

$lnPS_{j,t}$: Natural logarithm of prices of substitute destinations for tourists from China to country j year t

β_{0ij}, β_{1ij}, β_{2ij}, β_{3ij}, and β_{4ij} : The parameters to be estimated

ε: Error term

Because travelers from the original country to different countries' destinations would likely have varying elasticities of demand (Song *et al.*, 2000; Vanegas and Croes, 2000; Kulendran and Witt, 2001; Li *et al.*, 2006; Lim *et al.*, 2008a, 2008b; Gatta and Falzon, 2014), the chapter estimates separately tourism demand for countries in the Mekong downstream from originated China.

The number of arrivals has been commonly used as a proxy for tourism demand (Crouch, 1994; Song and Li, 2008; Untong *et al.*, 2014), and this study also uses it as a reliable demand proxy, consistent with many prior empirical studies on tourism demand (Vanegas and Croes, 2000; Greenidge, 2001; Song *et al.*, 2003a, 2003b; Song and Witt, 2003; Dritsakis, 2004; Lim, 2004; Croes and Vanegas, 2005; Mervar and Payne, 2007; Munõz, 2007; Lim *et al.*, 2008a, 2008b; Song *et al.*, 2010; Lee, 2011; Álvarez-Díaz *et al.*, 2015; Dogru *et al.*, 2017; Ramos *et al.*, 2017).

For the income variable, GDP and GDP per capita have been used to proxy tourist income. In this chapter, real GDP (constant GDP) per capita is also used for income as previous researches (Song *et al.*,

2000; Kulendran and Witt, 2001; Dritsakis, 2004; Lim, 2004; Lee, 2011) because it reflects not only GDP but also annual population size.

For tourism price variable, CPI index is often used as a basis for constructing tourism price data in case there is no data on tourism price (Song *et al.*, 2000, 2003a; Vanegas and Croes, 2000; Song and Witt, 2003; Croes and Vanegas, 2005; Gang Li *et al.*, 2006; Munõz, 2007; Seetaram, 2012; Álvarez-Díaz *et al.*, 2015; Seetaram *et al.*, 2016; Dogru, 2017). The relative price is used in this study as it reflects the cost of living in each country in the Mekong downstream. The formula to calculate the relative price (Mangion *et al.*, 2005; Song and Li, 2008; Munõz, 2007; Seetaram, 2012; Cheng, 2012; Gatta and Falzon, 2014; Seetaram *et al.*, 2016; Dogru *et al.*, 2017; Ramos *et al.*, 2017) is as follows:

$$PT_{j,t} = \frac{CPI_{j,t}}{CPI_{c,t} * ER_{c/j,t}} \tag{3}$$

where

$PT_{j,t}$: Relative price compared with origin China to destination j in year t

$CPI_{j,t}$: The consumer price index (CPI) in destination j in year t

$CPI_{c,t}$: The CPI of China in year t

$ER_{c/j,t}$: The exchange rate of Yuan to country j's currency in year t

There are several alternative destinations for the Mekong downstream nations from China and being identified as relative. They are usually countries with similar travel conditions. Therefore, this study assumes that when considering the travel demand from China to a country in the Mekong downstream, the remaining countries are alternative destinations in this study. The tourism price of intra-regional alternative destinations is also a substitute price and weighted as in the study of Dogru *et al.* (2017) and Ramos *et al.* (2017). The formula for calculating the substitute price is as follows:

$$PS_{c,t} = \sum_{s=1}^{n} W_{s,t} \frac{CPI_{s,t}}{CPI_{i,t} * ER_{i/s}, t} \tag{4}$$

where

$PS_{c,t}$: The substituting country's relative price compared with origin China in year t
$CPI_{s,t}$: The CPI in substitute destinations in year t
$CPI_{c,t}$: The CPI of China i in year t
$ER_{c/s,t}$: The exchange rate of Yuan to country's currency in year t

This study derived from the market share of tourists as shown in the study of Mangion *et al.* (2005), Song and Li (2008), and Ramos *et al.* (2017) to construct a weight for substitute pricing and it is determined by Equation (5) as follows:

$$W_{j,t} = \sum_{j=1}^{m} \frac{TA_{cj,t}}{TA_{c,t}} \tag{5}$$

where

$W_{j,t}$: The weights for substitute j in year t
$TA_{cj,t}$: The tourists from China traveling to country j in year t
$TA_{c,t}$: The total number of outbound tourists to substitute destinations from China in year t

3. Data and Methods

3.1. *Data*

Tourist data from China to Mekong countries downstream were collected from World Tourism Organization (2019) statistics for 1995–2018 and the countries' tourism authorities for 2019. The income per capita of Chinese people, CPI of China and the Mekong countries downstream, the exchange rate between the Chinese Yuan and US dollar, and the exchange rates between Mekong countries downstream's currencies and US dollar collected from data published by the World Bank (2020). Based on these rates, the bilateral exchange rate between the Chinese Yuan and the currencies of the Mekong countries is established. The CPI index is measured based on 1995, which means that the base year for the CPI is 1995, starting with an index number of 100. From these data, relative prices

Table 2: Descriptive statistics variables.

Variable	Country	Mean	Maximum	Minimum	Std. Dev.	Observations
LnDT	Cambodia	11.7397	14.6750	9.7574	1.5580	25
	Laos	11.3163	13.8353	8.3129	1.5009	25
	Myanmar	10.5669	13.5275	8.8941	1.2464	25
	Thailand	14.2959	16.2129	13.1735	1.0643	25
	Vietnam	13.7176	15.5745	11.0452	0.9716	25
LnIT	China	7.8802	9.2362	6.4129	0.9780	25
LnPT	Cambodia	6.6254	7.0543	5.6818	0.4198	25
	Laos	8.8266	9.7493	4.5680	1.6108	25
	Myanmar	6.6678	8.2803	4.4628	1.1564	25
	Thailand	1.6625	1.8275	1.0911	0.1975	25
	Vietnam	8.1675	9.0306	7.1660	0.6859	25
LnPS	Cambodia	7.3332	8.1803	4.9576	0.8133	25
	Laos	7.0957	7.9405	4.9982	0.6975	25
	Myanmar	7.3091	8.1190	5.0008	0.7879	25
	Thailand	8.1706	8.9657	6.8399	0.6826	25
	Vietnam	6.0868	7.5557	2.6814	1.5166	25

Source: Descriptive statistical analysis results.

and substitute prices at substitute destinations for countries in the Mekong downstream are determined by Eqs. (3) and (4). Descriptive statistics of variables (natural logarithms) are presented in Table 2.

3.2. *Methods*

Tourism demand is sensitive to uncertainty derived from crises such as political unrest, natural disasters, and epidemic outbreaks (Araña and León, 2008; Faulkner, 2001; Ritchie, 2004; Untong *et al.*, 2011). Therefore, stationarity tests should be carried out to prevent the phenomenon of spurious regression (Ramos *et al.*, 2017). The estimation of the long-run tourism demand model for inbound tourism from China to each country of the Mekong downstream is carried out through two steps.

Step 1: Unit root and cointegration tests

Unit root test is a standard method of testing stationarity for annual time series data. The literature suggests that the standard stationary tests for annual time series data are the Augmented Dickey–Fuller test (Said and Dickey, 1984), Phillips–Perrson test

(Phillips and Perrson, 1988), and Kwiatkowski–Phillips–Schidt–Shin (KPSS) test (Kwiatkowski *et al.*, 1992). If the time series is not stationary, a cointegration test needs to be conducted to consider the long-term relationship between the variables.

Step 2: Estimate the parameters in the long-term tourism demand model

Suppose time series is stationary at a level. In that case, the long-term tourism demand model parameters will be estimated using the ordinary least squares (OLS) model because OLS regression better captures the impact of time-invariant (stationary) variables. In the case of cointegration variables, techniques to estimate the coefficients of a single equation long-run model will be considered, such as fully modified ordinary least squares (FMOLS) (Phillips and Hansen, 1990), canonical cointegration regression (CCR) (Park, 1992), dynamic ordinary least squares (DOLS) (Stock and Watson, 1993), and ARDL (Pesaran and Shin, 1999). In the estimation process, eliminating will be applied to delete the variables when the statistical tests reveal insignificance and then select the final model.

4. Research Results and Discussion

4.1. *The test results of stationary and cointegration*

The first step comprises the stationarity tests for all variables by the Augmented Dickey–Fuller test. They were tested by both "Intercept" and "Intercept and trend" for the included test in the equation. The unit root test results are presented in Table 3 and suggest that the variables used in the model were stationary at different levels and that at least one independent variable was not stationary at I(0). Therefore, OLS estimation might be a spurious regression (Granger and Newbold, 1974), and a cointegration test is done to consider the long-term relationship among variables (Table 3).

The following proposed step is checking the existence of a long-run relationship among the variables. The cointegration test results

Table 3: Results of stationarity and cointegration test.

Country	LnDT		LnIT		LnPT		LnPS	
	Intercept	Intercept and Trend	Intercept	Intercept and Trend	Intercept	Intercept and Trend	Intercept	Intercept and Trend
Cambodia	I(1)***	I(1)***	I(1)***	I(0)**	I(0)**	I(1)**	I(0)***	I(0)***
Laos	I(1)**	I(0)**	I(1)***	I(0)**	I(1)***	I(1)***	I(0)***	I(0)***
Myanmar	I(2)***	I(2)***	I(1)***	I(0)**	I(1)***	I(1)***	I(0)***	I(0)***
Thailand	I(1)***	I(1)**	I(1)***	I(0)**	I(0)***	I(1)***	I(0)**	I(1)**
Vietnam	I(1)***	I(0)**	I(1)***	I(0)**	I(2)***	I(1)**	I(1)**	I(1)**

Note: ** and *** for significant at 0.05 and 0.01 levels, respectively.

Table 4: Results of cointegration test.

Origin Country	Trace Test	Max-Eigenvalue Test
Cambodia	2	2
Laos	4	1
Myanmar	1	1
Thailand	3	3
Vietnam	2	1

Note: Trend assumption: Linear deterministic trend; the number is the number of cointegrating eqn(s) at the 0.05 level.

in Table 4 by both Trace test and Max-eigenvalue test indicate that although there were different numbers of cointegration eqn(s) at the 0.05 level for each destination country, at least there was one cointegrating eqn(s) at the 0.05 level. Therefore, there is an equilibrium relationship at a statistically significant level of 0.05 among variables for all countries, meaning a long-run relationship among studied variables.

4.2. *Estimated results of the long-run tourism demand model*

Because there were long-run relationships among studied variables, FMOLS method estimation is applied for all countries. Table 5 presents the results of estimating the parameters in the model of long-run tourism demand from China to the Mekong downstream countries.

According to Table 5, in the first estimation step, the Adjusted R-squared in the cases of Cambodia, Laos, Myanmar, Thailand, and Vietnam are 96.63%, 93.62%, 92.72%, 71.71%, and 67.01%, respectively. These results show that the independent variables reflect a high ability to predict dependent variables, and all models are appropriate. The income variable is statistically significant at the 0.01 or 0.05 level for all countries except Vietnam.

Next, the variables with the highest p-value (statistically significant) are deleted first in the revised models. The final revised model

Table 5: Estimation results of the original model.

Variables		Cambodia	Laos	Myanmar	Thailand	Vietnam
LnIT	Coefficient	2.0843	1.5654	0.9332	4.0436	0.2440
	t-Statistic	7.8380***	6.0577***	2.3681**	3.9669***	0.3028
	Std. Error	0.2659	0.2584	0.3941	1.019337	0.8059
lnPT	Coefficient	−1.7245	−0.0297	0.8484	1.7920	0.9771
	t-Statistic	−1.8721*	−0.2706	2.1426**	1.3919	0.8748
	Std. Error	0.9212	0.1096	0.3960	1.287480	1.1169
lnPS	Coefficient	0.2500	−0.0141	−0.9161	−4.8063	−0.0755
	t-Statistic	0.4838	−0.0261	−2.1017**	−2.9359***	−0.6421
	Std. Error	0.5158	0.5403	0.4359	1.637070	0.1175
Constant	Coefficient	4.9331	−0.5865	4.3081	18.829	4.3354
	t-Statistic	1.7769*	−0.3576	2.3777**	4.8589***	1.4025
	Std. Error	2.7762	1.6400	1.8119	3.875240	3.0912
R-squared		0.9637	0.9468	0.9083	0.8254	0.7562
Adj *R*-squared		0.9582	0.9388	0.8945	0.7992	0.7196

Notes: LnDT is dependent variable; ordinary coefficient covariance method.
*, ** and *** for significant at 0.1, 0.05, and 0.01 levels, respectively.

is shown after taking steps to eliminate statistically insignificant variables from high to low until it reaches the statistical significance of 0.05 level. Table 6 presents the results of estimating the parameters of countries in the final revised models.

Table 6 indicates that the adjusted *R*-squared in the models ranges from 73.02% to 96.1%. This means that as the original models, the revised models are appropriate, and the independent variables reflect a high ability to predict dependent variables.

The income variable is statistically significant for the tourism demand function from China to all countries in the Mekong downstream. Besides, the relative price variable is only statistically significant for tourism demand from China to Cambodia and Myanmar. Meanwhile, the substitute price has statistical significance for tourism demand from China to Myanmar and Thailand. The income elasticities of demand from China to the Mekong downstream countries are positive, consistent with other prior studies, ranging from 0.7404 to 2.9561. More specifically, the income elasticities of China's tourism demand to Cambodia, Laos, Myanmar, Thailand, and Vietnam are 2.2378, 1.4284, 0.9332, 2.9561, and 0.7404, respectively. This result means that when per capita income increased

Table 6: Estimation results of the revised model.

Variables		Cambodia	Laos	Myanmar	Thailand	Vietnam
		FMOLS	FMOLS	FMOLS	FMOLS	FMOLS
LnIT	Coefficient	2.2378	1.4284	0.9332	2.9561	0.7404
	t-Statistic	8.7513***	14.1607***	2.3681**	3.4622***	5.0283***
	Std. Error	0.2557	0.1009	0.3941	0.8538	0.1473
lnPT	Coefficient	−1.7636	—	0.8484	—	—
	t-Statistic	−2.7533**	—	2.1426**	—	—
	Std. Error	0.6405	—	0.3960	—	—
lnPS	Coefficient	—	—	−0.9161	−3.0280	—
	t-Statistic	—	—	−2.1017**	−2.3813**	—
	Std. Error	—	—	0.4359	1.2715	—
Constant	Coefficient	5.8463	0.1528	4.3081	15.9038	8.0088
	t-Statistic	2.3498**	0.1895	2.3777**	3.9796***	6.8024***
	Std. Error	2.4880	0.8065	1.8119	3.9964	1.1773
R-squared		0.9644	0.9474	0.9083	0.8021	0.7419
Adj *R*-squared		0.9610	0.9450	0.8945	0.7833	0.7302

Notes: LnDT is dependent variable; ordinary coefficient covariance method.
*, ** and *** for significant at 0.1, 0.05, and 0.01 levels, respectively.

by 1%, Chinese tourism demand to Cambodia, Laos, Myanmar, Thailand, and Vietnam increased by 2.2378%, 1.4284%, 0.9332%, 2.9561%, and 0.7404%, respectively. The relative price elasticity of Chinese tourist demand in the case of Cambodia has a negative value consistent with many previous research's findings on the relationship between demand and relative price. Its value is −1.7636, which means that when the relative price increases by 1%, Chinese tourists' demand for Cambodia decreases by 1.763%.

The income variable is statistically significant for the tourism demand function from China to all countries in the Mekong downstream. Besides, the relative price variable is only statistically significant for tourism demand from China to Cambodia and Myanmar. Meanwhile, the substitute price also has statistical significance for tourism demand from China to Myanmar and Thailand. The income elasticities of demand from China to the Mekong downstream countries are all positive, consistent with most prior studies, ranging from 0.7404 to 2.9561. More specifically, the income elasticities of China's tourism demand to Cambodia, Laos, Myanmar, Thailand, and Vietnam are 2.2378, 1.4284, 0.9332, 2.9561, and 0.7404, respectively.

This result means that when per capita income increased by 1%, Chinese tourism demand to Cambodia, Laos, Myanmar, Thailand, and Vietnam increased by 2.2378%, 1.4284%, 0.9332%, 2.9561%, and 0.7404%, respectively.

The relative price elasticity of the demand for Chinese tourists to Cambodia is negative; by contrast to Myanmar, it is positive, at −1.7636 and 0.8484, respectively. Meanwhile, the elasticity of substitute price has a negative sign for the case of Chinese tourists going to Myanmar and Thailand, respectively −0.9161 and −3.0280.

4.3. *Discussions*

The results indicate that income plays a vital role in Chinese tourism demand to the Mekong downstream countries. Although the income elasticity coefficients vary from country to country, they all positively affect demand and are consistent with a general rule. Specifically, the income elasticity of Chinese demand decreases in Thailand, Cambodia, Laos, Myanmar, and Vietnam. The income elasticity of demand for Chinese tourists to Cambodia, Laos, and Thailand is greater than 1, implying that the demand is income-sensitive and that tourism services from China to these countries can be considered luxury goods. This supports many studies that suggest that most international tourism demand is income elastic (Lee, 2011; Seetaram, 2012; Cheng, 2012; Untong *et al.*, 2015; González-Gómez *et al.*, 2015; Seetaram *et al.*, 2016; Dogru *et al.*, 2017). Meanwhile, the income elasticity coefficient of Chinese tourists to Myanmar and Vietnam is less than 1, so tourism services from China to these countries can be considered necessary goods. Demand is less affected by income. Although not common, this issue is found in some cases such as from the Philippines and Taiwan to Hong Kong (Song *et al.*, 2010); from Japan and Malaysia to Thailand (Chaiboonsri *et al.*, 2010); from the UK to Italy, Portugal and Spain (Gatta & Falzon, 2014); from China to Hong Kong, Macao, Germany, Italy, Canada and USA (Lin *et al.*, 2015); from Singapore and Vietnam to Thailand (Ramos *et al.*, 2017). The different elastic demands can be explained by the attractiveness of destinations and the cost of travel in these countries. Myanmar and Vietnam share a border with China, so transportation costs will be lower than in Thailand and Cambodia. Chinese tourists can arrive by land, which significantly lowers the travel costs. The other two countries, namely Thailand and Cambodia, are far away from China, making tourism to these countries more expensive for Chinese tourists.

The relative price elasticity coefficient is significant for Cambodia with a downward slope, consistent with the general rule, and has an absolute value greater than 1, indicating a highly elastic demand by own price. Meanwhile, it has a positive sign for the destination Myanmar. This issue is also found in many tourism markets such as from the UK to the Republic of Ireland (Song *et al.*, 2000); from Malaysia and Singapore to Thailand (Chaiboonsri *et al.*, (2010); from the Philippines and UK to Hong Kong (Song *et al.*, 2010), from China to Hong Kong (Lee, 2011); from India, Malaysia, Singapore to Thailand (Kraipornsa, 2011); from Taiwan and Japan to Hong Kong (Cheng, 2012); from France, UK, Italy, and the US to Turkey (Dogru *et al.*, 2017). According to Crouch (1996), the sign of price elasticity could be positive if the income effect is strong and/or has a complementary relationship with substitute destinations. However, the income elasticity coefficient in the case of Myanmar is less than 1, which means that the income effect is not strong. However, the negative elasticity (−0.9161) of the substitute price is evidence supporting the favorable elasticity of relative price because it has a complementary relationship with substitute destinations.

A negative sign of the substitute price coefficient for tourists from China to Myanmar and Thailand is an indication that other destinations in the Mekong downstream countries could be additional destinations for these destinations. This sign is also found in markets from the UK to Germany and the US (Kulendran and Witt, 2001); from Korea Republic and the US to Thailand (Song *et al.*, 2003a); from the UK to Italy, Portugal, and Spain (Li *et al.*, 2006); China, Japan, Taiwan, and the US to Hong Kong (Song *et al.*, 2010); France and Singapore to Thailand (Kraipornsak, 2011). This result suggests that Mekong downstream countries compete with each other and cooperate to create transnational trips such as Indochina tourism or Mekong downstream tourism.

The issue of not finding related prices that have been signed for the tourism market from China to Laos, Thailand, and Vietnam and substitute prices have significant effects on the tourism market from China to Cambodia, Laos, and Vietnam in this study. The reason needs to be further researched. It can be explained by the strong income effect that makes the owner and/or substitutes price coefficients not statistically significant, as argued by Dogru *et al.* (2017).

5. Conclusion

China has the highest number of tourists to most Mekong downstream countries, so it plays an essential role in these countries' tourism industry. The study aims to analyze the impact of income, relative price, and substitute price on Chinese tourism demand. Before estimating the coefficients, the unit root test was used to examine the static and cointegration of all of the variables to identify the appropriate estimation method. The analysis of data of 25 years, from 1995–2019, shows that the income of Chinese tourists has a positive impact on demand for the Mekong downstream countries. Traveling from China to Thailand, Cambodia, and Laos can be considered luxury goods, especially to Thailand and Cambodia, while traveling to Myanmar and Vietnam is still necessary. This study found only the impact of relative price on the demand in Cambodia and Myanmar and the impact of substitute price on the tourism demand from China to Myanmar and Thailand. Also, the findings reveal that the effect of own price and substitute price on Chinese tourism demand in the remaining countries of the Mekong downstream is insignificant. Differences in tourism demand elasticity by price and income of China to the Mekong downstream countries are evidence to manifest that in addition to price and income, the destination choice of Chinese tourists to these countries depends on factors attracting tourists to the destination.

The contribution of this study is considered in two aspects. Firstly, from a theoretical perspective, this study enriches the role of income and tourism prices for inbound tourism in terms of destinations in Mekong downstream countries: Cambodia, Laos, Myanmar, Thailand, and Vietnam. From a practical perspective, the study points out that the income elasticities of Chinese tourism demand vary based on origin. The contributions of this study formulate tourism development policies as well as effective plans to attract Chinese tourists. Specifically, strategies for luxury goods in the case of Thailand, Cambodia, and Laos and necessity goods in the case of Myanmar and Vietnam.

Acknowledgment

This research was supported by the Ho Chi Minh City University of Industry and Trade, Vietnam.

Bibliography

Álvarez-Diaz, M., González-Gómez, M., and Otero-Giráldez, M.S. (2015). Research note: Estimating price and income dem and elasticities for Spain separately by the major source markets. *Tourism Economics*, 21(5), 1103–1110.

Araña, J.E. and León, C.J. (2008). The impact of terrorism on tourism demand. *Annals of Tourism Research*, 35(2), 299–315.

Baldigara, T., Štambuk, A., and Mamula, M. (2013). Contribution to e-tourism demand modelling. *Informatologia*, 46(4), 343–352.

Cambodia Ministry of Tourism (2019). Tourism Statistic Report, available at: https://www.tourismcambodia.com/tourist-information/tourist-statistic.htm (accessed March 15, 2020).

Chaiboonsri, C., Siroonjit, J., Sriwichailamphan, T., Chaitip, P., and Srioonchitta, S. (2010). A panel cointegration analysis: An application to international tourism demand of Thailand. *Annals of the University of Petrosani, Economics*, 10(3), 69–86.

Cheng, K.M. (2012). Tourism demand in Hong Kong: Income, prices, and visa restrictions. *Current Issues in Tourism*, 15(3), 167–181.

Croes, R. and Vanegas, M. (2005). An econometric study of tourist arrivals in Aruba and its implications. *Tourism Management*, 26, 879–890.

Crouch, G.I. (1992). Effects of income and price on international tourist demand. *Annals of Tourism*, 19(4), 643–664.

Crouch, G.I. (1994). The study of international tourism demand: A review of findings. *Journal of Travel Research*, 33(1), 12–23.

Diaz, M. and Otero-Giráldez, M.S. (2015). Research note: Estimating price and income demand and elasticities for Spain separately by the major source markets. *Tourism Economics*, 21(5), 1103–1110.

Dogru, T., Sirakaya-Turk, E., and Crouch, G.I. (2017). Remodeling international tourism demand: Old theory and new evidence. *Tourism Management*, 6, 47–55.

Dritsakis, N. (2004). Cointegration analysis of German and British tourism demand for Greece. *Tourism Management*, 25, 111–119.

Durbin, J. and Watson, G.S. (1951). Testing for serial correlation in least squares regression. II. *Biometrika*, 38(1/2), 159–179.

Faulkner, B. (2001). Towards a framework for tourism disaster management. *Tourism Management*, 22(2), 135–147.

Garín-Muñoz, T. (2009). Tourism in Galicia: Domestic and foreign demand. *Tourism in Galicia: Domestic and Foreign Demand*, 1–20.

Gatta, W. and Falzon, J. (2014). British tourism demand elasticities in Mediterranean countries. *Applied Economics*, 46(29), 3548–3561.

General Statistics Office of Vietnam (2018). Socio-economic Situation, available at: http://www.gso.gov.vn/ (accessed March 6, 2020).

Granger, C.W.J. and Newbold, P. (1974). Spurious regressions in econometrics. *Journal of Econometrics*, 2(2), 111–120.

Greenidge, K. (2001). Forecasting tourism demand: An STM approach. *Annals of Tourism Research*, 28(1), 98–112.

Kraipornsak, P. (2011). The world economy, competition, external shocks and demand for international tourist arrivals in Thailand. *International Journal Trade and Global Markets*, 4(1), 93–118.

Kulendran, N. and Witt, S.F. (2001). Cointegration versus least squares regression. *Annals of Tourism Research*, 28(2), 291–311.

Kumar, N., Kuma, R.R., Patel, A., and Shahzad, J. (2020). Modelling inbound international tourism demand in small Pacific Island countries. *Applied Economics*, 52(10), 1031–1047.

Kwiatkowski, D., Phillips, P., Schmidt, P., and Shin, Y. (1992). Testing the null hypothesis of stationarity against the alternative of a unit root: How sure are we that economic time series have a unit root? *Journal of Econometrics*, 54, 159–178.

Laos Ministry of Information, Culture and Tourism (2019). *Statistical Report on Tourism on Laos*, available at: https://www.tourismlaos.org/show.php?Cont_ID=43 (accessed March 8, 2020).

Lee, K.N.H. (2011). Estimating demand elasticities for intra-regional tourist arrivals to Hong Kong — the "bounds" testing approach. *Applied Economics Letters*, 18, 1645–1654.

Lim, C. (1997). Review of international tourism demand models. *Annals of Tourism Research*, 24(4), 835–849.

Lim, C. (1999). A meta-analytic review of international tourism demand. *Journal of Travel Research*, 37(3), 273–284.

Lim, C. (2004). The major determinants of Korean outbound travel to Australia. *Mathematics* and *Computers in Simulation*, 64, 477–485.

Lim, C., McAleer, M., and Min, J. (2008a). ARMAX modelling of international tourism demand. *Mathematics and Computers in Simulation*, 79, 2879–2888.

Lim, C., Min, J., and McAleer, M. (2008b). Modelling income effects on long and short haul international travel from Japan. *Tourism Management*, 29, 1099–1109.

Lin, V.S., Liu, A., and Song, H. (2015). Modelling and forecasting Chinese outbound tourism: An econometric approach. *Journal of Travel & Tourism Marketing*, 32(1–2), 34–49.

Lütkepohl, H. and Krätzing, M. (2004). *Applied Time Series Econometrics*. Cambridge University Press.

Mai, H. (2018). The Chinese tourist market coming to Vietnam and the issues raised in managing Chinese tourists in Vietnam. Institute for Tourism Development Research, available at: http://itdr.org.vn/nghien_cuu/thi-truong-khach-du-lich-trung-quoc-den-viet-nam-va-nhung-van-de-dat-ra-trong-quan-ly-khach-du-lich-trung-quoc-tai-viet-nam/ (accessed 12 January 12, 2020).

Mangion, M.L., Durbarry, R., and Sinclair, M.T. (2005). Tourism competitiveness: Price and quality. *Tourism Economics*, 11(1), 45–68.

Martin, C.A. and Witt, S.F. (1989). Forecasting tourism demand: A comparison of the accuracy of several quantitative methods. *International Journal of Forecasting*, 5(1), 7–19.

Mervar, A. and Payne, J.E. (2007). Analysis of foreign tourism demand for Croatian destinations: Long-run elasticity estimates. *Tourism Economics*, 13(3), 407–420.

Munõz, T.G. (2007). German demand for tourism in Spain. *Tourism Management*, 28(1), 12–22.

Neelu, S., Peter, F., and Larry, D. (2016). Measuring price elasticities of demand for outbound tourism using competitiveness indices. *Annals of Tourism Research*, 56(1), 65–79.

Otero-Giráldez, M.S., Álvarez-Díaz, M., and González-Gómez, M. (2012). Estimating the long-run effects of socioeconomic and meteorological factors on the domestic tourism demand for Galicia (Spain). *Tourism Management*, 33(6), 1301–1308.

Park, J. (1992). Canonical cointegrating regression. *Econometrica*, 60, 119–143.

Peng, B., Song, H., and Crouch, G.I. (2014). A meta-analysis of international tourism demand forecasting and implications for practice. *Tourism Management*, 45, 181–193.

Pesaran, M. and Shin, Y. (1999). An autoregressive distributed lag modelling approach to cointegration analysis. *Econometrics and Economic Theory in the 20th Century*, pp. 371–413. Cambridge University Press.

Phillips, P. and Hansen, B. (1990). Statistical inference in instrumental variables regression with I(1) processes. *Review of Economic Studies*, 57, 99–125.

Phillips, P. and Perron, P. (1988). Testing for a unit root in time series regression. *Biometrika*, 75, 335–346.

Qiu, H. and Zhang, J. (1995). Determinants of tourist arrivals and expenditures in Canada. *Journal of Travel Research*, 34(2), 43–49.

Ramos, V., Untong, A., and Kaosa-Ard, M. (2017). ASEAN's intra-regional tourism demand to Thailand. *Asia Pacific Journal of Tourism Research*, 22(9), 909–921.

Ritchie, B.W. (2004). Chaos, crises and disasters: A strategic approach to crisis management in the tourism industry. *Tourism Management*, 25(6), 669–683.

Said, S. and Dickey, D. (1984). Testing for Unit Roots in Autoregressive-Moving Average Models of Unknown Order. *Biometrika*, 71, 599–607.

Seetaram, N. (2012). Immigration and international inbound tourism: Empirical evidence from Australia. *Tourism Management*, 33, 1535–1543.

Seetaram, N., Forsyth, P., and Dwyer, L. (2016). Measuring price elasticities of demand for outbound tourism using competitiveness indices. *Annals of Tourism Research*, 56, 65–79.

Song, H. and Witt, S.F. (2003). Tourism forecasting: The general-to-specific approach. *Journal of Travel Research*, 42, 65–74.

Song, H. and Wong, K.K.F. (2003). Tourism demand modeling: A time-varying parameter approach. *Journal of Travel Research*, 42, 57–64.

Song, H. and Witt, S.F. (2000) *Tourism Demand Modeling and Forecasting: Modern Econometric Approaches.* Pergamon.

Song, H. and Li, G. (2008). Tourism demand modelling and forecasting — A review of recent research. *Tourism Management*, 29(2), 203–220.

Song, H., Kim, J.H., and Shu-Yang, S. (2010). Confidence intervals for tourism demand elasticity. *Annals of Tourism Research*, 37(2), 377–396.

Song, H., Romilly, P., and Liu, X. (2000). An empirical study of outbound tourism demand in the UK. *Applied Economics*, 32, 611–624.

Song, H., Witt, S.F., and Li, G. (2003a). Modelling and forecasting the demand for Thai tourism. *Tourism Economics*, 9(4), 363–387.

Song, H., Wong, K.K.F., and Chon, K.K.S. (2003b). Modeling and forecasting the demand for Hong Kong tourism. *International Hospitality Management*, 22(2), 435–455.

Stock, J. and Watson, M. (1993). A simple estimator of cointegrating vectors in higher order integrated system. *Economometrica*, 61, 783–820.

Studenmund, A.H. (2006). *Using Econometrics: A practical Guide*, 5th ed. Pearson Education.

Tea, B., Ana, S., and Maja, G. (2013). Contribution to e-tourism demand modelling. *Informatologia*, 46(4), 343–352.

Teresa, G.-M. (2009). Tourism in Galicia: Domestic and foreign demand. *Tourism Economics*, 15(4), 753–769.

The World Bank (2019). World Development Indicators, available at: https://data.worldbank.org/indicator/ (accessed March 11, 2020).

Untong, A., Ramos, V., Kaosa-Ard, M., and Rey-Maquieira, J. (2014). Thailand's long-run tourism demand elasticities. *Tourism Economics*, 20(3), 595–610.

Untong, A., Ramos, V., Kaosa-Ard, M., and Rey-Maquieira, J. (2015). Tourism demand analysis of Chinese arrivals in Thailand. *Tourism Economics*, 21(6), 1221–1234.

Untong, A., Ramos, V., Rey-Maquieira, J., and Kaosa-Ard, M. (2011). Impacts of crisis events on international tourism demand in Thailand (in Thai). *Applied Economics Journal*, 18(2), 45–64.

Uysal, M. and Crompton, J.L. (1985). An overview of approaches used to forecast tourism demand. *Journal of Travel Research*, 23(3), 7–15.

Vanegas, M. and Croes, R. (2000). Evaluation of demand: US tourist to Aruba. *Annals of Tourism Research*, 27(4), 946–963.

Vietnam National Administration of Toursim (2019). Domestic visitors 2000–2018, available at: http://vietnamtourism.gov.vn/2018/index.php/items/13460 (accessed March 6, 2020).

Witt, S. F. and Witt, C.A. (1995). Forecasting tourism demand: A review of empirical research. *International Journal of Forecasting*, 11(3), 447–475.

World Tourism Organization (2019). *Guidelines for the Success in the Chinese Outbound Tourism Market*. Madrid: World Tourism Organization, available at: https://www.e-unwto.org/doi/pdf/10.18111/9789284421138 (accessed March 10, 2020).

Part VIII
Digital Economy

https://doi.org/10.1142/9789811262258_0010

Chapter 10

Digital Transformation Experiences of the World's Top Countries: Experiences for Vietnam

Nguyen Phong Nguyen, Dang Khoa Tran, and Quoc Thy Pham

Abstract

Although Vietnamese digital platform businesses are making great efforts, they are under tremendous competitive pressure from foreign digital platforms, especially those operating across borders, and are facing competition right at their doorstep. Due to an incomplete legal corridor, we currently lack practical tools to fight monopoly, fight unfair competition, and protect Vietnamese businesses in cyberspace. We also lack legal tools to limit harmful forms of mergers and acquisitions, which can negatively impact the market. Besides, the digital economy market has not developed in the right direction. Creating and dedicating the domestic digital market, especially the Government digital market, so that Vietnamese businesses have the opportunity to train and grow to go global has not been implemented effectively.

The policy of creating and prioritizing the domestic digital market, especially the government sector market, to serve as a foundation for Vietnamese businesses to mature before expanding globally, has not yet been implemented effectively

Keywords: Digital economy; Digital platform; Digital transformation; Vietnam business

1. Introduction

Vietnam's digital economy and digital society have developed recently due to good telecommunications and IT infrastructure, comprehensive coverage, and high user density. This is because Vietnamese people are passionate about technology and like to use the highest level of technology in the region, and Vietnam's population is young, well educated, good at math, and hard-working. The Vietnamese also adapt quickly to change. This is Vietnam's advantage regarding digital transformation and the development of a digital economy and society.

We also have great opportunities to develop the digital economy. For the first time, Vietnam is part of the 4.0 industrial revolution — the digital transformation revolution. Vietnam is a large market with a lot of potential for new business models. It also has a large population, a large digital workforce, and a large number of Internet and smartphone users. Large and rapidly growing innovations will create attractive markets for the digital economy. Vietnam is also located at the heart of Southeast Asia, a region considered the center of global digital technology and economic development. COVID-19 is not only a global disaster but also functioned as a catalyst, dramatically accelerating the pace of digital transformation and digital economic development.

Vietnam successfully controlled the COVID-19 pandemic, using the pandemic as a great opportunity for making a breakthrough in the digital economy. We are also receiving the government's attention and fierce direction for digital transformation and economic development, which are shown through many essential documents recently issued.

2. Literature Review

The digital economy and the digital society are closely linked and mutually supportive. They are two inseparable aspects of the digital transformation process, so they often go hand in hand. International analysts and evaluators usually combine these two categories in their research. For example, the European Union combines these two areas in the Digital Economy and Society Index (DESI) to evaluate the development of member countries' digital economy and digital society.

There is no worldwide consensus on the definitions of digital economy, digital society, and digital transformation. Each country, depending on its economic and social development strategy, has different definitions of these terms.

Over the past few years, the conversation has shifted, focusing more on how digital technology, services, products, techniques, and skills are permeating economic sectors. This process is called industry digitalization, which is defined as the digital transformation process of businesses in traditional industries through the use of technology, products, and services. Reflecting this shift, recent research has focused on "digitization" and "digital transformation" (i.e., the ways in which digital products and services are disrupting traditional sectors) to explore various multisectoral digital economy trends (OECD, 2017; UNCTAD, 2017). The Digital Economy Cooperation and Development Initiative Forum of the World Economic Organization (WEF) and G20 countries (2016) stated that the digital economy includes economic activities that use (1) information and knowledge digitalization as a critical factor of production; (2) the modern information network, which is an important operating space; and (3) information and communications technology (ICT) as an important driver of productivity growth and economic structure optimization. OECD refers to the digital economy as the combination of all economic activities that rely on or are significantly enhanced by the use of digital inputs, including digital technology, digital infrastructure, digital services, and data, by all producers, consumers, and governments that use these digital inputs in economic activities. Oxford's Digital Economy Collaboration also refers to the digital economy as "an economy that operates primarily on digital technology, especially electronic transactions conducted via the Internet." Thus, the world is gradually unifying the content of the digital economy, including the core of the traditional ICT sector, along with new economic activities in cyberspace and the application of digital technology and the digital transformation of industries and traditional economic fields. This is especially relevant for developing countries where digital technology has begun to impact traditional sectors such as agriculture, tourism, and transportation.

Bukht and Heeks, in a study by the University of Manchester (2018), found that the definitions of digital economy include the Information and Communications Technology (ICT sector) economy and a category of IT consumption/application. It is this category that differentiates the definitions. From there, they proposed a conceptual framework for the digital economy consisting of three components: (1) core digital economy, (2) narrow-range digital economy, and (3) wide-range digital economy (Digitalized Economy, or economy that digitizes industries and fields).

- **Core digital economy:** Includes hardware manufacturing, information services, software, and IT consulting. This component is the traditional ICT field.
- **Narrow-scope digital economy:** Includes digital services and platform economy based on the core digital economy. The narrow-range digital economy also comprises a part of the sharing economy and the gig economy. This component can be collectively called the internet/platform digital economy
- **Wide-range digital economy:** Includes e-business, e-commerce, industry 4.0 (Industry 4.0), precision agriculture, algorithmic economy, the rest of economics, sharing economy, and an economy loosely linked to the digital economy. This component can be called the digital economy of sectors and fields.

The conceptual framework defining digital economy via three components of Bukht and Heeks is widely accepted in international organizations as well as many countries. The digital economy concepts of the World Economic Forum (WEF) and the organization of G20 countries, the organization of OECD countries, the IMF, UNCTAD, and the European Union, and many countries around the world vary and have different interpretations, but basically agree on the above-mentioned approach. Thus, the scope of the digital economy includes three components: information technology and telecommunications digital economy: includes the information technology industry and telecommunications services; platform digital economy: includes economic activities of digital platforms and information systems, connecting supply and demand through the Internet; and digital economy industry: includes economic activities of the industry, implementing digital technology applications, digital transformation or implementation on digital platforms and information systems connecting supply and demand through information, via the Internet.

3. Research Methods

3.1. *The approach combines theory and practice*

Combining theory and practice is a common approach in theoretical science.

Theoretically, the topic is based on updated international theories for digital economic development. From there, the study builds a theoretical framework for digital economic development suitable for the Vietnamese context, including concepts, components, impact factors, main development directions, and organizational methods. In addition, the topic researches the theoretical basis for digital economic development policies in developed countries in the context of globalization and the 4.0 industrial revolution. Important lessons are gathered from developed countries in the process of implementing the digital economy and the interrelationship between digital government, digital economy, and digital society in a country's digital transformation roadmap. These theoretical contents form an analytical framework to analyze the current situation and propose solutions.

3.2. *Multidisciplinary and multisector approach*

Multidisciplinary research approaches a problem from the perspective of several scientific disciplines. However, each discipline works stereotypically within itself, with very little cross-complementation or synergy in output.

Multidisciplinary, interdisciplinary, and transdisciplinary approaches are inevitable in economic science research. The digital economy is an integral part of a country's economy. Therefore, when researching the digital economy, the topic is approached by placing the digital economy in the general context of economies.

In addition, the multidisciplinary and interdisciplinary approach in the project are carried out as follows:

+ Determine the position of the digital economy in the entire economy.
+ Determine viewpoints on the role of digital economic development in the breakthrough and sustainable development of the economy.
+ Determine the perspective on the level of investment in the digital economy in relation to other economic fields.
+ Determine views on the development trend of the digital economy in relation to other economic fields.
+ Identify perspectives on the interrelationship between the digital economy and other economic fields.

3.3. *Interpretive approach*

A deductive approach is used to determine the theoretical framework for the topic. First of all, we briefly review theories on digital economic development to present concepts of digital economic development. From there, we provide a theoretical, analytical framework for digital economic development in Vietnam. This approach helps give the topic have a solid scientific basis. The topic inherits previously developed scientific knowledge about digital economic development. At the same time, we can apply scientific theories to suit the Vietnamese context and new development trends of technology.

3.4. *Experimental approach*

We research, analyze, and evaluate digital economic practices in Vietnam, thereby providing policy solutions based on the Vietnamese context, combined with experiences of implementing and developing digital economic policies around the world. With this approach, we will explore the methodology and policy tools shared by the studied countries, primarily focusing on (i) good practices, (ii) experiences drawn from current digital economic development orientations and policies, and (iii) knowledge from the success or failure of applied policies to avoid repeating past mistakes.

3.5. *Access to history*

This is a research topic on policy solutions for digital economic development in the domestic and international context. This approach will objectively show an overall picture of historical changes. Certain aspects are analyzed, evaluated, and compared to draw lessons, thereby recommending appropriate directions and solutions.

3.6. *Empirical approach*

All analyses, evaluations, and arguments of the topic must be based on convincing evidence, including the following:

- Scientific knowledge that has been tested and recognized,
- Documents from reliable sources,
- Strict survey data,
- Secondary data from reliable sources,
- Opinions of reputable experts,
- Data processing results from reliable research tools and methods.

4. Experiences of Global Digital Transformation Development

4.1. *The United States*

The United States is one of the world's leading countries in the field of digital economy and information and communications technology (ICT). America's strategy in this area has been formed and developed over many years since information technology and the internet became popular in everyday life. America is a unique country whose policies and environment are open and favorable for creative start-ups. In general, the US's digital economic development environment is based on many factors: the openness of the law, the government's supportive and encouraging policies, venture capital funds, etc. Some aspects of the US's outstanding policy in promoting the digital economy include (1) investing in research and development; (2) investing in start-up and firm development; (3) training human resources; (4) encouraging investment from technology corporations; (5) digital data development policies; (6) policy for developing critical digital technology products; and (7) business associate agreements.

The US has invested heavily in technological research and development, especially in the field of information and communications technology and the digital economy. Many extensive research and development (R&D) projects have been invested in to develop new technologies and improve existing technologies. The US government has also invested billions of dollars in research and development in areas such as artificial intelligence, machine learning, cloud computing, the Internet of Things (IoT), and other technologies to promote the development of the digital economy.

The US also funds research institutes, universities, start-ups, and other organizations to help increase the digital industry's power and innovation. Policies aimed at creating favorable conditions for businesses to invest in research and development, such as reduced tax payments and patent protection policies, have also been applied to encourage investment in industrial technologies and new advanced technologies.

The US has built a robust start-up ecosystem, with many opportunities and resources for start-ups, especially in the technology sector. The US government has applied many policies and support mechanisms for start-ups, such as tax reduction policies and start-up support programs.

The US government has introduced policies to encourage innovation and start-ups in the ICT field. This has created conditions for start-ups and new businesses to be born, thereby promoting the development of the country's digital economy and ICT.

Encouraging digital start-ups and other technology developers can help create new jobs, products, and services. The US has created an excellent start-up environment by providing favorable financial and institutional support for start-ups, as well as protecting intellectual property rights.

The US has a very good education system that trains and develops information and communications technology specialists. This helps the US have a workforce rich in skills and expertise, meeting the needs of the digital economy and ICT.

The US has also invested in training high-quality human resources in the digital economy and ICT sectors, including sponsoring training programs for students, teachers, and adult workers. These programs help provide workers with the latest skills and knowledge to meet the labor market's needs in the digital economy.

The US has encouraged investment from large technology corporations, such as Google, Apple, Facebook, Amazon, and Microsoft, to make essential contributions to the country's digital economy and ICT development.

Large corporations are also encouraged to develop digital infrastructure platforms, including telecommunications networks and other infrastructure, to support digital industrial development.

The US also promotes public–private cooperation in digital economic development. The government and private businesses can collaborate to develop digital and ICT solutions. Some policies, such as tax incentive programs, preferential loan credits, and public–private partnership contracts, can help enhance investment capacity and digital industry development.

The government also makes continuous efforts to create a favorable business environment for the digital economy and promote the development of businesses and the formation of unicorns.

4.2. *Australia*

The Australian government approved the Digital Economy Strategy 2030 in March 2021. Three main pillars of the strategy are (1) creating supporting foundations; (2) building capacity in new technologies; and (3) setting digital growth priorities. In the financial year 2021–2022, Australia spent 1.2 billion dollars on digital initiatives such as AI, new aviation technologies, tax incentives, protection of users' data rights, digital data development, digital skills training, deploying the myGov project, implementing the Electronic Health Record project, deploying the d-ID Digital Identity project, supporting small and medium-sized enterprises in digital transformation through the SMEdx project, promoting digital connection, creating the electronic invoice development project, establishing the ATANM Guarantee, and initiating a project to build a national digital map.

4.3. *The United Kingdom*

The UK has issued a Digital Strategy (UK Digital Strategy) and considers digital technology to be one of the country's most essential fields. The Strategy's ideology and ambition are to create a world-leading digital economy for everyone and ensure that the UK is the best place to start and grow a digital business, test new technology, or undertake cutting-edge research.

The seven pillars of the UK's Digital Strategy are as follows:

- Digital Skills (Aim: stronger digital skills at every level, for everyone, from bringing people online for the first time to attracting and training leading programming talent).
- Digital technology business development environment (Aim: make the UK the best place to start and grow a digital business).
- Transform every business into a digital technology enterprise (Purpose: increase the UK's global competitiveness).
- Data (Aim: unlock the power of data in the UK economy and improve public trust in the use of data).
- Digital infrastructure (Aim: building a world-class digital infrastructure for the UK, with widespread coverage, leaving no one behind, with enough capacity for now and the future).
- Cyber security (Aim: make the UK the safest place in the world to live and work online; give people the confidence to be part

of the digital world, as well as giving the UK a competitive advantage).
- Digital Government (Aim: make the UK government the world leader in serving its citizens online).

Laws/acts/regulations promulgated in the Strategy:

- **Digital skills:** Introduce regulations on the right to enjoy digital skills; develop a Tech Talent Charter to set out key measures that encourage organizations to think differently to support the tech workforce.

Digital technology business development environment: Issue preferential income tax policies for profits earned from patented inventions; reduce taxes for investors buying new shares in small, high-risk, and growing companies. The general ideology is that the regulatory environment is friendly toward innovation and creates a dynamic and flexible intellectual property regime that keeps pace with technological change.

- **Data:** Create legal frameworks that keep pace with new data technologies, support innovative business use of data, and provide protection for people's privacy while sanctioning data protection violations.

Digital infrastructure: Encourage investment in digital infrastructure, promote competition, and establish regulations to help operators build and develop digital infrastructure faster and cheaper. Also, improve consumer market regulation.

4.4. *Japan*

The world is facing global challenges, such as the depletion of natural resources, global warming, and increasing economic disparities. Therefore, ICT must be utilized to the fullest to gain new knowledge and create new values by creating connections between "People and

Things" and between the "real world and Cyberworld" as an effective and efficient means to solve problems in society, create a better life for people, and maintain healthy economic growth.

Big data collected from the process of connecting IoT, combined with AI technology, will create a new resource that reaches every corner of society. As we move to apply new technologies in the new society, the lives of all people will be more comfortable and sustainable, and we will be provided with products and services in specific quantities and at the required times.

To stay ahead of the global trend, "Society 5.0" is presented as a core concept in the 5th Science and Technology Basic Plan, approved by the Japanese Cabinet Office. A version (Japanese Cabinet) was passed in January 2016 and is identified as one of Japan's growth strategies. Society 5.0 or the super smart society is also a core part of the strategy "Investing for the future in 2017: Reform to achieve Society 5.0." Japan is the first country in the world to lead the construction of Society 5.0 — towards a new people-centered society.

- Society 1.0 is defined as groups of hunters and gatherers living in harmony with nature.
- Society 2.0 forms groups based on agriculture, strengthens organization, and builds nations.
- Society 3.0 promotes industrialization through the Industrial Revolution and mass production.
- Society 4.0 is an information society that realizes added value by connecting intangible assets in the form of information networks.
- Society 5.0 is an information society built on Society 4.0, aiming for a prosperous society centered on people.

The goal of Society 5.0 is to create a people-centered society, achieve economic development, and solve social challenges so everyone can enjoy a high-quality, fulfilling life and be comfortable. It is a society that will respond in detail to the different needs of people, regardless of region, age, gender, language, etc., by providing necessary items and services. The key to realizing Society 5.0 is a combination of cyberspace and the real world (physical space) to create new quality, value, and solutions for data, solving various social challenges and problems.

4.5. *Singapore*

The Singapore government approved the Digital Economy Framework for Action in early 2021. The structure of Singapore's Digital Economy Development Program is illustrated in Figure 1. Some key contents of Singapore's Digital Economy Development Action Program include the following:

Goal: to be a leading digital economy and continuously innovate itself.

Three pillars:

(1) **Acceleration:** Strong digital transformation of industries and fields. Focus on the digital transformation of businesses, especially SMEs.

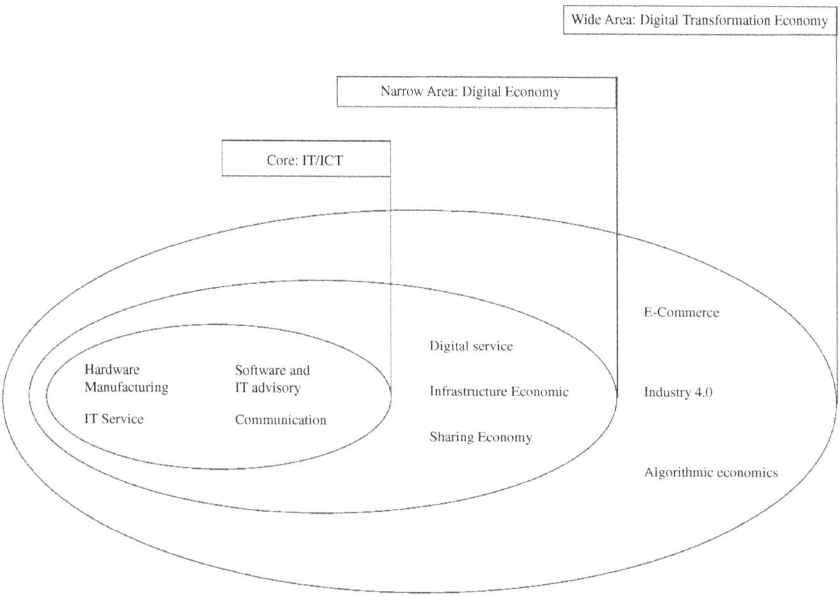

Figure 1: Core, narrow, and wide areas of the digital transformation economy.

(2) **Competition:** Increase national competitiveness with digital platforms (for new integrated ecosystems focused on customer needs) with the ability to go global.
(3) **Innovation:** Developing next-generation digital technology industries to create growth momentum and promote industry digital transformation.

Four foundational elements:

(1) **Human resources:** Continuously train and retrain digital skills and develop digital human resources.
(2) **Research and innovation:** Support businesses in creating and utilizing intellectual property to improve competitiveness and exploit the scientific community's capacity.
(3) **Policies, regulations, and standards:** Ensure that the legal environment and digital economy policies are the most competitive.
(4) **Digital and physical infrastructure:** Ensure that connection networks, platforms, data, and other digital infrastructure best support the digital economy.

Singapore's outstanding digital economic development policies include building digital infrastructure, building smart cities, developing electronic payment, and developing the information and communications technology (ICT) industry.

4.6. *Korea*

Korea has had policies to promote the development of the digital economy and digital society for many years. This is one of the leading countries in the hardware industry. The software and services industries are growing rapidly, especially high-value software and service combinations. The deployment of ecosystems built by large IT vendors, facilitated by an appropriate policy environment, is an important factor in helping Korea achieve great heights in IT industry development.

Since 2019, the Korean government has allocated 1.6 trillion Won (equivalent to 1.41 billion USE) annually to invest in developing the IT industry. This allocation especially focus on manufacturing industry bases on data, network, and artificial intelligence with emerging technology products such as 5G phones, IoT devices, virtual reality, augmented reality, products based on artificial intelligence, data analysis, big data, super high-resolution screens, etc. Support is provided for small and medium enterprises, especially start-up businesses.

Korea's digital economic development policy is reflected in the following highlights: universal internet, developing e-commerce, electronic entertainment development, ICT Convergence Act, 5G Strategy, and New Digital Technology Agreement.

4.7. *China*

China is now a major force in digital technology, both in the domestic and global markets. A report by the McKinsey Global Institute (MGI, 2017) affirms that China is currently a digital technology powerhouse with huge growth potential. According to MGI, China's e-commerce transactions are now larger than the combined figure of the world's top five economies of France, Germany, Japan, the UK, and the US. The total value of China's personal consumer mobile payments since 2016 has reached 790 billion USD, 11 times the figure of the US market. China is currently one of the top three destinations for venture capital investments in areas such as virtual reality, self-driving cars, 3D printing, robotics, drones, and AI. One-third of the 262 "unicorns" in the world today are Chinese, accounting for 43% of the total value of "unicorns" globally.

According to MGI, the three main pillars supporting China's extremely rapid development in the field of digital technology are (i) a huge and youthful market that allows rapid commercialization of business models number, (ii) a rich digital ecosystem expanding beyond the reach of a few giants, and (iii) the government creating conditions and space for digital businesses to experiment and be both investors and consumers of digital technologies.

China has implemented a number of policies to develop the ICT industry:

- Corporate income tax incentives for High and New Technology Enterprise (HNTEs). These incentives target three primary sectors: Electronic information, High technology service industry, and Innovation for high and new technology in traditional industries. The government also provides tax exemption for importing materials for production and interest subsidies on loans from commercial banks.
- Product and goods certification: China applies the CCC (China Compulsory Certificate) certification system that began to be applied in May 2002 and took effect widely from August 2003. This is a type of mandatory certification for many types of products and goods imported or circulated in the Chinese market. The CCC certification system is managed by a state agency, CNCA (Certification and Accreditation Administration of China), under the State Board of Supervision, Inspection and Quality Assurance (AQSIQ — Administration of Quality Supervision, Inspection, and Quarantine).

The government participates as an investor by providing investment capital in production projects (for example, chip production).

- Experience in IoT development: China has actively invested in the research and application of Internet of Things (IoT) technologies, integrating them into urban management, industrial automation, and consumer services
- Experience in developing centralized IT parks: China has developed centralized IT and innovation parks, such as Zhongguancun in Beijing and Shenzhen Hi-Tech Industrial Park, to concentrate technological resources, promote collaboration, and foster start-up ecosystems.

– Experience in attracting foreign investment: China has created favorable conditions for foreign investment through policy incentives, tax breaks, and the establishment of special economic zones that attract international technology companies and capital.

5. Conclusions

From the experiences of the countries analyzed, we can draw the following lessons on digital economic development for Vietnam:

First, many initiatives are increasingly relying on digital technology and can bring many socioeconomic benefits if deployed properly. It is clear that the potential contribution of digital technologies to the economy is huge, especially for Vietnam, which has a large number of internet and smartphone users who are passionate about technology. In this aspect, increasing awareness of the digital economy, its accompanying benefits and challenges, needs attention, especially through information from agencies, factories, and schools.

Second, the government needs to create an experimental space and support businesses in developing the digital economy. Digital technology applications will be a lever to promote innovation among individuals and businesses; thus, encouraging businesses to take full advantage of the power of digital technology must be set as a high priority. Accordingly, the experience of other countries shows that it is necessary to have strong support from the government with an open mindset to "untie" businesses, especially supporting small and medium-sized businesses to promote innovation. The current context shows that if management policies are not open and flexible, domestic enterprises and the national economy will weaken due to competition with foreign enterprises. In particular, Vietnam currently lacks a national plan for digital transformation to facilitate the development of the digital economy and form a national digital infrastructure. The first step is to develop and announce industry planning on information technology applications, which will serve as a foundation for establishing standards of information exchange between agencies and units, thereby ensuring connectivity and system synchronization. In the process of investing in and developing infrastructure based on these IT applications, it is essential to ensure consistency across platforms and compatibility between systems to support effective national digital transformation.

Third, both the government and the private sector need to make efforts to invest in upgrading digital infrastructure as well as modern digital technology solutions to deploy smartly connected digital applications and accelerate non-cash payment applications and e-government efficiency. Regarding digital infrastructure upgrades, the government and businesses need to urgently prepare plans to deploy 5G services to keep up with trends. In the first half of 2019, the world began to see the initial rollout of smartphones equipped with 5G capabilities, offering speeds many times faster than current 4G networks. 5G technology will create a good infrastructure for connecting to the Internet of Things, opening up many great business opportunities for Vietnamese businesses.

Fourth, in addition to improving the digital infrastructure, information technology human resources are critical. IT human resources training programs should attempt to accelerate the cultural integration of information technology education, especially by updating the IT training curriculum in response to emerging technological trends such as the Internet of Things (IoT), AI, and robotics technology. This will make it easier for students to get into this profession as soon as possible, while also promoting training and practice ties between schools and the corporate sector in IT applications.

Acknowledgments

This research was conducted, completed, and financially supported by the University of Economics Ho Chi Minh City (UEH), Vietnam.

Bibliography

AmCham. (2018). Workshop on Digital Economy and Cybersecurity Policy in Vietnam. The American Chamber of Commerce in Hanoi.

Budde, P. (2017). Singapore – Fixed Broadband Market, Digital Economy and Digital Media – Statistics and Analyses. Paul Budde Communication Pty Ltd.

Central Economic Committee. (2017). National Industrial Development Policy, National Economics University Publisher.

Central Institute for Economic Management Research. (2018). Research Topics on Digital Economic Development.

Deutsche Bank Research (DBR). (2015). Industry 4.0: China seizes an outstanding opportunity in the Year of Innovation, Talking point archive, DB.

He, Y. (2017). How China is preparing for an AI-power future, Research Paper, Wilson Centre, June/2017.

Institute for Security and Development Policy (ISDP). (2018). Made in China 2025: Backgrounder, June 2018, http://www.isdp.eu/.

Karabegovic, I. (2017). The role of 'Industry 4.0' in the modernisation of industrial production in China. *Journal of Scientific and Engineering Research*, 9(4), 177–186.

McKinsey Global Institute (MGI) (2017). China's digital economy: A leading global force, Discussion Paper, August, McKinsey & Company.

Ministry of Information and Communications. (2022a). Report on Building a Strategy for Developing Vietnam's Digital Economy and Digital Society.

Ministry of Information and Communications. (2022b). Report on Building a Strategy for Developing Vietnam's Digital Technology Industry.

MTI. (2017). The Digital Economy in Singapore. Ministry of Trade and Industry, Singapore. https://www.mti.gov.sg/ResearchRoom/SiteAssets/Pages/Economic-Survey-of-Singapore-Third-Quarter-2017/BA_3Q17.pdf.

OECD. (2017). OECD Digital Economy Outlook 2017. OECD Publishing, Paris. http://dx.doi.org/10.1787/9789264276284-en.

UNCTAD. (2017). The New Digital Economy and Development. United Nations Conference on Trade and Development, http://unctad.org/en/PublicationsLibrary/tn_unctad_ict4d08_en.pdf.

World Economic Forum (WEF). (2018). Readiness for the Future of Production, Report 2018, Geneva, Switzerland.

https://doi.org/10.1142/9789811262258_0011

Chapter 11

VR and AR in Vietnam: Theoretical Foundations and Marketing Applications

Thuy Trang Thi Pham and Xuan Vinh Vo

Abstract

This study examines the incorporation of virtual reality (VR) and augmented reality (AR) in enhancing customer interaction and marketing strategies, emphasizing Vietnam's rapidly evolving digital landscape. The theoretical framework incorporates multisensory integration, psychological theories (flow theory and situated cognition theory), and neurophysiological mechanisms. Grounded in Gibson's work, multisensory integration explores how visual, auditory, and haptic stimuli heighten user immersion in VR environments. Psychological theories highlight how flow and contextual learning foster deeper user interaction, while neurophysiological studies utilize tools like EEG and GSR to understand cognitive and emotional engagement. The paper also discusses practical applications of VR/AR in Vietnam's marketing sector, particularly across the pre-purchase, purchase, and post-purchase phases. With a focus on Vietnam's National Digital Transformation Program and infrastructure developments, the study identifies the key opportunities and challenges in AR/VR adoption, offering insights into the future of these technologies in Vietnam's consumer market.

Keywords: Virtual Reality; Augmented Reality; Consumer marketing; Vietnam; Digital transformation.

1. Introduction

Virtual Reality (VR) is a fully immersive, computer-generated simulation of a three-dimensional environment where users can explore and interact using specialized hardware such as headsets and controllers. VR typically replaces the physical environment entirely, offering users an interactive and fully immersive experience. In consumer marketing, VR is used to simulate product experiences, such as virtual tours in real estate or virtual test drives in the automotive industry.

Augmented Reality (AR), by contrast, blends virtual content with the physical world by overlaying digital elements onto a user's real-time view of their environment. AR enhances reality rather than replacing it, often through devices like smartphones or AR glasses. In marketing, AR is used to allow customers to visualize products in real-world settings, such as virtual try-ons in fashion or virtual furniture placement in home goods.

In the digital era, Virtual Reality (VR) and Augmented Reality (AR) have emerged as disruptive technologies with the potential to reshape industries globally. Defined as immersive, computer-generated experiences (VR) or the overlay of digital elements onto the physical world (AR), these technologies offer novel ways to engage consumers and enhance marketing strategies. Since the early 2010s, VR/AR technologies have steadily moved from niche applications in gaming and entertainment to mainstream adoption in areas such as retail, real estate, tourism, and education. By creating interactive, sensory-rich environments, VR/AR can significantly influence consumer behavior, offering personalized and immersive experiences that deepen engagement and increase brand loyalty.

The urgency of exploring VR/AR in consumer marketing is particularly pronounced in emerging markets like Vietnam. Driven by a young, tech-savvy population and government policies that foster innovation in the Fourth Industrial Revolution, Vietnam, one of Southeast Asia's fastest-growing economies, is undergoing rapid digital transformation. Recognizing the strategic importance of emerging technologies, the Vietnamese government has launched several initiatives to promote the adoption of VR/AR technologies as part of its broader vision for digital transformation and smart cities. Central to this effort is the National Digital Transformation Program to 2025, with a Vision to 2030, which seeks to integrate digital technologies across all sectors of the economy, including VR/AR, artificial intelligence (AI), and 5G.

The Ministry of Planning and Investment established the Vietnam National Innovation Center (NIC) to support the development of new technologies, including VR/AR, with a focus on fostering innovation and entrepreneurship, in alignment with this national strategy. The government has also emphasized the role of 5G networks in enabling high-speed data transfer, which is critical for delivering seamless, immersive VR/AR experiences. The launch of 5G services by Viettel and VNPT in major cities like Hanoi and Ho Chi Minh City reflects the government's commitment to building the digital infrastructure needed to support VR/AR applications (Nguyen and Nguyen, 2023).

The Prime Minister's 2017 Directive No. 16/CT-TTg, which prioritizes the development of smart cities, digital transformation, and the adoption of advanced technologies like VR/AR in key sectors like tourism, real estate, education, and retail, laid the foundation for Vietnam's strategy to embrace the Fourth Industrial Revolution. The Vietnam Smart City Development Plan 2025 complements these efforts by incorporating VR/AR into urban planning and public services, thereby accelerating the adoption of these technologies throughout the country (Vo, 2021).

Despite this progress, there remains a significant gap in the academic literature on the application of VR/AR technologies in Vietnam. Global studies have extensively explored the potential of VR/AR in consumer marketing, but it is crucial to examine the adoption and adaptation of these technologies in Vietnam's unique socioeconomic and cultural context. To fully understand how these technologies can be adapted to Vietnam's socioeconomic context, further studies are needed, particularly in consumer behavior and technology adoption. This is especially important as Vietnamese companies, from e-commerce platforms to real estate developers, increasingly utilize VR/AR to enhance consumer experiences, streamline operations, and differentiate themselves in a competitive marketplace.

2. Theoretical Framework

2.1. *Multisensory integration in VR*

Gibson (1966) first introduced the concept, emphasizing the significance of human perception of their environment through the integration of multiple senses. Gibson's theory provides the basis for understanding how VR leverages these sensory inputs to create a sense of presence.

Multisensory integration is a core component of Virtual Reality (VR) experiences, where visual, auditory, and haptic modalities combine to create an immersive environment that heightens user engagement. Visual stimuli play a foundational role by providing the primary interface through which users perceive and navigate virtual environments. Technologies such as advanced rendering systems offer photorealistic simulations that replicate the real world, improving the sense of presence (Flavián *et al.*, 2021). Coupled with auditory input, which spatially matches the virtual environment, these sensory cues enhance realism. Sound is particularly important in creating emotional responses, reinforcing the sense of immersion by guiding attention and emotional tone.

Haptic feedback, which simulates the sensation of touch, further deepens immersion by allowing users to physically interact with virtual objects. This feedback can range from subtle vibrations to sophisticated force-feedback systems that mimic the texture or weight of objects. Studies have demonstrated that the integration of these sensory inputs enhances both the psychological presence and emotional engagement of users, significantly improving their overall experience in VR. Together, the combination of these sensory modalities provides a more complete and engaging virtual experience, which is critical for applications in marketing, training, and entertainment.

A recent study by Flavián *et al.* (2021) introduced the element of scent into VR experiences, further demonstrating how integrating additional sensory inputs enhances immersion. This study showed how congruent sensory inputs, such as matching aroma with visual content, significantly heighten user engagement by enhancing the realism of the virtual environment. This is critical in areas like marketing, where creating an engaging and emotionally resonant experience is paramount.

2.2. *Psychological theories*

Understanding how users interact with VR environments requires the application of cognitive and behavioral theories. One key framework is Flow Theory, which explains how users enter a state of deep focus and immersion, often referred to as "flow," during optimal experiences. Flow occurs when users feel fully absorbed in the activity, lose track of time, and experience a high level of enjoyment. The seamless integration of multisensory inputs and the interactivity of the virtual environment facilitate flow in the context of VR. Users who achieve flow in VR are more likely to engage deeply with the content, leading to improved satisfaction and engagement.

Situated cognition theory (Hilken *et al.*, 2017) is another relevant framework that asserts the embeddedness of knowledge in the context of its use. In VR, users learn and make decisions based on the interactions they have with the virtual environment, which mirrors real-world experiences. This theory suggests that the virtual environment's design should align with users' real-world needs and contexts to foster meaningful engagement. In marketing, for example, AR applications allow consumers to interact with virtual products in their real-world environments, making product evaluations more intuitive and personalized (Hilken *et al.*, 2017).

2.3. *Neurophysiological theories*

Neurophysiological mechanisms can analyze the impact of VR on brain function, focusing on how VR stimulates cognitive and emotional responses. The first major breakthrough in measuring brain activity came from Berger (1929), who developed the electroencephalogram (EEG) to track brainwave activity. This technology remains a cornerstone in studying VR's impact on the brain.

Using tools like electroencephalography (EEG), galvanic skin response (GSR), and functional magnetic resonance imaging (fMRI), researchers can measure brain activation and physiological responses during VR tasks. These techniques provide real-time data on how users process sensory information, make decisions, and react emotionally in virtual environments (Kumar *et al.*, 2021).

In VR settings, researchers frequently use EEG to monitor neural engagement and cognitive load. Studies show that EEG can detect changes in brain wave patterns when users interact with VR environments, helping researchers assess levels of attention, focus, and emotional arousal. GSR, which measures skin conductivity in response to emotional stimuli, can provide additional insights into how VR experiences trigger emotional reactions, such as excitement or anxiety. Combining these techniques allows for a comprehensive understanding of how VR influences the brain's cognitive and emotional centers, ultimately improving the design of virtual experiences to maximize engagement and user satisfaction.

3. Applications of VR/AR in Consumer Marketing

3.1. *Pre-purchase stage*

VR/AR serves as a powerful tool for brand engagement during the pre-purchase phase, enabling consumers to interact with products in innovative ways. Virtual showrooms, product demonstrations, and AR-enhanced catalogs are just a few of the applications that have gained traction in industries like automotive, fashion, and beauty.

In addition to enhancing consumer interaction, VR/AR technologies significantly influence purchasing decisions by allowing potential customers to experience products more tangibly. This immersive engagement reduces uncertainty and increases confidence in their choices. For example, in the automotive industry, VR allows users to virtually "test drive" a car from the comfort of their homes, while AR-enabled apps in fashion let consumers visualize how clothing or accessories would look on them in real time. Similarly, in beauty, AR apps enable users to try on makeup or skincare products without physically applying them. These applications not only enhance the customer experience but also streamline the decision-making process, making it more convenient and personalized (Kim and Forsythe, 2008; Scholz and Smith, 2016).

3.2. *Purchase stage*

The purchase phase is where VR/AR applications can drive immediate sales by enhancing the retail experience. AR is particularly effective in brick-and-mortar retail environments, where it provides real-time product information, personalized recommendations, and virtual fitting rooms.

In the purchase phase, VR/AR not only improves the retail experience but also bridges the gap between online and offline shopping. For instance, AR can assist customers in making faster decisions by providing instant access to customer reviews, pricing comparisons, and product details through interactive displays. In physical stores, AR mirrors or apps allow consumers to visualize products such as furniture in their homes or try on different clothing styles without the need to enter a fitting room, increasing both convenience and satisfaction. Additionally, VR-based store environments in e-commerce allow users to explore virtual stores as if they were physically there, offering a more dynamic and engaging experience compared to traditional online shopping (Tom Dieck & Han, 2022). Research has shown that AR can significantly improve purchase intentions by reducing uncertainty, increasing engagement, and making the shopping experience more enjoyable.

3.3. *Post-purchase stage*

Post-Purchase Stage Traditional marketing strategies often overlook the post-purchase phase of the customer journey, but VR/AR presents new opportunities to boost customer loyalty and satisfaction. Companies can use these technologies to provide interactive product tutorials, personalized customer support, and even gamified experiences that keep customers engaged long after their initial purchase.

The post-purchase stage is crucial for fostering long-term customer relationships, and VR/AR can play a significant role in enhancing customer retention. Through VR-based tutorials or AR-enhanced instructions, companies can offer customers a more engaging way to learn how to use products, reducing frustration and ensuring greater satisfaction with their purchase. Additionally, AR can enable real-time customer support by allowing customers to visualize troubleshooting steps or receive remote assistance through augmented displays. Gamification, such as AR-based loyalty programs or VR experiences that reward customers for continued interaction, helps brands maintain top-of-mind awareness and can lead to increased repeat purchases and brand advocacy (Hilken *et al.*, 2017). By leveraging these technologies, businesses can cultivate a more immersive and satisfying post-purchase experience that strengthens customer loyalty.

4. Technological Advances Driving VR/AR in Marketing

4.1. *5G networks*

The deployment of 5G networks represents a fundamental advancement in enabling seamless VR/AR experiences by providing high-speed data transmission and low latency, which are critical for real-time interactions. In marketing, 5G allows for more fluid and immersive experiences, which are essential for campaigns that rely on VR/AR to engage consumers. Nguyen and Nguyen (2023) emphasize the role of 5G in promoting VR/AR applications in Vietnam, particularly in the retail and tourism sectors. Similarly, illustrate how 5G-enabled VR experiences in South Korea have transformed the entertainment industry by facilitating real-time, immersive virtual experiences. Additionally, Xu (2021) highlights how 5G has accelerated the adoption of AR/VR in China's retail sector, enabling virtual try-ons and interactive product showcases.

The incorporation of 5G enhances the functionality of VR/AR in marketing by ensuring uninterrupted and high-quality experiences, which are crucial for maintaining consumer engagement and satisfaction.

4.2. *Artificial intelligence (AI) integration*

The global proliferation of wearable VR/AR devices is expanding the reach of these technologies across a wider demographic. Wearables such as smart glasses, headsets, and AR-enhanced smartphones are becoming more affordable and accessible, allowing for the democratization of AR/VR experiences. AI has become integral to VR/AR in marketing, enabling personalized and dynamic content generation that enhances the relevance and effectiveness of marketing campaigns. AI-driven algorithms analyze consumer behavior to deliver customized VR/AR experiences, increasing engagement. Xu (2021) discusses the optimization of AR/VR experiences in China's retail sector through AI, highlighting its role in tailoring virtual interactions to individual consumer preferences. Furthermore, Scholz and Smith (2016) demonstrate how AI contributes to the design of immersive AR experiences that maximize consumer engagement by adapting content to user behavior. Kim and Forsythe (2008) explore how AI-powered virtual try-on technology enhances online shopping by offering personalized recommendations in virtual environments.

4.3. *Wearable devices*

Wearable devices such as AR glasses and VR headsets have become more accessible and affordable, broadening the reach of VR/AR technologies in marketing. These devices allow users to interact with virtual content hands-free, making the experience more immersive and engaging. Yeo *et al.* (2022) explore the use of wearable AR devices in healthcare and education in Singapore, demonstrating their effectiveness in creating highly interactive experiences. Tran and Do (2021) in Vietnam demonstrate the integration of wearable VR devices into marketing campaigns to enhance consumer engagement in virtual environments. Additionally, Tom Dieck and Han (2022) show that wearable VR devices enhance marketing effectiveness by providing more immersive and user-friendly experiences, particularly in retail.

4.4. *Cloud computing*

Another crucial technological enabler is cloud computing, which enables the scaled delivery of VR/AR applications without the need for high-end hardware, thereby enhancing accessibility. Cloud-based solutions enable real-time updates and collaborative experiences, making them ideal for marketing campaigns that require constant content refreshment and adaptation. Lee *et al.* (2020) highlight how cloud computing supports 5G-enabled VR applications in South Korea, allowing for broader access to immersive experiences. Gatter and Hodkinson (2018) discuss the role of cloud computing in improving the scalability and efficiency of VR/AR marketing by enabling seamless updates and enhanced performance. Pantano and Servidio (2012) investigate the use of cloud-based VR/AR solutions in retail, which enable the creation of innovative virtual showroom experiences.

4.5. *Advances in graphics and rendering*

Significant advancements in graphics and rendering techniques, such as ray tracing and photorealistic simulations, have greatly enhanced the realism of VR/AR environments. In marketing, high-quality visuals are essential for creating convincing and engaging experiences that can influence consumer behavior. Scholz and Smith (2016) emphasize that improved graphics in AR environments create more immersive experiences, leading to higher consumer engagement. (Tom Dieck & Han, 2022) further demonstrate that advancements in rendering techniques increase the realism and immersion of VR experiences, making them more impactful for marketing purposes. Kim and Forsythe (2008) also explore how realistic virtual try-ons improve customer satisfaction and influence purchase decisions, underscoring the importance of advanced graphics in creating effective VR/AR marketing experiences.

5. Applications and Research Context of VR/AR in Vietnam

5.1. *Vietnam's technological landscape and policy support*

Government initiatives that prioritize digital transformation and innovation are driving the rapid evolution of Vietnam's technological landscape and policy support. A cornerstone of this strategy is the National Digital Transformation Program from 2025 to 2030, which aims to integrate digital technologies such as AR/VR, artificial intelligence (AI), and 5G across all sectors of the economy. The Vietnam Smart City Development Plan, part of this larger national strategy, outlines the use of AR/VR in urban planning, infrastructure development, and public services. Smart cities aim to optimize urban management, provide real-time data for urban planning, and enhance citizen engagement by incorporating immersive technologies.

Moreover, the government's Fourth Industrial Revolution (4IR) strategy, outlined in Directive No. 16/CT-TTg, emphasizes the importance of adopting advanced technologies like AR/VR to enhance national competitiveness. Vietnam's focus on smart city development has placed AR/VR at the center of efforts to modernize urban infrastructure, with major cities like Hanoi and Ho Chi Minh

City implementing projects that use AR for traffic management, environmental monitoring, and public safety (Nguyen and Nguyen, 2023). These government-backed initiatives ensure that Vietnam continues to lead in the digital transformation race in Southeast Asia, creating fertile ground for AR/VR applications.

5.2. *Industry adoption of VR/AR in key sectors*

Vietnam's e-commerce, tourism, and real estate sectors have been at the forefront of adopting VR/AR technologies to enhance customer experiences. For instance, Vincom Retail has implemented AR in its malls to create interactive store displays and virtual fitting rooms that allow consumers to try on products digitally (Nguyen and Vu, 2021). Similarly, real estate companies like Vinhomes are utilizing VR to offer virtual property tours, enabling customers to view and explore properties remotely, a practice that became especially popular during the COVID-19 pandemic (Le and Pham, 2020).

The tourism industry is also leveraging VR/AR to create immersive experiences for potential visitors. The Vietnam National Administration of Tourism (VNAT) has been a pioneer in using VR tours to promote destinations such as Halong Bay, Hoi An, and Sapa. The design of these virtual experiences mimics on-the-ground exploration, enabling tourists to preview sites before booking trips (Phan, 2022).

5.3. *Academic research and development*

Vietnamese universities and research institutes are actively exploring the use of VR/AR technologies across various disciplines in the academic sphere. FPT University and RMIT University Vietnam are leading research on AR/VR applications in education and corporate training. FPT University, in collaboration with international partners, has developed neuro-marketing labs to study consumer behavior in VR environments using tools such as eye-tracking and EEG (Tran and Do, 2021). These initiatives highlight Vietnam's growing role in global VR/AR research and innovation.

In addition to higher education, vocational training centers in Vietnam are adopting AR/VR for skills training in fields such as automotive repair, healthcare, and construction. These immersive technologies provide hands-on, risk-free learning experiences, which have proven to be effective in improving skill acquisition and retention (Vu, 2022).

6. Discussion and Implications

6.1. *Challenges for AR/VR adoption in Vietnam*

6.1.1. *Infrastructure and technology gaps*

Despite significant improvements in Vietnam's digital infrastructure, particularly with the rollout of 5G networks, there are still technological gaps that could hinder the full adoption of AR/VR technologies. Rural areas and smaller cities often lack the high-speed internet connections required to support immersive VR/AR experiences, limiting the reach of these technologies primarily to urban centers like Hanoi and Ho Chi Minh City (Nguyen and Nguyen, 2023). Additionally, the cost of high-end VR/AR hardware, such as headsets and wearable devices, remains prohibitive for many consumers and businesses in Vietnam, especially for small and medium-sized enterprises (SMEs) that dominate the business landscape.

6.1.2. *High development costs and limited expertise*

The development of quality AR/VR applications requires significant investment in software development, content creation, and 3D modeling, areas in which Vietnam is still building its expertise. While large enterprises can afford the high initial costs associated with developing custom VR/AR platforms, smaller companies may struggle to justify the expense, especially in the absence of immediate returns. Furthermore, the lack of local expertise in advanced VR/AR design and development remains a significant barrier. Although universities and vocational institutions are beginning to offer training in these areas, the industry is still in its nascent stages, and finding qualified professionals can be challenging (Tran, 2022).

6.1.3. *Privacy and data security concerns*

As with many emerging technologies, AR/VR presents potential risks related to data privacy and security. VR/AR applications often collect personal data, such as biometric information, location data, and user interactions, to provide personalized experiences. Concerns arise regarding the storage, management, and protection of the data. Although the 2019 introduction of Vietnam's cybersecurity law addresses some of these concerns, consumers still harbor apprehensions about sharing personal data with companies, particularly as the country's cybersecurity regulations continue to evolve (Nguyen and Vu, 2021).

6.2. *Opportunities for AR/VR expansion in Vietnam*

6.2.1. *Young, tech-savvy population*

Vietnam boasts a young and digitally savvy population, with over 70% of the population under the age of 35. This demographic is highly receptive to new technologies and more willing to engage with digital experiences like VR/AR. With high levels of smartphone penetration and increasing internet access, Vietnam is well positioned to adopt immersive technologies in both consumer and enterprise settings. E-commerce platforms like Tiki, Lazada, and Shopee have already integrated AR features that allow consumers to virtually try on products, showing that tech adoption is well on its way, particularly among younger consumers (Le, 2023).

6.2.2. *Government support and policy initiatives*

The Vietnamese government has demonstrated proactive support for the development and adoption of AR/VR technologies. Policies such as the National Digital Transformation Program and the Vietnam Smart City Development Plan explicitly mention the role of

AR/VR in driving economic growth, particularly in education, urban planning, real estate, and tourism. These initiatives provide a favorable regulatory environment for businesses to experiment with and implement AR/VR solutions. Furthermore, the Vietnam National Innovation Center (NIC) offers grants and incentives for tech startups focusing on immersive technologies, making it easier for companies to develop VR/AR applications.

6.2.3. *Expanding into new sectors: Agriculture and manufacturing*

Beyond the typical sectors like retail and tourism, there are significant untapped opportunities for AR/VR technologies in Vietnam's agriculture and manufacturing sectors. AR in agriculture enables remote monitoring of crop conditions and virtual training on best practices for farmers, thereby boosting productivity and efficiency. The ability to visualize weather patterns, soil quality, and crop growth in real time through AR applications could revolutionize smart farming in rural Vietnam, where agriculture remains a critical part of the economy (Tran and Do, 2021).

Similarly, manufacturing, a rapidly expanding industry in Vietnam, can benefit from VR technologies to train workers in factory operations, machine repair, and safety protocols. These immersive simulations can reduce the risks associated with traditional on-site training while ensuring workers acquire the necessary skills more efficiently. The potential of AR-based remote maintenance could also revolutionize how manufacturers maintain equipment, reducing downtime and improving operational efficiency. These applications align with Vietnam's broader industrial modernization goals, as outlined in its Fourth Industrial Revolution strategy.

6.3. *Implications for future research and practice*

To bridge the digital divide, future studies should investigate how to adapt VR/AR to rural environments with limited infrastructure.

Addressing this issue is crucial to ensuring the equitable distribution of technological benefits across the country.

Additionally, businesses need to collaborate with educational institutions to develop local expertise in AR/VR technologies. By fostering partnerships between universities and tech firms, Vietnam can build a skilled workforce that is capable of innovating in this rapidly evolving space (Tran and Do, 2021).

From a regulatory perspective, data privacy and ethical considerations need further exploration. As AR/VR applications become more prevalent, companies must adopt transparent practices for data collection and usage. Furthermore, there is a need to investigate the potential psychological effects of prolonged VR use, including its impact on mental health and consumer behavior. Addressing these ethical concerns will help build consumer trust and encourage wider adoption of immersive technologies.

Despite significant challenges, the Vietnamese market has the potential to leverage AR/VR technologies, especially with government support and a young, digitally savvy population. By addressing infrastructural gaps, privacy concerns, and workforce limitations, Vietnam can emerge as a leader in AR/VR innovation in Southeast Asia.

7. Conclusion

Since the publication of Wedel *et al.* (2020), VR/AR technologies have continued to advance, offering new opportunities for consumer engagement and marketing strategies. The integration of neurophysiological measures, 5G networks, AI-driven personalization, and wearable devices has expanded the potential of VR/AR in consumer marketing, making these technologies more effective and accessible.

In Vietnam, the rapid adoption of VR/AR in industries such as retail, tourism, and education demonstrates the country's readiness to embrace digital transformation. While challenges such as privacy concerns, cost barriers, and user adoption remain, the future of VR/AR in Vietnam is promising, with significant potential for growth and innovation.

As the field of VR/AR research continues to evolve, scholars and practitioners must explore new avenues for understanding how these technologies influence consumer behavior. By addressing cultural differences, long-term impacts, and ethical considerations, future research can help businesses harness the full potential of VR/AR to create meaningful and lasting consumer experiences.

Acknowledgments

This research was supported by the University of Economics Ho Chi Minh City (UEH), Vietnam.

Bibliography

Berger, H. (1929). Über das elektroenkephalogramm des menschen. *Archiv für psychiatrie und nervenkrankheiten*, 87(1), 527–570.

Carmigniani, J., Furht, B., Anisetti, M., Ceravolo, P., Damiani, E., and Ivkovic, M. (2011). Augmented reality technologies, systems and applications. *Multimedia Tools and Applications*, 51, 341–377.

Csikszentmihalyi, M. (1990). *Flow: The Psychology of Optimal Experience (Vol. 1990)*. New York: Harper & Row.

Flavián, C., Ibáñez-Sánchez, S., and Orús, C. (2021). The influence of scent on virtual reality experiences: The role of aroma-content congruence. *Journal of Business Research*, 123, 289–301.

Gatter, K. and Hodkinson, C. (2018). The influence of immersive technology on marketing effectiveness: A focus on VR experiences. *Journal of Marketing Research*.

Hilken, T., de Ruyter, K., Chylinski, M., Mahr, D., and Keeling, D.I. (2017). Augmenting the eye of the beholder: Exploring the strategic potential of augmented reality to enhance online service experiences. *Journal of the Academy of Marketing Science*, 45, 884–905.

Kim, J. and Forsythe, S. (2008). Adoption of virtual try-on technology for online apparel shopping. *Journal of Interactive Marketing*, 22(2), 45–59.

Kumar, S., Sharma, A., Singh, P.K., and Mittal, M. (2021). Neurophysiological basis of virtual reality-induced emotions and its clinical applications: A comprehensive review. *Journal of Neuropsychology*.

Le, T.H. and Pham, N.T. (2020). Virtual tours as a response to COVID-19: The case of Vinhomes real estate. *Vietnam Journal of Digital Innovation*.

Le, T.H. (2023). The impact of AR on Vietnam's e-commerce: A case study on consumer behavior. *Vietnam Journal of Digital Commerce*.

Lee, H., Jung, T.H., tom Dieck, M.C., and Chung, N. (2020). Experiencing immersive virtual reality in museums. *Information and Management*, 57(5), 103229.

Li, H., Zhang, X., Wang, H., Yang, Z., Liu, H., Cao, Y., and Zhang, G. (2021). Access to nature via virtual reality: A mini-review. *Frontiers in psychology*, 12, 725288.

Ministry of Planning and Investment. (2020). National strategy on Fourth Industrial Revolution. Vietnam Government Publishing House.

Moorhouse, N., tom Dieck, M.C., and Jung, T. (2018). Technological innovations transforming the consumer retail experience: a review of literature. *Augmented Reality and Virtual Reality: Empowering Human, Place and Business*, 133–143.

Nguyen, M.T. and Vu, P.H. (2021). Integrating AR in retail environments: The case of Vincom Retail. *Southeast Asian Retail Review*.

Nguyen, H.P. and Vu, P.H. (2023). Vietnam's digital transformation: The role of emerging technologies in economic growth. *Journal of Technology in Southeast Asia*.

Phan, D.M. (2022). Vietnam's tourism sector embraces virtual reality: Opportunities and challenges. *International Journal of Tourism and Technology*, 15(2), 85–99.

Poushneh, A. and Vasquez-Parraga, A. Z. (2017). Discernible impact of augmented reality on retail customer's experience, satisfaction and willingness to buy. *Journal of Retailing and Consumer Services*, 34, 229–234.

Scholz, J. and Smith, A.N. (2016). Augmented reality: Designing immersive experiences that maximize consumer engagement. *Journal of Marketing Theory and Practice*, 59(2), 149–161.

Slater, M. and Sanchez-Vives, M. V. (2016). Enhancing our lives with immersive virtual reality. *Frontiers in Robotics and AI*, 3, 236–866.

Tom Dieck, M.C. and Han, D.-i. D. (2022). The role of immersive technology in customer experience management. *Journal of marketing theory and practice*, 30(1), 108–119.

Tran, Q.T. and Do, M.K. (2021). The role of VR in neuro-marketing: A study on consumer behavior in Vietnam. *Vietnam Journal of Marketing Science*.

Tran, T.P. (2022). Challenges in developing VR/AR technologies in Vietnam: A review of industry trends and educational initiatives. *Vietnam Journal of Digital Technology*.

Vo, H.T. (2021). Vietnam Smart City Development Plan 2025: The integration of AR/VR in urban planning. *Vietnam Journal of Urban Studies*.

Vu, K.H. (2022). Using VR/AR for vocational training in Vietnam: Challenges and future directions. *Vietnam Journal of Vocational Education*.

Yeo, S.F., Tan, C.L., Kumar, A., Tan, K. H., and Wong, J.K. (2022). Investigating the impact of AI-powered technologies on Instagrammers' purchase decisions in digitalization era: A study of the fashion and apparel industry. *Technological Forecasting and Social Change*, 177, 121551.

https://doi.org/10.1142/9789811262258_0012

Chapter 12

The Mediating Role of Organizational Citizenship Behavior in the Relationship between Locus of Control, Self-Efficacy, and Employee Performance at Tan Son Nhat International Airport

Thanh Truc Do Thi, Quoc Thy Pham, and Nguyen Phong Nguyen

Abstract

This study investigates the mediating role of Organizational Citizenship Behavior (OCB) in the relationship between Locus of Control, Self-Efficacy, and Employee Performance at Tan Son Nhat International Airport. The research examines factors influencing employee performance and provides management insights to improve operational efficiency and sustainability. The study highlights the airport's critical role in regional development, tourism, and export promotion, benefiting the local population and the broader Mekong Delta.

The research utilized both qualitative and quantitative methods, including a survey of 252 employees. The analysis employed Cronbach's Alpha, Confirmatory Factor Analysis (CFA), and Structural Equation Modeling (SEM) to validate the research model and test hypotheses. Results confirm that improving Locus of Control, Self-Efficacy, and OCB positively impacts employee performance, offering valuable implications for airport management and future research in the aviation industry.

Keywords: Organizational Citizenship Behavior (OCB); Locus of Control; Self-Efficacy; Employee performance; Tan Son Nhat International Airport; Aviation industry.

1. Introduction

In today's global service industry, effective management of human resources and technological assets is essential for enhancing competitiveness. Employees in service sectors, particularly aviation, play a crucial role in ensuring customer satisfaction and operational efficiency. Their interactions with customers often shape the organization's reputation, and their ability to go beyond formal job descriptions can significantly enhance performance and service quality.

Organizational Citizenship Behavior (OCB) refers to the voluntary behaviors employees exhibit that go beyond their formal responsibilities, contributing positively to the organization. Numerous studies have highlighted OCB's impact on improving work environments and employee performance. However, there is limited research on OCB within the aviation industry, especially in the context of airport staff, who operate in a demanding and fast-paced environment.

This study focuses on Tan Son Nhat International Airport, a strategic transportation hub for the Mekong Delta. Given the airport's growing importance in connecting the region with the rest of the world, enhancing employee performance is critical. Understanding the role of OCB, combined with factors like Locus of Control and Self-Efficacy, can provide valuable insights into improving employee effectiveness and overall service quality at the airport.

The research aims to explore the relationships between Locus of Control, Self-Efficacy, and employee performance, with OCB serving as a mediating factor. By examining these interactions, the study seeks to identify key drivers of employee performance and propose strategies to optimize human resource management. This will help airport managers create a more supportive work environment and improve service standards.

Ultimately, the findings of this study will contribute to the broader literature on organizational behavior in the aviation industry and offer practical management solutions for Tan Son Nhat

International Airport. These insights are expected to help enhance employee performance, improve customer satisfaction, and support the airport's long-term development and success in the competitive aviation market.

2. Theoretical Background

2.1. *Locus of Control (LOC)*

Locus of control refers to an individual's belief in their ability to influence events in their life, as defined by Strauser *et al.* (2002). In other words, Sardogan *et al.* (2006) describe it as a person's perception regarding whether their personal abilities or external forces beyond their control influence the positive or negative situations they encounter. According to Basım and Sesen (2006), this belief is shaped by experiences throughout an individual's life, specifically regarding outcomes such as rewards, successes, or failures. These beliefs are not only connected to external factors like chance, fate, or powerful figures outside one's control but also to the consequences of the individual's own attitudes and actions.

Robbins (2016) elaborates that locus of control is the extent to which individuals believe they are the masters of their own destiny. It is a personality trait that helps explain how behavior is influenced by personal expectations. Locus of control consists of two dimensions: internal and external factors. Internally oriented individuals believe they have control over what happens to them, attributing outcomes to their own actions and decisions. Conversely, externally oriented individuals believe their life events are governed by external forces such as luck, fate, or random chance. These two orientations play a significant role in shaping how people approach challenges and react to successes or failures in their personal and professional lives.

2.2. *Self-Efficacy (SE)*

Self-efficacy refers to an individual's belief in their ability to successfully organize and execute the actions required to achieve specific tasks in a given context. As described by Fattah (2017), self-efficacy involves the confidence a person has in mobilizing motivation, cognitive resources, and actions to perform successfully. It is not merely a reflection of one's actual abilities but a subjective evaluation of what one can accomplish. This belief is critical in shaping how individuals approach challenges and their persistence in achieving goals.

According to Bandura (1997), self-efficacy plays a central role in human behavior by influencing the level of effort and persistence a person applies when facing obstacles. It is a cognitive process where individuals assess their capabilities, which in turn impacts their emotional states, motivation, and actions. Importantly, self-efficacy is distinct from actual skills — it is about how confident a person feels in utilizing those skills to achieve desired outcomes. High self-efficacy leads to greater resilience and a proactive attitude, while low self-efficacy can result in doubt, anxiety, and avoidance of challenging tasks. Thus, fostering self-efficacy is essential for enhancing performance and success in both personal and professional contexts.

2.3. *Organizational Citizenship Behavior*

Organizational Citizenship Behavior (OCB), as defined by Ajabar (2020), refers to voluntary actions performed by individuals that are not formally recognized or directly rewarded by the organization's compensation system but contribute to the overall effectiveness of the organization. In other words, OCB encompasses behaviors where employees go beyond their required roles without expecting formal recognition or rewards. These behaviors enhance organizational performance by promoting a positive and productive work environment.

Organ and Bies (1989) and Podsakoff *et al.* (1990) identified five key components of OCB: altruism, conscientiousness, sportsmanship, courtesy, and civic virtue. These elements serve as a framework for evaluating how employees voluntarily engage in actions that go beyond their formal job requirements. Altruism involves helping colleagues, while conscientiousness refers to a high level of personal responsibility. Sportsmanship denotes a positive attitude despite challenges, courtesy ensures smooth interpersonal interactions, and civic virtue reflects an employee's participation in organizational life. Together, these components positively influence the work environment and contribute to improved organizational performance.

2.4. *Employee Performance (EP)*

Employee performance (EP), as defined by Dehaghi *et al.* (2014), refers to the measurable outcomes of an employee's work, reflecting both the quality and quantity of their achievements. It is a management process where the results are not only visible but can be assessed using various metrics. Employee performance contributes directly to the overall performance of an organization, and it can be evaluated through both financial and non-financial outcomes, as emphasized by Anitha (2014). EP is closely linked to how an employee's efforts influence the operational success of the company, either by meeting specific targets or by contributing to broader organizational goals.

According to Robbins *et al.* (2013), employee performance can be measured using five key indicators: quality, quantity, accuracy, efficiency, and independence. Quality refers to the extent to which the work meets perfection or aligns with ideal methods of achieving goals. This study adopts the definition of employee performance proposed by Robbins *et al.* (2013) and will apply these metrics — quality, quantity, accuracy, efficiency, and independence — to evaluate the performance of employees. By doing so, the research aims to assess current performance levels and propose strategies to enhance work outcomes within the organization, ultimately improving overall organizational effectiveness.

2.5. *Theory of Planned Behavior*

The Theory of Planned Behavior (TPB), developed by Icek Ajzen, expands on the earlier Theory of Reasoned Action (TRA) by incorporating the idea that human behavior is not solely governed by rational thinking. TPB explains how intentions to perform a behavior are influenced by three main factors: a positive attitude toward the behavior, supportive subjective norms (social pressures or perceived approval from others), and perceived behavioral control (belief in one's ability to perform the behavior). When these factors are strong, the intention to act is more likely to translate into actual behavior.

TPB has been widely applied across various fields, such as marketing, psychology, education, and health, to predict and understand human behavior in different contexts. Its comprehensive approach allows researchers and practitioners to analyze how attitudes, social influences, and perceived control work together to shape intentions and ultimately guide behavior, making it a powerful tool for studying decision-making and behavior prediction.

3. Hypotheses and Conceptual Framework

3.1. *Locus of Control and Employee Performance*

Locus of control refers to an individual's belief in their ability to control their own destiny. According to Listiani *et al.* (2017), this belief influences how employees perceive and approach tasks. Individuals with a strong internal locus of control believe that their efforts directly impact their outcomes, which makes them more motivated and proactive in improving their performance. They tend to feel more in control of work situations and believe that hard work leads to better results, enhancing their overall performance. In contrast, individuals with an external locus of control are more likely to attribute their successes or failures to external factors such as luck or fate, which can negatively affect their motivation and performance.

Machogu (2017) further emphasize that internal locus of control is positively correlated with better employee performance, as those individuals take more responsibility for their actions and outcomes. Employees with a strong internal locus are more likely to excel in their tasks, whereas those with a strong external locus may feel resigned to circumstances beyond their control, leading to lower performance. Abun *et al.* (2021) suggest that a well-developed internal locus of control motivates employees to approach their work with enthusiasm, reducing feelings of pressure. Based on Ajzen's (1991) Theory of Planned Behavior, employees with an internal locus believe they can control outcomes through personal effort, resulting in higher performance. This leads to the following hypothesis:

H_1*: *Locus of control has a positive effect on the performance of employees at Tan Son Nhat International Airport

3.2. *Self-Efficacy and Employee Performance*

Self-efficacy refers to an individual's belief in their ability to organize and execute actions required to achieve certain tasks. According to Feist and Feist (2012), individuals with high self-efficacy remain persistent and resilient in challenging situations, while those with low self-efficacy are more likely to give up. This self-regulating ability is essential for overcoming obstacles and achieving desired outcomes. In the workplace, self-efficacy impacts how employees approach their tasks, with those possessing high self-confidence feeling more capable and optimistic about successfully completing their responsibilities.

Ajabar (2020) points out that high self-efficacy leads employees to be more optimistic and efficient in performing assigned tasks, whereas those with low self-efficacy may struggle with feelings of inadequacy and uncertainty. Positive self-efficacy affects employee performance by enhancing their experiences of success, interpersonal interactions, verbal persuasion, and psychological state. Dyrbye *et al.* (2019) further argue that self-efficacy is critical for employees as it boosts their ability to handle tasks effectively, thus improving overall performance. Employees who trust in their capabilities are less emotionally affected by potential failures, while those with low self-confidence may experience anxiety about their work and fear of failure (Desiana, 2019; Wastuti, 2018).

Ajzen's (1991) Theory of Planned Behavior links self-efficacy to perceived behavioral control, where individuals who believe they have the necessary skills and competence are more likely to achieve desired outcomes. High self-efficacy also fosters a positive attitude toward tasks, leading employees to be more engaged and motivated to perform well. Based on these arguments, the following hypothesis is proposed:

***H_2*: Self-efficacy positively affects the performance of employees at Tan Son Nhat International Airport**

3.3. *Locus of Control and Organizational Citizenship Behavior (OCB)*

Locus of control, as defined by Sanga (2019), reflects the extent to which individuals believe that they can control events in their lives, with two opposing aspects: internal and external locus of control. Employees with a high internal locus of control believe that they have control over outcomes through their actions, making them more proactive and responsible in achieving goals. Locus of control plays a significant role in influencing Organizational Citizenship Behavior (OCB), as individuals with a strong internal locus of control are more likely to engage in OCB due to their belief in self-regulation and control over work-related outcomes. According to Ajzen's Theory of Planned Behavior (1991), perceived behavioral control, which is influenced by locus of control, determines whether employees decide to engage in voluntary behaviors like OCB. Internally controlled individuals are less swayed by social pressures, relying on their own abilities to guide their actions. In contrast, those with an external locus of control tend to be more influenced by social norms and the expectations of others, which can either hinder or enhance their engagement in OCB depending on external motivations.

Arshad and Amir (2021) suggest that the higher the level of internal locus of control, the more likely employees are to perform beyond their formal job roles, contributing to OCB. Employees who believe they have control over their work environment are more willing to go the extra mile for the organization, while those with a weaker internal locus of control are less inclined to engage in such behaviors. This leads to the following hypothesis:

H_3*: *Locus of control positively influences Organizational Citizenship Behavior among employees at Tan Son Nhat International Airport

3.4. *Self-Efficacy and Organizational Citizenship Behavior (OCB)*

Self-efficacy, or the belief in one's ability to accomplish tasks, is a critical factor influencing Organizational Citizenship Behavior (OCB). According to Ajzen's Theory of Planned Behavior (1991), an individual's attitude toward a particular behavior is heavily influenced by their belief in their ability to perform that behavior. When individuals are confident in their capabilities, they are more likely to focus their efforts on achieving goals and actively pursue those goals, as noted by Wijayanti (2014). High self-efficacy fosters a sense of control over one's actions, leading employees to engage more readily in OCB, where they voluntarily contribute beyond their formal job responsibilities.

Machogu (2017) emphasize that self-efficacy is the belief in one's ability to carry out tasks necessary to achieve specific goals. Individuals with high self-efficacy believe they can influence outcomes and take the necessary actions to affect their environment. This self-belief allows them to handle tasks beyond their formal duties, often leading to greater job satisfaction, which in turn positively impacts their engagement in OCB. Omar *et al.* (2016) assert that the higher an employee's self-efficacy, the more likely they are to demonstrate OCB, as they feel more capable of contributing to the organization in meaningful ways. Based on these arguments, the following hypothesis is proposed:

***H_4*: Self-efficacy positively influences Organizational Citizenship Behavior among employees at Tan Son Nhat International Airport**

Employee Commitment and Firm Competitive advantage.

3.5. *Organizational Citizenship Behavior (OCB) and Employee Performance*

Organizational Citizenship Behavior (OCB) refers to voluntary actions by employees that exceed formal job requirements, such as helping coworkers, taking on additional tasks, and following workplace rules. Titisari (2014) notes that OCB is a key factor in improving employee performance, as it fosters collaboration and efficiency, helping the organization achieve its goals. When OCB is regularly practiced, it leads to a more supportive and productive work environment, directly contributing to enhanced employee performance.

Ajzen's Theory of Planned Behavior (1991) suggests that social norms and perceived control influence whether employees engage in OCB. A workplace culture that encourages these behaviors can create positive social pressure for employees to contribute beyond their job descriptions. Rizki *et al.* (2019) add that OCB promotes social cohesion among employees, encouraging them to align personal values with organizational goals, which improves team dynamics and performance. Based on this, OCB is seen as a significant factor that positively impacts employee performance, leading to the following hypothesis:

***H_5*: Organizational Citizenship Behavior positively affects the performance of employees at Tan Son Nhat International Airport**

3.6. *Locus of Control and Employee Performance through the mediation of Organizational Citizenship Behavior (OCB)*

Locus of control refers to an individual's belief about the degree to which they can control events affecting their lives. This belief system reflects the extent to which a person takes responsibility for their outcomes. Individuals with a high internal locus of control believe that they are in control of their own success or failure and take responsibility for their actions. Such individuals tend to perform better in the workplace because they not only excel at their tasks but also engage in extra-role behaviors. As Robbins (2016) explains, employees with a strong internal locus of control are more likely to exhibit positive social behaviors, such as voluntarily helping colleagues and working extra hours without expecting rewards. These behaviors are classified as Organizational Citizenship Behavior (OCB), which goes beyond formal job requirements.

According to Ajzen's Theory of Planned Behavior (TPB), the perception of having control over one's actions (perceived behavioral control) and support from the work environment (subjective norms) encourages individuals to voluntarily engage in OCB. This helps explain why employees with a high locus of control often participate in OCB, thereby improving the work environment and contributing to organizational success. Therefore, it is hypothesized that locus of control positively affects employee performance through the mediation of OCB, leading to the following hypothesis:

***H_{6a}*: Locus of control positively influences employee performance through the mediation of OCB at Tan Son Nhat International Airport**

3.7. *Self-Efficacy and Employee Performance through the mediating role of Organizational Citizenship Behavior (OCB)*

Self-efficacy, first introduced by Bandura, refers to an individual's belief in their ability to organize and execute actions to demonstrate certain skills (Muis *et al.*, 2018). The better individuals apply their self-efficacy, the more satisfied they become in their jobs. This increased job satisfaction encourages employees to go beyond their formal roles, contributing to a higher level of cooperation among colleagues, which in turn boosts overall job performance. Employees with high self-efficacy feel more confident in their abilities, and this

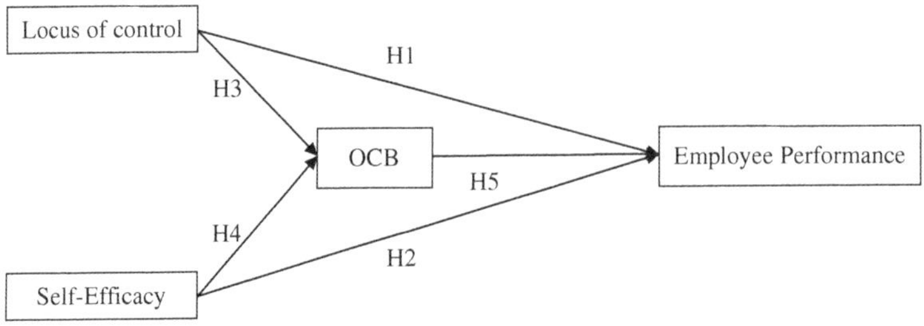

Figure 1: Proposed model.

self-assuredness leads to positive work behaviors that enhance both personal and organizational performance.

From the perspective of Ajzen's Theory of Planned Behavior (1991), high self-efficacy enhances perceived behavioral control, making employees more confident in performing extra-role behaviors like OCB. This increased engagement in OCB further improves their job performance. Employees with high self-efficacy not only approach tasks with a positive attitude but also believe in their ability to succeed, which drives them to actively participate in OCB. Their optimism and proactive behavior contribute to improved workplace dynamics and performance outcomes. Based on this, the following hypothesis is proposed:

H_{6b}: ***Self-efficacy positively influences employee performance through the mediation of OCB at Tan Son Nhat International Airport***

The relationships among the key variables in this study are depicted in Figure 1, which presents the proposed conceptual framework.

4. Methodology

4.1. *Sampling*

The authors collected 252 valid responses from employees at Tan Son Nhat International Airport through a combination of online and direct surveys. The online surveys were distributed via platforms such as Google Forms, Facebook, and Zalo, while direct surveys were conducted in person with airport staff. After gathering the data, the authors utilized SPSS 26.0 and AMOS 20 software for analysis, including descriptive statistics, reliability testing using Cronbach's Alpha, Exploratory Factor Analysis (EFA), Confirmatory Factor Analysis (CFA), and Structural Equation Modeling (SEM). Additionally, the Independent Sample T-Test and One-Way ANOVA were used to test for significant differences in the sample means. Upon completing the analysis, the authors provided insights into the studied factors, leading to conclusions and objective management recommendations. The goal of this process is to offer practical managerial implications aimed at improving and enhancing employee performance at the airport.

Table 1 show the descriptive statistics of respondents. Most participants were male, aged 25–35, held a university degree, earned 10–20 million VND per month, and had 3–10 years work experience.

Table 1: Descriptive statistics.

		Frequency	**Percentage (%)**
Gender	Male	148	58.7
	Female	104	41.3
Age	Under 25 years	26	10.3
	25–35 years	102	40.5
	36–45 years	85	33.7
	Over 45 years	39	15.5
Educational Level	Vocational	18	7.1
	College	38	15.1
	University	171	67.9
	Postgraduate	25	9.9
Income	Under 10 million VND	20	7.9
	10–20 million VND	192	76.2
	Over 20 million VND	40	15.9
Work Experience	Less than 3 years	31	12.3
	3–10 years	132	52.4
	Over 10 years	89	35.3

4.2. *Measurement*

The study utilizes established scales to measure key constructs related to employee performance. Locus of Control: Measured using Rotter's (1966) scale, this assesses whether individuals believe their outcomes are controlled by their actions (internal) or external forces like luck (external). Self-Efficacy: Bahtiar's (2023) scale is used to evaluate employees' confidence in their abilities to achieve goals and manage tasks, which influences their persistence and performance. Organizational Citizenship Behavior (OCB): Adapted from Yohanes *et al.* (2020), this scale measures voluntary, extra-role behaviors that enhance teamwork and organizational efficiency. Employee Performance: Using Yohanes *et al.* (2020), employee performance is assessed in terms of effectiveness, efficiency, and overall contributions to organizational success. These scales ensure reliable measurement of factors influencing employee performance at Tan Son Nhat International Airport.

5. Data Analysis and Findings

5.1. *Measurement model evaluation*

The reliability of the measurement scales was assessed using Cronbach's Alpha. As per Nunnally and Bernstein (1994), scales with an item-total correlation below 0.3 were excluded, and those with Cronbach's Alpha $\geq$0.6 were retained. All factors in this study exceeded 0.9, indicating high reliability. The model fit indices (Chi-square/df = 1.792, GFI = 0.900, CFI = 0.974, TLI = 0.970, RMSEA = 0.056) show a good fit for the measurement model. As shown in Table 2, composite reliability (CR) values ranged from 0.907 to 0.951, and average variance extracted (AVE) ranged from 0.660 to 0.797, indicating strong reliability and validity for all factors.

5.2. *Structural model evaluation*

The structural model evaluation reveals that the model fits the collected data well, based on several fit indices: Chi-square = 293.866,

Table 2: Discriminant validity testing.

	CR	AVE	MSV	MaxR(H)	OCB	LOC	SE	EP
OCB	0.949	0.788	0.540	0.953	**0.888**	—	—	—
LOC	0.907	0.660	0.428	0.910	0.654	**0.813**	—	—
SE	0.948	0.784	0.399	0.952	0.632	0.566	**0.885**	—
EP	0.951	0.797	0.540	0.958	0.735	0.595	0.607	**0.892**

Table 3: SEM results.

Relationship	Unstandardized Regression Coefficient	Standardized Regression Coefficient	S.E	C.R	P	Hypothesis Result
OCB <— SE	0.355	0.384	0.057	6.182	***	Accepted
OCB <— LOC	0.373	0.437	0.055	6.724	***	Accepted
EP <— OCB	0.604	0.512	0.083	7.262	***	Accepted
EP <— SE	0.220	0.202	0.068	3.245	0.001	Accepted
EP <— LOC	0.146	0.145	0.067	2.198	0.028	Accepted

df = 164, Chi-square/df = 1.792, P = 0.000, GFI = 0.900 ($\geq$0.8 is acceptable), CFI = 0.974 ($\geq$0.95 is excellent), PCLOSE = 0.160 ($\geq$0.05 is good), TLI = 0.970 ($\geq$0.9 is good), and RMSEA = 0.056 ($\leq$0.06 is good). These indicators collectively suggest that the model aligns well with the data collected from the survey.

Table 3 summarizes the SEM results. All hypothesis were supported, with significant effects of self-efficacy and locus of control on OCB and employee performance.

The parameter estimates for the structural model show that all relationships are statistically significant, with p-values less than 0.05. This means that all previously hypothesized relationships are supported. Specifically, both Locus of Control (LOC) and Self-Efficacy (SE) positively influence Organizational Citizenship Behavior (OCB), and OCB in turn significantly impacts Employee Performance (EP). Additionally, both LOC and SE have direct effects on EP, though the effects are more pronounced through OCB.

Table 4: Mediating effect.

Hypothesis	Indirect Effect	Standardized Indirect Effect	P	Hypothesis Result
H6a	EP <— OCB <— LOC	0.224	0.001	Accepted
H6b	EP <— OCB <— SE	0.197	0.002	Accepted

5.3. *Mediating effect*

To assess the mediating role of Organizational Citizenship Behavior (OCB) between independent variables and dependent variables, the authors used the Indirect tool to analyze the indirect relationships. Specifically, this study examines the mediating role of OCB in the relationships between Locus of control (LOC), Self-efficacy (SE), and Employee Performance (EP) at Tan Son Nhat International Airport. The analysis results are summarized as follows:

The results in Table 4, show that the indirect effects of OCB on the relationship between Locus of Control and Employee Performance, as well as Self-Efficacy and Employee Performance, are statistically significant, with p-values less than 0.05. Thus, both hypotheses H6a and H6b are accepted. This confirms that OCB plays a mediating role in these relationships, indicating that the impact of LOC and SE on EP is partially mediated by employees' engagement in OCB.

6. Discussion

The results of this study align with previous research by Syah *et al.* (2024), which demonstrated that Organizational Citizenship Behavior (OCB) serves as a mediating factor in the relationship between locus of control, self-efficacy, and employee performance. This study also provides specific reasoning for explaining the direct effects of these psychological factors on performance. Similarly, the findings of Rohmah *et al.* (2023) highlight the impact of self-efficacy, locus of control, and burnout on employee performance through the mediating role of OCB. These results confirm the complex interplay of psychological and behavioral factors in enhancing or diminishing employee performance, while underscoring the critical mediating role that OCB plays.

Specifically, OCB acts as a bridge between factors such as Corporate Social Responsibility (CSR) and work performance, while also boosting employee performance through increased work motivation. These studies suggest that OCB can optimize job performance by encouraging employees to maximize their capabilities, and it also facilitates the positive influence of other factors like CSR and work motivation. This research, therefore, provides a solid foundation for future studies to explore and expand on the role of OCB in organizational contexts.

7. Conclusion

7.1. *Theoretical implication*

This study developed a model that includes two independent variables locus of control and self-efficacy, one mediating variable Organizational Citizenship Behavior (OCB), and one dependent variable employee performance. Using a representative sample of 252 responses from Tan Son Nhat International Airport, the data were analyzed using SPSS 26.0 and AMOS 20 for reliability, confirmatory factor analysis (CFA), and structural equation modeling (SEM). The results confirmed that locus of control and self-efficacy significantly influence OCB, which mediates the relationship between these psychological traits and employee performance.

The study highlights that employees with higher self-efficacy and an internal locus of control are more likely to engage in OCB, improving both their individual performance and overall organizational effectiveness. The reliability of the measurement scales was confirmed with Cronbach's alpha values above 0.7, supporting their use in future research and strengthening the theoretical foundation for studies exploring similar variables in organizational contexts.

The findings emphasize the mediating role of OCB in the relationship between psychological traits (locus of control and self-efficacy) and employee performance. Employees with higher levels of self-efficacy and an internal locus of control tend to engage more frequently in OCB, which improves workplace cooperation, job satisfaction, and overall performance outcomes. This highlights the importance of fostering a work environment that supports and encourages OCB, as it not only boosts individual performance but also strengthens organizational effectiveness.

Moreover, this study reinforced the reliability and validity of the measurement scales for locus of control, self-efficacy, OCB, and employee performance. All scales achieved Cronbach's alpha values greater than 0.7, demonstrating high internal consistency and reliability. This provides a strong theoretical foundation for future research, validating the use of these scales in other organizational studies, particularly within the aviation industry or similar service-oriented sectors. The results contribute to the broader theoretical understanding of how psychological factors and voluntary employee behaviors like OCB can be leveraged to enhance performance and drive organizational success.

7.2. *Practical implication*

The findings of this study offer several practical implications for improving employee performance, particularly within the context of Tan Son Nhat International Airport and similar organizations.

First, organizations should focus on developing locus of control and self-efficacy among employees. By creating training and development programs that encourage employees to take responsibility for their actions and believe in their abilities, companies can foster a sense of control and confidence. This will not only enhance individual performance but also lead to more proactive and engaged behavior, such as Organizational Citizenship Behavior (OCB), where employees go beyond their formal duties.

Second, OCB plays a critical mediating role in improving employee performance. Managers should work to create a supportive organizational culture that encourages voluntary behaviors, such as helping colleagues or taking on extra tasks, without expecting immediate rewards. This could be facilitated through recognition programs, team-building activities, and fostering a collaborative environment where employees feel valued and motivated to contribute beyond their job descriptions.

Lastly, given the strong relationship between psychological traits and performance, human resource practices should incorporate assessments of locus of control and self-efficacy during recruitment and performance evaluations. Identifying and nurturing these traits in employees can lead to a more motivated and high-performing workforce. By leveraging these insights, organizations can better align employee behavior with overall strategic goals, leading to increased efficiency and organizational success.

7.3. *Limitations*

This study is one of the few to explore the mediating role of Organizational Citizenship Behavior (OCB) in the relationship between locus of control, self-efficacy, and employee performance in Vietnam, particularly within the aviation sector. However, being relatively new, the research has certain limitations that are hard to avoid. One notable limitation is that the study only gathered 252 quality responses from employees at Tan Son Nhat International Airport. The use of non-probability convenience sampling limits the representativeness of the results. For future research, a larger sample size would improve reliability and generalizability.

Second, due to constraints in budget and time, the study was confined to Tan Son Nhat International Airport. Therefore, the findings are only applicable to this specific airport and may not fully reflect conditions in other airports across Vietnam. In the future, expanding the research to include multiple airports nationwide would provide more comprehensive insights and broader applicability to the Vietnamese aviation market.

Finally, the respondents in this study were predominantly aged 25–35, which limits the scope of the findings across different age groups. In future research, the authors intend to include a more diverse range of ages to ensure the results are more objective and accurate. Further studies should also consider investigating additional factors affecting employee performance, providing managerial insights that contribute to improved service quality, customer satisfaction, and the economic development of Vietnam's aviation sector.

Acknowledgments

This research was conducted, completed, and financially supported by the University of Economics Ho Chi Minh City (UEH), Vietnam.

Bibliography

Abun, D., Nicolas, M.T., Apollo, E.P., Magallanes, T., and Encarnacion, M.J. (2021). Employees' self-efficacy and work performance of employees as mediated by work environment. *International Journal of Research in Business & Social Science*, 10(7), 01–15.

Ajabar. (2020). *Manajemen Sumber Daya Manusia. In EdisiRevisi Jakarta: Bumi Aksara.*

Ajzen, I. (1991). The theory of planned behaviour. *Organizational Behaviour and Human Decision Processes*, 50(2), 179–211.

Anitha, J. (2014). Determinants of employee engagement and their impact on employee performance. *International Journal of Productivity and Performance Management*, 63, 308–323.

Arshad, Z. and Amir, T.S. (2021). Locus of control as a mediating factor on the relationship between burnout and self-efficacy among university teacher. *Pakistan Journal of Education Research*, 4(1), 333–350.

Bahtiar, B. (2023). The effect of self-efficacy on organizational citizenship behavior (OCB) of science teacher candidates in technology based learning. *Journal of Research in Science Education*, 9(1), 390–401.

Bandura, A. (1977). Self-efficacy: Toward a unifying theory of behavioral change. *Psychological Review*, 84, 191–215.

Bandura, A. (1997). Self-efficacy: The exercise of control. W.H. Freeman/Times Books/Henry Holt & Co.

Basım, N.H. and Sesen, H. (2006). Politeness of employees and helping control the locus of the impact of behavior: A study in public sector. Selcuk University. *Journal of the Institute of Social Sciences*, 16, 159–168.

Dehaghi, M.R. and Rouhani, A. (2014). Studying the relationship between the effective factors on employees' performance in Iran's university and the students' satisfaction with regards to employees' performance. *Procedia — Social and Behavioral Sciences*, 141, 903–908.

Desiana, N.E. (2019). Pengaruh Efikasi Diri Terhadap Kinerja Karyawan Melalui Inovasi Sebagai Variabel Intervening (Studi Pada Divisi Sekretariat Dan Humas PDAM Surya Sembada Kota Surabaya) *Jurnal Ilmu Manajemen*, 7(2), 382–392.

Dyrbye, L.N., Shanafelt, T.D., Johnson, P.O., Johnson, L.A., Satele, D., and West, C.P. (2019). A cross-sectional study exploring the relationship between burnout, absenteeism, and job performance among American nurses. *BMC Nursing*, 18(1), 57. https://doi.org/10.1186/s12912-019-0382-7.

Fattah, H. (2017). *Kepuasan kerja & kinerja pegawai* (*Job Satisfaction & Employee Performance*). Elmatera.

Feist, J. and Feist, G.J. (2012). *Teori kepribadian* (*Personality Theory*). Salemba Humanika.

Listiani, K. and Kurniawati, S.L. (2017). Pengaruh financial knowledge, locus of control, dan financial attitude terhadap financial management behavior pada mahasiswa (The influence of financial knowledge, locus of control, and financial attitude on financial management behavior in students). *Jurnal Sekolah Tinggi Ilmu Ekonomi Perbanas*, 1(1), 1–11.

Machogu, A.M. (2017). Relationship between locus of control and employee performance: Internal and external locus of control. LAP LAMBERT Academic Publishing.

Muis, M.R., Nasution, M.I., Azhar, M.E., and Radiman, R. (2018). Pengaruh Kepemimpinan Dan Self Efficacy Terhadap Kelelahan Emosional Serta Dampaknya Terhadap Kepuasan Kerja Dosen. *Jurnal Riset Sains Manajemen*, 2(1), 131–142.

Nunnally, J.C. and Bernstein, I.H. (1994). *Psychometric Theory* (3rd ed.). New York: McGraw-Hill.

Omar, M.K., Hussein, N., and Azli, N. (2016). Role overload, self-efficacy, locus of control and job performance among employees of a printing company in Malaysia. *Information Management and Business Review*, 8, 61–69.

Organ, D.W. and Bies, R.J. (1989). Organizational citizenship behavior: The good soldier syndrome. *The Academy of Management Review*, 14, 294–297.

Podsakoff, P.M., MacKenzie, S.B., Moorman, R.H., and Fetter, R. (1990). Transformational leader behaviors and their effects on followers' trust in leader, satisfaction, and organizational citizenship behaviors. *Leadership Quarterly V*, 1, 107–142.

Rizki, V.L., Titisari, P., and Prihatini, D. (2019). The role of emotional intelligence and organizational commitment in increasing OCB and employee performance. *International Journal of Scientific Research and Management*, 7(5), 1139–1147.

Robbins, S.P. (2016). *Perilaku organisasi* (*Organizational Behavior*). Salemba Empat.

Robbins, S.P., Judge, T.A., and Vohra, N. (2013). *Organizational Behavior,* 15th Edition. India: Pearson Education Services Pvt Ltd.

Rohmah, R.M., Sularso, A., and Titisari, P. (2023). The role of organizational citizenship behavior (OCB) in mediating self-efficacy, locus of control, burnout on the performance of Bri Jember employees. *American Journal of Humanities and Social Sciences Research,* 7, 103–109.

Rotter, J.B. (1966). Generalized expectancies for internal versus external control of reinforcement. *Psychological Monographs: General and Applied*, 80(1), 1–28.

Sardogan, M.E., Kaygusuz, C., and ve Karahan, T.F. (2006). A human relations skills training program, university students' locus of control levels, Mersin University. *Journal of the Faculty of Education*, 2(2), 184–194.

Sanga, C. (2019). Locus of control vis-à-vis self-efficacy. *International Journal of English and Education*, 8(2), 1–9. https://doi.org/10.2139/ssrn.3447737.

Strauser, D.R., Ketz, K., and Keim, J. (2002). The relationship between self efficacy, locus of control and work personality. *Journal of Rehabilitation*, 68(1), 20–26.

Syah, A. and Safrida, S. (2024). The mediating role of organizational citizenship behavior (OCB) on employee performance: Locus of control and self-efficacy. *Qubahan Academic Journal* 4, 101–112.

Titisari, P. (2014). Peranan Organizational Citizenship Behavior (OCB).

Wastuti, S.N.Y. (2018). Efikasi diri terhadap kinerja karyawan PDAM Tirtanadi Unit Instalasi Pengolahan Air Sunggal (Selfefficacy on the performance of PDAM Tirtanadi Unit Instalasi Pengolahan employees at Air Sunggal). *Jurnal Kajian Konseling dan Pendidikan*, 1(2), 35–42.

Wijayanti, W. (2014). Pengaruh dukungan organisasi dan efikasi diri terhadap kepuasan melalui komitemen organisasi (The influence of organizational support and self-efficacy on satisfaction through organizational commitment). *Jurnal Bisnis dan Manajemen*, 6(2), 77–88.

Yohanes, L., Basana, S.R., and Panjaitan, T.W.S. (2020). The effect of organizational trust and organizational citizenship behavior on employee performance. *SHS Web of Conferences*, 76, 01058.

https://doi.org/10.1142/9789811262258_0013

Chapter 13

Vietnam on the Road to the Digital Economy

Xuan Vinh Vo

Abstract

Vietnam's digital economy and digital society have experienced rapid growth in recent years, driven by strong telecommunications and IT infrastructure, widespread technology adoption, and a young, tech-savvy workforce. The country's strategic position in Southeast Asia and government initiatives further support digital transformation. However, significant challenges remain, including legal and institutional barriers, regulatory gaps, and concerns about data protection and digital identity. Addressing these issues is crucial for sustainable digital economic development, fostering entrepreneurship, and ensuring inclusive growth.

Keywords: Digital economy; Digital society; Digital transformation; Entrepreneurship; Innovation; IT infrastructure; Regulatory challenges; Vietnam.

1. Introduction

Vietnamese digital economy and digital society have developed spontaneously in recent years but have grown quite rapidly due to good telecommunications and IT infrastructure, comprehensive coverage, and high user density due to the young, well-educated Vietnamese population, good at math and hard-working; Vietnamese people are passionate about technology and like to use technology in the highest category in the region and quickly adapt to change. These are

Vietnam's advantages regarding digital transformation and developing the digital economy and society.

We also have great opportunities to develop the digital economy. For the first time in history, Vietnam accompanies the world in the fourth industrial revolution, the digital transformation revolution, and has an excellent opportunity to break through and get ahead. Vietnam is a large market with much potential for new business models, with a large population, a golden population structure, a large digital workforce, and many Internet and smartphone users. A large and rapidly growing industry will create attractive markets for the digital economy. We are also located in the heart of Southeast Asia and Asia, which is considered the center of the development of digital technology and the global digital economy. COVID-19 is an international disaster and a hundred-year digital transformation and economic development push.

Vietnam has successfully contained COVID-19 and can fully take advantage of this opportunity to make a breakthrough in the digital economy. We are also receiving the attention and drastic direction of the Party, State, and Government for digital transformation and development of the digital economy, reflected in many essential documents issued over the past time.

However, Vietnam's digital economy and digital society are also facing significant shortcomings, limitations, and challenges, such as:

— *The legal and institutional system has not created favorable conditions for developing the digital economy and society.* Regulations for digital economic activities have not been synchronously formed and are slow to be completed, especially for the Internet/platform digital economy. There is no legal corridor for piloting the application of new business and service models. The system of legal documents has been promulgated many times but lacks synchronization, overlaps, and even conflicts, and is not suitable for the requirements of digital transformation and development of the digital economy. There is still a lack of regulations on data transactions, database protection, personal data, private information, and trust in the digital space, as well as a lack of rules on individual rights and ethics when applying artificial intelligence. Regulations on digital identity, identification, and electronic authentication for people are still slow to be promulgated.

The implementation of state management and the development and implementation of programs, plans, mechanisms, and policies to develop the digital economy and society is still inadequate. We have many ministries with functions and tasks related to the digital economy. Still, there is a lack of an agency responsible for leading and helping the Government perform state management and coordinate and promote the development of new potential fields with challenges. The Ministry of Information and Communications, which is actually implementing the state management of the digital economy, does not have a specialized unit in charge of this field. We also lack legal tools and technology systems capable of effectively monitoring and managing the operation of digital platforms and cross-border platforms in cyberspace to fight antitrust and limit unfair competition to support Vietnamese digital economy enterprises. The digital economy is changing our country's comparative advantage in terms of cheap labor, creating many new jobs requiring new skills and, at the same time, reducing many "traditional" occupations, leading to changes in the economy and employment structures. However, the development and implementation of mechanisms and policies to encourage the advantages of the digital economy and minimize the negative impact factors of this field are still embarrassing and inadequate.

Digital skills and digital human resources have not met the requirements of the digital economy and the development of the digital society. Digital human resources to meet the needs for research, development, and application of digital technologies are small and of low quality. Businesses still lack a technological workforce with enough knowledge and skills to apply digital technology to their production and business processes. The labor market is demanding a change in the quality of education and training to adapt to new requirements; meanwhile, university training and vocational training have not met the requirements in terms of both quantity and quality. The primary digital skills of the workforce are still low, and the ability to adapt to the digital environment is not high, while digital transformation is drastically reducing the demand for some traditional jobs and increasing the new requirements for basic digital skills. Educational institutions have not yet implemented the STEM/STEAM education model to equip students with digital baggage and essential digital skills to prepare for the future. Most people are still not equipped with the basic digital knowledge and skills to effectively exploit digital knowledge stores online and apply digital technology to their activities. Without a breakthrough in digital skills training and retraining for the technology workforce and basic digital skills training for people to keep up with the speed of digital transformation, our country may have to face the gap that disrupts digital transformation and the development of the digital economy.

The enterprise's digital transformation capacity is still weak; The force of business platforms is significant but not strong, and the young Made-in-Vietnam digital platforms face fierce competition from the outside. Except for enterprises operating in some fields that require digital transformation, such as finance and banking and information and communication technology, most companies still stop at the level of interest but have not yet implemented digital transformation. The capacity of enterprises to research, develop, and apply digital technology is still quite limited. Digital transformation helps Vietnam's international integration process go more smoothly, but the degree of benefit depends on the ability of digital transformation and the enterprises' internal resources. If the digital internal force fails, businesses will be more affected by the world economic instability, leading to having to accept a low position in the entire global value chain. Although Vietnamese digital platform businesses make great efforts, they are under excellent competition pressure from foreign digital platforms, especially those operating across borders, and even face unfair competition at home. Due to the incomplete legal framework, we currently lack practical tools to fight against monopoly and unfair competition and protect Vietnamese businesses in cyberspace. We also lack legal tools to limit malicious mergers and acquisitions that can adversely affect the market. Besides, the digital economy market has not developed in the right direction. Creating and saving the domestic digital market, especially the Government digital market, so Vietnamese businesses can practice and grow to go global has not been effectively implemented.

And especially, we do not yet have a national overall strategy for the digital economy and digital society development. Although we have resolutions and programs on digital transformation, we still do not have a national strategy, program, or plan for the development of the digital economy and digital society to define specific, clear views and visions as well as orientation of tasks, solutions, development, as a basis for ministries and local agencies to develop plans and schemes for implementation.

The development goal set by the Party and Government is for the proportion of the digital economy to reach 20% of GDP by 2025 and 30% by 2030. This goal is very challenging because, according to the standard development scenario, by 2025, Vietnam's digital economy will only reach 10.5% of GDP. To achieve this goal, we need to maintain an average annual growth of the digital economy of around 20%, three times the expected GDP growth (6.5–7%/year). This scenario is not easy to achieve, and it has very high goals for the digital society, requiring the drastic intervention of the whole political system and the worthy investment of all ministries, sectors, and localities for digital transformation and digital economy development.

In that context, it is necessary to study international experiences to draw lessons on digital economic development for Vietnam.

2. Conceptual Background

2.1. *The development of the digital economy around the world*

The digital economy and digital society are closely linked and mutually reciprocal, and they are two inseparable aspects of the digital transformation process; therefore, they often go hand in hand. Analysts and international reviewers usually pair this category in their research. For example, the European Union combined these two fields in the Digital Economy and Society Index (DESI)[1] to assess the level of digital economy and digital society development of member countries.

There is no common consensus on the definitions of digital economy, digital society, and digital transformation. Each country, depending on its economic and social development strategy, has different definitions of these terms.

In the late 1990s, the analysis was mainly concerned with Internet adoption and its economic impact (about the "Internet Economy") (Brynjolfsson and Kahin, 2002). As Internet use expanded, reports from the mid-2000s onward focused more and more on the conditions under which the Internet economy could emerge and develop (Figure 1).

Johansson *et al.* (2006) assert that the rapid development of information and communication technology (ICT) and the use of ICT have created the image of the digital economy today. The rapid spread of ICT has brought about significant changes in how products and services are produced, the nature of products and services made,

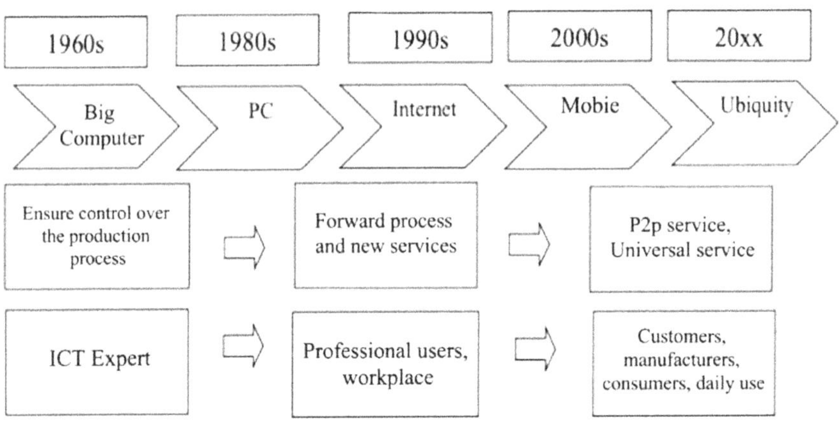

Figure 1: The development of ITC and the digital economy over time.

[1]https://ec.europa.eu/digital-single-market/en/digital-economy-and-society-index-desi.

and how products and services are delivered to the market and distributed to customers. During the 1990s, the digital economy was the dominant factor, leading to structural changes and economic growth at both the national and regional levels in developed and developing countries. However, due to different ICT development and adoption levels, countries differ in their distances and paths to the digital economy.

Atkinson and Mckay (2007) define the digital economy as an economy with the widespread use of ICT (hardware, software, applications, and telecommunications) in all aspects of the economy, including activities within organizations (businesses, governments, non-profit organizations), transactions between organizations, and transactions between individuals.

Similar to the views of most other researchers, Malecki and Moriset (2008) describe the digital economy by a pyramid shown in Figure 2. The top triangle includes products such as the semiconductor and silicon industries. It's not a big industry in itself. Still, it is essential because its product is at the heart of computers and

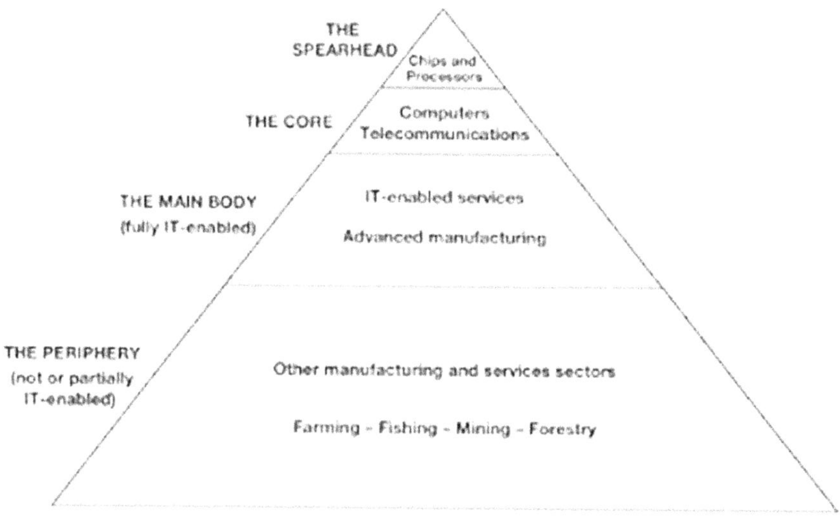

Figure 2: The pyramid of the digital economy.
Source: Malecki and Moriset (2008).

electronic devices, which continue to be integrated into many other products such as consumer electronics, automobiles, machinery, and other industrial equipment. The computer and telecommunications industries, including manufacturing and services, are at the second level of the pyramid. These are the digital economy's core sectors because they allow the industries to function at two lower tiers. The third layer is the main body of the digital economy, including services and manufacturing industries that rely heavily on digital technology. Employees in these industries require skills in using information technology devices a lot. At the bottom are the industries that are the slowest to digitize. Sectors such as agriculture, especially in developing countries, and household services such as garbage collection, hair care, etc., rarely or only use a small part of information and communication technology.

Over the past few years, the discussion has changed again, focusing on how digital technologies, services, products, techniques, and skills are pervasive across industries. This process is often called industry digitization or industry digital economy, which is defined as the digital transformation process of businesses in traditional industries using digital technologies, products, and services (Brennen and Kreiss, 2014). Regarding this change, recent studies have focused on "digitization" and "digital transformation" (i.e., how digital products and services are disrupting traditional sectors) to explore various multisectoral digital economy trends (OECD, 2016 and 2017; UNCTAD, 2017). The Digital Economy Cooperation and Development Initiative Forum of the World Economic Organization (WEF) and G20 countries (2016) addresses the digital economy, including economic activities using (1) information and knowledge be digitized as the main factor of production; (2) the modern information network is an essential operational space; and (3) effective use of information and communication technology (ICT) as an essential driver of productivity growth and economic structural optimization. The OECD (2016) refers to the digital economy as the combination of all economic activities based on or significantly enhanced by using digital inputs, including digital technologies, digital infrastructure, digital services, and data, including all producers, consumers, and governments that use these digital inputs in their economic activities. The Oxford Digital Economy Collaborative Group also refers to the digital economy as "an economy that operates primarily on digital technologies, especially electronic transactions conducted via the Internet." Thus, the world is gradually unifying the content of the digital economy, including the traditional ICT field as the core, new economic activities in cyberspace, the application of digital technology, and the digital transformation of traditional sectors and industries. This is especially relevant for developing countries where digital technology has already begun to affect traditional sectors such as agriculture, tourism, and transportation.

Heeks and Bukht, at the University of Manchester study[2] (2018), found that digital economy definitions all include the Information Technology — Communication economy (ICT sector) and the same category of ICT consumption/applications. This category differentiates the definitions. From there, they proposed a conceptual framework for the digital economy consisting of three components: (1) core digital economy, (2) narrow digital economy, and (3) Digitalized Economy (see Figure 3).

— Core Digital Economy: includes hardware manufacturing, information services, software, and IT consulting. This component is the traditional ICT sector.
— Narrow scope — digital economy: This includes digital services and platform economy based on the core digital economy. The narrow digital economy also includes a part of the sharing economy and the gig economy. This component can be collectively referred to as the internet/platform digital economy.
— Broad scope — digitalized economy: This includes e-business, e-commerce, industry 4.0, precision agriculture, algorithmic

[2]https://www.researchgate.net/publication/327356904_Defining_Conceptualising_and_Measuring_the_Digital_Economy.

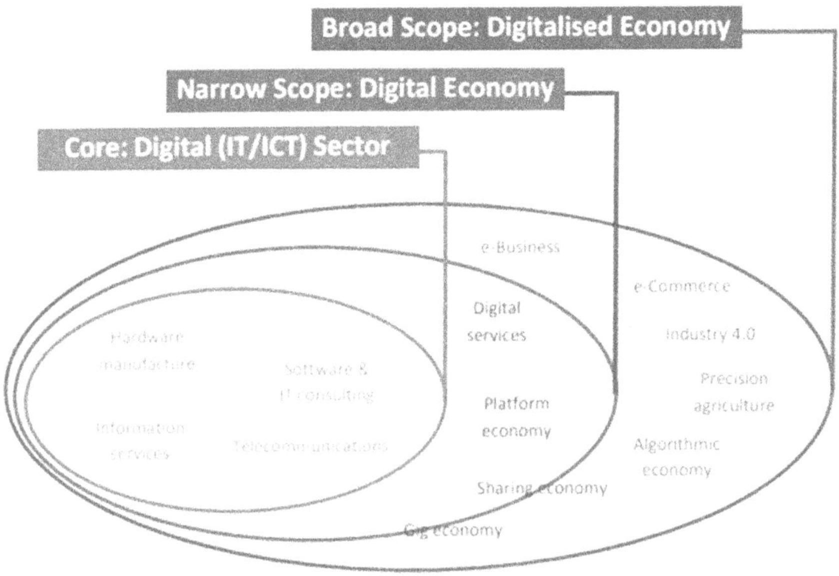

Figure 3: Digital economy definition.
Source: Bukht and Heeks (2010).

economy, the rest of the sharing economy, and the gig economy. This component can be called the sectoral digital economy.

The approach to the digital economy with three components as above by authors Bukht and Heeks in the study of the University of Manchester is now widely accepted in international organizations and many countries. Digital economy concepts of the World Economic Forum (WEF) and the organization of G20 countries, organization of OECD countries, IMF, UNCTAD, and although there are different interpretations of the European Union and many countries in the world, they agree on the above approach. Thus, the primary digital economy scope consists of three components: Information technology — telecommunications digital economy, which includes the information technology industry and telecommunications services; Platform digital economy, which consists of the economic activities of the digital platforms and the information systems connecting supply and demand through the Internet; Sector — field digital economy, which includes economic activities of the industry, the field of implementing the digital technology application, digital transformation or implementation on the digital platforms and information systems connecting supply and demand through the Internet.

Along with the abovementioned digital economy approach, most countries also use the above connotation to measure the digital economy. For example, according to the Digital Economy Report 2019 of the United Nations Trade and Development Forum (UNCTAD),[3] the contribution to the worldwide national account of the ICT digital economy in 2017 was 4.5% of GDP. The contribution of the total digital economy (including the IT economy and the digital economy) is 15.5%; the corresponding figures in the US are 6.9% and 21.6% of GDP, respectively, and in China is 6% and 30%, respectively.

Huawei and London Economics (2017) argue that applying digital technology and digital transformation in traditional economic activities (digital economy of industries and fields) can create a much more significant impact than its contribution to the output of the core digital economy. These impacts are called digital spillover, affecting the industry's digital economy through three channels: internal channel, horizontal channel, and vertical channel). The internal channel determines the spillover effects within an organization that invests in ICT products and services. The horizontal channel represents the spillover effects from enterprises applying ICT to enterprises in the same industry. The vertical channel represents the spillover effects from enterprises applying ICT to enterprises along the product value chain.

Cameron *et al.* (2019) pointed out some characteristics of the digital economy compared to the traditional economy:

Firstly, data is a source of value in the digital economy: The rise of digital technology means that data can now be collected from multiple sources, from smartphones to millions of sensors in home

[3]https://unctad.org/system/files/official-document/der2019_en.pdf (trang 48, 69).

machines, vehicles, and individuals. These massive data streams and big data analytics can create value in all operations.

Secondly, the advancement of hardware and software related to ICT: The Digital Economy results from the development of new digital technologies and has digital transformation impacts beyond the ICT sector — such as robotics, the Internet of Things, and digital platforms. Transformation occurs across all industries, from finance to transportation, manufacturing, media, education, healthcare, and other fields.

Thirdly, new business models facilitate growth and disrupt existing business: Digital-based business models allow different groups of people to interact, thus creating network effects and increasing efficiency by reducing transaction costs. For example, e-commerce facilitates orders for goods and services that can be delivered through a conventional channel or entirely electronically. Online advertising is another emerging area where the Internet has become a vehicle for delivering targeted messages to segmented customers. Meanwhile, the sharing economy gives individuals employment opportunities and access to underutilized assets and services.

Fourthly, the consumer's new role: Digital technology has put the consumer at the center. The ability to communicate and share reviews with others not only changes the customer's buying experience but also dramatically affects the business's reputation. The Internet also empowers consumers with a new way to create and share ideas. Consumers can become a significant source of new creative ideas for manufacturers.

UN (2019) points out that there is still a gap between different countries regarding the digital economy. However, the economic geography of the digital economy does not show the traditional North–South divide. The digital economy is continuously led by one developed and one developing country: the United States and China. For example, these two countries account for 75% of all blockchain technology-related patents, 50% of global IoT spending, and more than 75% of the world's public cloud market. And perhaps most strikingly, these two countries account for 90% of the market capitalization of the world's 70 most significant digital platforms. Europe's market share is 4%, and Africa and Latin America have just 1%. Seven "super-platforms" — Microsoft, followed by Apple, Amazon, Google, Facebook, Tencent, and Alibaba — account for two-thirds of the total value market. This points to challenges for latecomers and indicates opportunities for developing countries along the Traditional North-South axis like Vietnam.

3. Context of the Digital Economy

The digital economy is economic activities that use digital information, knowledge, technology, and data as the main factors of production; use telecommunications networks, the Internet, and computer networks as operating spaces; and use digital technology and digital platforms to increase labor productivity and optimize the economy. In simple terms, the digital economy is related to digital technology.

The Ministry of Information and Communications has deeply researched the digital economy concept of many organizations and countries worldwide, such as the University of Manchester,[4] the World Economic Forum (WEF), the G20 countries, OECD countries, and the European Union.

As analyzed above, a commonly used definition of the digital economy in many countries and international organizations today is that a digital economy is an economy based on digital technology and digital data, taking place in a digital environment, with three main components: digital economy and information technology and telecommunications; platform digital economy and online business; and digital economy in industries and fields.

On that basis, Vietnam inherits the definitions and contents of the digital economy that have been agreed upon by most countries and international organizations and rewritten in the "language" of Vietnam as follows:

[4]https://www.researchgate.net/publication/327356904_Defining_Conceptualising_and_Measuring_the_Digital_Economy.

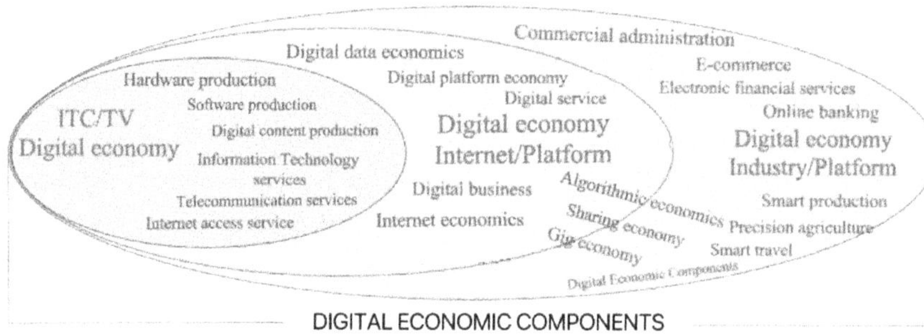

Figure 4: Components of the digital economy.
Source: Strategy for Vietnam's digital economy and digital society to 2025, vision to 2030.

A digital economy is an economic activity that uses digital technology and data as its main inputs, the digital environment as its primary operating space, and information and telecommunications technology to increase labor productivity, business model innovation, and economic structure optimization.

Figure 4 shows the digital economic component model.

As shown in Figure 4, the digital economy consists of three components: ICT/VT (ICT Digital Economy), Internet/Platform Digital Economy (Basic Digital Economy), and Industry/Field Digital Economy (Digital Economy), in which:

— Digital economy ICT: It is the information technology industry and telecommunications services, including producing electronic products, hardware, software, and digital content, providing IT services and telecommunications services.
— Platform digital economy: It is the economic activities of digital platforms, online systems, and online services, using digital technology and digital data as the main input, and the Internet is the primary operating space, such as data economy, platform economy, online business.
— Sectoral digital economy: It is a significantly increased economic activity of industries and fields thanks to digital technology and

digital data inputs, with the digital environment being the main operating space, including activities such as e-value, e-commerce, smart agriculture, smart manufacturing, smart tourism, etc.

According to research by many prestigious international organizations, the digital economy is one of the main drivers for global growth in the coming period. The digital economy helps increase labor productivity, opening up new growth spaces for the economy. The digital economy also helps sustainable development and inclusive growth because it uses more knowledge than resources, lower costs of joining the digital economy, creating business opportunities for more people; digital economy helps to improve the competitiveness of the economy, contributing to solving socio-economic problems; digital technology is borderless; hence it will reduce the gap between rural and urban areas; Digital technology also gives us new approaches, new solutions to effectively solve long-standing problems of humankind, such as environmental pollution, the gap between rich and poor, measuring social mood, citizen participation in policy-making, etc.

4. Experience Developing Digital Economy in the World

4.1. *The situation of digital economy development in the world*

The digital economy increasingly asserts its role as a core driver of global growth. No longer confined to an elite group of "high-tech" countries, the digital economy is being promoted worldwide in both developed and developing countries and bringing huge profits for many businesses and countries. Governments and policymakers are trying to research and find the best way to take advantage of the opportunities of the digital transformation revolution to accelerate the development of their country's digital economy, bringing the best benefits to their citizens. Many countries are trying to transform traditional economic structures, promote the ICT/VT and internet/platform digital economy, promote the digital transformation of industries and fields, and support businesses to transform the country into a consistent, dynamic, innovative, and growing digital powerhouse.

According to the Digital Economy Report of the United Nations Forum on Trade and Development (UNCTAD),[5] in 2019, the ICT/VT digital economy contributed about 4.5% of global GDP, and the internet/platform digital economy contributed 15.5% of the global GDP. The corresponding figures in the US are 6.9% and 21.6% of GDP, and in China it is 6% and 30% of GDP. A study by Microsoft also indicates that the digital economy contributed to the GDP of the Asia-Pacific region by about 6% in 2017, about 25% in 2019, and about 60% in 2021.

China is a successful example of digital economy development, with a very high growth rate, and is mainly based on the Internet/platform digital economy components and the industry/sector digital economy. According to the International Monetary Fund, the size of China's digital economy has increased from 15% of GDP in 2008 to 37% in 2019, in which the ICT/VT digital economy component accounts for a small and stable part of the country, around 6%–7% of GDP annually, while the Internet/platform digital economy component has multiplied from 7% of GDP in 2008 to 30% of GDP in 2019.

In the ASEAN region, according to the e-Conomy SEA 2020 Report,[6] the Internet/platform digital economy component alone in 2020 has reached about 105 US billion dollars (up 5% compared to 2019) and is expected to reach 309 US billion dollars by 2025. Indonesia has the highest revenue from the Internet/platform digital

[5]https://unctad.org/system/files/official-document/der2019_en.pdf.

[6]https://storage.googleapis.com/gweb-economy-sea.appspot.com/assets/pdf/e-Conomy_SEA_2020_Report.pdf (Report by Google Temasek and Bain& Company).

economy with 44 US billion dollars in 2020, followed by Thailand with 18 US billion dollars and Vietnam with 14 US billion dollars.

To see the global digital economy development trends, look at the performance areas of the top 20 companies in the world by market capitalization according to the UNCTAD Digital Economy Report. In 2009 among the world's leading companies, 35% were oil, gas, and mining economic companies, while only 15% were digital economy companies; however, by 2018, the picture has changed *significantly*: The number of top digital economy companies in the world increased by 40%, while the number of oil, gas and mining companies in the top decreased to only 10%. This change is even more noticeable when measured by market capitalization: In 2009, oil, gas, and mining economic companies accounted for 36% of the total market capitalization of the world's top 20 companies, while the digital economy group accounted for 16%, but by 2018, the digital economy group had increased to 56% of the total market capitalization, whereas the proportion of oil, gas, and mining economic companies decreased to only 7%.

The United States and Asia are the two fastest-growing regions in the digital economy, with a high concentration of the world's leading digital technology companies in these two regions.

4.2. *Development orientation of countries*

In the face of the strong wave of the digital transformation revolution and the rapid development of the digital economy and digital society, several countries, recognizing the opportunity, have soon issued strategies and programs for digital transformation and growth. It's a digital economy and digital society, for example, the UK (Digital Economy Strategy), Canada (Canada's Digital Economy Strategy), Australia (National Digital Economy Strategy), Nigeria (National Digital Economy Policy and Strategy), and Kenya (Digital). Economy strategy), Taiwan (DIGI 2025 Creative Economy Development Plan), Singapore (Digital Economy Framework for Action), and Thailand (Thailand Digital Economy and Society Development Plan). Along with the urgent promulgation and implementation of strategies and programs to develop the digital economy and digital society, countries have also strongly transformed their institutions, promulgated legal documents, and created a legal corridor suitable for digital economic development.

Many countries are well aware of the content of the digital economy and digital society and have made efforts to transform and improve the management system of the Information and Communication industry to promote development because the characteristics of the digital economy and digital society are associated with the role, position, and development of this industry. Two of the three components of the digital economy are under the direct management responsibility of the Information and Communication industry, namely the ICT/VT digital economy and the internet/platform digital economy. The digital economic component of the industry/field also needs support, promotion, infrastructure creation, and technical conditions for this industry to develop. For the digital society, of the seven basic characteristics mentioned in Section 2.1, there are also the first five criteria that fall under the management responsibility of the Information and Communication industry.

Therefore, many countries have changed the name and organizational structure of the Ministry of Information and Communications Management to a new Ministry with the phrase "Digital" prominently in the name of the Ministry to carry out state management of the digital economy and digital transformation. For example, Thailand changed the name of the Ministry of Information and Communications to the Ministry of Digital Economy and Society (Ministry of Digital Economy and Society), Austria changed its name to the Ministry of Digital Transformation and Digital Economy (Ministry for Digital and Economic Affairs), Russia changed its name to the Ministry of Communications and Digital Development (Ministry for Digital Development, Communications and Mass Media), etc.

5. Experience of Digital Economy Development of Some Countries

5.1. *America's digital economy development experience*

The United States is one of the world's leading countries in the field of digital economy and information and communication technology (ICT). The US strategy in this area has been formed and developed over the years since information technology and the internet began to spread in daily life. The US is a specific country where the policies and environment are open and favorable for innovative startups. In general, the US digital economy development environment combines many factors, from the transparency of the law, the government's supportive and encouraging policies, venture capital funds, etc. Prominent US policy aspects in promoting the digital economy include:

5.1.1. *Invest heavily in research and development*

The US has invested heavily in technology research and development, especially information and communication technology. Research and development of new technologies, especially in the digital economy and ICT, should be one of the top priorities. Many significant research and development (R&D) projects have been invested to develop new technologies and improve existing technologies. The US government has invested billions of dollars in research and development in areas such as artificial intelligence, machine learning, the Internet of Things, cloud computing, the Internet of Things (IoT), and other technologies to promote the development of the digital economy.

The US also spends a lot of its budget funding research institutes, universities, startups, and other organizations to help strengthen the digital industry's power and creativity. Policies for creating favorable conditions for businesses to invest in research and development, such as reduced tax payments and patent protection policies, have also been introduced to encourage companies' investment in new advanced technology.

5.1.2. *Promoting innovative start-ups and business development*

The US has built a robust startup ecosystem, with many opportunities and resources to start a business, especially in the technology sector. The US government has applied many policies and support mechanisms for start-ups, such as tax reduction policies and startup support programs.

The US government has introduced policies to encourage innovation and entrepreneurship in the ICT sector, which has created conditions for startups and new businesses to be born, thereby accelerating the development of the country's digital economy and ICT.

Incentivizing digital startups and other technology developers can help create new jobs, products, and services. The US has made an excellent start-up environment by providing startups with favorable financial and institutional support and protecting intellectual property rights.

The US creates many favorable conditions for startups and businesses in the digital economy and ICT field. The US government has provided loans and grants to help start-ups develop new services and products. In addition, the US government has created a favorable business environment by providing clear legal regulations and supporting business registration procedures.

The US also introduced policies to support and encourage businesses to enter the digital economy and ICT market. The US government has launched training programs and financial support for new companies entering the market, thereby promoting the development of the digital economy and ICT.

5.1.3. *Training and developing human resources*

The US has an excellent education system that trains and develops specialists and specialists in information and communication technology. This helps the US have a skilled and specialized workforce that meets the needs of the digital economy and ICT development.

The US has invested in training high-quality human resources in digital economy and ICT, including sponsoring training programs for students, teachers, and adult workers. These programs help provide workers with the latest skills and knowledge to meet the needs of the labor market in the digital economy.

5.1.4. *Encourage investment from large technology corporations*

The US has encouraged investment from extensive technology corporations, such as Google, Apple, Facebook, Amazon, and Microsoft, to make essential contributions to the development of the digital economy and ICT of the country.

Large corporations are also encouraged to develop digital infrastructure platforms, including telecommunications networks and other infrastructure, to support the development of the digital industry.

The US also promotes public–private cooperation in developing the digital economy. Governments and private businesses can collaborate to develop ICT and digital solutions. Policies such as tax incentives, preferential loan credits, and public-private partnerships can help increase investment capacity and develop the digital industry.

The government also makes constant efforts to create a favorable business environment in the digital economy and promote the development of businesses and the formation of unions.

5.1.5. *Digital data development policy*

— Regulation: There is no general personal data privacy framework that each State regulates. However, a strict localization policy applies to security and defense data. For cross-border data, the US approach is to maintain leadership in the global digital market and further expand into new markets, which advocates against data and digital protectionism.

Strategy: Promote the expansion of global digital technology corporations, support the promotion of free data flow, and hinder data localization requirements in trade agreements.[7]

5.1.6. *Key digital product development policy*

Introduce measures to restrict the export of technology such as algorithms and drones... and may expand in the future.

A good example of a key product development policy is the plan of the Government of President Biden in 2021 to invest 258 US million dollars with technology companies AMD, Cray, HP, IBM, NVIDIA to produce products Supercomputer.

5.1.7. *Procurement Act (BAA) of the United States*

This act primarily governs domestic preferences in federal government procurement. The BAA does not prohibit the purchase of foreign goods. Instead, it establishes preferences that apply to American materials and products. The BAA requires the federal government to buy only products and materials mined and manufactured in the United States and only under certain circumstances.

According to BAA, a product is considered made in the US if "most" of the components made up of materials, materials, and supplies are exploited and manufactured in the US. According to federal government regulations, the product must be manufactured in the US, and the cost of input materials in the US must account for more than 55% of the total cost. If this level is not met, it is considered

[7]Specifically: When drafting regulations such as the Law on Cybersecurity, the draft Decree 72, etc., organizations and alliances whose members are US businesses often speak out strongly about the requirements. require a server in Vietnam, have a copy of the data in Vietnam, or some content related to data localization.

a foreign product and can only be purchased in exceptional circumstances.

Exceptions to the US Procurement Act include:

(1) The purchase of domestic products would not be in the public interest, mainly: The US Department of Defense uses the public interest provision to bypass BAA regulations that apply to countries that signed a Memorandum of Understanding on Reciprocal Procurement with the United States. This memorandum of understanding includes defense goods not covered by trade agreements.
(2) The price of the domestic product is unreasonable: To determine whether the domestic price is absurd, the BAA uses the price differential. A spread of 6% is used for most procurement contracts. However, a spread of 12% applies if the lowest domestic price is offered by a small business. Particularly, the Ministry of Defense uses 50% of the difference in its procurement activities. This difference is added to the lowest price in the country compared to the price of foreign suppliers. It is considered unreasonable if the domestic price is still higher than the foreign price.
(3) Domestic product does not meet quantity or quality requirements: BAA does not care whether a product has not been manufactured in the United States or does not meet commercial requirements in quantity or quality. Instead, it is based on the FAR catalog of goods. According to FAR, this provision does not mean that there is no domestic product; instead, it means that domestic resources can only meet 50% or less of total demand. Government agencies also have the power to determine the non-availability of regulated goods on their own.
(4) The purchased product is used outside the United States: The Ministry of Defense, in particular, applies the Balance of Payment Program (Balance of Payment Program).
(5) Procurement costs are lower than the minimum purchase threshold of 3,000 US dollars.
(6) Commercial products in FAR's list of information technology products.

5.2. *Australia's digital economy development experience (Australia)*

The Australian Government approved the Digital Economy Strategy 2030 in March 2021. Some of the critical points of Australia's 2030 Digital Economy Strategy include:

(a) *Vision*: As a leading digital economy and digital society in the world.

(b) *Goals to 2030*:
- 100% of Government services are online;
- The digital technology industry uses 10% of the workforce;
- Graduated digital technology students increase by 15,000/year;
- All enterprises are technology enterprises since their inception;
- All enterprises continuously improve the capacity of ATANM;
- 90% of small and medium enterprises (SMEs) use e-commerce tools.

(c) *The three main pillars of the strategy*:

Pillar 1: Building supporting platforms
Includes main contents:

(1) Digital infrastructure;
(2) ATANM and digital trust;
(3) Digital skills and digital human resources;
(4) Legal and Systematic;
(5) Digital trade and international agreements.

Pillar 2: Building capacity in new technologies
Includes main contents: AI, IoT, Data analytics, Blockchain, and Quantum Computing.

Pillar 3: Establish digital growth priorities
Includes main contents:
(1) Transformation of the number of SMEs;
(2) Digital transformation of modern industries and industries with competitive advantages;
(3) Create a dynamic emerging technology industry;
(4) Building a Digital Government.

(d) *Structure*: The structure of Australia's 2030 Digital Economy Strategy is shown in Figure 5.

(e) *Action programs and funding*: The fiscal year of 2021–2022 spent 1.2 US billion dollars on digital initiatives such as Artificial Intelligence AI; New aviation technology; tax incentives; protection of the data rights of the user; digital data development; digital skills training; myGov project implementation; Implementing the project of Electronic health records; Implementation of the d-ID Digital Identity project; Support small and medium enterprises in the digital transformation of SMEdx; Project to promote digital connection; E-invoice development project; Guaranteed ATANM; National digital map construction project.

5.3. *Experience in Developing the UK's Digital Economy (UK)*

The UK has issued a UK Digital Strategy and considers digital technology one of the country's most important sectors. The Strategy's ideology and ambition are to create a world-leading digital economy to ensure the UK is the best place to start and grow a digital business, test a new technology, or undertake cutting-edge research.

The seven pillars of the UK's Digital Strategy include:

- Digital Skills (Purpose: Stronger digital skills at every level, for everyone, from getting people online for the first time to attracting and training programming talent) top in the world).
- Digital business development environment (Purpose: Make the UK the best place to start and grow a digital business).
- Transform every business into a digital technology enterprise (Purpose: Increase the UK's global competitiveness).
- Data (Purpose: Unlocking the power of data in the UK economy and improving public confidence in the use of data).
- Digital Infrastructure (Purpose: to build a world-class digital infrastructure for the UK, with comprehensive coverage, no one left out, and enough capacity for the present and the future).

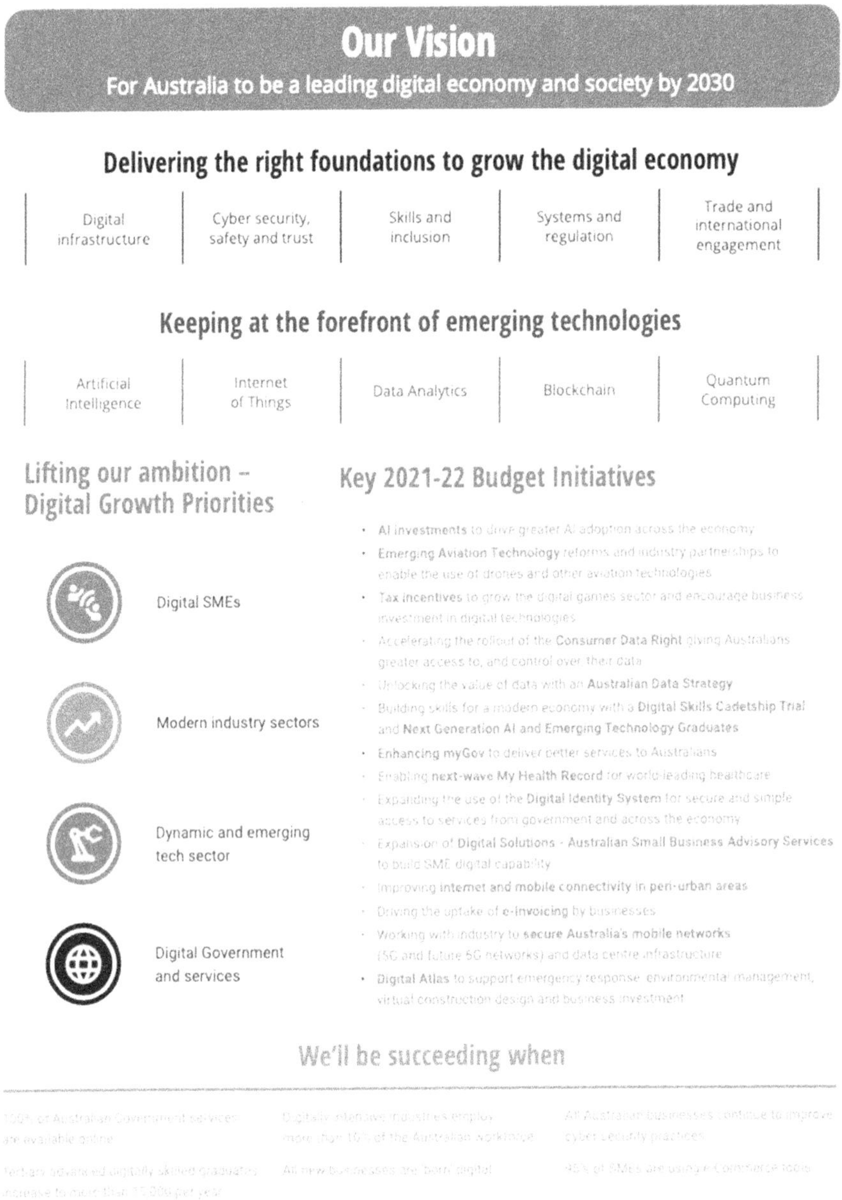

Figure 5: Australia's digital economy strategic structure.

- Cybersecurity (Purpose: to make the UK the safest place to live and work online in the world, give people the confidence to be part of the digital world and the digital world, and give the UK a competitive advantage).
- Digital Government (Purpose: to maintain the UK government as a world leader in serving its citizens online).

The following laws/laws/regulations are oriented and promulgated in the Strategy:

- Digital skills: Putting regulations on the Right to enjoy digital skills into the law; developing the Tech Talent Charter to set out key measures to encourage organizations to think differently to support the technology workforce.
- Environment for developing digital technology enterprises: Promulgating income tax incentives for profits earned from patented inventions; tax relief for investors buying new shares in small companies, high-risk companies, and growing... The general idea is that the regulatory environment is friendly to innovation and creates a dynamic and flexible intellectual property regime that keeps up with technological changes.
- Data: Create regulatory frameworks that keep pace with new data technologies, support innovative enterprise uses of data, and protect people's privacy; sanctions for data protection breaches.
- Digital infrastructure: Encourage investment in digital infrastructure; promote competition; create regulations to help operators build and develop digital infrastructure faster and cheaper; improve the regulation of the consumer market.

Some UK successes: The digital technology industry grew six times faster than any other sector in the UK in 2019, a bright spot in the UK economy. The UK's tech sector growth beat both the US and China in 2019. The number of tech unicorns created in the UK is second only to the US and China. Eight billion-dollar companies were founded in the UK in 2019 — bringing the total number based in the UK to 77, double the total in Germany (34) and almost four times that of Israel (20).

5.4. *Japan's digital economy development experience*

5.4.1. *Digital transformation in Japan*

The wave of digital transformation has become the mainstay of Japan's industrial policy. This country wants to pioneer in the new era of the world, the era of globalization and the rapid development of digital technologies such as the Internet of Things (IoT), artificial intelligence (AI), and machine learning are bringing significant changes to the entire society.

The world is facing challenges on a global scale, such as the depletion of natural resources, global warming, growing economic disparities, etc. Therefore, it is imperative to make the most of ICT to gain new knowledge and create new values by building connections between "People and Things" and between the "Real world and Cyberworld," as an effective and efficient means of solving problems in society, creating better lives for people and maintaining healthy economic growth.

Big data collected from IoT and AI technology will create a new resource that reaches every corner of society. As we adopt new technologies in the new society, our lives will all be more comfortable and sustainable, and products and services will be provided in specific quantities when needed.

To stay ahead of the global trend, "Society 5.0" is presented as a core concept in the 5th Science and Technology Basic Plan, approved by the Japanese Cabinet in January 2016; it is identified as one of Japan's growth strategies. Society 5.0 — Super Smart Society, is also a core part of the Strategy "Investing in the Future 2017: Reforms to Achieve Society 5.0." Japan is the first country in the world to lead the construction of Society 5.0 — Toward a new people-centered society.

— Society 1.0 is defined as groups of hunters and gatherers living in harmony with nature;

— Society 2.0 forms groups based on farming, strengthening organization, and building nation;
— Society 3.0 is a society that promotes industrialization through the industrial revolution and mass production;
— Society 4.0 is an information society that realizes added value by connecting intangible assets in the form of information networks;
— Society 5.0 is an information society built based on Society 4.0, geared toward a prosperous society centered on the people.

The goal of Society 5.0 is to create a people-centered society, achieve economic development, and solve social challenges so that everyone can enjoy a high-quality and comfortable life. It is a society that will respond in detail to the different needs of people, regardless of region, age, gender, language, etc., by providing necessary items and services. The key to realizing Society 5.0 is the combination of cyberspace and the natural world (physical space) to create new quality, value, and solutions for data, solving challenges and various social problems.

Following the Cabinet's decision on the 5th Science and Technology Basic Plan, the Japan Economic Recovery Headquarters established the "Investment Council for the Future" to promote its growth strategy and rapid structural reform to increase "investment for the future." In June 2017, "Investing in Future Strategy 2017" to realize the Cabinet approved Society 5.0 as a concrete measure to achieve Society 5.0. According to this strategy, the key to achieving medium- and long-term growth is to realize Society 5.0, addressing various social challenges by incorporating the innovations of the 4th Industrial Revolution into every area of social life, such as the Internet of Things (IoT), Big data, artificial intelligence AI, robotics and the sharing economy in all areas of social life. That way, the future society will be one in which new values and services are created continuously, improving people's lives.

Japan has selected five main areas that can take advantage of its strengths and attract investors in the world such as: "Promoting health," "Prolonging life," "Realizing the mobile revolution," "Creating Next Generation Supply Chains," "*Building and Developing*

Infrastructure" and "*Leveraging Technology in FinTech Operations and Financial Services.*" With the challenge of an aging population, Japan is bearing the growing health and social security costs of caring for older people. Japan is one of the first countries in the world to move toward an aging society, establishing a "new health system" to extend people's life expectancy through medical care, and nursing care with a focus on health management, disease prevention, and self-help. Effective medical treatment based on data is delivered by connecting and sharing medical data currently distributed in different hospitals. Telemedicine helps older adults no longer have to go to the hospital as often. In addition, it is also possible to measure and manage health data, such as measuring heart rate at home, so that people's life expectancy can be extended.

In December 2017, the "New Economic Policy Package" was adopted to implement the measures in the "Investment for the Future Strategy 2017," including the revolution of human resource development and innovation of the supply system, which are essential policies in Japanese society. By promoting human resource development, the Japanese government aims to build a society in which all citizens, including young and old, women and men, people with disabilities, and people with disabilities terminally ill, have a whole life. In the supply system revolution, new value will be created by technological innovations such as IoT, big data, robotics, and AI in autonomous driving, health, medical care, long-term care, financial and commercial transactions, construction, transportation, agriculture, forestry and fisheries and tourism, sports, culture, and the arts. Japan is promoting Society 5.0 by introducing digital technologies in various systems and accelerating the implementation of digital technologies to achieve a society where all citizens can actively participate in all sectors of society.

5.4.2. *Strategy for the development of Japan's digital society*

With the digital transformation policy aimed at building a society of 5.0, in Japan's view, the digital economy is harmonized with developing a digital society. The Japanese Government issued the Strategy for developing Japan's Digital Society in January 2021. The main contents of this Strategy include:

5.4.2.1. Vision

Building a digital society where people can choose the right service for each person and have more happiness through digital transformation, with the motto "Leave no one behind, human-friendly digital transformation."

Toward establishing the Digital Department, based on "Basic orientation of reforms to realize digital society," accelerating efforts on digital governance such as bringing digital governance content into the digital transformation guide for the State/local.

5.4.2.2. The main contents of the strategy

(a) Service design/radical business reform (BPR):

- ✓ Stemming from the needs of users, administrative services "can be used immediately," "simple," "and convenience" ... based on 12 principles of service design from the point of view of End-to-End.
- ✓ For users, realize 100% digital transformation of administrative services so that all administrative services are digitized from the beginning to the end.
- ✓ Thorough business reform (BPR), capturing and analyzing differences between users and actual business details.

(b) State/local digital transformation guide:

Implemented based on "Personal Code System and Report of Working Group on Fundamental Improvement of State and Local Digital Infrastructure" (including progress).

- ✓ Building a "Gov-Cloud" system (temporary name), which is the common foundation of state and local information systems.
- ✓ Information linkage and beyond the three areas of social security, tax, disaster, and automatic notification system review for Once-Only implementation, fundamentally review the architecture related to information linkage.

- ✓ Fundamentally review state and local network structure (high speed, low cost, large capacity ...).
- ✓ Standardize/share/use "Gov-Cloud" (temporary name) of the local business system.
- ✓ Establishing the Digital Department as a Command, transforming J-LIS into a legal entity jointly managed by the state and local authorities.
- ✓ Forming a mechanism to register state/local money-receiving accounts, a mechanism to facilitate the association of personal identification numbers with savings deposit accounts.
- ✓ Bringing the function of the personal identification number card to the smartphone application, resetting the security code of the electronic certificate at the post office, submitting an application for a card with a 2-way barcode for those who do not have a code, synchronizing all types of cards (driver's license, residence card, national certificates).
- ✓ Improve UX-UI of Myna Portal (connecting localities), enhance information center function.
- ✓ Reviewing legal regulations on personal information security (synchronizing laws, reducing the burden on private enterprises).
- ✓ Institutionalize the transcription of names in the household registration book (using English phonetic characters on the card, speeding up the processing speed of the system).

(c) Completing infrastructure to deploy e-government:

- ✓ Completing the shared system in Government, platform, and function (digital infrastructure).
- ✓ Consider using Cloud services to promote network security assessment mechanism (ISMAP).
- ✓ Thoroughly implement the policy of ensuring information security, the privacy of personal information, ensuring the continuity of business.
- ✓ Completing the essential registration (legal entities, primary data related to land) based on the new Data Strategy, building administration as a platform, and promoting strengthening the agency's open data system administrative management.

(d) Digital transformation of administrative procedures, promoting a 1-stop service:
  - ✓ Along with reviewing documents, seals, and direct contact, promote the transition to online administrative procedures.
  - ✓ For certificates (information linkage has been started), and household registration books (from 2023), based on information linkage between administrative agencies, gradually remove documents attached to administrative procedures.
  - ✓ Implement One Stop Service for procedures such as child care, elderly care, house moving, death/inheritance, employee social insurance, tax, and business establishment.
  - ✓ Enhancing the convenience of procedures for businesses, such as expanding the functionality of Digital Platform for businesses.

(e) Solutions to the digital divide/implementation of propaganda:
  - ✓ Basic implementation of a staffed mechanism to support the use of digital to be able to consult in the most convenient way.
  - ✓ Easy-to-understand propaganda through the message/image system, organizing events with the participation of the people.

(f) Deploy the construction of e-Government in the locality:
  - ✓ Speeding up the standardization/sharing of the local professional system (state support, including financial resources).
  - ✓ Implement the transformation to the online form of local administrative procedures through the use of Myna Portal (including administrative procedures based on terms/regulations).
  - ✓ Support local efforts based on the "Local Digital Transformation Implementation Plan."
  - ✓ Using Cloud services, promoting the efficiency of operations using AI and RPA.
  - ✓ Securing/developing digital human resources using "Local Informatization Advisor."

(g) Enhance centralized project management:
  - ✓ Toward establishing the Digital Department to strengthen the centralized project management from pre-budget to implementation involving the entire government information system.

✓ To increase efficiency and modernize the government information system, expand the scope of one-time allocation of the budget related to the information system (consider a one-time allocation to the Digital Bureau of the entire budget associated with all systems).
✓ To improve the system in a mobile and efficient way, test new procurement and contract methods so that technical discussions on the proposed content can be discussed with many businesses before signing the contract.
✓ Toward the fiscal year 2025, to reduce 30% of operating costs of government information systems, and expenses related to system improvement (compared to 2020).
✓ Mechanism to use highly specialized human resources from outside, soon apply the mechanism to recruit IT human resources through civil service exam.

5.5. *Singapore's digital economy development experience*

5.5.1. *Singapore's digital economy development action plan*

Singapore Government approved the Digital Economy Framework for Action in early 2021. The structure of Singapore's Digital Economy Development Program is shown in Figure 6. Some of the critical contents of Singapore's Digital Economy Development Action Agenda include:

(a) *Target*: Being a leading digital economy and continuously reinventing itself.
(b) *Three pillars*:
    (1) *Acceleration*: Strong digital transformation of industries and fields. Focus on the digital transformation of businesses, especially SMEs.
    (2) *Competition*: Increase national competitiveness with digital platforms (for a new integrated ecosystem focusing on customer needs) that can go global.

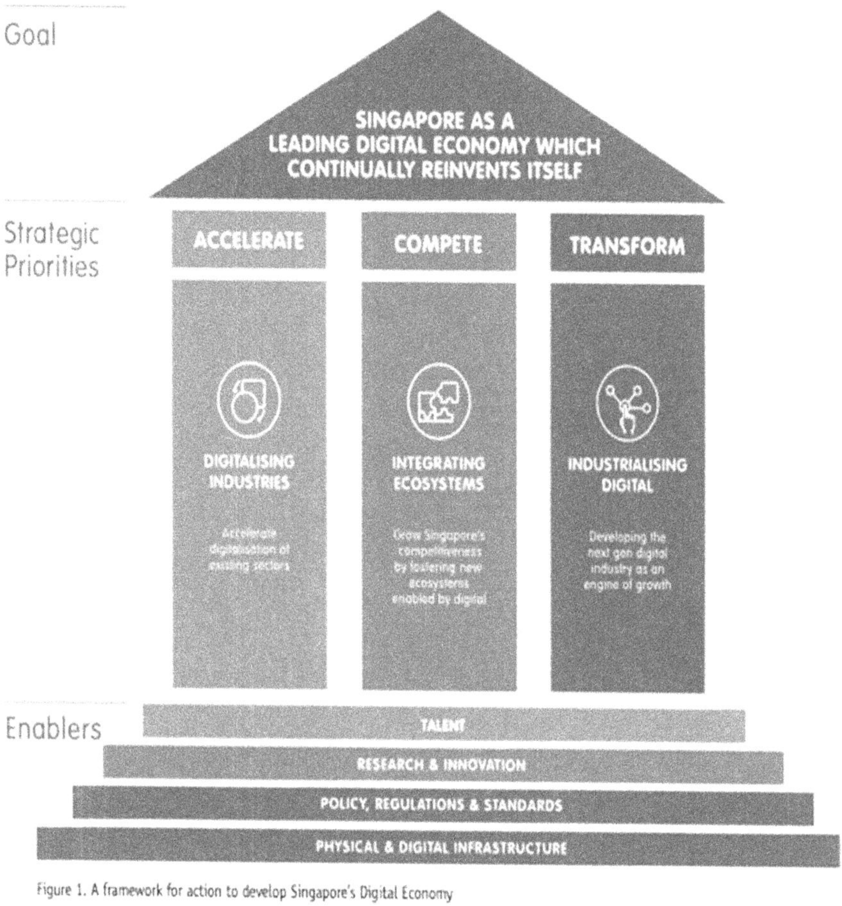

Figure 6: Structure of Singapore's Digital Economy Development Program.

(3) *Innovation*: Developing next-generation digital industries to drive growth and promote industry digital transformation.

(c) *Four fundamental factors*:

(1) *Human resources*: Continuously training and retraining digital skills and developing the digital workforce.

(2) *Research and innovation*: Support enterprises in creating and utilizing intellectual property to improve competitiveness and exploit the scientific community's capacity.

(3) *Policies, regulations, and standards*: Ensure that the digital economy policy and regulatory environment are the most competitive.
(4) *Digital and physical infrastructure*: Ensure that connectivity networks, platforms, data, and other digital infrastructure best support the digital economy.

5.5.2. *Singapore's outstanding digital economy development policies*

5.5.2.1. Building digital infrastructure

Singapore has made significant progress in improving its digital infrastructure, thereby promoting capacity building and expanding digitalization in households and businesses. Typically, the development of optical fiber systems and 4G networks significantly increases the speed of information transmission. Thanks to the fiber optic network, Singapore's average Internet connection speed has risen from 5.4 megabits per second (Mbps) in 2012 to 20 Mbps in 2016, on par with Japan and Finland. Similarly, Singapore is among the top countries with the fastest 4G connection speeds globally, thanks in part to continuous investment in improving network infrastructure. Total fiber broadband and 4G subscriptions in Singapore have doubled in the past five years. Faster internet speeds spur Singaporean households to move more of their activities into the digital space. Findings from the annual survey by the Information and Communications Development Authority of Singapore (IMDA) show that between 2010 and 2015, the number of people engaged in Internet activities such as online shopping and online financial transactions increased significantly. In the corporate sector, investments in digital assets to strengthen the digital capabilities of businesses are also growing. Between 2013 and 2015, total capital expenditure on digital assets[8] increased by an average of 7.1% annually. Accordingly, businesses also increase the use of digital tools in daily business activities

[8]Including computers, peripheral devices, and information — telecommunications equipment.

and the application of electronic payments and mobile services in the industry.

In addition to the prominent trends, the application level of digital tools and capabilities such as cloud computing services, intelligent factories, etc., has also increased rapidly in recent years. With many efforts from the Singapore government toward digitizing the economy (such as through the Smart City Initiative), the level of digitalization of households and businesses is maintained and growing.

5.5.2.2. Building a smart city

Smart Cities Program office to coordinate efforts from various government agencies toward the ambitious goal of becoming the world's first Smart City. The "Smart City" project aims to solve five main challenges that countries worldwide face: high urban population density, population aging, increasing demand for health care, difficult urban traffic, and lack of energy. By applying digital technologies to solve these problems, Singapore hopes its "Smart City" model can become a model for other countries. The Singapore Smart City model aims to include the following contents: a greener, cleaner, and safer living environment for urban residents; more choices of means of transportation; better home health care for older people; Public services are more convenient, and there are better living opportunities for citizens. Jurong Lak, a district west of Singapore, was chosen as a testbed for innovative city initiatives.

The Smart City platform has many important features that support individuals, governments, and businesses. It focuses on three aspects: connection, collection, and understanding.

In the first phase, Singapore identified five critical areas for any citizen and society in which digital technology can participate: transport, housing and environment, business performance, health, and public services. The government is committed to creating conditions for infrastructure and policies so that all initiatives and ideas have the opportunity to form and test, including possible risks.

Information technology (IT) is identified as the core to realizing the Smart City goal, which focuses on three priorities: technology to support society, mobility and intelligent transportation, and secure data environment. The government also commits to investing about 1% of GDP annually in research and development.

Those decisions have yielded impressive results. IT has become a part of life in Singapore, where 75% of households have at least one computer and over 50% have a broadband connection to surf the net. The IT industry contributes up to 6.5% to the country's GDP. More than 172,000 people working in the IT sector are ready to support the economy and society's information, communication, and telecommunications needs.

5.5.2.3. Electronic payment development

Singapore is the fastest-growing e-payment market among ASEAN countries, with an internet population of about 80% and an e-commerce index of about 56%–57%. Singapore is a country that quickly adopts new technology with the number of e-wallet users, which since 2015 has accounted for 23% of the country's total population and more than 41% of the total number of online shoppers.

Singapore is one of the first countries to apply e-commerce in the world. E-commerce activities develop at a relatively fast rate. However, up to now, Singapore still lags behind many other countries, such as China, in applying e-commerce technology. Most people in Singapore have a smartphone, but nine out of 10 people still want to pay for their day-to-day transactions in an old-fashioned way with cash. 43% of Singaporeans surveyed said they use cash the most, almost double the 25% in China. The reason is that Singapore has many e-commerce programs, but there is a lack of connection and connection between these payment systems, so it causes a lot of trouble, especially people have to carry many cards and businesses also have to pay expensive bills to install multiple systems.

Advocacy to turn Singapore into a cashless society is unanimously needed to simplify and unify the different payment systems. To accelerate the roadmap, the Monetary Authority of Singapore has launched an initiative with 2,000 POS systems (machines that accept card payments for customers to swipe cards) for uniform payment at more than 650 retail stores nationwide. These POSs support various payment options, including Samsung Pay and Apple Pay. POS has the advantage of being compact, occupying only a small area, and can be easily installed in many places. In addition, the Singapore government plans to develop a fast payment system using a standard QR code (a type of code that can be scanned with a smartphone) to conduct e-commerce nationwide. The working group responsible for this is coordinated by the Monetary Authority of Singapore and the Infocomm Media Development Authority (Infocomm Media Development Authority), and many stakeholders are included, such as banks, payment schemes, QR payment service providers, and government agencies. In fact, QR codes offer a cheaper and less infrastructure alternative to debit and credit card schemes. Therefore, QR codes are increasingly used in e-commerce, contributing to the promotion of cashless payments.

Many businesses have been implementing innovative initiatives in response to the government's policy of promoting e-commerce. Technology company Razer proposes a unified e-payment initiative. The solution is to use RazerPay, a type of electronic wallet based on cloud technology, which can be deployed in many different forms, from a VSF (Stored Value Facilities) card to a mobile wallet app, a chip, or more. Ride-hailing app Grab company aims to roll out its QR payment system at 1,000 retail stores and small merchants. Nets Payment firm also announced plans to roll out the NetsPay mobile wallet, which can digitize six banks' credit, debit, and ATM cards, helping reduce the hassle for users due to the need to download multiple mobile apps. This solution allows users to perform direct payments from their bank account by scanning a QR code using a personal smartphone or by contactless swiping if the device is within the range that allows short-range wireless connectivity (NFC). Nets' network currently has about 10 million ATM cards; in addition, Nets supports accepting ATM cards from DBS, OCBC Bank, and United Overseas Bank. ATM cards of foreign banks such as HSBC, Maybank and Standard Chartered Bank can also be used at 100,000 retail points that accept Nets payments by directly deducting from people's bank accounts.

5.5.2.4. Development of information and communication technology (ICT) industry

Singapore develops the ICT industry as the fundamental driving force for the development of the digital economy. ICT includes 12 sub-sectors that produce or promote the development of digital goods and services (including hardware, telecommunications, IT services, software, games, online services, printing, and postal services and courier, publishing, broadcasting, film and video, and music), thereby playing an essential role in facilitating the adoption of digitization among households and businesses in Singapore. For example, companies in the telecommunications industry provide Internet access services, while the IT services subsector serves businesses with computer programming services.

The increase in demand for digital goods and services among individuals and businesses has fueled the growth of the ICT industry. The ICT industry's nominal value added (VA) grew at an average rate of 7.2% annually, faster than the average growth rate of 4.2% for the whole economy. The growth rate of employment in the ICT sector in the same period reached 2.5% per year, although it was slower than the overall employment growth of the economy (3.2% per year). Accordingly, the productivity of the ICT industry in VA per worker increased by more than 4.6%/year, much higher than the overall productivity growth of the economy (0.6%/year).

The vigorous development of the ICT industry has increased the industry's contribution to the economy from 7.4% of nominal GDP in 2011 to 8.3% in 2015. The industry's nominal VA reached 32 US billion dollars, and three sub-sectors account for the majority of nominal VA, including hardware 40%, telecommunications 16%, and IT services 15%.

5.6. *Korea's digital economy development experience*

Korea has a policy to promote the development of the digital economy and digital society from a very early age. It is one of the leading countries in the hardware industry. The software and services industries are proliferating especially the high-value associated software and services. The deployment of ecosystems built by large IT suppliers, facilitated by an appropriate policy environment, is essential in helping Korea achieve achievements in IT industry development.

From 2019, every year, the Korean Government spends a budget of 1.6 trillion won (equivalent to 1.41 billion US dollars) to invest in the development of the IT industry, especially the manufacturing industries based on Data–Network–AI with emerging technology products such as 5G phones, IoT devices, virtual reality, augmented reality, artificial intelligence based products, data analytics large data sets, super high-resolution screens, etc. The support is provided by supporting small and medium enterprises, especially forming start-up businesses.

Korea's digital economic development policy is reflected in the following highlights:

5.6.1. *Universal Internet access*

The percentage of the Korean population using the Internet since 2016 has reached 88.3%. In particular, the number of older adults using the Internet has increased sharply, with one in two people over 60 years old. The rate of Internet use in the age group from 10 to 40 years old reaches 100%. The means to access the internet is shifting from computer to smartphones. The rate of smartphone ownership per household reached 88.5% in 2016. The percentage of Korean households connected to the Internet reached 99.2%, ranking first among the 175 Telecommunications Union International (ITU) countries. According to Akamai — an Internet research organization, Korea is currently the country with the fastest internet connection speed in the world, surpassing both Japan and the US. The success in popularizing high-speed internet in Korea is linked to five key factors that are linked together, including: (i) Government planning; (ii) promoting fair competition; (iii) urban population density; (iv) growth of the private sector; and (v) Korean culture. Korea is currently focusing on boosting the number of internet users, increasing the percentage of smartphone users, and increasing the rate of households with fiber and 4G connections to 5G.

From a planning perspective, thanks to the implementation of the Government's initiatives on education and information technology infrastructure, about 84% of the Korean population has access to the Internet, of which about 94% use broadband. Timely planning and vigorous implementation of Internet policies made a perfect start, and they continue to be effective.

The second success factor is that the Government maintains a healthy competitive environment and encourages innovation. In parallel with establishing the public sector Internet network, the Korean Government retains its support for investment in the private sector through consistent regulatory policies. These policies reduce obstacles to new Internet service providers (ISPs), promoting a competitive environment. These policies allow private sector operators to expand the Internet from a core framework into a nationwide system and speed up the Internet through fierce competition.

The third factor in creating favorable conditions for Korea to deploy high-speed Internet widely is that Korea has an urban population density as high as 83%, concentrated in urban apartment buildings. Therefore, constructing broadband fiber optic infrastructure becomes easy and significantly reduces costs while reducing the loss of Internet transmission performance.

The fourth factor contributing to the successful Internet universalization in Korea is the strong partnership between the government-backed private and public sectors in infrastructure construction. Today, the private Korean industry is conducting some of the most cutting-edge technology research, with Samsung as one of the key players behind developing the upcoming 5G network.

The fifth factor contributing to Korea's world-leading internet development lies in its cultural characteristics. Accordingly, Korean culture focuses on the importance of morality and perseverance; once the goal of technological development is set, Koreans do not back down. At the same time, the Korean Government strives to promote the Internet as a tool for education and progress, focusing on connecting education to the Internet and seeing it as a helpful way to develop thinking in the 21st century.

5.6.2. *E-commerce development*

E-commerce has been strongly applied in Korea. Since 2015, it has accounted for over 40% of all commercial transactions and is now estimated at around 60%.

Electronic banking (E-banking) was introduced in Korea in 1999. Most banks increased the deposit interest rates by 0.1–0.5 percentage points for customers registering for Internet banking and 0.5 percentage points discount on the loan rate. By 2010, 42.3% of internet users aged 12 and overused e-banking services. The average usage for Internet banking is 4.9 times per month. Most Internet banking users use computers (96.2%), while 9.2% use mobile phones.

Korea's e-commerce boom is driven by the extent to which broadband Internet access has been developed and widely accepted. Regarding the legal corridor, due to a landmark move in 1999, the Korean Government has regulated online signatures in e-commerce with full legal status, such as fresh signatures on documents. This regulation allows electronic signatures to be used as evidence in legal matters.

To enhance information security in e-commerce, the Government has also developed regulations related to protecting personal information and guided the private sector in using encryption technology. In addition, since 2000, about 15 organizations related to e-commerce have launched the Integrated E-Commerce Forum to promote domestic and international standardization of e-commerce platforms.

Since 2003, Korea has adopted a uniform standard for defining digital content to promote e-commerce and make the most of Korea's broadband infrastructure. Accordingly, applying a common national standard for classifying digital content is necessary to accelerate the purchase, sale, and use of Internet-based content. This standard is applied primarily to digital content in the public sector, with an intergovernmental committee established to support digital content transactions.

In summary, e-commerce in Korea was developed very early based on solutions to promote e-banking and online payment; regulations allowing the use of electronic/digital signatures in e-commerce with full legal status, such as fresh signatures on paper documents; rules related to the protection of personal information and guidelines for the private sector to use encryption technology to enhance security in online transactions; allows the use of different software for identification and authentication in e-banking and shopping services online, thereby promoting competition and keeping up with technological advancements.

5.6.3. *Electronic entertainment development*

The online game market in Korea has more than 15 million registered players. Many games are designed in the fantasy world with online multiplayer. The popularity of gaming portals such as Netmarble, Hangame, and Pmang brings the network in big revenue, and an estimated 10 million Korean adults play games through these portals monthly.

The majority of online games are free to play and profits are generated through the sale of virtual items. The leading online gaming companies are NHN, Nexon, NCsoft, Neowiz, and CJ Internet. Since 2010, the Supreme Court of Korea has ruled that virtual currencies can be exchanged for real money and transactions using "virtual currency" will be taxed.

In summary, Korea develops electronic entertainment through policies to promote the development of the online game market; accept virtual assets in video games such as goods, allow trading and exchange; authorize and recognize virtual currencies that can be exchanged for real money and transactions using "virtual currency" will be taxed.

5.6.4. *ICT Convergence Act*

Korea promulgated the ICT Convergence Act (Special Act to Promote ICT, Promote Convergence, effective January 2019), which contains regulations to develop the ICT industry such as: deploying new products, services, and models; Human resource development (training, fostering, and attracting human resources); R&D; Quality management; Support small and medium enterprises, start-ups; Establish an apparatus to support ICT development; Market support, product commercialization, technology. This act contains several sandbox provisions to support the development of new technologies and new paradigms. Accordingly, if the current legal system has prohibitions or unclear/unreasonable regulations to apply to new ICT enterprises/new ICT-related activities, the ICT Convergence Act provides that the applicant Sandbox applications can apply for a temporary "trial" waiver. Under this waiver, sandbox registrants can test a new model/digital product under specific time, territory, and scope limitations.

5.6.5. *5G strategy and new digital technology agreement*

Korea has also issued a 5G Strategy and a New Digital Technology Agreement (5G + Strategy and The Digital New Deal) with the following essential contents:

Vision:

— Consider digital technology as a critical industry to boost the Korean economy;
— Establish a foundation to continue maintaining and be a leading power in digital technology.

Deployment solution:

— 5G plus: nationwide coverage of 5G and business support policies focusing on industries (AR/VR, CCTV, Wearables, robots, ATTT, Cloud computing, drones, smartphones, networks) and services (smart factories, self-driving cars, healthcare, digital content ...) based on 5G;
— Develop a DNA digital ecosystem (data technology, networking, and artificial intelligence) to drive growth in productivity and

production of digital goods and services. Convergence technologies such as 5G, AI, and data analysis apply to almost all fields;
— Focus on investing in chip and semiconductor manufacturing technology to compete with China, Japan, and Taiwan;
— Promote a "quick-quick" *pali-pali* culture: challenging work spirit; patriotism in the use of domestic products and services; open and receptive to technological innovation; promote early technology learning (kindergarten learns coding technology) so that the future will have many talents in the technology field.
— Chaebol is the backbone of the Korean economy, leading in R&D investments, technological innovation, and South Korea Silicon Valley.

5.7. *China's digital economy development experience*

5.7.1. *Promoting the development of the digital economy*

China is already a significant force in digital technology, both in the domestic and global markets. A report by the McKinsey Global Institute (MGI, 2017) confirms that China is currently a digital technology powerhouse with tremendous growth potential. According to MGI, China's e-commerce transactions are now more significant than the combined number of the world's top five economies, including France, Germany, Japan, the UK, and the US. The total value of China's personal consumer mobile payments since 2016 has reached 790 billion US dollars, 11 times more than this in the US market. China is currently one of the top three destinations for venture capital activities in virtual reality, self-driving cars, 3D printing, robotics, drones, and AI. One-third of the 262 "unicorns"[9] in the world today are Chinese, accounting for 43% of the total value of "unicorns" globally.

[9]Startups valued at over 1 US billion dollars.

According to MGI, the three main pillars supporting China's extremely rapid development in digital technology are (i) a huge and young market enabling rapid commercialization of digital business models; (ii) a rich digital ecosystem expanding beyond a few "giants;" (iii) The government creates conditions and space for digital businesses to experiment and be both investors and consumers of digital technologies.

The MGI report forecasts that digital technology could change and generate between 10% and 45% of China's industrial revenue by 2030. MGI also reckons that the Internet has the potential to contribute an additional one percentage point to China's GDP growth rate from 2013 to 2025, resulting in a 22% increase in GDP during this period, equivalent to RMB 14 trillion.

China has strongly developed the digital economy to meet the needs of a huge online population, especially for information search, communication, and commerce in the early stages. China's digital economy is characterized by the strong growth of digital media and e-commerce with the presence of three giant domestic suppliers, including Alibaba (e-commerce), Tencent (online games and social networks), and Baidu (search engine). Each year, the e-commerce group Alibaba handles more purchases than eBay and Amazon combined. With strengths in online games and social networks, Tencent is currently the 10th most valuable company globally (about 275 US billion dollars). Baidu is the company that dominates the search engine segment in the domestic market after Google had to withdraw from the market due to censorship.

Since 2015, China has risen to the top of e-commerce worldwide, with online shopping accounting for 18% of total retail sales, compared with just 8% in the US. It can be said that China's three leading technology platforms, Baidu, Alibaba, and Tencent, have developed to the point where they can compete with the US tech giants Amazon, Apple, Facebook, Google, and Netflix.

China is also developing a digital economy in banking and financial services, public administrative services, health services, and educational services. In China, the online population is becoming more affluent thanks to steady economic growth and rapid urbanization. China also encourages the development of the digital economy and sees it as a solution to help rebalance the economy, avoid over-reliance on infrastructure construction, and promote domestic consumption.

A report by the China Institute of Information Technology and Communications (CAIT) and the Ministry of Industry and Information Technology (MIIT) shows that China's digital economy has grown tremendously since 2016, with an annual growth rate of 19%. Since 2016, China's digital economy has reached 3.4 US trillion dollars in size, ranking second globally, accounting for about 30.3% of GDP of the whole economy. These two agencies' reports also show that China's digital economy will reach 4.8 US trillion dollars by 2020, accounting for 35% of China's GDP. The digital economy will continue to grow rapidly, accounting for approximately 50% of GDP by 2030. One of the highlights of China's digital revolution is mobile payments. In 2016, 790 US billion dollars in third-party payments were made via mobile transactions, 11 times more than the US.

With the growing infrastructure and awareness related to mobile payments, China has a great opportunity to surpass many major powers and become the world's first cashless economy in the near future. The tremendous growth in mobile and payment technologies and their acceptance in currency transactions are helping China close the gap quickly with economic powerhouses such as the US, UK, and France.

Research by Forex Bonuses organization shows that since 2017, the percentage of Chinese people aware of mobile payment services has increased to 77%, far ahead of many other economies such as Australia, Germany, Japan, and Russia. This achievement is mainly due to the explosion of smartphones in the world's most populous market. It also comes with the acumen of many retail and financial service operators when they accept mobile payments quickly.

China is the world's largest smartphone and internet market. From shopping and dining to taking a taxi or playing games, it all comes with online and mobile payment options. Thanks to that, users do not need to worry about carrying cash whenever they go out. China is considered one of the world's most advanced mobile payment markets, with widespread coverage of WeChat Pay and Alipay. Even owning credit and debit cards in China is now gradually becoming redundant when just a smartphone and a WeChat or Alipay payment account, users can pay for almost any service, the necessities of life without needing cash. Therefore, it is not an exaggeration to think that China has a great advantage in moving toward a cashless market in the not-too-distant future.

5.7.2. *Promote ICT industry development*

China has implemented several policies to develop the ICT industry, such as:

- Implement preferential policies such as CIT incentives for high and new technology enterprises (HNTEs), including Electronic information; High technology service industry; Innovation for high and new technology in traditional industries. Exemption from import tax on materials for production. Subsidizing interest rates on loans from commercial banks.
- Product and goods certification: China applies the CCC (China Compulsory Certificate) certification system, a mandatory certification for many types of products and goods imported or circulated in the Chinese market. The system was applied in May 2002 and became widely effective in August 2003. The CCC certification system is managed by a state agency, CNCA (Certification and Accreditation Administration of China), under the Commission of Administration of Quality Supervision, Inspection, and Quarantine (AQSIQ).
- The government participates as an investor in capital contributions to production projects (for example, chip production).

- Experience in IoT development.
  - * At a national scale, IoT is officially mentioned in an essential document of China, the 12th and 13th Five-Year Socio-Economic Development Plan for the period 2011–2015 and 2015–2020. IoT is identified as the focus of investment with the expectation of leaps and bounds.
  - * The State Council has issued "Guidelines on tracking and ordering to promote the development of IoT."
  - * China established an Advisory Committee on IoT development and issued 10 action plans, including developing a roadmap for IoT development and application, developing standards, R&D, promoting applications through incubation projects, supporting business development, researching information security, increasing government support in IoT development, developing legal documents and related legislation, and human resource development.
  - * Period 2015–2020: Priority areas for investment and IoT applications include: modernization of the agricultural sector, modern and optimized industrial systems, cyber economy, modern infrastructure network, new urban background.
- Experience in developing centralized IT zones.

  In China, the incentives for businesses in the concentrated IT zone are similar to those in the high-tech zone, including incentives for corporate income tax exemption and reduction; permitting the establishment of joint stock enterprises in development zones; reducing import duties and taxes on imported products and products used for processing or assembling for export; reducing export tax for exported products; reducing import tax for equipment and machinery that cannot be produced domestically; allowing businesses in the zone to quickly depreciate equipment and machinery to encourage technological innovation; creating conditions for technicians and managers in the hi-tech development zone to go abroad many times a year.
- Experience in attracting foreign investment.

  After becoming a big attraction for FDI, in 1995, China divided FDI into four categories: Encourage, allow, restrict, and prohibit.

Accordingly, the type of incentive is for projects on technology transfer, technology capacity improvement of domestic enterprises, etc. These projects enjoy many incentives:

* Tax reduction policy for multinational companies: CIT exemption for the first two years after getting the first profit and 50% reduction for the next three years, this number can be up to 6 years for CNC enterprises.
* Imported equipment and technology for R&D of Labs are exempt from import tax.
* Income from technology transfer from domestic FDI laboratories is accounted separately and not subject to CIT.
* If an FDI enterprise spends at least 10% on R&D in the previous year, it is considered to deduct 50% of the total cost of technology development in the current year's CIT.
* FDIs with R&D Centers in China are allowed to import and sell small quantities of high-tech products for testing in the local market if they are produced from the parent company's R&D.

In addition, China has also issued the Made in China 2025 Strategy, according to which

Vision:

— Comprehensive upgrade of the ICT industry;
— China can be self-sufficient and meet 70% of domestic high-tech needs and then, by 2049, China will rise to become the world leader in technology, especially in telecommunications technology, pine;
— Consider new generation information — Telecommunications technology as a top priority to help this country realize its goal of becoming the world's No. 1 technology superpower;

Making:

— Associate technology with all development strategies in all socio-economic fields;

— Development of huge public and private telecommunications enterprises;
+ Alibaba (TMDT)
+ Tencent (Game online, NDS, software)
+ Baidu (online search)
+ Byte Dance (MXH)
+ Huawei, Xiaomi (CNC products, chips, ...)

5.7.3. *Promote online activities*

Thanks to the rapid development of the Internet and digital technology, China strongly promotes online activities with diverse and large users. Typical shopping and social networking applications such as QQ, WeChat, Taobao, and Alibaba make connecting with Chinese users easy, affordable, and easy to use.

Notably, online consumption in China has reached RMB 3.9 trillion since 2016, contributing 0.26 percentage points to the GDP growth rate of 6.7%. Online consumption has become one of the most innovative, fastest growing, and most widely accepted economic sectors, becoming a major driver of domestic consumption demand, creating many jobs, and promoting industrial structure upgrading.

The Chinese government promotes spending online users with the goal of an average annual growth rate of at least 11% with a total revenue of 6 trillion RMB (about 900 billion US dollar). This is an important part of the Chinese government's efforts to stimulate domestic consumer demand and promote economic growth. China is also determined to provide incentives and support for areas such as smart technology, online medical education and treatment, e-commerce, 5G mobile networks, and telecommunications services in China's rural areas.

5.7.4. *E-commerce development*

Online commerce has become one of the most popular online activities in China, with more than half of all Internet users engaged in online shopping. The means of connecting to online shopping are mainly desktop computers and mobile phones. Online shopping in China has evolved in line with the end user's needs. Increased demand for high-quality foreign products has led to an increase in cross-border B2C transactions.

The popularity of e-commerce comes from the growing number of Internet users in China. China's e-commerce industry is dominated by online platforms like Taobao (Alibaba), Tmall and Jingdon.com (JD.com). The sheer size of China's e-commerce market has attracted significant brick-and-mortar retailers such as Suning Appliance Company (which operates the website suning.com) as well as major international competitors such as Amazon (which operates the website amazon.cn) and Walmart (with a large customer base through the website yihaodian.com). The e-commerce industry attracts over 2.5 million direct workers and over 18 million indirect workers and is growing in number at a high rate.

5.7.5. *Development of e-banking*

E-banking services are becoming increasingly popular in China as the banking system modernizes traditional peer-to-peer (P2P) lending by adopting Internet-based technology and improving regulations to support SMEs to access credit. The former SME sector often has difficulty accessing finance from China's state-owned banking system. P2P programs are very popular in China and the Internet has expanded access to finance through P2P activities with about 2,000 such websites established since 2007.

In another initiative to support the financial needs of small businesses, since 2014 the China Banking Regulatory Commission (CBRC) has approved a pilot plan to set up five private banks. One of the five pilot banks — WeBank — has opened its first operation since early 2015 as a pure Internet bank with a registered capital of RMB 3 billion. The main shareholders include Tencent (30% stake), Baiyeyuan (20%) and Liye (20%). Next, Alibaba Group also successfully became a shareholder of the pilot bank Mybank through its subsidiary Ant Financial with a 30% stake in the joint venture with Fosun International (25% stake) and Wanxiang Group (18%).

Before Mybank, in mid-2013, Alibaba opened a mutual fund under the Yuebao brand for Alipay users, which was managed by its subsidiary, THFund. In just six months of operation, more than 43 million people have joined Yuebao. Yuebao's popularity is due to its convenience, as Alipay users can transfer money with just one click and withdraw cash at any time for shopping. Subsequently, similar Internet-based mutual fund models, including Baidu, Netease, and WeChat, were established.

5.7.6. *Promoting electronic payments*

The era of popular cash payments in China seems to be coming to an end. Credit card payments also seem to be gradually becoming a thing of the past. Chinese people increasingly prefer non-cash payment methods, such as scanning QR codes and paying with e-wallets. Many essential consumer products allow mobile payments. China's two most popular daily electronic payment applications are Tencent's WeChat Pay (Tenpay) and Alibaba's Alipay. This payment type uses an e-wallet via mobile phone, requiring users to register with their real name and connect to a bank account. At banks, staff can assist customers with the entire process of linking and activating e-wallets. CNBC said that less regulation and a less developed financial system are also factors that push China to surpass developed countries in mobile payments. The size of the mobile payment market in China more than doubled to 5,570 US billion dollars in 2016. This is almost 50 times that of the US. Many countries, such as Norway, Finland, and Sweden, no longer use much cash but still prefer cards.

The rapid growth of mobile payments in China is supported by a large number of smartphone users. As of mid-2017, WeChat has over 960 million users, and Alipay has 520 million. According to some studies, the scale of electronic payments in China is predicted to quadruple to RMB 300,000 billion by 2021. According to experts, the high percentage of the population using the internet via mobile and e-commerce and the underdeveloped traditional financial markets will be the driving forces behind high mobile payments growth in China.

5.7.7. *China's success factors*

Three basic factors contributing to the strong development of the digital economy in China can be mentioned: (i) the huge market size with a large number of young, passionate and dynamic internet users; (ii) a strong competitive environment in the rich digital ecosystem that was initially created around the group of companies core BAT (Baidu, Alibaba and Tencent) and is now diversified and widely developed; and (iii) strong Government support through flexible regulatory frameworks, encouraging innovation, and supporting investment attraction and application of the latest technologies.

Since 2016 China has had 731 million internet users, more than the EU and US combined. China also has 695 million mobile phone users (95% of whom use the Internet), compared with 343 million in the EU (79%) and 262 million in the United States (91%). The large market size with many young, dynamic, and enthusiastic mobile users facilitates the rapid development and application of digital technologies. In the field of e-commerce, the percentage of Internet users using mobile payment services accounts for 68% compared to only 15% in the United States. Mobile payment sales in China account for 70% of all e-commerce sales compared to only about 30% in the United States. In addition, the large number of populous cities in China — 22 cities with over 5 million inhabitants compared to just one city in the US and 4 cities in the EU — is also a big attraction for investors. In addition, the large scale of users also increases the diversity in consumption and shopping, resulting in sales fluctuating very differently from time to time, posing many challenges and stimulating innovation with many unique solutions to meet the diverse needs of a huge market on the basis of improving digital infrastructure, optimizing algorithms, improving processing speed, storage capacity, as well as applying AI.

The large market size and outdated and inefficient traditional business models and methods have created opportunities for BAT companies and new competitors to set world-class standards and build a strong, diverse, and effective digital ecosystem thanks to constant learning and innovation, expanding customer service coverage across the country. Encouraged by the government to experiment with Internet-based business models, Chinese companies are revolutionizing how they do business, putting great pressure on the traditional way of doing business. This change is happening so quickly that even governments are feeling the pressure to catch up with businesses by adopting new technologies like blockchain and AI.

Another angle to the success of the development of the digital economy in China is due to the combination of physical and digital technologies and new business models, combined with a strong commitment to support from the Government. According to a recent study conducted by Bruegel, China spends more on R&D (as a percentage of GDP) than the EU. China now publishes as many scientific publications as the US and has more PhDs in the natural sciences and technical. By simplifying information exchange and facilitating coordination between complex tasks, China's WeChat social networking application, with 938 million users as of the first quarter of 2017, has contributed to improving outstanding labor productivity.

From the perspective of government support, it can be said that the Chinese Government is the Government of action. The government not only issues policy but also plays the role of investors, innovators, and consumers in efforts to support digitization. The Chinese government strongly supports the digital economy with a system of policies designed to strengthen the digital economy's capacity as a new tool for economic development. Since 2015, the Chinese government has announced the concept of "Internet Plus" and realized it with a detailed action plan to integrate the internet, cloud computing, big data, IoT with traditional industries and consumers. So far, the Internet Plus program has been widely deployed in many industries such as logistics, social security, and manufacturing.

The government is also actively facilitating investment attraction in digital technology. Since 2016, China's National Development and Reform Commission — the government's economic planning agency — has published a "Three-Year Action Plan for Internet Development Combined with Artificial Intelligence" with the hopes to build an AI application market worth more than 100 billion RMB (about 15 billion US dollars) by developing nine major AI ecosystems, including home appliances for smart homes, smart cars, smart wearables, and intelligent terminals. Under this plan, government agencies can fund specific projects from central and local budgets. Besides, the government also provides funding for new internet businesses. Since 2014, the Chinese state has encouraged citizens to engage in start-ups and innovation activities through support measures such as tax exemptions and start-up support funds.

5.8. *Overview of Vietnam's digital economy*

According to international organizations, Vietnam's digital economy has made rapid and promising developments compared to the region and the world.

According to the e-Conomy SEA Report 2020, only the Internet/platform digital economy component alone, Vietnam has reached 14 US billion dollars, ranking third in ASEAN, but is the country with the highest growth rate in this field with an increase of 16%, the country with the subsequent highest increase is Indonesia with 11%, and Thailand with 7% (see Figure 7). This report also forecasts that by 2025, Vietnam's Internet/platform digital economy will reach 52 US billion dollars.

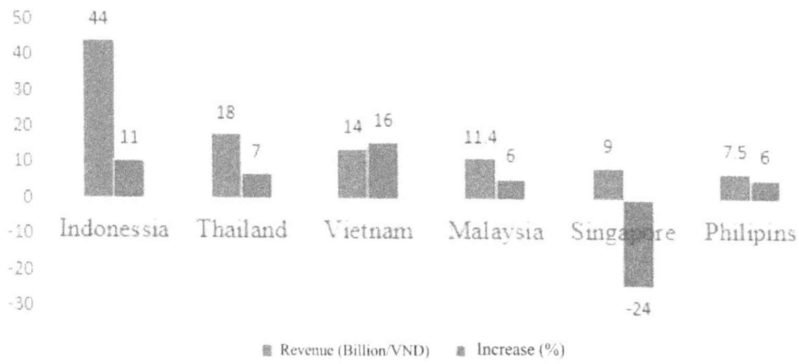

Figure 7: Internet digital economy revenue and growth in ASEAN countries (2020).

The measurement and complete statistics of the digital economy are currently a big challenge for almost all countries, even Vietnam. The General Statistics Office is making great efforts to coordinate with relevant agencies to research and develop specific targets to organize surveys and statistics on this new field. Although there is no official and complete data on Vietnam's digital economy, preliminary synthesis from domestic and foreign reports shows that Vietnam's digital economy in 2020 will reach about 163 billion USD, accounting for about 163 US billion dollars, about 8.2% of the country's GDP, of which the ICT/VT digital economy component reached 126 US billion dollars, accounting for 5.5% of GDP, the Internet/platform digital economy reached 14 US billion dollars, accounting for 1% of GDP, and the digital economy/sectors reached about 23 US billion dollars, accounting for 1.7% of GDP.

Analysis of the strengths, weaknesses, opportunities, and challenges of Vietnam's digital economy development shows that:

- **Strengths:** (1) The Party and Government's timely and correct awareness and policy on the fourth industrial revolution and digital transformation; (2) The will and aspiration of the political system, businesses and people of Vietnam to build a strong and powerful Vietnam; (3) Telecommunications — IT infrastructure is quite good, comprehensive coverage, high user density; (4) Vietnamese people are passionate about technology, like to use technology among the highest in the region; (5) Vietnam's population is young, well-educated, well-educated and hard-working; (6) Vietnamese personality quickly adapts to change.
- **Weak points:** (1) The legal and institutional system has not yet created favorable conditions for the development of the digital economy and digital society; (2) The implementation of state management, development and implementation of programs, plans, mechanisms, and policies to develop the digital economy and digital society are still inadequate; (3) Digital skills and digital human resources have not met the requirements of the digital economy and digital society development; (4) The

enterprise's digital transformation capacity is still weak; The force of enterprise platforms is significant but not vital, and the young Made in Vietnam digital platforms face fierce competition from the outside; (5) We do not yet have an overall national strategy on digital economy and digital society development.

— **Opportunities:** (1) Vietnam is going with the world in the fourth industrial revolution, the digital transformation revolution, and we have an excellent opportunity to break through and get ahead; (2) Vietnam is a large and potential market for new business models, with a large population, a golden population structure, a large workforce, a large and rapidly growing number of smartphones and Internet users which will create attractive markets for the digital economy; (3) Vietnam is located in the center of Southeast Asia, of Asia, which are assessed to be the center of development of digital technology and the global digital economy; (4) COVID-19 is a global disaster but also a hundred-year push for digital transformation and digital economic development; (5) Vietnam has basically successfully contained COVID-19, and can fully take advantage of this opportunity to make a breakthrough in the digital economy; (6) The intense attention and direction of the Party, State and Government for digital transformation and development of the digital economy, reflected in many vital documents issued over the past time.

— **Challenges:** (1) Risk of being left behind special subjects, needing care without an overview of the entire development process; (2) Lack of human resources if they are not trained and regularly updated with new skills and knowledge; (3) The risk of high-tech crimes, network insecurity leading to the decline of users' trust in transactions in the digital environment; (4) The risk of loss of budget revenue if transactions in the digital environment are not strictly controlled.

The vigorous development of the Internet and technology is expected to create a supporting platform for the fast-growing digital economy and make an increasing contribution to Vietnam's economy in the coming time. However, for the digital economy to develop sustainably, it is necessary to have synchronous support solutions and efforts from many sides.

5.8.1. *Lessons from the experiences of other countries*

From the experience of the countries analyzed above, some lessons can be drawn about the development of the digital economy for Vietnam as follows:

First, initiatives increasingly rely on digital technology and can bring many socio-economic benefits if implemented properly. The potential contribution of digital technologies to the economy is enormous, especially for Vietnam, which has many Internet and smartphone users and a passion for technology. In this respect, increasing the awareness of people and businesses about the digital economy, the benefits, and challenges associated with it, with specific content for each industry and field, is also very much in need of attention, primarily through offices, factories, and schools.

Second, the government must create a testing space and support businesses in developing the digital economy. Digital technology applications will be a lever to promote innovation of individuals and companies, so encouraging businesses to make the most of the power of digital technology must be a high priority. Accordingly, the experience of other countries shows that it is necessary to have strong support from the Government with an open management mindset to "untie" businesses, primarily to support small and medium-sized enterprises, promoting innovation. The current context shows that if the management policy is not open, flexible, and open, it will weaken domestic enterprises and the national economy in competition with foreign enterprises and economies worldwide. Especially, Vietnam currently lacks a national plan for digital transformation to facilitate the development of the digital economy and synchronously form the national digital infrastructure. The first action is to develop and publish a sector plan on information technology applications as a basis for promulgating standards for information exchange between agencies and units, thereby creating linkages and synchronization.

in the infrastructure investment and development process based on information technology applications.

Third, the government and the private sector need to invest in upgrading digital infrastructure and modern digital technology solutions to deploy smartly connected digital applications, accelerate cashless payment applications, and improve e-government efficiency ... Regarding upgrading digital infrastructure, the government and businesses need to urgently prepare plans to deploy 5G services to keep pace with the trend. In the first half of 2019, there will be smartphones with 5G integrated with high-speed steaming many times to the current 4G network. 5G technology will create a good infrastructure for connectivity, opening up many substantial business opportunities for Vietnamese businesses.

Fourth, besides focusing on upgrading digital infrastructure, information technology human resources also play a vital role. The IT human resource training program should aim to accelerate the socialization of information technology education, especially updating the IT training curriculum in association with new technology trends such as the IoT, AI, and robotics technology creating conditions for students to access this field as soon as possible, promoting training and practice linkages between schools and the business sector in IT application.

5.8.2. *Lessons from the Chinese experience*

Through the experiences of China's digital economy development, some lessons learned for Vietnam as follows:

First, it is necessary to recognize both the randomness and the effectiveness of proactive state policies in the story of digital market development in China. No country seems to have predicted the development of CN4.0. Information technology has developed enormously in the first decade of the twenty-first century, but awareness and policies are still behind the technological innovation steps of enterprises. Therefore, it is difficult to say that the decision to close the market for technology corporations like Google and Facebook at that time was China's calculation for the future development of the digital economy. However, it can be said that this policy shows China's initiative when they are not caught up in the play of multinational corporations. It may be due to the position of a large country, but they clearly show self-control over the domestic market. This comes from an economic philosophy rather than a deliberate calculation. Of course, that policy only becomes the right decision when leading businesses and digital technology markets are developed. The impact of this policy difference is difficult to quantify, but if we ask again the question of a market of a similar size: if India also closes the market, will it grow its digital economy like China? There is no satisfactory answer, but it is evident that, with the opposite policy, India does not seem to be a powerhouse in digital technology. The fact shows that large corporations still need China's domestic market just as China's enterprises have begun to expand overseas.

For Vietnam, the story of opening or closing the market seems to be very different because the market size of 90 million people is much smaller than the two countries mentioned above. However, compared to the world, the population of our country stands at 13 at the top of the list is not small. However, any research can only assess the benefits/costs of market opening if both the benefits of that market and the development potential of domestic enterprises are considered. Considering the context of globalization (no other country besides China has such a market closure policy), the benefits of export activities for our country, and the choice of opening or closing the market is not easy to identify.

Second, the way to develop the digital economy and policies at the later stage, precisely China's MIC2025 strategy, shows that their policies always focus on practicality and pragmatism, not stereotypes. It seems that this helps them assess their capabilities and potential very accurately, so they should set out policy stages according to subjective and objective conditions. China's digital economy has developed very quickly, and they have strong businesses, but they are still aware of their huge gap with developed economies.

Each country needs to design its policies in accordance with the characteristics, conditions and needs of the domestic economy. In addition, our country's technological development level will need to be recognized as an even greater distance than the world's CN4.0. Such an assessment is not to discourage businesses but to choose the right areas to develop first. For example, China seems to have the right choice when it comes to e-commerce, which requires moderate technology and then moves into more complex areas such as AI and Robot.

Third, the above statement is not necessarily true if we consider the meaning of CN4.0 is to allow taking shortcuts. So, the question remains, will Vietnam's domestic enterprises and human resources allow us to enter the most advanced fields? Here, it is necessary to mention the role of businesses. Vietnam has large-scale leading technology enterprises with international development prospects, but it does not seem to have achieved such an effect. The trio of businesses such as VNPT, Viettel, and FPT has chosen to go in different directions: Viettel focuses on telecommunications business and invests abroad; FPT aims to export software... As a result, the e-commerce and e-payment market has been left open for a long time. Until this segment is focused, domestic enterprises like Vingroup (with Adayroi!) have to compete with firms acquired by foreign enterprises (Lazada, tiki. vn). FPT had a well-developed social network ttvnonline, but it was not later expanded into a commercial product. Viettel owns a huge number of mobile subscribers, but only develops a money transfer service via scratch cards, not a form of e-wallet. Regardless of inefficient investments outside the industry in the financial sector, many large enterprises diversified into television and game markets but failed to achieve the corresponding market share. VNPT is still in a more passive position, while smaller businesses like BKAV struggled to find a way to manufacture mobile phones without any support.

Fourth, the experience of developing the digital economy in China shows that Vietnam needs to create a comprehensive ecosystem for businesses to develop and consumers to become the center of products, services, and services. The workforce is trained to participate in entrepreneurship and innovation. Thus, the role of capital markets, venture capital activities for innovative startups, legal institutions and regulations on technical standards, availability of technology research and development institutes, and Cooperation between universities are very important.

In addition to economic policies, social policies, such as social security for workers in industrial parks, consumer protection policies, environmental protection, and balanced and inclusive development, also play a big role in developing a modern, efficient digital economy that benefits all population groups.

Acknowledgment

This research was supported by the University of Economics Ho Chi Minh City (UEH), Vietnam.

Bibliography

AMCHAM (2018). *Workshop on Digital Economy and Cybersecurity Policy in Vietnam.* The American Chamber of Commerce in Hanoi.

Atkinson, R.D. and McKay, A. (2007). Digital prosperity. *Understanding the Economic Benefits of the Information Technology Revolution.* Washington, DC: Information Technology and Innovation Foundation.

Brennen, J.S. and Kreiss, D. (2016). *Digitalization. In The International Encyclopedia of Communication Theory and Philosophy* (eds K.B. Jensen, E.W. Rothenbuhler, J.D. Pooley and R.T. Craig).

Brynjolfsson, E. and Kahin, B. (2002). *Understanding the Digital Economy: Data, Tools, and Research.* MIT press.

Budde, P. (2017). *Singapore — Fixed Broadband Market, Digital Economy and Digital Media — Statistics and Analyses.* Paul Budde Communication Pty Ltd.

Bukht, R. and Heeks, R. (2010). Defining, conceptualising and measuring the digital economy (Working Paper No. 68). University of Manchester, Centre for Development Informatics, Global Development Institute.

Central Institute for Economic Management (2018). *Research Topics on Digital Economic Development.* CIEM.

Deutsche Bank Research (DBR). (2015). Industry 4.0: China seizes an outstanding opportunity in the Year of Innovation, *Talking Point archive*, DB.

Economic Committee of the Party Central Committee (2017). *National Industrial Development Policy*. National Economics University Publishing House.

He, Y. (2017). How China is preparing for an AI-power future. *Research paper*, Wilson Centre.

Heeks, R. and Bukht, R. (2018). Digital economy policy in developing countries (DIODE Working Paper No. 6). SSRN. https://doi.org/10.2139/ssrn.3540027.

Institute for Security and Development Policy (ISDP). (2018). Made in China 2025: *Backgrounder*, June 2018, www.isdp.eu.

Johansson, A., Heady, C., Arnold, J., Brys, B., and Vartia, L. (2006). Taxation and economic growth (OECD Economics Department Working Papers No. 620). OECD Publishing.

Karabegovic, I. (2017). The Role of "Industry 4.0" in modernizing industrial production in China. *Journal of Scientific and Engineering Research*, 9(4), 177–186.

Malecki, E.J. and Moriset, B. (2008). *The Digital Economy: Business Organization, Production Processes and Regional Developments* (1st ed.). Routledge.

MGI (2017). *China's Digital Economy: A Leading Global Force*. McKinsey Global Institute, McKinsey&Company.

Ministry of Information and Communications (2022a). *Report on Developing a Strategy for the Development of Digital Economy and Digital Society in Vietnam*. MIC.

Ministry of Information and Communications (2022b). *Report on Developing a Strategy for the Development of Vietnam's Digital Technology Industry*. MIC.

MTI (2017). *The Digital Economy in Singapore*. Ministry of Trade and Industry.

OECD (2016). *OECD Digital Economy Outlook 2016*. OECD Publishing.

OECD (2017). *OECD Digital Economy Outlook 2017*. OECD Publishing.

UNCTAD (2017). *The New Digital Economy and Development*. United Nations Conference on Trade and Development.

World Economic Forum (WEF). (2018). Readiness for the future of production, *Report 2018*, Geneva, Switzerland.

https://doi.org/10.1142/9789811262258_0014

Chapter 14

The Influence of Social Interactions on the Impulse Buying Behavior of Generation Z Customers on Vietnam's Digital Platforms

Tran Thanh Trung, Nguyen Duy Thuc, and Xuan Vinh Vo

Abstract

The purpose of this study is to determine the impact of online social interactions on impulse buying behavior among Generation Z customers in Vietnam. The study is based on an SOR framework and has constructed a research model with seven components and 12 research hypotheses. The results of a survey of 310 consumers in Vietnam show that review quality and observational learning are important factors in perceiving the enjoyment and usefulness of online reviews. Positive affect and perceived enjoyment have direct and indirect effects on impulse buying behavior through the impulse to buy impulsively on digital platforms. However, the study did not find a significant relationship between review quality and perceived usefulness. Additionally, there is insufficient statistical evidence to support a positive effect on online impulse buying behavior. Based on the analysis, management implications are proposed to improve impulsive shopping behavior among Generation Z on digital platforms in Vietnam.

Keywords: Impulse buying behavior; Review quality; Observational learning; Positive affect; Perceived usefulness; Perceived enjoyment; Digital platforms; Vietnam.

1. Introduction

Digital retailing has gained significant attention in recent years due to its potential impact on both buyers and sellers. In Vietnam, the use of mobile devices and social media, as well as online purchasing, has become commonplace among consumers, particularly the younger generation. In the context of live streaming on digital platforms, also known as social commerce, it is crucial for sellers to understand and capitalize on impulsive buying behavior (Wang *et al.*, 2022). Social commerce websites influence over 70% of online customers, leading to impulsive buying behavior (Chen *et al.*, 2016). This type of behavior is primarily seen in consumers who have a lack of control when exposed to online stimuli (Anh and Trung, 2022).

Impulse buying involves a specific and complex shopping process. In other words, the belief about the potential risks of online shopping serves as the initial motivation that influences a consumer's continued stay on the online store's website (Chen *et al.*, 2019). In addition, online customers can play the role of both system users and impulse buyers in subsequent stages of shopping (Wu *et al.*, 2016). Online customers must assess the potential risks of buying from online websites, so the perceived image of an online sales website helps to promote buys (Chen and Zhang, 2015). When playing the role of system users, online consumers engage with online shopping websites to find information about products, online reviews, and information sources through observational learning and positive affect. They are also influenced by website attributes, such as visual appeal, secure communication style, and safety (Aladwani, 2018).

Zafar *et al.* (2021) believed that impulse buying was a hot issue in consumer behavior, with various influencing factors. Previous scholars found that many factors affected online impulse buying behavior, mainly focusing on personality traits and behavioral situations (Wang and Chapa, 2022), such as consumer factors (Bellini *et al.*, 2017), marketing factors (Liu *et al.*, 2013), or situational factors (Park *et al.*, 2012). They also focused on online chatting and general social media platforms (Akram *et al.*, 2018). Nevertheless, the impacts of various social factors on impulse buying on social commerce websites have not been fully uncovered (Leong *et al.*, 2018; Xu *et al.*, 2020). In addition, although scholars have recognized the important role of review quality (Xu *et al.*, 2020), few of them have examined the effect of online review quality, as a social factor, on online impulse buying behavior.

Gulfraz *et al.* (2022) researched online impulse buying behavior through psychological and functional aspects. Goel *et al.* (2022) researched and evaluated customers' intention to continue online impulse buying during and after the global pandemic. Islam *et al.* (2021) studied markets in the U.S, China, India, and Pakistan. Many other researchers from around the world have also studied this issue, such as Chen *et al.* (2016), Lin *et al.* (2018), Sihombing *et al.* (2020), Zhang *et al.* (2020), Wu *et al.* (2021), Sarah *et al.* (2021), and Zhang *et al.* (2021). In the Vietnamese market, there have been several studies conducted on the factors influencing consumer impulsive shopping behavior. For example, Nguyen-Viet and Diep (2022) conducted research in Ho Chi Minh City, focusing on convenience value and refreshing value as factors affecting impulsive purchases. Similarly, Anh and Trung (2022) studied the impact of social interaction on impulsive online shopping behavior in Vietnam. Additionally, Lan and Trung (2023) explored the effects of reliability, visual appeal, spontaneity, advertising, interactivity, review quality, and price and discounts on impulsive buying behavior among young people in Ho Chi Minh City.

Therefore, this study was conducted to determine and evaluate the influence of consumer-generated stimuli (i.e., social interactions) on impulse buying and social interactions, which did not take into account the effect of product prices, product availability, and marketing stimuli. To understand the role of such social interactions in the consumer impulse buying process, this paper follows the stimulus–organism–response framework (SOR framework) and dual systems theory. In addition, most previous studies delved into the relations between social interactions and impulse buying behavior using partial least squares (PLS), focused on structural equation modeling (SEM). The method of assessing the model's predictive relevance is by using PLS predict, as proposed by Shmueli (2019), which is not common in existing studies.

2. Literature Review and Hypotheses

2.1. *Theoretical basis*

To explain the research model in this study, we rely on the following theoretical foundations: the S-O-R framework (Stimulus-Organism-Response), dual systems theory (which includes the reflective and impulsive systems), and the Technology Acceptance Model (TAM).

The technology acceptance model was first discovered by Davis in 1989. This model is widely applied to explain and predict the adoption and use of technology as a platform for online commerce. The model's two fundamental components are perceived usefulness and perceived usability.

Dual systems theory suggests that human social behavior is guided by two parallel and competing information processing systems (Evans, 2008; Strack and Deutsch, 2004). The impulsive system generates automatic and unconscious urges to perform the behavior. However, the reflexive system employs syllogism principles (stimulus–organism–response) to make decisions that are considered (Strack and Deutsch, 2004). According to the dual systems theory's information processing scheme, the impulsive system is frequently active at the start of processing, whereas the reflective system is typically triggered following the activation of the impulsive system or may even become disengaged (Strack and Deutsch, 2004).

The SOR model describes the connection between stimulus (such as external factors) that will affect organisms (cognition and emotions of people) and the response people have to the stimulus (such as behavior). This model has been used extensively in studies about online impulse buying behavior across the world (Chan *et al.*, 2017; Zhang and Benyoucef, 2016). Stimulus from external elements might trigger a subject's internal perceptions or emotions, and then in turn can cause response behaviors in the context of buying on digital platforms.

This study proposes that social interactions, such as review quality and observational learning (stimulus), can stimulate perceived enjoyment, perceived usefulness, and positive affect (organism). Finally, the reaction will create an urge to buy impulsively and result in online impulse buying behavior on a digital platform.

2.2. *Research model and hypotheses*

2.2.1. *Review quality*

Review quality refers to how customers perceive information quality based on reviews on digital platforms (Jiang *et al.*, 2021). A quality review functions both as an informant and as a recommender, and is important in making purchase decisions as well as for product sales (Park *et al.*, 2007). Jiang *et al.* (2021) have shown a direct positive influence of information quality on willingness to receive the information. When customers believe that the reviews on a digital platform are reliable, they will apply these reviews and utilize them as a guide to make buying decisions. In addition, Cheung *et al.* (2009) indicated that the receiver's attitude will be affected by information quality. If consumers believe the information on a digital platform is trustworthy, they will use it to aid in decision-making; otherwise, they will not. According to Park *et al.* (2012), in addition to the pragmatic purpose of finding information, consumers consider looking for information as a form of enjoyment. According to Erkan and Evans (2016) and Anh and Trung (2022), consumer adoption is positively influenced by high-quality information. Similar to how good online reviews give consumers security when they buy, reviews can also have a positive affect on digital buying platforms. Therefore, this study expects that if consumers discover high-quality online evaluations on a digital platform, they are likely to have a significant positive affect on that platform. As a result, this study proposes the following hypothesis:

Hypothesis 1a: Review quality is positively associated (+) with positive affect.

Additionally, perceived usefulness is the extent to which consumers believe that using specific digital platforms will increase their buying productivity (Koufaris, 2002). According to the research of Jiang *et al.* (2021) and Anh and Trung (2022), information quality has a positive affect on the receipt of information, leading to the feasibility of information and the acceptance of this information by consumers. Previous research has also demonstrated that consumers frequently seek out detailed online product reviews and self-assess that these reviews are more reliable and useful than information received directly from the seller about the product (Cheung *et al.*, 2009). Fiore and Yu (2001) thought that interesting information can be elicited if people read useful texts. If digital platforms have a lot of good reviews, customers will find them useful. Therefore, this study proposes the following hypothesis:

Hypothesis 1b: Review quality is positively associated (+) with perceived *usefulness.*

2.2.2. *Observational learning*

Observational learning refers to how much a consumer observes other customers who have made purchases on a digital platform (Chen *et al.*, 2011). In the context of commerce on social media platforms, Cheung *et al.* (2015) emphasized that consumers can use prior purchase data offered by other customers on a social commerce platform as the basis for making product selections, and this information can positively affect a customer's decision on an upcoming purchase. Products that have been sold a lot online tend to attract additional purchases from customers (Xu *et al.*, 2020). Therefore, this study proposes that an individual establishes a positive affect on digital platforms where products/services are sold with high sales. From that, this study proposes the following hypothesis:

Hypothesis 2a: Observational learning is positively associated (+) with positive affect.

Research by Chen *et al.* (2011) suggests that observing other consumers' purchases serves as a behavior-based social interaction in e-commerce settings. Because consumers frequently have imperfect information about the thing they are looking to buy, they frequently observe and learn from the buying behavior of others (Park and Lessig, 1977). Information collected by other customers regarding the product can be an additional source combined with their own experiences, leading to more accurate buying decisions. Positive observational learning (which boosts sales) has more of an impact than negative observational learning (Chen *et al.*, 2011), and observational learning is positively influenced by perceived usefulness (Anh and Trung, 2022). Observational learning suggests that people will consider a product's high or low sales on a digital platform as useful and interesting information to assess the product's quality and finally decide whether to buy or not. Therefore, this study proposes the following hypothesis:

Hypothesis 2b: Observational learning is positively associated (+) with perceived usefulness.

Zhang *et al.* (2021) studied the relationship between perceived enjoyment and online impulse buying behavior during shopping on the occasion of "Singles' Day" in China. According to Lee and Chen (2021), consumers are more likely to make impulsive purchases when buying and selling through live-streaming, driven by the streamer's professional and engaging presentation within a short time frame. Additionally, customer enjoyment is influenced by factors such as attraction, trust, and specialized knowledge (Lee and Chen, 2021). As a result, this study aims to examine the following hypothesis:

Hypothesis 2c: Observational learning is positively associated (+) with perceived enjoyment.

2.2.3. *Positive affect*

Positive affect is defined as positive emotions, such as excitement and amusement, when using digital platforms to buy. Positive affect refers to the way a person perceives a pleasant and enjoyable buying experience on a digital platform (Beatty and Ferrell, 1998).

According to Holbrook and Batra (1987), decisions are influenced by perception, which then results in behavior. Perceived usefulness has a positive affect on perceived enjoyment (Parboteeah *et al.*, 2009). Hoch *et al.* (1991) showed that negative perceptions will arouse negative emotions, disrupting the impulse buying process. According to earlier research (Weinberg and Gottwald, 1982), perception is a key factor in purchasing. In the context of purchasing on digital platforms, according to a convincing argument made by Parboteeah *et al.* (2009), customer excitement and amusement in interacting with digital platforms have a significant influence on the perceived usefulness of online shopping platforms. Moon and Kim (2001) also show that consumers feel comfortable and experience amusement (positive emotions) when they use digital platforms because they feel that the platform is useful to them. Previous research on impulse buying also posited positive effects on positive affect and perceived usefulness (Zhang *et al.*, 2014). Therefore, this study suggests the following hypothesis:

Hypothesis 3a: Positive affect is positively associated (+) with perceived usefulness.

In the study by Mohan *et al.* (2013) and Anh and Trung (2022), it was shown that positive affect has an effect on the urge to buy impulsively, while negative affect has no significant effect. Liu *et al.* (2013) suggest that immediate purchase intention will be effectively activated by satisfaction. In addition, recent studies have shown that positive affect, including enjoyment, arousal, shopping preference, and satisfaction, will also immediately affect the buying behavior of consumers on digital platforms (Floh and Madlberger, 2013). So, this study expects that if a consumer who buys online has a positive affect by utilizing online shopping platforms, they will be more inclined to buy impulsively and exhibit online impulse buying behavior. Hypotheses H3b and H3c are as follows:

Hypothesis 3b: Positive affect is positively associated (+) with the urge to buy impulsively on digital platforms for consumers in Vietnam.

Hypothesis 3c: Positive affect is positively associated (+) with online impulse buying behavior on digital platforms for consumers in Vietnam.

2.2.4. *Perceived enjoyment*

Perceived enjoyment is thought to be the degree to which buying behavior on technology platforms is perceived as pleasurable and predictable (Davis *et al.,* 1992). In addition, Mullins and Sabherwal (2020) described enjoyment as "the most important consumer interaction goal."

Lee and Chen's (2021) study indicated that, out of the two variables, perceived usefulness and perceived enjoyment, only perceived enjoyment has been demonstrated to positively affect the urge to buy impulsively. Lee and Chen (2021) concluded that the streamer's professional and engaging presentation, within a short time frame, significantly influences consumers, making them more likely to make impulsive purchases during live-streaming buying and selling. Sihombing *et al.* (2020) also demonstrated that perceived enjoyment has an indirect influence on the urge to buy impulsively by consumers. The study by Xiang *et al.* (2016) demonstrated that perceived enjoyment has a direct influence on the urge to buy impulsively by consumers. Therefore, this study proposes the following hypothesis:

Hypothesis 4a: Perceived enjoyment is positively associated (+) with the urge to buy impulsively on digital platforms by consumers in Vietnam.

The experimental results of Zhang *et al.* (2021) show that both perceived enjoyment and social interaction have a strong influence on online impulse buying behavior, which is consistent with previous studies such as those by Chan *et al.* (2017), Xiang *et al.* (2016), and Zhang *et al.* (2014). Therefore, the following hypothesis is proposed:

Hypothesis 4b: Perceived enjoyment is positively associated (+) with online impulse buying behavior on digital platforms by consumers in Vietnam.

2.2.5. *Perceived usefulness*

In the context of the adoption of advanced information technology systems, perceived usefulness is defined as the likelihood that potential users believe a specific application will enhance their job performance (Davis, 1989). This definition fits the context of e-commerce. Perceived usefulness of digital platforms is the degree to which consumers believe their buying productivity will increase by using particular digital platforms (Koufaris, 2002).

Research by Lee and Chen (2021) has demonstrated a positive affect of perceived usefulness on perceived enjoyment. Through perceived enjoyment, factors like attractiveness, reliability, and knowledge also have an indirect effect on perceived usefulness. The study by Xiang *et al.* (2016) demonstrated that perceived usefulness has a positive relationship with perceived enjoyment in the Chinese market. Sihombing *et al.* (2020) show that perceived enjoyment is affected by external impressions. Product variety, price attributes, and information quality were not correlated with perceived enjoyment. However, these three factors have a positive influence on perceived usefulness, and perceived usefulness is positively correlated with perceived enjoyment. Therefore, this study proposes the following hypothesis:

Hypothesis 5: Perceived usefulness is positively associated (+) with perceived enjoyment.

2.2.6. *Urge to buy impulsively*

Urge to buy impulsively refers to the sudden and spontaneous desire to buy, for consumers, after reading product reviews or seeing how many products have been sold. An urge to buy impulsively can result in out-of-control actions when people try to satisfy their needs and wants right away. In addition, impulse buying behavior is a consumer behavior that is stimulated by a sudden, strong, and persistent urge to buy something immediately (Rook and Fisher, 1995). Chen *et al.* (2017) therefore argued that before engaging in an impulsive purchase behavior, customers first feel the temptation to do so. Accordingly, the urge to buy impulsively arises from an intense interest in a specific good or service (Zhang *et al.*, 2022). This interest is typically based on non-reflective thinking related to the attributes of goods and services, which fuels an immediate desire for enjoyment and ultimately leads to a purchase (Xu *et al.*, 2020). Although the urge to buy impulsively may not always lead to impulse buying behavior, as certain situational constraints (time, money, and willpower) can interfere with the impulse buying process, the predictability of the urge for real behavior has been well established in previous studies. Therefore, it has been asserted that individuals can engage in impulse buying only after the urge to buy impulsively is triggered by a set of stimuli, according to studies by Anh and Trung (2022), Zheng *et al.* (2020), and Feng *et al.* (2023). Therefore, this study proposes the following hypothesis:

Hypothesis 6: The urge to buy impulsively is positively associated (+) with online impulse buying behavior on digital platforms by consumers in Vietnam.

2.3. *Research model and hypotheses*

Utilizing the study results of the above-mentioned authors, along with previous studies on impulse buying behavior, this study proposes to divide the impulsive system in consumer behavior into three groups of factors: (1) Stimulus: review quality and observational learning; (2) Organism: positive affect, perceived usefulness, and perceived enjoyment; and (3) Response: urge to buy impulsively and online impulse buying behavior. These three groups of factors are presented by the authors in the proposed research model as shown in Figure 1.

3. Methodology and Data

The purpose of this qualitative research phase is to serve as the process of building a survey questionnaire with relevant scales suitable for Vietnam. Based on the translation process proposed by Craig and Douglas (2005), the scales are translated and checked; then, the draft

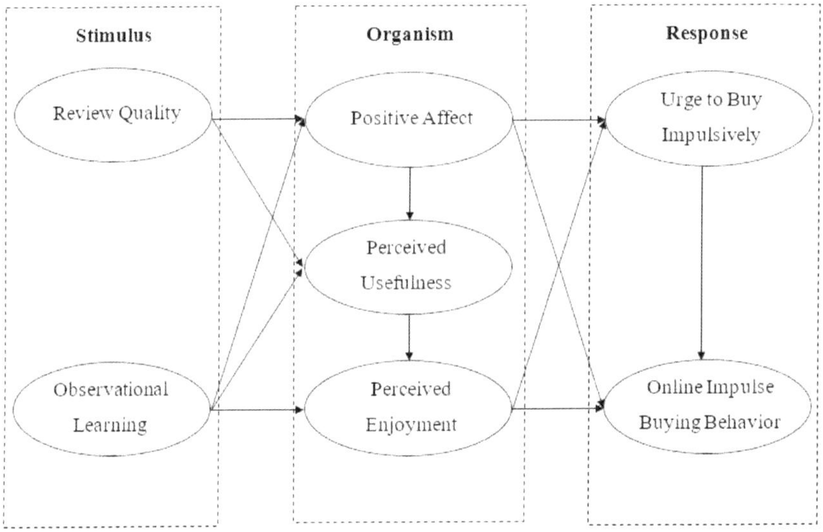

Figure 1: Proposed research model.

questionnaire is discussed using the group discussion method (group of 10 members) to check the appropriateness of the statements and correct (add or remove) any questions that are not relevant to this study.

This study uses a seven-point Likert scale ranging from 1 "strongly disagree" to 7 "strongly agree" to observe the seven concepts mentioned. We developed an online questionnaire for this study. Because we conducted the online survey in Vietnam, we performed a translation and "back-translation" process to ensure the translation quality. All measurement items were adapted from prior research (for details of the scale, see Table A1 in the Appendix). Non-probability sampling is the technique used in this study. The survey questionnaire was sent to consumers who know about e-commerce and have bought on digital platforms in provinces in Vietnam from January to June 2023. To prevent duplication, we also asked each respondent to fill in their email address in the questionnaire. Finally, 310 valid questionnaire responses were received.

The sample size needed for SEM is quite large; in many references, it is recommended to have 100–200 samples. The minimum sample size should be 10 times the largest number of structural paths leading to a particular latent construct in the structural model. (Barclay *et al.*, 1995; Hair Jr *et al.*, 2016). Hair Jr *et al.* (2016) recommend that researchers should choose Cohen's (1992) standard sample calculation formula. Thus, this study decided on a sample size of 310 in order to guarantee the reliability of the research results. The methods used in this study are Cronbach's Alpha (CA), Composite Reliability (CR), Average Variance Extracted (AVE), Convergent Validity, Discriminant Validity, HTMT, and Structural Equation Modeling (SEM).

4. Results

4.1. *Respondent profile*

The sample includes those who are studying and working in Vietnam. There are 310 people, including 60.3% female and 39.7% male respondents. The age group of 18 to 30 years old accounted for the majority, representing 83.9% of the total. The age group under 18 years accounts for 10.6% of the respondents, and the group with the lowest percentage in the sample is the group of 31–40 year olds with a rate of only 5.5%. The majority of people surveyed have college or university degrees (61%). In terms of monthly income, the group with the highest percentage in the sample (26.1%) is the group with an income range of 700–1,200 USD. The group with an income range of 200–700 USD and the group with an income range of 1,200–1,700 USD both account for the same rate of 20.3%. Nearly 18.1% of respondents have an income range of over 2,200 USD and 13.5% of respondents have an income range of 1,700–2,200 USD. The low-income group (mostly trainees and students) with an income of less than 200 USD accounts for about 1.3% of respondents. This study uses a convenient sampling method through online surveys, so survey respondents come from many different provinces and cities in Vietnam.

4.2. *The results of scale reliability testing*

4.2.1. *Testing the reliability of the scale using Cronbach's Alpha, Composite Reliability (CR), and Average Variance Extracted (AVE)*

Table 1 shows that all scales are reliable using Cronbach's Alpha (CA), Composite Reliability (CR), and Average Variance Extracted (AVE), and no observed variables are excluded from the scale.

4.2.2. *Testing the scale using Convergent Validity*

The results show that the factor loading of all factors is greater than 0.7 and AVE is greater than 0.5 (Table 1). According to Fornell and Larcker (1981), the proposed scales reached convergent validity. The results of testing the values of Cronbach's Alpha, CR, and AVE of all variables show that these indicators and scales have research value.

4.2.3. *Testing the scale using Discriminant Validity*

Discriminant validity refers to the degree to which a specific latent variable is distinct from other latent variables (Henseler *et al.*, 2009). The evaluation results show that the square value of the Average

Table 1: Construct reliability and validity.

Variables	ID	Number of Items	CA	CR	AVE	Conclusion
Review Quality	RQ	04	0.921	0.942	0.802	Valuable for research
Perceived Usefulness	PU	03	0.804	0.884	0.718	Valuable for research
Perceived Enjoyment	PE	03	0.712	0.840	0.637	Valuable for research
Online Impulse Buying Behavior	OIBB	03	0.715	0.833	0.625	Valuable for research
Observational Learning	OL	03	0.623	0.792	0.559	Valuable for research
Urge to Buy Impulsively	UBI	03	0.893	0.933	0.824	Valuable for research
Positive Affect	PA	04	0.870	0.912	0.721	Valuable for research

Variance Extracted (AVE) of each concept is greater than the correlation coefficients between the corresponding variables. As a result, the research model's concepts gain discriminant validity. In Table 2, the correlations between perceived usefulness and perceived enjoyment, as well as between online impulse buying behavior and the urge to buy impulsively are all quite high; however, the correlations between these pairs of variables are all lower than the square root of the AVE value (Sqrt(AVE)), so these scales do not violate discrimination and the scale still ensures discrimination. However, Henseler *et al.* (2015) provided convincing evidence that the method proposed by Fornell and Larcker (1981) would not truly assess the discriminant validity of a scale (e.g., lack of foundation in inferential statistics). Therefore, this study proceeds with analyzing the Heterotrait–Monotrait (HTMT) ratio for the scale.

In addition, we can also test the Heterotrait–Monotrait Indicator (HTMT) in order to assess the discriminant validity of the scale. Table 3 shows that the HTMT indicators are all smaller than 0.9, showing that the concepts are distinct from each other (Hu and Bentler, 1999). Table 3 shows that the correlations between perceived enjoyment and perceived usefulness as well as perceived enjoyment and online impulse buying behavior are quite high ($0.85 < \text{HTMT} < 0.9$). However, all HTMT indexes were lower than 90%, so the scale still achieved a discriminatory value among latent variables.

Table 2: Fornell–Larcker's Discriminant Validity.

Variables	RQ	PU	PE	OIBB	OL	UBI	PA
Review Quality	**0.896**	—	—	—	—	—	—
Perceived Usefulness	0.008	**0.847**	—	—	—	—	—
Perceived Enjoyment	−0.025	0.700	**0.798**	—	—	—	—
Online Impulse Buying Behavior	0.060	0.499	0.659	**0.791**	—	—	—
Observational Learning	0.197	0.336	0.256	0.447	**0.747**	—	—
Urge to Buy Impulsively	−0.004	0.459	0.707	0.748	0.250	**0.908**	—
Positive Affect	0.265	0.235	0.137	0.252	0.447	0.122	**0.849**

Table 3: Heterotrait–Monotrait ratio (HTMT) for discriminant validity.

Variables	RQ	PU	PE	OIBB	OL	UBI	PA
Review Quality	—	—	—	—	—	—	—
Perceived Usefulness	0.058	—	—	—	—	—	—
Perceived Enjoyment	0.131	0.818	—	—	—	—	—
Online Impulse Buying Behavior	0.102	0.648	0.883	—	—	—	—
Observational Learning	0.268	0.434	0.338	0.660	—	—	—
Urge to Buy Impulsively	0.024	0.533	0.877	0.863	0.309	—	—
Positive Affect	0.274	0.294	0.174	0.347	0.616	0.137	—

Table 4: Results of SRMR.

Variables	Saturated Model	Estimated Model
SRMR	0.094	0.098
d_ULS	2.433	2.672
d_G	0.839	0.863
Chi-Square	1448.78	1471.767
NFI	0.695	0.690

SRMR indicators (indicators best match for the model) are the difference between the actual data part and the predicted model part. Table 4 shows that the predictive model fits the data.

4.2.4. *Testing the Structural Equation Modeling (SEM)*

The R^2 Indicators in Table 5 are all greater than 0.2. In it, the scale of positive affect has the lowest R^2 Indicator of 0.232 and the scale of online impulse buying behavior is the highest (61.5%). The structural equation modeling of the study meets the stated requirements.

Additionally, the Durbin–Watson coefficient (d) test shows no autocorrelation when $1 < d < 3$, and the Variance Inflation Factors (VIF) are below 3, indicating the absence of multicollinearity (Hair *et al.*, 2016).

The research used the partial least squares path model (PLS-PM) approach to test the appropriateness of the structural model using the PLS algorithm provided by SmartPLS 3.3.9 (Henseler *et al.*,

5. Discussion and Managerial Implications

5.1. *Discussion*

Research results show that there are two factors affecting perceived usefulness: observational learning (β = 0.297) and positive affect (β = 0.121). Observational learning both directly and indirectly affects perceived usefulness through the mediating factor of positive affect (β = 0.411) (for details, see Figure 2). However, this study did not have enough statistical evidence to accept the correlation between review quality and perceived usefulness, observational learning and perceived enjoyment, and positive affect and urge to buy impulsively (hypothesis H1b, H2c, and H3b are rejected). Different from the studies conducted by Cheung *et al.* (2009) and Jiang *et al.* (2021), this study does not prove the relationship between review quality and perceived usefulness. The reviews that are detailed and of high quality are more prone to lead to information overload than simple or low-quality reviews (Xu *et al.*, 2020). Hence, high-quality reviews may not trigger perceived usefulness. Observational learning has a positive impact on perceived usefulness in accordance with previous research by Chen *et al.* (2011) and Xu *et al.* (2020). Thus, it can be seen that consumers tend to observe other people's purchasing decisions and learn about other people's purchasing behavior because they often have imperfect knowledge about the product they are buying. Product knowledge learned from other consumers can be a complementary resource combined with one's own experience, leading to more accurate purchasing decisions. Additionally, observational learning positively influences affect, which aligns with previous research by Cheung *et al.* (2015). Furthermore, purchase information shared by other users on digital platforms, such as the number of people who have bought the product or its sales figures, can serve as a reference for future consumers (Xu *et al.*, 2020). This information can, in turn, positively influence consumers' purchasing decisions. On the other hand, people tend to develop more favorable attitudes toward products that are widely sold on online shopping platforms.

Different from previous studies by Beatty and Ferrell (1998), Floh and Madlberger (2013), Liu *et al.* (2013), Mohan *et al.* (2013), and Xu *et al.* (2020), the results of this study did not prove a relationship between positive affect and the urge to buy impulsively. Therefore, it is possible that positive affect, such as joy, stimulation, shopping enjoyment, or satisfaction, will not greatly affect the online urge to buy impulsively in Vietnam.

Similar to the research results of Lee and Chen (2021), Sihombing *et al.* (2020), and Xiang *et al.* (2016), the results of this study demonstrated that perceived usefulness had a positive impact on perceived enjoyment ($\beta = 0.694$). This study also confirmed that review quality positively affects positive affect ($\beta = 0.184$). However, the relationship between review quality and positive affect was not proven by Xu *et al.* (2020), but this result was proven by Cheung *et al.* (2009), Erkan and Evans (2016), and Jiang *et al.* (2021). High-quality reviews and source credibility are important factors of positive affect; therefore, online retailers can also offer incentives to product experts to comment on and recommend products to others.

Besides, there are also 3 factors that positively influence online impulse buying behavior on digital platforms: urge to buy impulsively ($\beta = 0.568$), perceived enjoyment ($\beta = 0.239$), and positive affect ($\beta = 0.146$). In addition, perceived enjoyment has a direct impact on the urge to buy impulsively ($\beta = 0.707$), and the urge to buy impulsively has a significant positive effect (56.8%) on online impulse buying behavior on digital platforms. The positive relationship between perceived enjoyment and the urge to buy impulsively was also demonstrated in prior studies (Xiang *et al.*, 2016). This study shows a consistent result confirming this positive relationship. That is to say, individuals who have a higher propensity to perceive enjoyment are more likely to experience increased urges. However, in this study, there was not enough statistical evidence to show a positive affect on the urge to buy impulsively. The findings of this study will bring forth noteworthy insights regarding how online reviews and observational learning may induce consumers' impulse buying on social commerce websites.

The research results indicate a positive correlation between the urge to buy impulsively and online impulse buying behavior, which is consistent with previous studies conducted by Feng *et al.* (2023). This finding is further supported by research conducted by Xu *et al.* (2020) and Zheng *et al.* (2020), who also found a significant connection between the urge to buy impulsively and online impulse buying behavior. This study concludes that although the desire to buy impulsively may not always lead to impulse buying behavior due to situational constraints such as time, money, and willpower, the predictability of the urge for impulse buying is well established. Therefore, consumers may only engage in impulse buying at a later time when they are exposed to stimuli that trigger an impulsive purchase.

In addition, this study's results reconfirmed that online review attributes (review quality) and observational learning are the two main determinants of "unplanned" behavior of consumers on digital platforms. Therefore, the findings of this study enrich the theoretical basis for the influence of online reviews on Vietnamese consumers' buying behavior on online sales platforms.

5.2. *Managerial implications*

Firstly, the research results demonstrate that observational learning and review quality, particularly those of high quality, can influence customer purchasing decisions in social commerce. Therefore, marketing managers should incorporate elements of online social interaction, including online reviews, transaction history, and product sales, into their digital platform. Then, it is important to ensure the quality of the online reviews and the reliability of the review sources, possibly by inviting renowned and trusted reviewers to participate in positive reviews of products, thereby increasing the authenticity of the reviews as well as increasing observational learning by consumers.

Secondly, this study explores how the quality of online reviews has a positive impact on positive affect (pleasure and excitement while searching for information on the digital platform) so that merchants can keep customers longer on their platforms and increase the chances of these customers buying. When it comes to giving customers a "real feeling" or a "natural feeling" for the information in the reviews, this is also a matter that needs to be handled very delicately; avoid giving customers the "feeling of being paid to write or review." Moreover, businesses that sell products or services online can establish online communities for the categories of goods or services they provide. In these communities, customers can report any negative online reviews and evaluate the reliability of all review sources on the unit's website. This means that just like communities in real life, online commerce systems must be able to foster social connections and aid these communities in actively trading multi-dimensional information. Most crucially, these online systems must develop reviews of goods and services that are comparatively independent to give consumers an "objective feeling" when they interact with these online communities.

Thirdly, according to the research results, observational learning has a favorable impact on perceived usefulness (i.e., a factor that improves purchasing performance), so it can boost sales for digital platforms. Online retailers should offer transparent data that reflect the volume of sales and transaction history for all products and services that are featured on an online trading platform in order to improve the observational learning of consumers. On the one hand, this fosters objectivity and gives customers complete information; on the other hand, consumers may easily recognize the buying behavior of prior purchasers and, as a result, develop shopping requirements for categories of goods and services that have already been purchased by many other individuals. This tactic is also applied by online sales sites when offering a limited number of sold goods and publicizing the number of sold/remaining goods. This creates the psychology of "fear of missing out" (FOMO) for consumers and stimulates them to make buying decisions faster.

Fourthly, businesses should increase customers' positive emotions such as happiness or love. Businesses can also expose people to instantly and easily interactive stimuli by integrating a livestream from social websites such as Facebook, TikTok, and Instagram into the e-commerce platforms in order to more effectively make people purchase. This increases the customer's awareness of the product and enables the seller to take care of any of the client's questions and concerns right away, thus motivating the customer to make a decision to buy the product.

Finally, the urge to buy impulsively deeply influences the online impulse buying behavior of consumers. Besides, with a huge amount of information available on social interactions from such online communities, it will be an invaluable source of data for companies that sell products online. This data source will help retail businesses analyze customer segmentation aspects not only relating to demographics but also to psychographics. Smart cameras and other data-collecting equipment used in physical stores will provide retail businesses with an overall view of their customers. To stimulate impulsive buying, online businesses should focus on analyzing the data of each customer group to understand their preferences and consumption habits. This will allow them to predict customer needs and present products at the right moment, thereby increasing the likelihood of impulsive purchases.

5.3. *Limitations and opportunities for future research*

In spite of these results, this study still has many limitations. The first limitation is that the sample size is relatively small, so it is difficult to represent the impulse buying behavior of consumers in Vietnam. Further research should be conducted with a larger sample and wider distribution. The second limitation is that although this study looked at persons who had previously made online purchases, it did not precisely examine any particular product, sector, or online sales platform. Future studies can focus on a particular product, commodity, retail industry, or online shopping platform to further investigate specific aspects. The third limitation is that there are not many explanatory variables that can influence impulse buying behavior, necessitating more analysis. Another limitation is that this study emphasizes the influence of consumer-generated stimulus (social interactions) on online buying. Future research can therefore also include these elements in the study model. Scientific can also research whether different types of stimuli have different impacts on online purchases.

Acknowledgments

This research was supported by the University of Economics Ho Chi Minh City.

Bibliography

Akram, U., Hui, P., Khan, M.K., Yan, C., and Akram, Z. (2018). Factors affecting online impulse buying: Evidence from Chinese social commerce environment. *Sustainability*, 10(2), 352. https://doi.org/10.3390/su10020352.

Aladwani, A.M. (2018). A quality-facilitated socialization model of social commerce decisions. *International Journal of Information Management*, 40, 1–7. https://doi.org/10.1016/j.ijinfomgt.2018.01.006.

Anh, L.N.T. and Trung, T.T. (2022). Anh huong cua tuong tac xa hoi den hanh vi mua hang ngau hung truc tuyen tai Vietnam [Influence of social interaction on impulsive online shopping behavior in Vietnam]. *Review of Finance*, 787(2), 103–106 (In Vietnamese). https://doi.org/10.31219/osf.io/dcz4b.

Barclay, D., Higgins, C., and Thompson, R. (1995). The partial least squares approach to causal modeling, personal computing adoption and use as an illustration. *Technology Studies*, 2(2), 285–309. Retrieved from https://www.researchgate.net/publication/242663837_The_Partial_Least_Squares_PLS_Approach_to_Causal_Modeling_Personal_Computer_Use_as_an_Illustration

Beatty, S.E. and Ferrell, M.E. (1998). Impulse buying: Modeling its precursors. *Journal of Retailing*, 74(2), 169–191. https://doi.org/10.1016/S0022-4359(99)80092-X.

Bellini, S., Cardinali, M.G., and Grandi, B. (2017). A structural equation model of impulse buying behaviour in grocery retailing. *Journal of Retailing and Consumer Services*, 36, 164–171. https://doi.org/10.1016/j.jretconser.2017.02.001.

Chan, T.K., Cheung, C.M., and Lee, Z.W. (2017). The state of online impulse-buying research: A literature analysis. *Information and Management*, 54(2), 204–217. https://doi.org/10.1016/j.im.2016.06.001.

Chen, J.V., Su, B., and Widjaja, A.E. (2016). Facebook C2C social commerce: A study of online impulse buying. *Decision Support Systems,* 83, 57–69. https://doi.org/10.1016/j.dss.2015.12.008.

Chen, X., Huang, Q., and Davison, R.M. (2017). The role of website quality and social capital in building buyers' loyalty. *International Journal of Information Management,* 37(1), 1563–1574. https://doi.org/10.1016/j.ijinfomgt.2016.07.005.

Chen, Y. and Zhang, L. (2015). Influential factors for online impulse buying in China: A model and its empirical analysis. *International Management Review,* 11(2), 57–69. Retrieved from http://americanscholarspress.us/journals/IMR/pdf/IMR-2-2015/IMR-v11n2art5.pdf.

Chen, Y., Lu, Y., Wang, B., and Pan, Z. (2019). How do product recommendations affect impulse buying? An empirical study on WeChat social commerce. *Information & Management,* 56(2), 236–248. https://doi.org/10.1016/j.im.2018.09.002.

Chen, Y., Wang, Q., and Xie, J. (2011). Online social interactions: A natural experiment on word of mouth versus observational learning. *Journal of Marketing Research,* 48(2), 238–254. https://doi.org/10.1509/jmkr.48.2.238.

Cheung, C.M., Liu, I.L., and Lee, M.K. (2015). How online social interactions influence customer information contribution behavior in online social shopping communities: A social learning theory perspective. *Journal of the Association for Information Science and Technology,* 66(12), 2511–2521. https://doi.org/10.1002/asi.23340.

Cheung, M.Y., Luo, C., Sia, C.L., and Chen, H.P. (2009). Credibility of electronic word-of-mouth: Informational and normative determinants of online consumer recommendations. *International Journal of Electronic Commerce,* 13(4), 9–38. https://doi.org/10.2753/JEC1086-4415130402.

Cohen, J. (1992). Quantitative methods in psychology: A power primer. *Psychological Bulletin,* 112(1), 155–159. https://doi.org/10.1037/0033-2909.112.1.155.

Craig, C. and Douglas, S. (2005). *International Marketing Research,* 3rd Edition. West Sussex: John Wiley and Son.

Davis, F.D. (1989). Perceived usefulness, perceived ease of use and user acceptance of information technology. *MIS Quarterly,* 13(3), 319–339. https://doi.org/10.2307/249008.

Davis, F.D., Bagozzi, R.P., and Warshaw, P.R. (1992). Extrinsic and intrinsic motivation to use computers in the workplace. *Journal of Applied Social Psychology,* 22(14), 1111–1132. https://doi.org/10.1111/j.1559-1816.1992.tb00945.x.

Erkan, I. and Evans, C. (2016). The influence of eWOM in social media on consumers purchase intentions: An extended approach to information adoption. *Computers in Human Behavior,* 61, 47–55. https://doi.org/10.1016/j.chb.2016.03.003

Evans, J.S.B.T. (2008). Dual-processing accounts of reasoning, judgment, and social cognition. *Annual Review of Psychology,* 59(1), 255–278. https://doi.org/10.1146/annurev.psych.59.103006.093629.

Feng, Z., Al Mamun, A., Masukujjaman, M., and Yang, Q. (2023). Modeling the significance of advertising values on online impulse buying behavior. *Humanities and Social Sciences Communications,* 10(1), 1–17. https://doi.org/10.1057/s41599-023-02231-7.

Fiore, A.M. and Yu, H. (2001). Effects of imagery copy and product samples on responses toward the product. *Journal of Interactive Marketing,* 15(2), 36–46. https://doi.org/10.1002/dir.1009.

Floh, A. and Madlberger, M. (2013). The role of atmospheric cues in online impulse-buying behavior. *Electronic Commerce Research and Applications,* 12(6), 425–439. https://doi.org/10.1016/j.elerap.2013.06.001.

Fornell, C. and Larcker, D.F. (1981). Evaluating structural equation models with unobservable variables and measurement error. *Journal of Marketing Research,* 18(1), 39–50. https://doi.org/10.1177/002224378101800104.

Goel, P., Parayitam, S., Sharma, A., Rana, N.P., and Dwivedi, Y.K. (2022). A moderated mediation model for e-impulse buying tendency, customer satisfaction and intention to continue e-shopping. *Journal of Business Research,* 142, 1–16. https://doi.org/10.1016/j.jbusres.2021.12.041.

Gulfraz, M.B., Sufyan, M., Mustak, M., Salminen, J., and Srivastava, D.K. (2022). Understanding the impact of online customers' shopping experience on online impulsive buying: A study on two leading E-commerce platforms. *Journal of Retailing and Consumer Services,* 68, 103000. https://doi.org/10.1016/j.jretconser.2022.103000.

Hair Jr, J.F., Hult, G.T.M., Ringle, C.M., and Sartedt, M. (2016). *A Primer on Partial Least Squares Structural Equation Modeling (PLS-SEM),* 2nd Edition. Los Angeles: SAGE Publications Ltd.

Henseler, J., Ringle, C.M., and Sarstedt, M. (2015). A new criterion for assessing discriminant validity in variance-based structural equation modeling. *Journal of the Academy of Marketing Science*, 43, 115–135. https://doi.org/10.1007/s11747-014-0403-8.

Henseler, J., Ringle, C.M., and Sinkovics, R. (2009). The use of partial least squares path modeling in international marketing. *Advances in International Marketing,* 20(4), 277–319. https://doi.org/10.1108/S1474-7979(2009)0000020014.

Hoch, S.J. and Loewenstein, G.F. (1991). Time-inconsistent preferences and consumer self-control. *Journal of Consumer Research,* 17(4), 492–507. https://doi.org/10.1086/208573.

Holbrook, M.B. and Batra, R. (1987). Assessing the role of emotions as mediators of consumer responses to advertising. *Journal of Consumer Research,* 14(3), 404–420. https://doi.org/10.1086/209123.

Hu, L. and Bentler, P.M. (1999). Cutoff criteria for fit indexes in covariance structure analysis: Conventional criteria versus new alternatives. *SEM,* 6(1), 1–55. https://doi.org/10.1080/10705519909540118.

Islam, T., Pitafi, A.H., Arya, V., Wang, Y., Akhtar, N., Mubarik, S., and Xiaobei, L. (2021). Panic buying in the COVID-19 pandemic: A multi-country examination. *Journal of Retailing and Consumer Services,* 59, 102357. https://doi.org/10.1016/j.jretconser.2020.102357.

Jiang, G., Liu, F., Liu, W., Liu, S., Chen, Y., and Xu, D. (2021). Effects of information quality on information adoption on social media review platforms: Moderating role of perceived risk. *Data Science and Management,* 1(1), 13–22. https://doi.org/10.1016/j.dsm.2021.02.004.

Koufaris, M. (2002). Applying the technology acceptance model and flow theory to online consumer behavior. *Information Systems Research,* 13(2), 205–223. https://doi.org/10.1287/isre.13.2.205.83.

Lan, T.T.N. and Trung, T.T. (2023). Yếu tố ảnh hu'ở'ng đền hành vi mua hàng ngẫu hú'ng qua thu'o'ng mại điện tử' của gió'i trẻ tại Thành phố Hố Chí Minh [Factors influencing impulse shopping behavior through e–commerce of young people in Ho Chi Minh City]. *Review of Finance,* 1(802), 188–191 (In Vietnamese). https://doi.org/10.31219/osf.io/j43c9.

Lee, C.H., and Chen, C.W. (2021). Impulse buying behaviors in live streaming commerce based on the stimulus-organism-response framework. *Information,* 12(6), 241. https://doi.org/10.3390/info12060241.

Leong, L.Y., Jaafar, N.I., and Ainin, S. (2018). The effects of Facebook browsing and usage intensity on impulse purchase in f-commerce. *Computers in Human Behavior,* 78, 160–173. https://doi.org/10.1016/j.chb.2017.09.033.

Lin, C.T., Chen, C.W., Wang, S.J., and Lin, C.C. (2018). The influence of impulse buying toward consumer loyalty in online shopping: A regulatory focus theory perspective. *Journal of Ambient Intelligence and Humanized Computing,* 1–11. https://doi.org/10.1007/s12652-018-0935-8.

Liu, Y., Li, H.X., and Hu, F. (2013). Website attributes in urging online impulse purchase: An empirical investigation on consumer perceptions. *Decision Support Systems,* 55(3), 829–837. https://doi.org/10.1016/j.dss.2013.04.001.

Mohan, G., Sivakumaran, B., and Sharma, P. (2013). Impact of store environment on impulse buying behavior. *European Journal of Marketing,* 47(10), 1711–1732. https://doi.org/10.1108/EJM-03-2011-0110.

Moon, J.-W. and Kim, Y.-G. (2001). Extending the TAM for a World-Wide-Web context. *Information and Management,* 38(4), 217–230. https://doi.org/10.1016/S0378-7206(00)00061-6.

Mullins, J.K. and Sabherwal, R. (2020). Gamification: A cognitive-emotional view. *Journal of Business Research,* 106, 304–314. https://doi.org/10.1016/j.jbusres.2018.09.023.

Nguyen-Viet, B. and Diep, T. (2022). Factor drving online impulse buying behavior of consumers in Ho Chi Minh City. *Science & Technology Development Journal: Economics-Law & Management,* 6(3), 3205–3215 (In Vietnamese). https://doi.org/10.32508/stdjelm.v6i3.1015.

Parboteeah, D.V., Valacich, J.S., and Wells, J.D. (2009). The influence of website characteristics on a consumer's urge to buy impulsively. *Information Systems Research,* 20(1), 60–78. https://doi.org/10.1287/isre.1070.0157.

Park, C.W. and Lessig, V.P. (1977). Students and housewives: Differences in susceptibility to reference group influence. *Journal of Consumer Research,* 4(2), 102–110. https://doi.org/10.1086/208685.

Park, D.H., Lee, J., and Han, I. (2007). The effect of on-line consumer reviews on consumer purchasing intention: The moderating role of involvement. *International journal of electronic commerce,* 11(4), 125–148. https://doi.org/10.2753/JEC1086-4415110405.

Park, E.J., Kim, E.Y., Funches, V.M., and Foxx, W. (2012). Apparel product attributes, web browsing, and e-impulse buying on shopping websites. *Journal of Business Research,* 65(11), 1583–1589. https://doi.org/10.1016/j.jbusres.2011.02.043.

Rook, D.W. and Fisher, R. (1995). Normative influences on impulsive buying behavior. *Journal of Consumer Research,* 22, 305–313. https://doi.org/10.1086/209452.

Sarah, F.H., Goi, C.L., Chieng, F., and Taufique, K.M.R. (2021). Examining the influence of atmospheric cues on online impulse buying behavior across product categories: Insights from an emerging e-market. *Journal of Internet Commerce,* 20(1), 25–45. https://doi.org/10.1080/15332861.2020.1836593.

Shmueli, G., Sarstedt, M., Hair, J.F., Cheah, J.H., Ting, H., Vaithilingam, S., and Ringle, C.M. (2019). Predictive model assessment in PLS-SEM: Guidelines for using PLSpredict. *European Journal of Marketing,* 53(11), 2322–2347. https://doi.org/10.1108/EJM-02-2019-0189.

Sihombing, E.S., Budi, I., and Munajat, Q. (2020). Factors affecting the urge of impulsive buying on social commerce Instagram. *International Journal of Internet Marketing and Advertising,* 14(3), 236–257. https://doi.org/10.1504/IJIMA.2020.108716.

Strack, F. and Deutsch, R. (2004). Reflective and impulsive determinants of social behavior, personality and social psychology review. *An*

Official Journal of the Society for Personality and Social Psychology, 8(3), 220–247. https://doi.org/10.1207/s15327957pspr0803_1.

Wang, D., Luo, X.R., Hua, Y., and Benitez, J. (2022). Big arena, small potatoes: A mixed-methods investigation of atmospheric cues in live-streaming e-commerce. *Decision Support Systems,* 158, Article 113801. https://doi.org/10.1016/j.dss.2022.113801.

Wang, P. and Chapa, S. (2022). Online impulse buying behavior and marketing optimization guided by entrepreneurial psychology under COVID-19. *Frontiers in Psychology,* 13, 939786. https://doi.org/10.3389/fpsyg.2022.939786.

Weinberg, P. and Gottwald, W. (1982). Impulsive consumer buying as a result of emotions. *Journal of Business Research,* 10(1), 43–57. https://doi.org/10.1016/0148-2963(82)90016-9.

Wu, L., Chen, K.W., and Chiu, M.L. (2016). Defining key drivers of online impulse purchasing: A perspective of both impulse shoppers and system users. *International Journal of Information Management,* 36(3), 284–296. https://doi.org/10.1016/j.ijinfomgt.2015.11.015.

Wu, Y., Xin, L., Li, D., Yu, J., and Guo, J. (2021). How does scarcity promotion lead to impulse purchase in the online market? A field experiments. *Information & Management,* 58(1), 103283. https://doi.org/10.1016/j.im.2020.103283.

Xiang, L., Zheng, X., Lee, M.K., and Zhao, D. (2016). Exploring consumers' impulse buying behavior on social commerce platform: The role of parasocial interaction. *International Journal of Information Management,* 36(3), 333–347. https://doi.org/10.1016/j.ijinfomgt.2015.11.002.

Xu, H., Zhang, K.Z., and Zhao, S.J. (2020). A dual systems model of online impulse buying. *Industrial Management & Data Systems,* 120(5), 845–861. https://doi.org/10.1108/IMDS-04-2019-0214.

Zafar, A.U., Qiu, J., Li, Y., Wang, J., and Shahzad, M. (2021). The impact of social media celebrities' posts and contextual interactions on impulse buying in social commerce. *Computers in Human Behavior,* 115, 106178. https://doi.org/10.1016/j.chb.2019.106178.

Zhang, K.Z., Zhao, S.J., Cheung, C.M., and Lee, M.K. (2014). Examining the influence of online reviews on consumers' decision-making: A heuristic–systematic model. *Decision Support Systems,* 67, 78–89. https://doi.org/10.1016/j.dss.2014.08.005.

Zhang, K.Z.K. and Benyoucef, M. (2016). Consumer behavior in social commerce: A literature review. *Decision Support Systems,* 86, 95–108. https://doi.org/10.1016/j.dss.2016.04.001.

Zhang, L., Shao, Z., Li, X., and Feng, Y. (2021). Gamification and online impulse buying: The moderating effect of gender and age. *International*

Journal of Information Management, 61, 102267. https://doi.org/10.1016/j.ijinfomgt.2020.102267.

Zhang, Z., Zhang, N., and Wang, J. (2022). The influencing factors on impulse buying behavior of consumers under the mode of hunger marketing in live commerce. *Sustainability*, 14(4), 2122. https://doi.org/10.3390/su14042122.

Zheng, Y., Yang, X., Zhou, R., Niu, G., Liu, Q., and Zhou, Z. (2020). Upward social comparison and state anxiety as mediators between passive social network site usage and online compulsive buying among women. *Addictive Behaviors*, 111, 106569. https://doi.org/10.1016/j.addbeh.2020.106569.

Appendix

Table A1: Measures of constructs.

Code	Items
Review Quality (*modified from Park et al., 2007*)	
RQ1	The reviews on the digital platform are complete.
RQ2	The reviews on the digital platform are accurate.
RQ3	The reviews on the digital platform are credible.
RQ4	The reviews on the digital platform are objective.
Perceived Usefulness (*modified from Parboteeah et al., 2009*)	
PU1	Using the digital platform can improve my shopping performance.
PU2	Using the digital platform can increase my shopping productivity.
PU3	Using the digital platform can increase my shopping effectiveness.
Perceived Enjoyment (*modified from Parboteeah et al., 2009*)	
PE1	I enjoy my interactions on the digital platform.
PE2	My interaction on the digital platform leaves a good impression on me.
PE3	My interaction on the digital platform is exciting and pleasurable.
Positive Affect (*modified from Floh and Madlberger, 2013*)	
PA1	When shopping on a digital platform, I feel excited.
PA2	When shopping on a digital platform, I feel enthusiastic.
PA3	When shopping on a digital platform, I feel inspired.
PA4	When shopping on a digital platform, I feel happy.
Observational Learning (*modified from Zhang et al., 2014*)	
OL1	It is easy for me to observe that products on the digital platform are purchased by a lot of people.
OL2	I observe that the sales volumes of products on the digital platform are high.
OL3	I observe that many people buy products on the digital platform.

(*continued*)

Table A1: (*continued*).

Code	Items
Urge to Buy Impulsively (*modified from Parboteeah et al., 2009*)	
UBI1	I have the urge to purchase items other than or in addition to my shopping goals on the digital platform.
UBI2	I have a desire to buy items that do not pertain to my shopping goals on the digital platform.
UBI3	I have the inclination to purchase items outside my shopping goals on the digital platform.
Online Impulse Buying Behavior (*modified from Rook and Fisher, 1995*)	
OIBB1	I had the urge to purchase items other than or in addition to my specific shopping goal on the digital platform.
OIBB2	I had a desire to buy items that did not pertain to my specific shopping goal on the digital platform.
OIBB3	I had the inclination to purchase items outside my specific shopping goal on the digital platform.

https://doi.org/10.1142/9789811262258_bmatter

Index

www.ingramcontent.com/pod-product-compliance
Lightning Source LLC
Chambersburg PA
CBHW060543050126
37699CB00004B/97